T0274008

YOU CAN
GO HOME
AGAIN

YOU CAN GO HOME AGAIN

RECONNECTING WITH YOUR FAMILY

3RD EDITION

MONICA McGOLDRICK
TRACEY LASZLOFFY

W. W. NORTON & COMPANY
Independent Publishers Since 1923

Important Note: *You Can Go Home Again* is intended to provide general information on the subject of health and well-being; it is not a substitute for medical or psychological treatment and may not be relied upon for purposes of diagnosing or treating any illness. Please seek out the care of a professional healthcare provider if you are pregnant, nursing, or experiencing symptoms of any potentially serious condition. As of press time, the URLs displayed in this book link or refer to existing sites. The publisher and author are not responsible for any content that appears on third-party websites.

For information about permission to reproduce selections from this book, write to Permissions, W. W. Norton & Company, Inc., 500 Fifth Avenue, New York, NY 10110

For information about special discounts for bulk purchases, please contact W. W. Norton Special Sales at specialsales@wwnorton.com or 800-233-4830

Manufacturing by Marquis Book Printing
Production manager: Gwen Cullen

ISBN: 978-1-324-03014-0 (pbk)

W. W. Norton & Company, Inc., 500 Fifth Avenue, New York, NY 10110
www.wwnorton.com

W. W. Norton & Company Ltd., 15 Carlisle Street, London W1D 3BS

1 2 3 4 5 6 7 8 9 0

CONTENTS

ACKNOWLEDGMENTS AND DEDICATION

DEDICATION (McGOLDRICK)

I dedicate this book to my mother, who taught me that it is possible to repair a cutoff and come to love someone with whom you have had profound conflicts. I believe that it is not so much our mothers who have let us down, as the yardsticks by which we have measured them. I dedicate this book to her for her courage as a woman and for her willingness to keep growing until her last breath. She lives in my heart every day.

This book is also dedicated to Betty Carter, my mentor, soulmate, and sister, with whom I thought through so many of the issues discussed here about how to reconnect with your family. I dedicate this book to her in gratitude for her love, humor, and brilliance in thinking systems, and for the blessing of over 30 years of collaboration with her.

And I dedicate this book also to my lifemates and soulmates, whom I have loved for so many decades, Carol Anderson and Paulette Moore Hines. They were my friends, compatriots, and advisors through thick and thin, and their presence, guidance, and friendship I now miss every day.

ACKNOWLEDGMENTS (McGOLDRICK)

I am very grateful also to my husband Sophocles Orfanidis, who has been a crucial part of my sense of "home" since we first met in 1968. I thank him for his support and for our many years together. Our wonderful son John went from birth to almost midlife over the decades of the three editions of this book. I have been so blessed to have him in my life over these past 38 years and he has "grown me up" as I hope I helped him grow up. It has been the greatest joy of my life. And he brought my much-loved daughter-in-law, Anna DePalma, into our lives and together they brought us our magnificent grandson, Owen William Orfanidis. Anna was already a great help with the pictures of the previous edition, but now she has her own amazing and creative projects! I thank also my beloved in-laws Renee Psiakis and Bill DePalma, who have also been loving and generous in their general and specific support through the evolution of this third edition, for which I am deeply grateful, and who have also become my dear friends, for whom I am so grateful.

I thank also my sisters, Neale and Morna, for all they have meant to me through my life and for their role in my sense of home for the whole journey of our lives, and our beloved Margaret Bush and our Aunt Mamie, both of whom I still miss every day.

My nephews Guy and Hugh, and my niece-in-law Maria Sperling and grand-nephew Renzo have been, I always know, among my greatest supporters. Though far away, they are always a deep part of my sense of rootedness and belonging. Guy has been my graphics consultant for many years and I thank him specifically for his suggestions on photos, genograms, and stories for this book. He has been a great resource. And Hugh came through for me for this edition's genograms right when I desperately needed him. I greatly appreciate his talents, speed, and willingness to help me out in my desperation.

My formal and informal godchildren have also been major inspirations: Stefan, Ariane, and Natalie Baer; Irini and Angeliki Syrcos; Maria Anderson Rubin; Claire Whitney; Patti, Gina, Ryan, Terry, and Christiana Thanos; Irene and Gabe Berkowitz, and Ava Lee-Green. This book is also for them and their children of the next generation.

Many dear friends and colleagues have offered direct and indirect support throughout the years of writing and rewriting this book. Carol Anderson, Froma Walsh, Nydia Garcia Preto, Paulette Hines, Nollaig and Henry Byrne, Imelda McCarthy, Elaine Pinderhughes, Barbara Petkov, Sueli Petry, Roberto Font, Ken Hardy, John Folwarski, Jayne Mahboubi, Kalli Adamides, Fernanda Fihlo, Jane Hart Tollinger, Charlotte Fremon Danielson, Jane Sufian, Jim Michener (my friend since earliest childhood), Nancy Boyd and A. J. Franklin, Glenn Wolf, Doug Schoeninger, Ron Arons, Liz Nicolai, and Salome Raheim were all important resources for me, though they may not have realized the role they were playing.

I am especially grateful to Sueli Petry for her dedication to genograms and specifically to the hard work she has shared with me over the past decade to define and expand our understanding of genograms. She came first as a student with a strong interest in genograms and grew into a friend and colleague and a steadfast support in thinking through the issues of genograms and many other personal and professional issues.

My renowned friend and soulmate, Fernando Colon, provided inspiration, help, and affirmation particularly regarding the importance of nonbiological kin networks. I thank also my friend Robert Jay Green for challenging my unquestioning belief in the relevance of genograms, in almost every conversation we have, helping me to clarify for myself the deepest meanings of family and of "home."

I am grateful to many people for their help in the development of this project. I owe special thanks to Randy Gerson, for the formative efforts he made to describe genogram patterns and make them universally accessible through his creativity in computer applications and through his concerted efforts and those we made together toward the computerizing of genograms, even though we never accomplished our goals. I am so sorry we lost him much too soon.

I also thank my friend and colleague of many years and many professional projects and personal experiences, Michael Rohrbaugh, who persuaded me to write about genograms in the first place, challenging my assumptions and helping me clarify my thinking about genograms and their potential as a research and clinical tool, and who helped me develop research projects to learn about genogram patterns.

I also thank Dan Morin, the developer of Genopro (www.genopro.com), for his support. I am very eager for what he is developing for the future of genograms. It is with his Genopro program that the genograms in this book were produced. Dan's program, which not only draws genograms but also creates a database, has the potential to help us study patterns in multiple families over generations. Creation of such a program to develop a database to study genogram patterns has been a dream of mine since 1980, when I first discovered that Randy Gerson had developed a computerized genogram graphic. Randy and I sought support for years to develop a computerized genogram database with which we could research families. Dan's program is the start of such a system, which will hopefully become fully developed over the next few years for this exact purpose. I am very grateful for his efforts to make his program conform to the conventions that have been worked out and for his creativity in improving his system for the use of clinicians.

Meanwhile, during the years of developing this edition, Jamie Quiros has kept our office going, which left me free to focus on this project, and for her support I am very grateful. And Ben Forest, our enthusiastic computer consultant, spent many hours helping us figure out and coordinate the genograms and the text for this and several other books over the past many years. His support has also been essential for this project.

And Tracey Laszloffy, a respected colleague for many years, has become a trusted friend and a wonderful collaborator on this third edition. I am deeply grateful for her brilliance, writing skills, enthusiasm for this book, and collaboration.

Finally, the Norton editorial team and especially my editors Deborah Malmud, Mariah Eppes, and Jamie Vincent supported us to bring this book to fruition for this third edition as Norton has supported so many of our other projects in the past—on genograms, on loss issues on women, and on revisioning family therapy. I was also extremely fortunate to find Liz Seramur as my picture person, just when I was in desperate need of help. She was extremely generous in her efforts with picture permissions, which could have been a real nightmare. Her work on permissions has made a tremendous difference in the ability of this book to convey the stories of those discussed. I am extremely grateful for her help and support. Overall, we are very grateful for Norton's commitment to this project and the enormous help and support they have given us in bringing this book to fruition.

I hope one day our grandson, along with our grandnephew Renzo Livingston and others of their generation, will come to share our enthusiasm for genograms and for our genogram in particular. I look forward to how our genograms will continue as the next generations expand our families.

And, of course, there would have been no book without the underlying support of my parents and all our other family who have gone before us— whether connected through biology, legal ties, or spiritual and physical affinity—who are a part of my genogram. I stand on the shoulders of many supportive, creative, and generous kin, without whom I would not be writing this book. With their support, I write for all those who will come after— whether connected through biology or through intellectual, emotional, or spiritual ties.

DEDICATION (LASZLOFFY)

This book is about our families and how they shape us. As such, I want to dedicate this book to my family. First and foremost, I dedicate it to my parents June and Jerome Laszloffy. Though they are gone now, their love continues to nurture me every day of my life. It is through their love that I learned the meaning of home as a place of genuine acceptance, belonging, safety, security, connection, and comfort. In particular, I want to acknowledge my mother for giving me the greatest gift a parent can give a child—nondefensive acknowledgment of the inevitable wounding that paves a pathway to healing. I want to also acknowledge my father, who from my earliest years, spoke of the importance of family history and knowing where you came from. Through his disciplined efforts to record family members talking about their lives, and his amassing and cataloguing a rich collection of family photos, he taught me about the importance of knowing our family history. I believe he laid the foundation that led me to become a family therapist and to become a passionate advocate for studying family histories.

I also dedicate this book to my sister Joyce, who has been my most trusted companion, confidante, conspirator, challenger, and closest ally since childhood. Like most siblings we have had our fair share of tussles, but never at the expense of our care for and commitment to each other. Our connection affirms for me the strength of family bonds and the enrichment they bring to our lives.

ACKNOWLEDGMENTS (LASZLOFFY)

In addition to my parents and my sister, I want to acknowledge my extended family members. I am grateful for the depth of their love and for the ways they supported me during difficult times and celebrated and shared joy during happy times.

Very importantly, I want to acknowledge my partner, Bill, who has for many years patiently listened to and gently supported me as I have struggled through my various writing projects. I am deeply thankful for his support.

Lastly, I want to acknowledge Monica McGoldrick, who has been a source of inspiration and affirmation. I am grateful for her mentorship and the many invaluable opportunities she has given me over the years, the greatest of which has been the chance to collaborate with her on this book. I am so proud of *You Can Go Home Again* and I hope it helps people do just that.

YOU CAN
GO HOME
AGAIN

INTRODUCTION
Our Own Homecoming Journeys

Know whence you came. If you know whence you came, there is no limit to where you can go.

—JAMES BALDWIN
The Fire Next Time

You live without history as if you throw no shadow behind you.

—TOM STOPPARD
Leopoldstadt

This book aims to inspire and guide you in deepening your understanding of your family relationships and, where possible, to change your part in problematic family patterns of conflict, tension, and cutoff. We believe that the key to understanding who we are in this world is, as James Baldwin put it so well, to "know whence you came." As a basic tool to that end, we use a family tree, along with whatever we can learn from conversations, pictures, and stories about our history.

The particular family tree we use to map our family's history and patterns is called a genogram. A group of family doctors once wrote a paper called "If You Meet a Buddha on The Road, Take A Genogram" (Garrett, Klinkman, & Post, 1987), suggesting the importance of genograms or family trees as orienting maps for understanding ourselves and each other through paying attention to what our history is, especially our family history. We are passionate about the use of genograms to map family systems and identify patterns and dynamics across multiple generations. In fact, we are so passionate about genograms that we never watch a movie or read a novel or a biography without working out the family tree or "genogram" for the characters involved. Hence, one of the things we will do in this book is encourage you to create a genogram for your own family, to deepen your understanding your family system, and yourself.

Having produced two editions of this book since 1995, I am joined for this edition with my friend and colleague, Tracey Laszloffy. She and I have been collaborating on writing projects on the life cycle and cultural issues for many years. I am delighted that she has become a major collaborator for this third edition of *You Can Go Home Again*.

But, before we start laying out how to embark on the journey to go home, we want to share our own journeys. We hope this will demonstrate why we believe so deeply in this process and inspire you to do the same.

MONICA McGOLDRICK

This book grew out of my efforts to "go home again" at a point in my life when I was feeling ready to cut off my family, because I could not find a way to feel connected. My going home journey began in 1972, when I first heard Murray Bowen give a talk about his conceptual framework and the importance of being able to sit and have a calm conversation with your mother. I concluded that either he was very wrong (because he had never met my mother) or that I had to learn what he was talking about. That very week I started my journey to understand myself and my family differently and change my role in my own family, hiring one of Bowen's students, Phil Guerin, to coach me through the reconnection. Through exploring my own family history, I came to love my difficult, powerful, and vulnerable mother more deeply and to acknowledge my sweet, brilliant, funny father's limitations in ways that did not make me love him less, but did enable me to love my mother more. I then spent many years doing genealogical research on my family, tracking down relatives from Wyoming to Ballybofey, Donegal, and Leap near Skibberean in County Cork, Ireland. My personal journey helped me realize that I am a part of all that came before and appreciate the legacy we leave to those who come after us, so that, in the words of Seamus Heaney, "hope and history can rhyme."

I am the middle of three sisters, a fourth generation Irish American. Born in Brooklyn in 1943 (raised on the Brooklyn Dodgers), I grew up from age six on a farm in Solebury, Pennsylvania. In 1972, I married a Greek immigrant and by now have become a mother, and aunt, and a grandmother.

My mother was one of the most interesting women I have ever known, and I struggled with her for all the years of my childhood, adolescence, and young adulthood. She graduated from Barnard, class of 1934, and then gave up a successful career in public relations to marry my father, whom she adored for all of their thirty-eight years together. My father was a well-known reform politician in New York City. He was the longest serving New York City Comptroller in the La Guardia administration. He was also a lawyer and professor of political science. In fact, I come from a family of teachers; including my husband, my father, both my sisters, my three aunts, an uncle, and my maternal grandfather.

My adored caretaker, for all the years of my childhood, was Margaret Phifer Bush, an African American from Asheville, North Carolina. Because of racism, she did not learn to read until after I did, but ran our family along with my mother, despite being the "servant"—in that pernicious racial arrangement of family relationships common among privileged white families in the U.S.

She was the person to whom I was closest throughout childhood. My father was a beloved visiting dignitary on weekends.

My great Aunt Mamie, who used to visit for weeks at a time, was our "Santa Claus." And our Uncle Raymond shared with me his enjoyment of the Russian language and of music and he was thrilled when I married my Greek husband, Sophocles, thereby bringing another physicist into the family.

We also had a wonderful "informal family." Elliot Mottram, my uncle's high school friend, and his wife Marie (who convinced my father to buy the farm next to theirs in Solebury) were lifelong friends of my parents, and informal "godparents" to my sisters and me.

In terms of our extended family, we were close only to Aunt Mamie. Our mother's mother could charm us with her piano rendition of "Golliwog's Cakewalk," but only much later did I take any interest in my extended family or find out that my grandmother had been the first woman on Staten Island to drive a car.

I knew that I was technically Irish, but that fact meant nothing to me. I thought I was just a regular American person. I had no concept of culture or

Morna, Monica, and Neale with their beloved Margaret

of my ancestors—who they were or what they did. It was only after meeting Murray Bowen and learning about genograms that I began to wonder who I really belonged to and began to make connections with my extended family and my Irish ancestry. When I did begin creating my genogram and asking

Morna and Monica with their Santa Claus: Aunt Mamie Cahalane

my mother about our background, she said there was nothing to tell. When I pressed her, which I always tended to do, she said, "They were just peasants, Monica. We're Americans now, so forget it!"

But I kept pushing. Within a couple of years my parents had shifted their response to my curiosity about our history and they arranged to have our whole family spend their thirty-fifth wedding anniversary at Ballymaloe, in Cork, Ireland. This was a huge awakening for me. I had never even thought of going to Ireland, though I had gone several times to Greece with my husband. But from the moment we landed in Ireland, I had a deep realization that these were my people. They looked like my parents, my Aunt Mamie, and my Uncle Raymond, and their ways of interacting were remarkably familiar, in spite of their accent. I was struck, for example, by their way of using humor to challenge a speaker or keep children in line. This and other reactions were strikingly familiar behaviors to me.

From then on I have had great curiosity about everyone's cultural background. I can never resist asking people where they come from and how they think their customs and values have been shaped by their heritage.

During that trip to Ireland I made many connections with McGoldrick cousins in Donegal, including Hughie McGoldrick, from whom I learned several important family secrets, which helped me understand myself and my family more deeply. All the McGoldricks from the Glen now live in my heart, as do the Cahalanes from my mother's side of the family in Leap, County Cork: Patsy and Michael Cahalane (who both remembered my great grandfather's brother, to whom they brought wood to when they were very young) and Tadg Wholley (who told us great stories about our Cahalane ancestors going way back in history).

My educational background had been in Russian studies in college and graduate school, so I had always had an interest in culture, but I thought I was "regular" and it was other people who had "culture." My theses in college and graduate school were on Pushkin and Dostoevsky, which probably reflected my attraction in psychology. Then I fell in love with therapy and switched to social work. My social work thesis focused on children's use of humor in psychotherapy. This was in the late 1960s, which was the heyday of community mental health and family therapy.

I became enamored with family therapy, moving to New Jersey in 1972 for a job teaching family therapy at Rutgers Medical School and its Community Mental Health Center, which were both just opening. That was the same year I heard Murray Bowen give the talk about his conceptual framework and realized I had to learn what he was talking about, and when I joined Phil Guerin's newly formed Bowen Family Institute in Westchester and began "coaching" with him to understand the Bowen approach which forms the basis of this book, and of all my other writings.

My interests have included culture, social class, gender, race, couples, the life cycle, schizophrenia, remarried families, sibling relationships, intermarriage, family therapy with one person, and the impact of loss on families. For many years I was on the faculty of the Psychiatry Department and Community Mental Health Center of Robert Wood Johnson Medical School of Rutgers University, before becoming the director of the Multicultural Family Institute in central New Jersey in 1991.

What I learned about multigenerational family systems and how they are embedded within broader cultural contexts changed my life. I became able to explore and unearth many family stories, secrets, and patterns that had influenced my identity and development, but I also learned how to transform my own role in my family, so that I could relate in healthier and more satisfying ways and help others to do the same.

As a therapist and as a coach I have worked for many years to help clients and students take their own journeys of learning, healing, and transformation, which is why we are writing this book: to share these understandings with you.

TRACEY LASZLOFFY

As for me (Tracey), (see **Genogram I.1: Laszloffy Family**), both sets of my mother's grandparents immigrated to American from Russia, while my father's parents immigrated from Hungary.

On my mother's side, I know almost nothing of the time in Russia other than the fact that they were all Jews and the persecution they faced was the basis for their immigrating to the U.S. The one story I have is that during one of the pogroms, my great-grandmother Elizabeth and her younger brother were directed by their parents to flee and try to get to a port city in the hopes of making their way to America. They ran during the night and hid during the day. On one occasion they even hid in a grave to escape detection. After passing through Ellis Island, Elizabeth settled in Brooklyn, where she worked as a milliner (hat maker). Eventually, she met a fellow Russian Jew, Boris, who had just graduated from pharmacy school. Within a year they were married and had their first child, Ruth—my grandmother. Seven years later they had a second child, Paul. Ruth adored her father and wanted to follow in his footsteps, enrolling in the pharmacy program at Brooklyn College. I was always proud of the fact she pushed against the social barriers of that time by pursuing her education in a male-dominated field. However, during her college years she began corresponding with a doctor (Morris, who was also of Russian Jewish ancestry) that her aunt had introduced her to just weeks before he was shipped overseas to serve in World War II. Upon his return home, despite their seventeen-year age difference, Ruth and Morris were secretly married. Ruth dropped out of college to become a full-time wife, and soon, a mother. Their firstborn child was my mother, June, and a year later they had a second child, Arnold.

My father's parents grew up in neighboring towns in Hungary. My parents' families knew each other, but they did not meet until after they had immigrated to America and established their new lives in New York City. My grandmother, Elizabeth, told me she did not really want to marry my grandfather, Julius, but agreed to because she had been heartbroken when the man she really loved disappeared from her life. When he returned several years later, their relationship could not resume, because she was already married. I believe she felt great loss about that for the rest of her life.

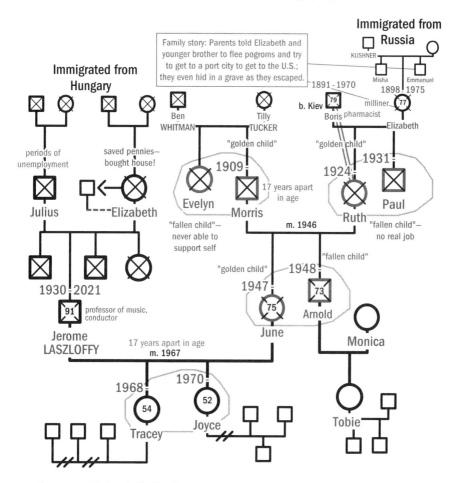

Immigrated from Russia

Family story: Parents told Elizabeth and younger brother to flee pogroms and try to get to a port city to get to the U.S.; they even hid in a grave as they escaped.

Immigrated from Hungary

KUSHNER

Misha 1898 milliner

Emmanuel 1975

1891-1970

b. Kiev 79

Boris pharmacist 77

Ben WHITMAN

Tilly TUCKER "golden child"

Elizabeth

"golden child"

periods of unemployment

saved pennies— bought house!

1909

1931

1924

Julius

Elizabeth

Evelyn

Morris

17 years apart in age

Ruth

Paul

"fallen child"— never able to support self

m. 1946

"fallen child"— no real job

1930-2021

"golden child"

1947

"fallen child"

1948

73

Arnold

91 professor of music, conductor

June

Monica

Jerome LASZLOFFY

17 years apart in age m. 1967

1970

1968

54

52

Joyce

Tobie

Tracey

Genogram I.1: Laszloffy Family

My grandparents had three sons, of whom my father, Jerome, was in the middle. Later came a daughter, my aunt Carole. The family went through times of boom and bust because my grandfather went through periods of unemployment. My grandmother, to manage during the times without income, became a skilled saver of pennies that she secretly collected over time. Eventually she saved enough to put a down payment on a home that had long been her dream.

My grandfather was initially enraged when he realized his wife had been hiding money from him, money he would surely have gambled away, had he known of it. My father described his father as a man of extremes. He could be jovial and good-humored, but if something rubbed him the wrong way, he was prone to fits of violent rage. Perhaps, as a way to escape the tensions of the family, my father fell in love with the classical music he heard on the radio at a very young age. That passion carried him to pursue a career as an orchestra conductor, and later, a professor of music.

My parents met in the fall of 1966 at the University of Connecticut, where my father was a new professor of music assigned to conduct the student orchestra. My mother, a sophomore, was seated in the first violin section. My parents, like my mother's own parents, had a seventeen-year age difference. My father was thirty-six and my mother was nineteen. Six months after they met they were married at Carnegie Hall in New York City. Given the brevity of their courtship, their difference in age, and difference in social standing (she was his student), the odds were stacked against them. Amazingly, they were a good fit and remained happily married for over fifty years.

I was born a year after my parents married and my sister Joyce was born two years later. I grew up living in a home that my father designed and built in Mansfield, Connecticut. I had a happy childhood, benefiting from the security and privileges that our being white and solidly middle class bestowed upon us. While ethnically Jewish, we have always been an atheist family, but our family's Jewish background sensitized my parents to social justice issues, and they encouraged this consciousness in my sister and me.

As an adolescent I became friends with a group of African Americans and Latinos—my first exposure to the realities of racial inequities. Until that point my social activism had been focused on animal rights and environmental justice, but my adolescent experiences expanded my vision to include a passion to work on behalf of racial, class, and gender justice. I knew that I wanted to become a healer and a change agent at both the micro and macro levels. In 1988, when I took a course in marriage and family therapy, the professor introduced systems theory, and I knew I had found my pathway. The emphasis on context and relationships was music to my ears. I saw an opportunity to become a healer and a change agent while working with family systems and addressing broader social and environmental contexts.

That was the beginning of my genogram journey and the process of "going home." I still remember the exhilaration I felt when I started to identify the family patterns transmitted across generations. One of my earliest discoveries involved a high-low functioning sibling dynamic that was especially pronounced on my mother's side of the family. My mother's maternal grandparents had two children, my grandmother Ruth and my great uncle, Paul. Ruth was the golden child, the loyal, loving, utterly devoted good daughter. In contrast, my great-uncle Paul was the "fallen" child who had an "other than honorable discharge" from the army, never married or had children, and never held down a job. Instead, he lived most of his life in and out of VA hospitals. My mother's paternal grandparents also had two children, my grandfather Morris and my great-aunt Evelyn. Morris was the golden child who, after being denied entry into medical school in New York because he was Jewish, earned his medical degree in Bern, Switzerland (learning German at the same time), and went on to become a radiologist who worked for the VA after serving his time in the army. As the golden child, he became the caretaker of his parents, while his sister was the fallen sibling: having had two short marriages and no means of supporting herself.

My mother's parents—who were each the golden children in their families—had two children of their own, my mother June and my uncle Arnold. My mother was the golden child, the adored daughter who did everything right, while my uncle was the fallen child, having dropped out of medical school, then dropped out of a chemistry doctoral program just before writing his dissertation. Despite having a brilliant mind, he was never able to succeed in building his business as an investment advisor, and thus was financially dependent on his parents for his whole life. Recognizing this golden/fallen sibling split in my early twenties helped me see elements of this dynamic between me and my sister. While the disparities between us were not nearly as extreme as in previous generations, the splitting was still present, and it required a lot of intentional work to communicate with my family about this so we did not replicate the dysfunction of the past generations. Some of this work included sharing this intergenerational pattern directly with my family and hearing their reactions to and feelings about it. I had many conversations with my parents and sister about behaviors that ran the risk of reinforcing this pattern and making conscious efforts to challenge it. For example, my family regarded it as a pride issue that I went to college and then graduate school, while my sister had rebuffed college for herself. But after examining this family pattern, she decided her decision had been driven by forces beyond her own desires, and in her late twenties earned her college degree, which altered the golden child/fallen child dynamics we had been at risk of repeating.

In studying my family, I was especially interested in the influence of my Russian and Hungarian Jewish roots. My studies helped me see, for example, how certain traits expressed by my paternal grandparents, my father, and myself, reflected our Hungarian cultural ancestry. More specifically, my grandmother's proclivity to tell highly imaginative stories that involved a lot of embellishment, and my grandfather's intense emotional extremes between joviality and rage were expressions of their Hungarian roots. I saw how my father's artistic creativity as a musician and his intense emotionality, often defined by extremes, was not only modeled by his parents but also from his Hungarian culture. It was helpful to understand this since, I also recognized some of these traits in myself.

This "going home" journey that began in my early twenties has continued to this day. The process of exploration, reflection, and reconnection continues to be illuminating, healing, and growth-enhancing.

If you are reading this now, it means you are considering embarking on this journey for yourself. We hope you will choose to engage in this process and that our suggestions will encourage you.

Chapter 1
Why Go Home Again?

To go home may be impossible, but it is often a driving necessity, or at least a compelling dream. . . . Home is a concept, not a place. It is a state of mind where self-definition starts; it is origins—the mix of time and place and smell and weather wherein one first realizes one is an original. . . . Home . . . remains in the mind as a place where reunion, if it were ever to occur, would happen. . . . It is about restoration of the right relations among things—and going home is where that restoration occurs, because that is where it matters most.

—A. BARTLETT GIAMATTI
Take Time for Paradise

At least 27 percent of Americans are estranged from a member of their own family and research suggests about 40 percent of Americans have experienced estrangement at some point.

—DAVID BROOKS
The New York Times

If you embark on the going home journey that we outline in this book, you will be exploring your family over many generations, coming to understand how your family related and where they got stuck, as well as your own role, not simply as victim or reactor to your experiences, but as an active player and a definer of your own future behavior. We believe that deepening our understanding of our families and their history makes us better able to change problematic patterns and choose the values by which we want to live.

Our families are, except in rare circumstances, the most important emotional systems to which we ever belong; they shape us and continue to influence us over the course of our lives. Even the worst most painful family experiences—addiction, violence, sexual abuse, suicide—are part of our accumulated identity. Understanding what led to these behaviors can help us make sense not only of the dark side of ourselves, but most importantly, learn about our sources of resilience. It is therefore profoundly important to examine our relationships and develop the best connection we can with those to whom we belong. Relationships and functioning (physical, social, emotional, and spiritual) are interdependent; change in one part of a system leads to compensatory change in other parts. This can, of course, make the family our greatest source of stress as well as potentially our greatest resource.

We use a systemic perspective to guide the journey to go home. This perspective assumes that all things are interconnected and the more we understand about the whole, the more we will understand about each part. All human beings are embedded in family, social, and ecological contexts, which shape our lives in every dimension: physically, emotionally, and in our values, beliefs, and behaviors throughout time, from the past and into the future. We are a part of all that came before and all that will come after, so we do our best when we focus on understanding of ourselves in the broadest possible context.

James Baldwin   © SZ Photo / Brigitte Friedrich / Bridgeman Images

We are at risk of losing our center if we do not appreciate that we are all linked to each other in our life journey and we need to find ways to hold on to our connections. As James Baldwin (1998) once said, in a quote we have remembered all our lives: "The moment we cease to hold each other, the sea engulfs us and the light goes out" (p. 706).

As teachers of family therapy, we have come to use the examples of famous families to learn about family process. The families we discuss in this book were chosen primarily because biographical information was available over several generations, which illustrated the patterns we consider most important. We have been astounded how often biographers ignore the family context of their subjects. It has indeed often been difficult to find families for whom relevant family history was even available. We regret any inaccuracies in our information, but as we know, family histories are always incomplete, and information is always skewed by the forgetfulness, secrecy, misremembering, distortion, fantasy, and elaboration of family members as well as biographers. We must do the best we can with whatever we can learn. We also use examples from famous families because the natural curiosity about the lives of famous people and their families helps to draw in readers' attention and interest. In addition, since famous people are often idealized, we have found it helpful to see that famous families deal with the same struggles and complexities as other families. Although each family is unique, families seem to have certain similar underlying patterns. All families have basic ways of dealing with love, pain, conflict, making sense of life, moving through the life cycle, and bridging time, social class, and cultural barriers. All families must find ways to deal with loss and integrate new members. Thus, in terms of emotional process, famous families may be as "ordinary" or "unique" as the rest of us.

We hope you will be as inspired as we have been by the stories of the families, famous and otherwise, discussed in this book and empowered to learn and understand as much as you can about your own family, and will work to have the most meaningful relationships possible with them.

THE IMPORTANCE OF UNDERSTANDING OUR FAMILY HISTORY

In his profound historical story, *Roots*, Alex Haley speaks of Omoro Kinte telling his son Kunta, after the death of his beloved grandmother:

> He said that three groups of people lived in every village. First were those you could see—walking around, eating, sleeping, and working. Second were the ancestors, whom Grandma Yaisa had now joined.
>
> "And the third people—who are they?" asked Kunta.
>
> "The third people," said Omoro, "are those waiting to be born." (Haley, 1977, p. 24)

Alex Haley
ZUMA Press, Inc. / Alamy Stock Photo

We believe deeply in encouraging people to pay attention to those to whom we belong, those who came before, and those who will come after us. A wise colleague once suggested to us that among the most helpful questions to ask ourselves when we feel stuck include: what would your unborn great-granddaughter want you to do now? And what would your long-lost great grandfather want you to do now?

However, many people prefer to downplay family history. Sigmund Freud, who has probably influenced psychological thinking about human behavior more than any other psychologist, focused almost exclusively on the importance of childhood fantasies about parents, ignoring the realities of parents' lives, the extended family, cultural history, and even the role of siblings. In fact, he wrote a whole autobiography in which he never even mentioned that he had siblings.

Sigmund Freud with his wife, Martha Bernays
Chronicle / Alamy Stock Photo

He destroyed many of his personal and family records, embarrassed, as so many of us are, by the mental illness and criminal acts of various family members. At least one of his secrets, his affair with his sister-in-law, Minna, was kept secret for almost 100 years and only confirmed recently by a serendipitous finding in a hotel record where they had stayed, which made the front page of *The New York Times*. Freud's biographers have gone along with his negative attitude about exploring family history, never bothering, as far as we know, to interview his siblings or even his mother, though she lived to be 95 and mothers featured centrally in his psychological theories.

While we can try to hide our history, it lives on inside us, probably the more powerful for our attempts to bury it, which may tend to fester, influencing others born long after the original painful experiences. Later family members may feel mystified by feelings they cannot understand because of the secrecy.

Almost fifty years ago now, Alex Haley's tracing of his own African American roots back to Africa in his book *Roots*, inspired not only African Americans but a whole generation to learn about their family and cultural history. And by the beginning of this century, genealogy had become the number one hobby in the U.S. with Ancestry.com, 23 and Me, MyHeritage.com, Familysearch.org, and many other resources available. People are developing access to history we never thought we would be able to assemble, both through DNA and through groups collecting public records from around the world in retrievable form.

THE DNA AGE: THE PAST IS NOT OVER

The recent availability of DNA evidence on our knowledge about family connections has also been enormous and promises to teach us even more about how we are biologically connected to our ancestors. We can learn that our father is not our father or that we have more siblings than we knew. Even more extraordinary, some sperm donors have created hundreds of children, and there are, apparently, even clubs of children who have the same sperm donor.

But learning the secrets of one's family history through DNA results can also be traumatic. Children may learn their parents are not their parents or that they are the product of an affair rather than of the parent they thought they had. They may have to rethink the history they thought they knew. Perhaps they have DNA connected siblings elsewhere that they have never heard of. This is well illustrated in the book *Inheritance: A Memoir of Genealogy, Paternity and Love* (2019), by Dani Shapiro, an only child who learned through sending a sample of her DNA for analysis after both her parents died that her father, to whom she had been close, was not her father, and her mother, with whom she had always struggled, had had her through in vitro fertilization by a medical student. She managed to find her biological father, who was married to a woman from Brazil with whom he had four children. Meeting them, she was struck that her resemblance to her biological father was actually stronger than his resemblance to any of his other children. Resemblance does not necessarily fit with closeness, just as the stories we learn growing up do not always fit with the way we have experienced our lives. Once DNA discrepancies are discovered, family members may need to rethink their whole history with a parent, a spouse, a child, or with the whole family as they realize the connections are not what they had thought. Secrets revealed through DNA can be both fascinating and profoundly disturbing.

The situation of children switched at birth as in the Benson–Collins families (**see Genogram 1.1: Benson–Collins Family**), illustrates such a discovery that affected multiple generations of two large families, but also their creativity in rethinking themselves and organizing a family reunion to celebrate their surprising and newfound identities and relationships.

Jim Collins, born in 1913 at a Bronx New York hospital to Irish immigrant parents, had been mistakenly switched at birth with Philip Benson, a Jewish baby, delivered the same day by the same doctor. The Jewish baby Philip Benson became the Irish Jim Collins, while the Irish Jim Collins became the Jewish Philip Benson. Sadly, "Jim's" parents died when he was very young and as result, he grew up in an orphanage. He went on to have a family of seven children, who grew up traveling around the world, settling eventually in California.

Philip Benson, who was raised as Jim Collins
Courtesy Alice Collins Plebuch

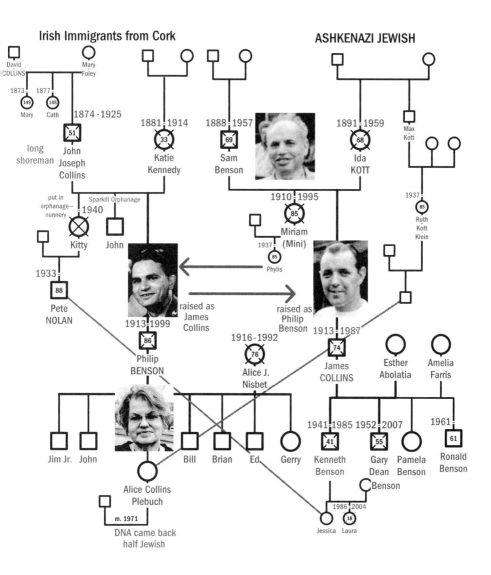

Genogram 1.1: Benson–Collins Family (Switched at Birth)

It wasn't until almost 100 years later, in 2012, that Jim's oldest daughter, Alice Collins Plebuch, at age sixty-four and retired, became inspired "just for fun" to get her DNA tested. Both her parents had died and she did not know much about them. She did know that her father's mother had died when he was still a baby and that he had grown up in a Catholic orphanage in the Bronx.

To Alice's great surprise, her DNA test results said she did not have much Irish ancestry but was 50 percent Ashkenazi Jewish! Having no known Jewish family connections anywhere in her history, Alice, along with several of her siblings, were mystified and began to dig into their family's DNA. All of Alice's siblings also did DNA tests and came out to be half Jewish. What could the explanation for this be? Had their mother had an affair and gotten pregnant all seven times with her paramour?

Alice Collins Plebuch
Courtesy Alice Collins Plebuch

John Collins with his three children, John, Kitty, and baby Jim Collins, who was born Philip Benson and mistakenly switched at birth
Courtesy Alice Collins Plebuch

They began to realize that their father, Jim Collins, was not related to his parents. It left them feeling a loss of identity. Who were they? Alice was motivated eventually to take a course in DNA and through enormous effort and some clever sleuthing, which genealogy often entails, the siblings discovered that their father, Jim, whom everyone always thought was remarkably short compared to all his relatives, had been switched at birth at Fordham Hospital in the Bronx with Philip Benson, a six-foot-tall man, raised in the Jewish Benson family. His birth certificate revealed that both he and Jim Collins had been delivered by the same doctor on the same day. The connection had come through another woman who had done a DNA test to learn about her Ashkenazi Jewish ancestry, only to find out she was mostly Irish!

Born Jim Collins (six feet tall) but accidentally switched at birth and raised as Philip Benson—with his father Sam Benson (five foot two)
Courtesy Pam Benson

Philip's father, Sam, had been five foot two and his mother four foot nine. When Philip married, his Jewish wife's parents had insisted he bring his birth certificate, because they didn't think he looked Jewish!

Not surprisingly, the discovery of the baby switch, which unfortunately came after both men had died, led to a great deal of family rethinking about who they were and what their history was. The cousins began calling each other "swapcuz." In a very creative readjustment move, the children, cousins, and grandchildren held a large Collins–Benson "reunion" allowing both sides to see for the first time many relatives who looked much more like them and their fathers than those they had thought were their relatives!

WHO IS FAMILY?

Family used to be a "tribe" who lived in relatively close proximity and continued from generation to generation in pretty much the same place or migrated together when circumstances required. Since the industrial revolution people have moved to pursue employment opportunities, while advances in transportation have expanded our tendency to move more frequently. While the configuration of families and degrees of physical proximity have changed, the notion of "family" remains an anchoring concept that is still deeply tied to the sense of who we are in the world. We generally resemble other members of our family. Their quirks and gestures are likely similar to our own. Our family members have been there, or we believe they *should* have been there, at all the important occasions of our lives—birth, marriages, graduations, illness, death. The meaning of family also expands far beyond our DNA connections to include those who become family through long connection and bonds of affection.

However, we often feel that if our families cannot acknowledge us, love us, and support us, no one else will. No matter how old we are, or how distant emotionally or physically, family still seems to matter. These relationships are our most important in life. Yet we often fail to connect with family members. At the end of Robert Anderson's play, *I Never Sang for My Father*, the son says: "What does it matter if I never loved him or he never loved me? But still, when I hear the word 'father' it matters." This is the point—family matters. However far we travel in miles or achievements, our family belongs to us and we belong to them. Indeed, our family is likely to come back to haunt us—in our relationships with our spouses, our children, our friends, and even at work. Beneath each family's particular idiosyncrasies lie patterns that cut across culture and time. Many of the basic ways families relate are universal.

EVERYONE IN A FAMILY MATTERS

Not only does family matter from a family systems point of view, but all family members are equally important—the renegades, the sinners, the villains, and the heroes. As a good friend, Ron Arons (2016) demonstrates in his research that began with his great grandfather, who had spent time in Sing Sing Prison, we can learn as much from the black sheep, the skinflints, and the hypochondriacs as we can from the saints and the martyrs. Those who became drunkards or addicts must be viewed in relation to their illustrious brothers who became U.S. presidents, as in the case of George Washington, John Quincy Adams, Theodore Roosevelt, Jimmy Carter, Bill Clinton, George Bush, and others. Sometimes the ne'er-do-wells make the heroes look more heroic. The failures can provide lessons about the cracks in our family's relationship system. We need to know about everyone, because, since everything is connected, without the whole, it is impossible to understand the individual parts. Those who have not had a voice, because they were poor, female, disabled, mentally ill or for whatever reason, are still important in a family's psychological reality, even if they lacked visibility within or outside the family.

Problems in our families of origin are often repeated in the families we create ourselves, however much we may wish it were not so. Even people with remarkable abilities in other areas may lose all objectivity when they return to their childhood homes. It is often especially difficult to notice how our own thinking and behavior may perpetuate problems that already have a long history in our families. Family problems can easily lead to cutoffs, whether they are about culture, race, social class, abuse, or other trauma. This book is about helping overcome such cutoffs and reconnecting with our history to free us up for our future.

THE POWER OF MEMBERS OF A SYSTEM IS NOT EQUAL, BUT THE SYSTEM IS STILL A SYSTEM

Although we are all affected by each other, the power that family members have to change relationships or resolve problems is not equal. Factors like gender, age, skin color, class standing, sexual identity, health status, and sibling position, influence the power that family members have to influence relationships and events.

It is important to take into account the power differentials of family members in relation to each other and their position in society (see also Pinderhughes, 2017). Relationships generally do not occur on an even playing field. This does not mean that relationships are not reciprocal, but that we must factor the dimension of unequal power into our understanding of each person's participation in the family and how we might change our own role. Efforts to change ourselves and our role in the family system often trigger family reactivity, but this is even more likely in the case of those who have less power within the family or within the larger social system.

THE PRICE OF CUTOFF AND TAKING OPPORTUNITIES TO RECONNECT

More than a hundred years ago, Abraham Lincoln, who did so much to create the right relations among people, refused to be in contact with his dying father, whom he had not visited in twenty years, saying that: "If we could meet now, it is doubtful whether it would not be more painful than pleasant" (Oates, 1977, p. 103).

Abraham Lincoln
Library of Congress, Prints and Photographs Division, LC-DIG-ppmsca-19301

Lincoln's hopelessness about changing his relationship with his father, who had apparently been abusive to him in childhood, is surely familiar to many of us. In spite of his brilliance and clarity on the dangers of cutoff affecting our nation as a whole, his pessimism about his father led him, in our view, to miss the possibility that a visit to his dying father might have offered. Of course, there is no guarantee the father would have responded differently to him, but he missed the opportunity to check that out. Our point is that it is only by making the effort to reconnect that we can see if the other person might have had a change of heart. We have found that there is almost always something to learn from reaching out across a divide to reconnect. If the effort is never made, this chance will be lost. We believe that even when there has been a long cutoff from a key family member for serious reasons, it is worth it to make an effort to reconnect every once in a while, which also gives the message you are leaving the door open.

This may be the hardest message of this book: that we do not believe in writing anyone in your family off forever. Rather, we suggest always keeping your heart open to the other person in case they become willing to change their behavior. This doesn't mean spending your weekends sitting in the bar with your abusive alcoholic father. Indeed, we believe it is important to find ways to leave any abusive situation. Never tolerate abuse, but do not be the one to create a forever cutoff with any key member of your family.

We hope you will find inspiration from the stories in this book of those who transformed their understanding of difficult family members as they strove to understand their history differently: James Baldwin's efforts to understand his abusive stepfather, Jennifer Teege's effort to understand her avoidant mother and her Nazi concentration camp director grandfather, Susan Faludi's efforts to get to know her abusive transgender father, and Amy Tan's efforts to get to know her self-centered, abusive mother's history.

What is it that makes approaching our families so hard? Why is it that so many people seem locked in boring or painful routines or cutting off from their families? Why do we sometimes become obsessed with how we are doing with our partners and our children, while ignoring our parents and siblings? And may we not then put too much pressure on our relationships with the next generation and jam the circuits with them, without realizing how all the generations are connected.

Many people fail to recognize until it is too late, the emotional price they pay for maintaining a "non-relationship" with important family members. Not to be in contact with your family may be an intense experience, even while it looks blank, because deep down most of us long for something different. Two sisters who do not speak for 40 years may experience a profound emptiness. They may resemble each other, have the same voice and mannerisms, and share a history that belongs only to them. Yet, anyone who suggests they both appear at the same family event will realize the painful intensity of their sense of wound behind their lack of connection. Children not getting to know their aunts and cousins or share their history is also a major, if at times hidden, loss to the family.

THE CONNECTION BETWEEN CLOSENESS, FUSION, CONFLICT, AND CUTOFF

People often mistakenly assume that a cut-off relationship means there is a lack of emotional connection. But in many cases cutoff is a reaction to extreme emotional intensity, or what we think of as fusion. Healthy closeness includes a balance between an emotionally warm and caring connection and clear boundaries that allow each person to also maintain their individuality. Fusion on the other hand involves an unhealthy degree of closeness, defined by weak boundaries that compromise the individuality of each person. Eventually fusion may lead to cutoff if the pressure to agree becomes too intense. The problem is that cutoff does not resolve the fusion. It just hides it from clear view. Under the surface the fusion persists, and it can only be resolved by each person finding ways to stay connected while maintaining a boundary that allows them to have their own opinions and identity. This is a central thesis of this book. As you will see in the chapters that follow, over and over we will make the case that to live your best life, it is important to find ways to be connected to your family while maintaining a clear boundary between yourself and others. This involves balancing the forces of separation and closeness so that you can relate to others while not losing yourself.

Queen Victoria grew up as an only child of a single mother. She slept with her mother every night until she was eighteen, sharing everything with her, and was almost completely isolated from other close relationships. Her German mother had immigrated alone to England to marry, and after the very early death of her husband, her British relatives left her isolated with her daughter, with whom she spoke German in a foreign land. As Victoria matured, she began to feel smothered by her exiled mother's demands for a kind of emotional fusion. When Victoria at eighteen acceded to the throne, she turned her back on her mother and replaced their earlier intense mother–daughter bond with a passionate and turbulent relationship with her first cousin and soon to be husband, Prince Albert.

Queen Victoria
IanDagnall Computing/Alamy Stock Photo

Twenty-four years later, when her mother died, Victoria went into paroxysms of grief, experiencing deep remorse over her long cutoff. As she sorted her mother's papers, she found that her mother had saved every scrap of Victoria's childhood memorabilia. Realizing too late how deeply her mother had loved her, she felt intense regret. In a typical response to such pain, she now blamed outsiders, especially her governess and her mother's advisor, for the cutoff she had affected herself: "Her love for me. It is too touching: I have found little books with the accounts of my babyhood, and they show such unbounded tenderness! I am wretched to think how for a time two people estranged us. . . . To miss a mother's friendship, not to be able to have her to confide in when a girl most needs it . . . drives me wild now" (cited in Woodham-Smith, 1972, p. 412).

Victoria, though already in middle age, described herself here as a "girl," elsewhere calling herself a "poor orphan child," who felt as if she were no longer cared for after her mother's death. She seemed, as one observer noted, "determined to cherish her grief and not be consoled" (Weintraub, 1987, p. 290). For weeks she took all her meals alone, considering her children "a disturbance," and leaving all the business of government to her husband, who was himself already terminally ill.

While Victoria and her mother had had almost no contact for nearly a quarter of a century, the underlying emotional dynamics that defined their earlier fused relationship had not really changed. They remained emotionally fused and thereby lacked a clear sense of themselves as individuals separate from each other. Given their fusion, it is understandable that Victoria cut off her mother when she took the throne, in part replacing her fusion with her mother with the intensity of her relationship with her husband. In addition, her position as queen made her mother's intrusions very difficult to manage. But when her mother died, it was for Victoria as if she had lost a part of herself. Now she thought of herself as "a poor orphan child" cherishing her grief for her mother as an unbearable loss, perhaps in part because she had never evolved the relationship from the fusion of her childhood to a mature closeness.

When Albert died a few months later, Victoria was overwhelmed completely. She had made him the centerpiece of her life, having moved from fusion with her mother to fusion with him. Every other relationship was secondary. She did not attend his funeral, yet for years she slept with his nightshirt in her arms. She made his room into a "sacred room" to be kept exactly as it had been when he was alive. Every day for the rest of her long life she had his linens changed, his clothes laid out afresh, and water prepared for his shaving. To every bed in which she slept, she attached a photograph of Albert as he lay dead. For the next forty years she wore a mourning dress in the style of the year he died. Years before, Victoria had written, "How one loves to cling to grief" (Benson, 1987, p. 96), and she certainly did. She developed an obsession with cataloguing everything, so that nothing would be changed. She surrounded herself with mementos of the past and gave orders that nothing ever be thrown away. There were to be no further changes or losses, and as long as she lived, these orders were obeyed (Strachey, 1921).

Victoria's reactions, constricted and rigid as they are, reflect understandable human reactions to distress, especially when closeness has devolved into fusion. Loss can then create a situation where it feels as if time stops. Families may close down, attempting to control those aspects of their world over which they still have some power, because in the one area that matters most—human relationships—they have lost their sense of control.

Queen Victoria was a great and remarkable woman whose personality dominated the nineteenth century, and in many ways, continued to do so through the twentieth. Ruler of England for two thirds of a century, she wrote more than any monarch in history, her total production the equivalent of 700 volumes! She was by all accounts a woman of many paradoxes—difficult, demanding, and capricious, but also gentle, passionate, humble, and scrupulously honest. On the other hand, she suffered, as many people do, from the deep-seated effects of her family problems. Her isolated childhood seemed to limit her relationships with her own children, with whom she said she never felt at ease. But then she had grown up as a child alone and had no real experience with children.

We know that Victoria refused to make any accommodation to her oldest son's need to learn how to rule, treating him like a child until her last breath, when he was sixty. A hundred years later, King Charles III was in a similarly ambiguous position while waiting to ascend to the throne. It may be a particularly unusual paradox that his "professional" life could not begin until his mother died, but it is not uncommon for children to see themselves as unfree until a parent dies, instead of viewing the time they do have together as the important part.

RUNNING AWAY FROM YOUR FAMILY MAY TRAP YOU IN THE PAST

Most people avoid confronting family issues because they cannot see a way to change relationships that they find frustrating. This often leads them to seek new relationships to make up for whatever has gone wrong earlier. If these new relationships don't bring fulfillment, their general bitterness and pain are likely to increase. Running away from home emotionally or physically typically traps people in the past rather than freeing them for the future. As the saying goes, "The thread to your past is the ladder to your future."

Perhaps the most famous runaway in American history was Benjamin Franklin. He was bitter about family conflicts, especially with an older brother, James, to whom he had been apprenticed as a printer at twelve. James had beaten and humiliated him whenever he did not tow the line. When James was sent to prison for his writings a few years later, Franklin took over and ran the press, but when James returned, Ben could not stand to be under his thumb again. Nor could he tolerate, apparently, the lack of his parents' support. In 1724, at the age of seventeen, Franklin left his family in Boston and moved to Philadelphia, telling no one of his whereabouts. Eventually a brother-in-law tracked him down and persuaded him to return to Boston to reconnect. He returned, hoping also for some money, but when he was unsuccessful with both the reconnection and the money, he left again. He remained estranged for the rest of his life. Although his parents lived for twenty-five more years, Franklin rarely communicated with them and appears never to have repaired his relationships with them in any but the most superficial way. In all his prodigious writings he hardly mentions them.

In the next generation, Franklin had an out-of-wedlock son, William, to whom in early years he was very attached. William became his companion and collaborator, and it was for him that Franklin began writing his famous autobiography. However, just as his relationship with his family of origin ended in cutoff, this relationship also ended in a bitter and forever unreconciled cutoff. Even when you try to do the opposite of what your parents did, you may unwittingly repeat the same pattern.

In an almost uncannily similar way, Franklin's son William ended up with a cutoff from his own son, Temple Franklin. Like his father, William had his son out of wedlock, and like his father, he tried to fashion his son into a companion. But William and his son also ended up bitterly estranged. Franklin's grandson then fathered two children out of wedlock, from whom he, too, became cut off. Another multigenerational pattern repetition accompanied these cutoffs in the Franklin family: after cutting off his son, Franklin doted on his grandson, Temple; in the next generation, William doted on *his* grandchild, Ellen, to such an extent that he pretended she was his own daughter.

These sad patterns are surprisingly common in families. Cutoffs tend to beget first fusion in the next generation, and then, perhaps because of the intensity of the need for connection, more cutoffs.

Whatever has happened in your family shapes you. Events that occurred long before your birth, never mentioned in your family during your lifetime, may influence you in powerful, hidden ways, sometimes fostering resilience, other times creating patterns of secrecy, anxiety, and more cutoff. When, for example, a child dies before another's birth, the "replacement" child may manage until he or she tries to leave home, at which point the family may go into a crisis, triggered by the original loss, though no one may link the upheaval to the first child's death years earlier.

Every experience in your family's biography is part of the many-layered pattern that influences your identity. If your aunt dies by suicide, it will affect most immediately her husband and children (your uncle and cousins), who may be left with a legacy of pain, anger, guilt, and social stigma. However, it will also affect her parents (your grandparents), who may forever wonder where they went wrong. It will affect her aunts and uncles and her siblings (including your parents), who will share the family pain, wondering what they might have done differently to keep her from killing herself. But those are only the obvious people affected. Your aunt's suicide will also affect her nieces and nephews (you, your siblings, and cousins), who will have to wonder whether your parents might ever, like their sister, decide on such a course of action, and her grandchildren, perhaps not even born at the time of the suicide, who will be influenced by their parents' pain over the loss as well as by their own fears about the meaning of their grandmother's death. Your own children will probably have similar doubts about whether suicide runs in your family and how it might again come into their lives. In addition, each family member will have to respond to the reactions of the others. Inevitably, the impact of such an experience tends to ripple throughout the whole family for generations into the future.

The antidote to the transmission of pain, however silently it flows, is to face the secrets and traumas to take away their power and learn about the family's resilience in response to such a loss, which is just as important. No matter what traumas have occurred in your family in the past, every family's very existence is a testament to their survival of previous traumas, and thus also a source of resilience.

FAMILY PATTERNS OVER THE LIFE CYCLE

To understand your family it is important to track family patterns over time, in life-cycle perspective, noting especially those transitions at which families tend to be more vulnerable because of the necessary readjustment in relationships. It helps to explore problems in the context of a family's trajectory in their past, the tasks they are presently trying to master, and the future toward which they are moving, although, of course, any family is more than the sum of its parts. The individual life cycle from birth to death takes place within the family life cycle, which takes place within the larger cultural and societal life cycle. Problems are most likely to appear when there is an interruption or dislocation in the process, whether because of an untimely death, a chronic illness, a divorce or migration that forces family members to separate, or because the family is unable to launch a child or tolerate the entry of a new in-law, grandchild, or grandparent into the family home. Major conflicts and cutoffs often occur also in relation to major life-cycle transitions such as marriage, having a child, divorce, remarriage, adolescence, launching, aging, disability, illness, and death.

The patterns of the current family life cycle are changing rapidly. It is easy to lose a sense of connection with what has come before in our families, which can be a serious loss. With advances in audio, video, and internet technology, however, we now actually have, for the first time, new capabilities for transmission of the culture and history from one generation to the next. Yet families often fail to share their cultural and family stories and history, though these are such wellsprings for social and personal identity and have such potential to inspire families.

We are living a great deal longer than human beings ever lived before, so we have much more ability to connect with previous generations. But at the same time, we have become so mobile that we often suffer from disconnection. For a variety of reasons, separations and cut-offs are common in families. Family roles are also changing. While working fathers, homemaker mothers, and several children was the model for families 100 years ago, families have shrunk, couples are having fewer children, divorcing more frequently and re-partnering into other constellations, and traditional gender roles often no longer apply. So families now look very different from even one or two generations ago. We require very different patterns of caretaking for children, older family members, and the disabled, who were traditionally taken care of primarily by women in the home.

FAMILY ROLES TEND TO GET FIXED

Usually, people take on certain roles in families—hero, villain, joker, caretaker, victim. These characterizations tend to reinforce basic family messages by indicating who the "good guys" and "bad guys" are. As we become aware of a family's stories and the messages embedded in them, we can evaluate whether to maintain these "labels" or not. It is not unusual for people to feel acute embarrassment, shame, or even despair about certain details of family history. They worry that negative traits may be inherited or that they are doomed to repeat family mistakes. Family skeletons may remain in the closet because some people don't want to know the truth and others don't want to tell. But, of course, avoidance of painful memories tends to distort family relationships, causing more ongoing problems in family relationships even generations after a trauma has occurred. When families keep secrets, their relationships may become dishonest and insecure.

MAKING THE CONNECTIONS BETWEEN EVENTS AND RELATIONSHIPS

At times the coincidences in events and relationships in families over the generations may seem uncanny. How does it happen that patterns repeat without the participants' awareness of the earlier experience? In one family, an aunt had committed murder of another family member and then suicide. The rest of the family moved away, changed their names, and never spoke of the trauma. But years later a grandniece in her teens attempted suicide on the exact date of her grandaunt's suicide, not even knowing the family's history. How such family secrets get transmitted is a mystery, but the more we can learn about our family's history, the more perspective we will gain to address the present issues.

STARTING YOUR JOURNEY TO GO HOME AGAIN

This book discusses making efforts to change your relationships in your immediate and extended family and social systems by changing yourself. A good place to start is to ask yourself about your own beliefs and life goals, and what family patterns you see as dysfunctional. This is the starting point for taking the journey to learn as much as possible about how family relationship patterns have evolved. This book will guide you in the process of identifying family patterns and themes over the course of multiple generations and within the context of culture, class, race, religion, gender, sexual orientation, and critical life experiences, especially trauma, untimely loss, family resilience, secrets, and cutoffs. We will emphasize expanding your perspective beyond just your own assessment of each person to learn the views of others.

Before things can start to change in your family, you will need to become an observer and researcher of stories and patterns in your family. We aim to guide you in deepening your knowledge of your family's patterns over time so you can decide how to bring your own behavior more in line with your own deepest values. Change does not begin with pressing others to change their views or behaviors, but rather with considering deeply what views you want to live by and which of your own behaviors you might want to change. For example, directly challenging a family member's anti-humanistic beliefs, such as racism, sexism, homophobia, or physical or psychological abuse, would most likely provoke reactivity toward you. Instead, you might begin by seeking to empower yourself to have the best possible connection with each other family member, while holding on to your own sense of self. Once you have maximized your connection to another family member, you begin to consider when and how to broach a challenging topic in the most respectful and diplomatic way.

It makes sense to explore individual symptoms and problems in the context of the entire spectrum of functioning and relationships, emphasizing overall patterns in the network of relationships, rather than viewing them primarily as an individual's psychological process. This can be surprisingly difficult, since most of us have been socialized to think in a very individualistic way about human problems, and to assume that they reside inside the individual rather than being part of the larger context. Furthermore, our political and economic systems operate on the belief that one can pull oneself up by one's bootstraps, in spite of the widespread evidence that our social system largely defines our options right down to our longevity.

In some cases, it may be tempting to remain distant from your family, or parts of your family, and yet, when there are cutoffs, the ghosts of our families can haunt us—voices in our head, sounding disapproval, threats of further abandonment, or loss of self. These ghosts can stand between you and all that you cherish in life, or they can taint an otherwise productive and satisfying life with pain and sadness. By remaining unaware of family ghosts, a family can be locked in these formative experiences, unable to move beyond them.

The main work of going home again involves looking at your relationships in context and then thinking and planning how you want to change your ways of relating to family members. You begin by trying to connect your feelings and reactions back to family emotional patterns and relationships. This does not discount the impact of the internal psychological or physiological system on your functioning. Rather, you start with the assumption that external systems influence internal feeling states. But you still have a choice about how you will ultimately respond to others. The focus here is on helping you choose responses that honor your values, rather than simply reacting to how others are relating to you. The book aims to guide you in making informed choices about the kinds of family relationships you want to have with your family members. Once you get comfortable in relating in new ways, with less reactivity, your confidence in your relating will increase and, hopefully, the relationships in your family will begin to change.

A few questions that may help you get started on your family journey:

- How do family members think about each other? What characteristics are mentioned? What are the roles and labels in the family? Is one "weak, boring, slow" and another "brilliant, domineering, and manipulative"? Make a list of the different ways family members are described, noting especially the opposites in role or label.
- Who was named for whom in the family and why? Do names reveal the roles people have played? Who chose the names? Why were they chosen? If names have no apparent rhyme or reason, could there be hidden meanings? Was someone named for a mother's lost sweetheart? If members are named for the dead, have they taken on their characteristics? Were the family's naming patterns reflected in the structure or have they influenced psychological patterns?
- How did migration influence the family's experience? How did financial changes influence the family? How did illness and death influence them at different ages?
- Which family members did not conform to expected gender roles and how were they viewed by others? What can we learn about the family's flexibility or inflexibility from their history of allowable gender roles?

Chapter 2
Culture: Ethnicity, Race, Class, Religion, and Historical Period

The ache for home lives in all of us, the safe place where we can go as we are and not be questioned. It impels mighty ambitions and dangerous capers. . . . Hoping that by doing these things home will find us acceptable or, failing that, that we all forget our awful yearning for it.

—MAYA ANGELOU
All God's Children Need Traveling Shoes

Our relationships can destroy us, but they can change us too, and restore us, and without us ever seeing it happen, they can define us.

—ROBERT KOLKER
Hidden Valley Road

The world has learned over and over again that the wounds of the ancestors make the children bleed. I do not know if anyone will ever be forgiven or if the harm that was done will ever be undone.

—LOUIS DE BERNIERES
Birds Without Wings

To best understand our families, we must also look deeply into their cultural context. When and where in history were our family members born and what life circumstances, migrations, local or societal political and economic events circumscribed their lives? These are crucial questions for understanding who we are as human beings.

Genograms help us contextualize kinship networks and family processes in terms of culture, class, race, gender, sexual orientation, religion, and migration history. What is the impact of having ancestors who immigrated from Europe and headed westward to be homesteaders in Nebraska on lands the government stole by breaking treaties with the Native peoples who were torn from their homelands? What is the impact of having ancestors who were members of the Kickapoo or Omaha nations whose treaties with the U.S. government had been broken and who had been forcibly relocated from lands they had inhabited for many generations? What might be the impact of having ancestors who grew wealthy on the work of other human beings they bought and sold?

By learning the cultural, religious, and class stories of our families, we can place our present issues in the context of our family's evolutionary cultural patterns of geography, migration, and social context.

What we think, how we act, and even our language are transmitted through our family and the wider cultural context in which we are embedded. And culture itself is not a monologue, but a dialogue. Our families are themselves made up of many cultural roots. No matter what a person's background is, it is effectively multicultural, as all marriages are at a level intercultural. To understand your family, you need to know about their cultural roots.

Families differ in their sense of their cultural roots. Whether or not they feel connected to their cultural history, these roots shape the family's identity, patterns, and dynamics, influencing our attitudes toward life, death, sex, food, men, women, children, the elderly, birth, and death. Have family members conformed to what is expected of men and of women in their cultural group? How much closeness is expected or desired between family members? Patterns vary greatly from one cultural group to another. Italians may tend to be close and enmeshed, sharing a great deal and spending holidays and free time together and tending to believe that if you lose your family you might as well be dead. Scandinavian families often maintain a greater distance and are less likely to demonstrate anger or affection, even among close relatives.

Families exist in a sociocultural context, and thus, part of understanding your family must include understanding how factors like ethnicity, race, religion, class, economic and political circumstances, historical events, geography, and migration have influenced their values, beliefs, and behaviors.

A family's xenophobia or open curiosity about outsiders probably reflects their cultural history. If your family members were poor, politically oppressed for centuries, or were adventurers who moved about, gathering energy as they went, those patterns are undoubtedly still embedded in you. If they were members of the ruling class of the land, the dominant "tribe" in their cultural context or the object of another group's colonizing or discriminatory efforts, that history will have its impact as well. If they were extremely nationalistic, they may have felt oppressed as a minority within a larger community. Sometimes there is an attempt to hold on tightly to cultural traditions, even if this closes them to new experiences. Seeing their attitudes about culture from a systemic perspective can help you understand how your family's history may have led them to hold onto certain beliefs or shift to others. Under pressure from the dominant society, family members may try to "pass," renouncing their heritage, or they may cling to it unduly. For all of these reasons, it is important to try to identify your family's cultural roots and to examine how culturally based issues and experiences shaped their evolution over time.

COMING HOME

Critic and author bell hooks has written about the way that our sense of home is tied not only to our families of origin, but also to place and space (geography), and to broader social factors such as race, gender, and class. If we remember home as a place where we experienced devaluation, either within our families or from external forces such as poverty, racism, homophobia, or other oppression, this can prevent us from making the journey home again. In her book *Belonging: The Culture of Place* (2009), bell hooks explains that

she left her family and her home state of Kentucky when she was eighteen to escape the pain of a dysfunctional family and of the racism and classism she felt growing up there. "Since my native place was indeed the site and origin of the deep dysfunction that had damaged my spirit, I did not believe I could be safe there" (p. 18). . . . "My own deep wounds, the traumas of my Kentucky childhood are marked by the meeting place of family dysfunction and the disorder produced by dominator thinking and practice, combined with the effect of racism, sexism, and class elitism" (p. 52).

bell hooks
*Monica Almeida/The New
York Times/Redux*

Within her family, her father's sexism and her mother's acquiescence to it were wounding to hooks, but this was not the only source of her childhood pain. When she was eight, her parents moved the family from the country to the city in their attempt to "move up" in the world. They rejected the ways of the elders and traditions of the ancestors that they perceived as backward. They wanted their children to be modern and sophisticated, which was all about trying to "enhance" their class status, and distance from the shame they associated with being poor, rural, and Black. But for hooks the move to the city and the loss of connection with nature, the land, and the old ways was traumatizing. Moreover, in the city she experienced intensive and consistent racism that also inflicted deep wounds.

When she was eighteen, she left Kentucky and her family to attend college in California at Berkeley. She was trying to escape the pain that had haunted her as a child. Yet in leaving home, she became an exile, and that too hurt. "Living away from my native place, I became more consciously Kentuckian than I was when I lived home. This is what the experience of exile can do, change your mind, utterly transform . . . (your) perception of the world of home" (hooks, 2009, p. 13). However, as exiled as she felt for thirty years, she did not feel that she could go home. "Like many writers, especially southerners, who have stayed away from their native place, who live in a state of mental exile, the condition of feeling split was damaging, and caused a breaking down of the spirit. Healing that spirit meant for me remembering myself, taking the bits and pieces of my life and putting them together again. In remembering my childhood and writing about my early life I was mapping the territory, discovering myself and finding homeplace" (p. 15).

In writing about belonging, hooks explains that it is common for people to try to distance themselves from their past, their families, and their cultural legacies, in an effort to start anew. Yet these efforts to reinvent ourselves have a way of continually looping us back to our past. When we can finally stop fighting this and see our history as a resource that we can learn from, it can give us the power to find what we have been seeking all along—home.

How many of us have been trying to distance ourselves from home, both in terms of our family of origin, and of the experiences we and our families had with respect to our racial, ethnic, and religious background, class status, gender and sexual identities, and experiences with migration and geographic location? How many of us, like bell hooks, have been haunted by past pain related to dysfunction in our family that is tied to our cultural identities, whether we consciously recognized it or not? Probably most of us have struggled with how to find a way home that is honest yet healing and transformative. What is vital to bear in mind is that the journey to go home again is not about regressing into sentimentalism. As hooks cites anthropologist Carol Stack: "No one, however nostalgic, is really seeking to turn back the clock. . . . What people are seeking is not so much the home they left behind as a place that they can change, a place in which their lives and strivings will make a difference—a place in which to create a home" (Carol Stack, cited in hooks, 2009, p. 221).

For hooks, it was only by facing what she had left behind and allowing herself to see the good and the bad, that she was able to finally find herself: "To return home was to come back to the pain and hurt that I had spent years of my life trying to make go away. My hurt was rooted in trauma experienced in the dysfunctional family and the pain of growing up in a racially segregated world in the midst of racial apartheid . . . (but) I cannot live a grounded life without being grounded in a place" (hooks, 2009, p. 59, 68). And this grounding cannot occur unless and until we allow ourselves to go home again—to see, explore, investigate, expose and ultimately understand and accept our families of origin and our cultural legacies, which for better and for worse, are always a part of us.

Linda Burton and her colleagues have argued that it is essential to take into account the concept of homeplace, which they define as "the multilayered, nuanced individual and family processes that are anchored in a physical space that elicits feelings of empowerment, belonging, commitment, rootedness, ownership, safety, and renewal. This includes the ability to develop relationships that provide us with a solid sense of social and cultural identity" (Burton, Winn, Stevenson, & Lawson Clark, 2004, p. 397).

The notion of homeplace is relevant for people of all cultures throughout the life cycle. This is especially true for immigrants, who are away from their homes, networks, communities, and rituals. Homeplace also serves as the site of resistance against the oppressive forces of our society (Burton et al., 2004). Home provides security and safety to develop self-esteem, political consciousness and resistance to societal invalidation, racism, and other oppression. Those who are gay, lesbian, bisexual, or transgender may need special adaptive strategies to find a place they can feel at home, because the very place that others rely on as home has often become the place of greatest danger. This is true as well for many children whose families suffer from mental illness, violence, addictions, and other negative forces.

We all need to experience a sense of belonging—to feel safe and secure, especially when living in a multicultural society, where connecting with others who are different from us may be particularly challenging. Indeed, the most challenging aspect of development involves our beliefs about, and interaction with others who are different from ourselves: men from women; young from old; Black from white; wealthy from poor; heterosexual from LGBTQ. Our level of maturity on this crucial dimension of tolerance and openness to difference is strongly influenced by how our families, cultures of origin, community, and society as a whole have dealt with difference. To find our way back home we must explore the ways our sense of home may have been disrupted exploring and reconnecting with our multicultural familial roots.

HOW CULTURE SHAPES FAMILY PATTERNS

Ethnicity refers to the group, clan, or tribe from which one's family has descended. Groups share cultural customs, values, and usually language and national origins, but not always. Jewish groups, for example, come from two major subgroups, Ashkenazi (Eastern European) and Sephardic (Spanish and Middle Eastern) and may have neither a common country of origin nor a language in common; they may be Orthodox, Conservative, Reform, or nonreligious, but still share cultural origins. National boundaries are often the result of political decisions by colonizing powers and may be a poor reflection of ethnic distinctions. The boundaries between countries in Africa, the Middle East, or between India and Pakistan are recent creations and rarely reflect the ethnicities of the multiple cultural groups within their boundaries. In the U.S. we have a tendency to define Native Americans as a monolithic group with little regard for the hundreds of different tribal cultural groups that existed here long before white colonizers arrived and established arbitrary and imperialist boundaries between the U.S., Mexico, and Canada. It is important to understand where your family members come from and what their intergroup relationships have been, going back as far as possible.

For African Americans the issue of ethnicity is complicated by the legacy of slavery, which forcibly transported Africans from their homes across the Atlantic and deprived them of any knowledge of their history or even their names. This holocaust forever changed the lives of generations of families, giving them no opportunity to connect with the specific tribal groups from which their ancestors descended. What stands in its place is a shared identity rooted in a multigenerational legacy of racial oppression and genocide. Nevertheless, with DNA testing, some people can at least learn their generic cultural roots if not their specific family and cultural history, which can help them expand their sense of "home."

Many Native American groups have been deprived by U.S. policies of maintaining their cultural connections, but DNA may help them as well to confirm basics of their cultural origins. We may also be able to learn enough about general cultural history to speculate about its influence on our particular family's history. The cultural stories of others of the same background may give meaningful clues as well. The evolution of the Black Church as a cultural unifier for the descendants of slaves is a great example of threads of cultural continuity that have followed down the generations, in spite of the dominant society's efforts to cut them off from their heritage (Gates, 2021).

Ethnicity patterns our thinking, feeling, and behavior in both obvious and subtle ways, although generally operating outside of our awareness. It plays a major role in determining what we eat, how we work, how we relate, how we celebrate holidays and rituals, and how we feel about life, death, and illness (McGoldrick, Giordano, & Garcia Preto, 2005). When asked to consider ethnicity most of us can come up with a list of characteristics that we associate with various ethnic groups. Doing so may run the risk of generalizing at best and stereotyping at worst, and yet there is some truth reflected in these characterizations. In our work with families, we have found that it is helpful to have people identify the ethnic groups from which they are descended and to consider the traits that are generally associated with those groups to see if any of these fit their own family and life experience. Doing so is one way to contextualize values, beliefs, and behaviors.

There are so many ways ethnicity may shape family patterns: Some groups may value active verbal engagement, while others may place a premium on keeping to yourself. Some cultures value open, expressive displays of emotions while others prefer to keep a stiff upper lip. Some value individuality, while others emphasize group identity and loyalty to the community above individual identity. Some are comfortable addressing illness and death while for others, this arouses anxiety and discomfort. Some groups live primarily in the present while others pay more attention to the past, and still others focus mostly on the future. Consideration of the role of our ethnic background is a starting point for exploring what dynamics may be related to our current family patterns. Couples from different ethnic groups may indeed be drawn to each other by their very differences. But these very ethnic differences may eventually become "the rub." For example, some groups tend to be highly expressive, leaning toward intense, passionate relationships, while others are often conflicted about expressing emotions, particularly angry or sexual feelings. For example, during a marital argument, a spouse, who happens to be Italian, might make outrageous dramatic accusations or threats, to convey the depth of her passion, which her partner, who happens to be Irish, might experience as an overwhelming "attack" that he responds to with immobilization and a stony silence. His response, or lack thereof, is devastating for his partner who is seeking connection through her passionate argument. While there are many variables that may account for their differing emotional styles, ethnic background may be one of them, and we encourage you to factor this in when you assess the different ways that members of your family respond to conflict and the intensity of emotional expression.

Katharine Hepburn, from an upper-middle-class New England liberal Protestant family of Anglo heritage, and Spencer Tracy, from an ultra-conservative, urban, Midwestern, working-class, Irish Catholic family, illustrate how cultural differences may be compounded by class differences as well. In fact, Tracy's mother's background was more similar to Hepburn's, as she was Anglo, not Irish, and descended from founders of Brown University. Yet, as often happened to women, in her marriage to a hard driving, hard drinking, Irish Catholic truck salesman who was the son of immigrants in Milwaukee, she moved into his social context and adapted to his cultural location.

Irish Spencer Tracy and
Anglo Katharine Hepburn
Album/Alamy Stock Photo

Hepburn and Tracy differed dramatically in their emotional expression. She preferred restraint, decorum, logic, and stoicism. Dorothy Parker once said Hepburn ran "the gamut of emotion all the way from A to B," while with Tracy it was impossible to know when he was pretending and when he was telling the truth (Kanin, 1988, p. 17). His family was more erratic, less predictable, and much less interested in logic. He would go from violent drunken rages to merry times, to sullen withdrawal in roller coaster fashion.

These contextual factors were probably compounded by Tracy and Hepburn's sibling positions: She was a functional oldest and he a younger brother of an older brother whom he seems to have loved and hated with equal intensity all his life.

While Hepburn was careful, thorough, methodical, and analytical, Tracy was an instinctive, intuitive actor, who thought you went stale by over-rehearsing, and preferred to trust his intuition. Hepburn's values of cleanliness (she took seven to eight showers a day!), frugality, hard work, and rugged individualism were legendary. Tracy was a fighter and a rebel, most comfortable in working-class contexts, dropping out of fifteen schools before finishing eighth grade, whereas for Hepburn, work was never a chore. Tracy saw fun in everything, except his religion, but was full of unpredictable highs and lows, a full-scale hell-raiser from his youth, whereas a friend said that with Hepburn: "When you enter her world . . . you arrive on time and leave as early as possible; . . . you do not gossip; you agree with . . . her many opinions; . . . you do not get drunk no matter how much you drink . . . you do not complain (you may, however, rail); you refrain from lies, dissemblances, and exaggerations, you omit discussion of your physical state, symptoms, or ailments (unless preparatory to asking her advice); you take her advice; you do not use obscene, coarse, or lewd expressions" (Kanin, 1988, pp. 11–12). The couple even differed in what "home" meant to them. Kate was a "house person," viewing even an apartment as "an artificial and temporary abode." Spencer was perfectly content in a hotel room and liked to live in small places "because I live a small life" (Kanin, 1988, p. 13).

RACE AND SKIN COLOR

Racial minorities tend to recognize the significance of race and skin color, because society never lets them forget it. They must be attuned to the realities of race and teach their children how to survive in the face of racial discrimination and devaluation. Race and skin color are powerful organizing principles in the U.S., where there is great racial diversity as well as a long history of inequitable treatment of those who were not white.

Be mindful of the extent to which culture shapes relationships among family members of color. In their book *The Color Complex*, Russell, Wilson, and Hall (1993) explained that, "even in families where color does not seem to be much of an issue, siblings learn to use their differences as ammunition in ordinary rivalries. . . . In healthy families, such sibling conflict may actually relieve pent-up feelings and make the whole issue seem less serious or threatening. It is when color remains an unspoken concern that children may suffer the most" (p. 96).

Most whites think of race as an issue only for people of color, failing to recognize the ways in which their own racial identity has shaped their lives as well. The privilege of whiteness makes it possible not to think about race and as a result, most whites do not consider the relevance of race until a family member dates or marries someone of color. As the United States becomes increasingly diverse, more and more people are marrying out of their ethnic and racial group. This is significant, given that until the past generation insidious laws prohibited people from marrying across racial lines. Even in the twenty-first century, the British royal family still worried that their latest grandson might be too dark skinned to be a prince and he was denied the title. The point about white privilege is that it enables most white people to live without noticing how race influences their lives.

Barack Obama
Library of Congress,
Prints and Photographs
Division, LC-DIG-ppbd-00603

Barack Obama discussed this dynamic in considering how his maternal grandparents from Kansas came to allow their daughter, however grudgingly, to marry an African, a question that always puzzled him. He explained that in his grandparents' memories, when Black people appeared they were "shadowy, silent presences" that elicited "neither passion nor fear" (Obama, 1995, p. 18). He thought they probably never gave Black people any consideration at all under the belief one should keep contact between the races to a minimum. Several years after they were married, Obama's grandparents (Stanley and Toot) moved to Texas and it was there that they first became aware of racism. Stanley Dunham was warned not to serve Mexican and Black customers as a furniture store salesman, and Toot was accosted by a secretary in the bank where she worked for referring to the Black janitor as "Mister Reed." Experiences like these shocked and offended them, but were likely the only times they thought about race overtly. While Stanley insisted they leave Texas because they were disturbed by the racism there, Toot said they actually left in search of better work.

Once Barack was born, of course, his grandparents were forever part of an interracial family. Racial diversity in Hawaii was also much more a part of the local culture than on the mainland U.S., which may have made things easier. Nevertheless, this once white family now had to deal with race overtly as an undeniable part of their everyday experience.

It is important to be curious about how couples in your family came together—couples from different class backgrounds, religions, ethnic or racial groups, and to explore how family members thought about and responded to interracial or other intergroup differences. Who was supportive of their relationship and who was against it? What reasons did they offer and how directly or indirectly were various opinions, beliefs, and reactions communicated? How did triangles, coalitions, alliances, or distance and cutoffs develop in response to racial issues or other differences?

Within families of color, how overtly are issues of race and skin color addressed by family members? And in white families, how and what are children taught about race? How have children been socialized with respect to racial awareness and coping with racism? How are some family members valued or devalued based on complexion? Have triangles, alliances, coalitions and cutoffs developed around issues of race/skin color? Be curious about how your family has reacted to differences of all kinds, including those related to race and skin color.

If your family has remained exclusively white (as far as you know), it will still increase your understanding to know how they thought about and dealt with people of other races, cultures, religions, and social locations. These questions remain relevant because we never know who our children may choose to connect with and bring into our family and how soon we may be challenged to find ways to connect beyond our comfort zone.

HISTORICAL CONTEXT: YOUR FAMILY'S PLACE IN TIME

When trying to understand your family from an intergenerational perspective, consider how the historical context shaped family members in the particular time and place where they lived. This is similar to the concept of cohort that refers to a group of people who grew up during a particular period in time, and/or have a shared geographic, political, or social location. The same behaviors have different meanings and provoke differential reactions depending on the historical period in which one grew up. For example, how people view various issues tends to differ depending on whether they grew up during the Depression Era, World War II, the Vietnam Era, or the "Covid Era."

Migration is also an important factor in any family's history. In the United States, everyone except Native Americans and African Americans migrated to this country intentionally from somewhere else in the world, and that history tends to impact your worldview and ways of relating significantly. Pay attention to how old people were at the time they migrated. A family that migrates in the middle of the mother's childbearing years may have two different sets of children. The children born after the migration may have been raised in a much more hopeful context or, on the other hand, in a more stressed family, struggling to acculturate and learn the language and missing their own culture and family members left behind.

The experiences people have had along the path of their migration also shape family dynamics. The reasons why individuals or families migrate, and their relationship with the family members and cultures they have left behind, passed through, and resettled in are essential factors in their character and developmental processes.

Groups may also have particular histories of trauma associated with their migration. Jewish families, for example, were oppressed for hundreds of years before coming to the U.S. The Freud family was forced to migrate twice, before coming to Vienna, and never again returning to their home in what is now the Czech Republic. Although they maintained their Jewish identity, they experienced continuous anti-Semitism, which limited Freud's professional development, and then in the 1930s the family were forced to flee again for England to escape the Nazis. The family of Gustav Mahler experienced a very similar migration, coming to Vienna from the same region as the Freuds. In their case, Gustav also left behind his Jewish identity under the pressure of the times, to succeed musically in Vienna. One wonders what the Mahler family lost in the pain of migration and what price they paid emotionally and spiritually in giving up their religion and coming to a country that would never accept them for who they truly were. Even today, the city of Vienna seems limited in its celebration Mahler's role in the history of music, although his music is still played throughout the world. What does it cost a family in terms of a sense of belonging and identity to live in a place where their heritage and talents are not recognized?

All too often, migration experiences are tied to stories of suffering and trauma, which may leave an indelible impact on the family for multiple generations. As already mentioned, the traumatic case of African Americans, whose ancestors were violently uprooted from their cultures and families of origin and relocated thousands of miles away as slaves still affects African American families, and our society as a whole today. Not only did they endure a devastating physical separation from their homes, families, and communities, but they also had to endure the trauma of being forbidden to maintain any overt association with their cultural traditions. We also need to ask what is the impact of this history on any family over time who participated in the enslavement of African Americans?

Scott Joplin (see **Genogram 2.1: Scott Joplin Family**) was another gifted composer whose talent was not acknowledged as a result of the racist context in which he lived. His life, like that of all African Americans, was profoundly affected by his not being able to feel at home in the cultural context and the historical period in which he lived. The first African American composer to fully develop his compositions into an American idiom, he was also the first of his family's children to be born after the end of slavery in Texas, where the family lived. Might that have influenced his special place as the only one of his highly gifted musical family to become a successful musician and composer? Both parents and all children were extremely musical.

Scott Joplin
*The History Collection /
Alamy Stock Photo*

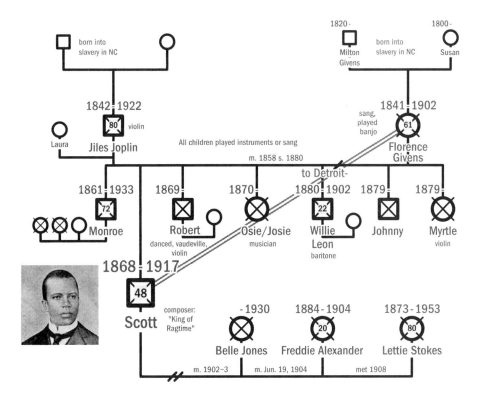

Genogram 2.1: Scott Joplin Family

While there is no doubt that Scott was extremely talented, perhaps there also were family patterns linked to their broader social context as an African American family living in the South during the era of Emancipation, that contributed to his special development and eventual success, as well as to the limitations on his musical accomplishments.

As a Black artist living during such a racially oppressive period, Joplin was forced to migrate several times, from Texarkana to St. Louis, then to Chicago, and finally on to New York. His publishers refused to accept his operas, claiming they did not suit him as a Black man, considering ragtime the only acceptable music allowed him. Had he been able to develop the whole range of his talents, his musical innovations would likely have been even more amazing. He spent years trying to find a way to publish and produce his opera *Tremonisha*, finally exhausting his resources in the process. The opera was not fully performed until 1972, almost sixty years after Joplin's death! His life is an illustration of both the possibilities of the timing of his birth historically, and the limitations of his cultural context that prevented him from developing his talents to the fullest.

Other groups have also suffered from traumatic migrations related to fleeing poverty or persecution. Russian Jews fled from the pogroms, and later the horrors of the Holocaust; the Irish fled starvation during the Irish famine in the mid-nineteenth century; in the 1980s thousands died under the brutal Pol Pot regime in Cambodia; Mexicans and others in the Americas have risked their lives for decades to migrate the U.S. in search of a livelihood.

Families' migration experiences often have many chapters. The more you can understand your family's history, the better you can understand their ensuing patterns. For example, while most Latinos/as are keenly aware of the migration stories that led them from countries within Central and South American and the Caribbean, there tends to be less awareness of the earlier migrations over many generations that culminated in the convergence of three incredibly diverse groups of people; the Black Africans who were brought to the Americas as slaves, the Indigenous Americans who originally migrated to the Americas from Asia thousands of years ago, and the Spaniards who came as colonists and conquerors.

It is also important to consider the life-cycle stage at which family members migrated. Did they have resources to begin building a new life? Was there a serious language barrier? How well have different generations adapted and acculturated to their new environment? For example, if children in a family learn English before their parents, which often happens, parents tend to lose status, which may happen in the migration process itself as well. In other cases, immigrants may increase their status by succeeding in ways they had hardly dreamed of when they came. Both patterns will likely influence family relationships for generations.

Whatever your family's migration history, try to understand how it has affected different family members over time, whether they came or were left behind. What dreams, fears, and losses did people have?

FRIDA KAHLO AND DIEGO RIVERA

It would be hard to make sense of the lives of painters Frida Kahlo and her husband Diego Rivera without considering the historical and cultural context in which they lived. Kahlo was a revolutionary artist born in Coyoacán, Mexico, amid political chaos in her homeland, who so identified with her political era that she used to claim she was born in 1910, the year of the Mexican Revolution, although she was actually born three years earlier! Her life was fully caught up in the sociopolitical struggles of her culture and times, which are reflected in her work (McGoldrick, Gerson, & Petry, 2021) (**see Genogram 2.2: Kahlo–Rivera Family**).

Diego Rivera
Bettmann/Getty Images

Frida Kahlo
GL Archive/Alamy Stock Photo

Diego Rivera and Frida Kahlo, portrait by Frida Kahlo
GL Archive/Alamy Stock Photo

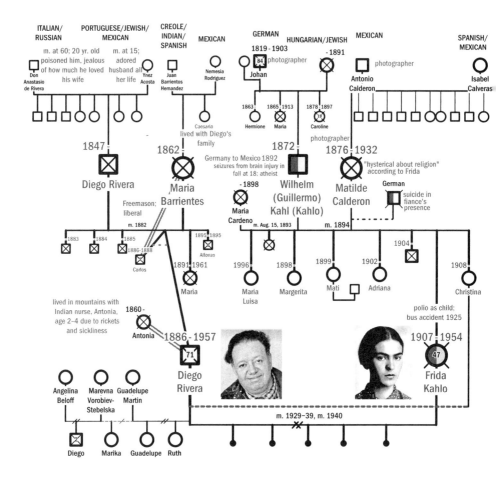

Genogram 2.2: Kahlo–Rivera Family

Kahlo's father was a Hungarian and German Jewish émigré artist himself, who deeply embraced the cultures of Mexico. Kahlo's mother was his second wife, and the daughter of a native Michoacán woman (descendant of an empire that rivaled the Aztec Empire) and a Spanish General. She was thus the embodiment of Mexican culture, which had been forged through the clash between the Spanish Conquistadors and the local Indigenous peoples of ancient Mexico. Kahlo's works are a testament to the clash between the ancient Indigenous ways of life and the modernizing and sophisticated artistic and political context of her times.

We often think of Kahlo as having been the creator of the first genogram, because she painted a diagram of her family with portraits of each member.

Kahlo's portrait of her family tree or "genogram," going back to her grandparents
Frank Nowikowski/Alamy Stock Photo

Her picture conveys the complex cultural heritage of both her parents, as well as some of the complex legacies of the children.

In fact, this portrait was inspired by genealogical charts used by the Nazis to prove "racial purity." By 1936, Nazi-oriented manuals on how to conduct genealogical research were distributed in the German School of Mexico City, where many of the teachers joined the Nazi Party and encouraged their students to chart their family trees. Kahlo transformed this Nazi device to highlight rather than hide her interracial origins. Her painting was an act of rebellion—reflecting her strong identification with her Jewish and multi-racial roots. Beyond this, her art reflects her passion and attunement to the complexities of Mexican culture, which combined ancient Meso-American and European roots. Her art incorporated religious symbols that were Jewish, Catholic, and Indigenous, further emphasizing her family's mixed cultural roots.

Her father grew up in Germany where he expected to go to university, but at eighteen he suffered a serious accident, which left him with seizures

and unable to pursue his university education. His mother's death the following year, compounded by his father's quick remarriage, led him to emigrate to
Mexico where he changed his name from Wilhelm Kahl to Guillermo Kahlo
and became a photographer, in spite of ongoing sequelae from his accident.
He soon married a first wife and had three daughters, but one died and then
his wife died tragically in childbirth.

Kahlo seems to have met his second wife the very night of his first wife's

death and married her soon after. She,
however, did not want to have to raise
his two surviving daughters from his
first marriage, so they were sent away
to a convent, and he and Mathilda
"started over."

Over the next years Mathilda and
Guillermo had two daughters, a son

Wedding photograph of Frida's German/
Hungarian immigrant father and her
Michoacán/Spanish mother
Album/Alamy Stock Photo

Frida Kahlo as an adolescent dressed as a male
Guillermo Kahlo, 1926, GRANGER

who died, and then two more daughters. Frida was the first daughter born after the lost son. As a teenager she indeed looked like a son, demonstrating again her ability to incorporate many different cultural possibilities. She seems to have had a strong awareness of not only her cultural heritage, but also of the hidden trauma history of her family, including those family members who had died or been cut off, which we will be discussing in Chapter 6.

Frida's "genogram" portrait appears to show in birth order her two older sisters, and then a baby (the brother who died?) and then herself and her sister Christina. But on the right are two faceless people and below a boy crossed out. Could the two faceless people be her two sisters who had been extruded from the family and then her dead brother, who was still a family member as well?

She does seem to have been, in many ways, a replacement for her lost brother. She became her father's favorite daughter, demonstrating a remarkable ability to transform traumatic experiences into hope and beautiful art despite her own severe disabilities, which had begun when she got polio at six, leaving her right leg weaker and smaller. At eighteen she was impaled on a metal pipe in a horrific bus accident, which went completely through her pelvis, fracturing her spine, leaving her with chronic pain for the rest of her life, in spite of numerous operations.

Frida became an artist, like her father and her maternal grandfather. Three years after her accident she married Diego Rivera, who was already a successful artist, twenty-one years older than she. Rivera was also from a very diverse background, Russian, Italian, Portuguese, Spanish, Creole, and Mexican, including ancestors who had been forced to convert from Judaism to Catholicism.

Like Kahlo, Rivera's family had experienced many traumas. His parents had lost three baby boys before he and his twin brother were born. His twin died at two, as did the youngest son. Diego and one younger sister were the only two out of seven children to survive. After his twin brother Carlos died when they were two, Rivera's mother became so distraught that

Diego Rivera and his twin brother
NortePhoto.com/Alamy Stock Photo

she spent all her time at the cemetery and was unable to care for him. Though two aunts lived in the household, the father gave Diego to a Native caretaker, Antonia, to live in the mountains with her for the next two years. Diego wrote in his autobiography that from that time on he loved Antonia more than his mother.

Indeed, years after he had grown and left home, he made a surprise return visit to his family in Mexico. That week his early nursemaid, Antonia, had a dream about him and walked for eight days from the mountains, sure that he was coming home. Diego's mother was shocked when Antonia showed up: "I am certain you dreamed this news about him. I know you possess him because I never have. That is why I have been so sick and unhappy. It is only because I gave birth to him from my own body, that you shall never be able to claim him truly as yours" (Rivera, 1991, p. 42). Antonia's reply: "You gave birth to him, but if it were not for me, he would not be alive. You were not able to keep his life going. I was. That is why he is more mine than yours. Were you able to see him when he was far away and count your steps, so that you could meet him the moment he arrived?" (p. 43). At that, the mother's voice broke and she took Antonia in her arms. They both began to cry. Watching them, Diego said he felt small and insignificant compared to their "stupendous expression of love, and then we began to laugh and hug each other" (p. 43).

They all connected, realizing their love was not a competition. Surely, no genogram for Rivera would be complete without Antonia. He, in fact, quotes her as saying "As long as the sun shines, I will be with you always" (Rivera, 1991, p. 44).

By the time Kahlo fell in love with him, he had already been married several times and had several children. She too had already had various other relationships. She had four miscarriages during the marriage, which were extremely painful for her emotionally and physically.

Rivera appears to have been the love of her life, but he was never faithful, having multiple affairs, including with her sister Christina. The couple divorced and remarried, and Frida herself had lovers, both male and female, including with the famous Russian revolutionary Leon Trotsky. The couple eventually lived in separate but connected homes in Mexico City. Both were extraordinary artists. Despite her physical and psychological suffering throughout her life, Kahlo was one of the most remarkably inventive, colorful, and creative artists of the twentieth century. She and Rivera demonstrate the importance of attending to both the cohort to which spouses belong in time and place, the cultural groups their families have come from, and the creative power of their individual and family struggles and resilience.

SOCIAL CLASS, MONEY, AND
SOCIAL LOCATION

Social class is one of the most powerful factors in organizing systems. In some societies, class is an openly acknowledged and overt way of structuring relationships. For centuries in India, explicit caste rules structured societal relationships and prevented different castes from intermarrying. In the United States, we tend to operate on the myth that we are a classless society, but class rules have covertly always regulated family relationships.

In spite of the many barriers to our changing class, most families have in fact moved from one class to another over the past few generations. And people in the U.S. are trying to move up in class all the time.

Class values permeate all sorts of everyday activities such as what car you drive (or would even feel comfortable driving, and, of course, whether you even have a car!), what music you listen to, what leisure activities you engage in, what foods you prefer, and where and how you are comfortable eating. Symbols of class including money tend to show up in family rituals, especially around weddings. Upper-class and working-class families may go all out for a wedding while upper-middle-class families may see such display as "gauche." Social location is likely to influence whether your family prefers bowling, golf, a Philharmonic concert, or a country and western band. Family members' taste in music may also reflect the cohort or generation you are from and what music you grew up with. We urge you to consider how your family's cultural and social class history may influence their comfort in various social situations, school, work, or in community social settings.

Changes in class status are among the most profound social changes families can experience, though they are generally not talked about. Social class differences are constantly played out in couple conflicts, among siblings, and in in-law, and parent–child relationships. Siblings may shift class, depending on their gender, profession, education, income, level of functioning or who they marry, especially sisters who marry up or down.

The identical twins Ester Pauline (Eppie) and Pauline Esther Friedman, who for decades wrote competing newspaper advice columns "Dear Abby" and "Ann Landers," had been emotionally connected at the hip from birth to adulthood. Eppie even changed partners in time to keep plans for a joint wedding in place. But after the wedding they had to separate for the first time because Eppie's husband couldn't afford to continue their joint honeymoon.

The twins and their two older sisters were the children of Russian Jewish immigrant parents who came to the U.S. with almost nothing, and at first, neither spoke English. They settled in Sioux City, Iowa, peddling chickens

Identical twins "Dear Abby" and "Ann Landers"
AP Photo/John Gaps III

from a pushcart until they could buy a grocery store and leave the poor section of the city. Eventually the father became an entrepreneur, owning almost all the movie theaters in the area. The daughters were close growing up, attending high school and college together. Yet, class tensions related to their husbands' class differences appear to have contributed to their falling out in adulthood.

The younger twin, Pauline, married Mort Philips whose family had gone from rags to riches and was heir to a Minnesota-based family fortune. After the wedding, they moved into a luxurious home with several servants and were groomed to take over the family business. Eventually Mort offered his brother-in-law, Jules, a job selling pans for one of his companies.

Eppie eventually took over the role of advice columnist Ann Landers, for which she became famous. Soon afterward, Pauline began her own advice column as "Dear Abby." That intensified the twins' competition. The long cutoff that followed was undoubtedly fueled by their divergent social-class standing, tied to their husbands' vastly different socioeconomic status, a common source of resentment in families over who deserved more and got more.

Parent–child resentments and cutoffs may also develop if children are upwardly mobile or have less education than their parents. It helps to consider what circumstances in your family may have influenced members to move toward a different class or cultural group: a sense of inadequacy, financial success or failure, education, sibling position, temperament, talent, ability or disability, a family legacy, a secret alliance, or some other factor.

Class differences created when a child is the first to have a college or professional education may create a painful chasm, especially when the loss created by social distance is not acknowledged, as often happens. The same is true when a child is downwardly mobile through disability—addiction, mental illness, or other dysfunction. Families often feel shamed by their children's consequent loss of class status, especially because our society does not generally acknowledge or deal directly with social-class issues.

Family cutoffs often get played out in stereotypes about class difference: "They've gotten above themselves," "They've got no manners," etc. The difficulty we have talking about class distance makes it even harder to contend with, as people feel obliged to hide their origins, whether because of their financial straits or their privilege. Family members of lower social class or cultural background may cut off from the family, out of shame or embarrassment.

Class difference is about power. While denying that class matters, families tend to be extremely conscious of class in their interactions, especially in relation to outsiders. Children tend to measure their family in relation to their age mates' families. Family members may have been embarrassed because their parents didn't speak "correctly." Did parents seem snobbish or intimidated when introduced to school friends? Social class tends to play a key role in how we assess ourselves in relation to others, and how we measure our families in relation to the rest of the community. In a letter that Ann Landers wrote to her daughter Margo, decades after she had to abandon her joint honeymoon because of her finances, she stated: "I remember my own resentment against my parents. . . . When I didn't do well in school one day, I came home and said to my father: 'You failed your children. You didn't give us CULTURE. There is never anything to read in this damn house but *Elks* magazines.' I can remember the hurt in his eyes. After all, what did (he) . . . know about 'culture'? Nothing, I can assure you. But he knew an awful lot about how to love people and make them love him. He was a master at this. And he taught me a great deal that has made me able to do the work I am doing today" (Howard, 2003, p. 14).

Landers's poignant disclosure exposes how class dynamics impacted her relationship with her parents. Her angry attack on her father's reading only

Elks magazine also, of course, masked her feelings of vulnerability, shame, and inadequacy related to not feeling "good enough" in relation to others she knew.

Class aspirations may even have more influence on families' perspective on the acceptability of a marriage partner than by the new spouse's character. It may take years for a family to revise its initial perceptions of a spouse of "lower class" who marries in—if ever.

Education has historically been the most secure way of changing class. Our society often operates on the notion that all options are open through education, but we still have a remarkably stratified system of access to education, as well as of judging schools along class lines: from the Ivy League to state universities, to community colleges, with virtually no acknowledgment of the racial and gender components that have perpetually kept people from being able to move up in class through education.

Money and occupation are other indicators of class, with medicine, the law, and sometimes the clergy, acting, music, art, or politics elevating in certain professions to a higher-class status.

As for money, we all recognize the different value various cultural groups place on money. It can be a clue about a family's most deeply held views about the meaning of life. It may represent love, security, happiness, success, power, shame, pride, fear, and many other things. Conflicts between the "tightwad" and the "spendthrift" may dominate family interactions, causing children to collude with one parent against the other, disrupting and distorting family relationships.

Nor are attitudes toward money always based on "reality." Although class power is usually a reflection of money and earning power, some millionaire family members may be unable to enjoy a meal for fear of the expense, while others, who barely have two nickels, feel quite secure that they will always have enough—and indeed always seem to manage.

Money also often plays a role in underlying family dynamics tied to conflicts and cutoffs. For example, where a family business or a will has left family money unequally divided among siblings, relationships are likely to be impaired or even cut off, often for generations. Therapists may be brought in to help family members work through such difficulties. They may coach clients to "let go of the rope" to free themselves emotionally from money conflicts. Of course, this is unlikely to work unless people are prepared to lose an inheritance in order to keep the relationship.

Since money can be extremely dangerous to other values in a family, assessing your family's attitudes about money can help you to assess how power operates in relationships. As Tom Wolfe said, if the "money nexus" becomes the primary determinant of class, all other ties and values, like kith and kin may be out the window. And this money nexus does seem to be taking hold, as the distance between the haves and the have-nots becomes more extreme year by year.

RELIGION AND SPIRITUALITY

Whether or not a family defines their ethnicity in terms of a religious group, religion is a powerful dimension of culture that shapes family patterns over time. Your family's spiritual values are a part of the bedrock that shapes them. In adolescence and young adulthood especially, family members may rebel against traditional practices and customs of their parents, seeking to coalesce their own religious and spiritual beliefs. This may create deep strains within the family. Parents may feel threatened at a personal level and for the continuity of their family. Understanding your family involves pushing past the polemics of family arguments over religion to understand the roots of family members' most cherished beliefs. Why has Uncle Joe become an atheist? Why does your mother hold so tightly to saying the rosary every day? Why did your grandparents "sit shiva" (a mourning ritual for the dead) for their son when he married a "shiksa" (a non-Jewish woman)? Unless you can imagine your way into the mindset of other family members, you will not really be able to understand them.

Families in which different religious and spiritual orientations are represented present children with both a challenge and an opportunity. On one hand, being exposed to diverse ways of experiencing religiosity can encourage the exploration of different perspectives and having the freedom to define your religion and spirituality for yourself. On the other hand, parents' different religious orientations can be a source of tension and conflict, and children may feel divided loyalties. When parents are of different faiths, how their children come to define themselves spiritually often hints at underlying family triangles, coalitions, or alliances.

Oftentimes, a person's experiences with religion while growing up foster either an identification and loyalty to that group, or a reaction against their religious community. The role of the Black Church as a cultural safe haven for African Americans is an example of the former. The Kennedy family, where all members embraced their Catholic roots, is another, while the examples of Erik Erikson, who disavowed his Jewish roots, and the Nehru family who turned away from their Hindu roots, are examples of the latter.

Jawaharlal Nehru as a child with
parents Motilal and Swanup
Keystone/Getty Images

Jawaharlal Nehru as a child with parents
Motilal and Swanup
Keystone/Getty Images

Jawaharlal Nehru, the first Prime Minister of India, was the son of parents
with very different orientations (**see Genogram 2.3: Nehru–Gandhi Family**). Nehru's mother was a deeply devoted Hindu, while his father rejected
religion in favor of secular humanism. Of these two dramatically different
perspectives, Nehru eventually followed in his father's footsteps, proclaiming that all religion and spiritualism were absurd and defining himself as an
agnostic. Nehru's identification with his father's perspective and disavowal of
his mother's may say something about his relationship with each. Although
he felt closer to his mother, his father's approval was more important to him,
leading him to model his own beliefs in concert with his father's. What is
especially intriguing is that Nehru married a woman like his mother, a
devout Hindu, Kamala.

Yet like his father had done with him, he openly expressed to his daughter
Indira his ideas about the dangers of religion and the value of secularism. In a
letter he wrote to her when she was ten, he explained: "Religion first came as
fear, and anything that is done because of fear is bad. Religion, as you know,
tells us many beautiful things. When you grow up, you will read about the
religions of the world and of the good things and the bad things that have

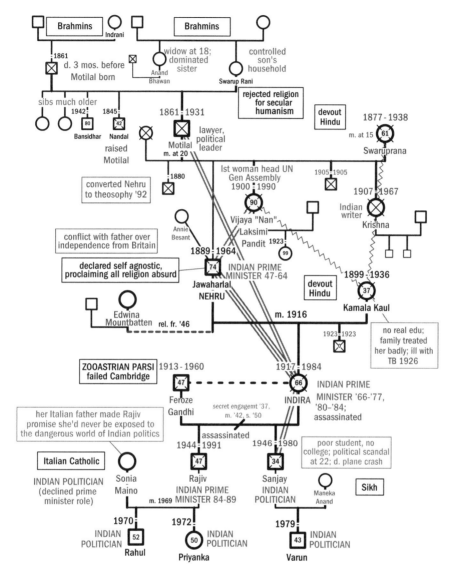

Genogram 2.3: Nehru–Gandhi Family

been done in their name. However much it may have grown, we see even today that people fight and break each other's heads in the name of religion. And for many people it is still something to be afraid of. They spend their time in trying to please some imaginary beings by making presents in temples and even sacrifices of animals" (p. 72).

Indira seems to have experienced the same religious divide between her parents as her father had experienced between his parents. And she followed

Indira Gandhi with her sons, daughter-in-law, and grandchildren
AP Photo

in her father's footsteps, rejecting religion. Hence it should not be surprising that she married a non-Hindu man, Feroze Gandhi, who was Parsi. Their two children married neither Hindus nor Parsis. Rajiv married Sonia, an Italian Catholic, and his brother Sanjay married Maneka, who is Sikh.

MARILYN MONROE: RELIGIOUS IDENTIFICATION AND DISIDENTIFICATION

Religious experiences in childhood may also produce effects that are more complex than merely identifying or dis-identifying with one's religious community of origin. Marilyn Monroe appeared to both connect with and disconnect from her primary religious community of origin. She was born Norma Jean Baker in 1926. Both her mother and her grandmother were zealous Pentecostal evangelicals, but she spent most of her childhood living in a series of foster homes. Her first and most consistent home was with Ida and Wayne Bolender, whom she lived with from the time of her birth until the age of seven. They were Christian Scientists, and like her mother, fanatically religious. The Bolenders were extremely strict with her, believing that a strong moral and religious background would benefit her as an impressionable little girl throughout her life. It is ironic that they condemned movies and warned about the sinfulness of sexuality, and yet Norma Jean grew up to become Marilyn Monroe, one of the world's most famous movie stars and sex symbols. It is as if her life became a reaction against the deeply restrictive and repressive religiosity she was subjected to in childhood. However, as much as Marilyn came to embody things that were condemned by her religious community of origin, she remained a Christian Scientist until the age of thirty. At that point, she married Arthur Miller and converted to Judaism. Though neither he nor his family apparently cared about this issue, she insisted on the conversion and even after her divorce from Miller she maintained her Jewish identity until her death. It is perhaps also relevant that Miller and Monroe witnessed a traumatic, fatal accident the day before their wedding, which precipitated their marriage and may have influenced Monroe's need for a spiritual home as well.

Marilyn Monroe and Arthur Miller
New York Daily News Archive/Getty Images

Marilyn Monroe experienced a sense of alienation and homelessness on many levels all her life. Her experience with religion in childhood was one of isolation, repression, and loneliness, despite the fact that religion could have provided her with a sense of community and connection. Her conversion to Judaism may have reflected a desire to become part of an extended family community, an attempt to find "homeplace." In Judaism she may have been seeking to fulfill her underlying spiritual and emotional hunger, her yearning to be a part of a community with a sense of historical continuity and connection (Zimroth, 2002), which were unfulfilled desires deeply rooted in childhood that haunted her throughout her life.

CULTURALLY-BASED SECRETS AND SHAME

Within many families, issues related to culture form the basis for family secrets that are tied to feelings of guilt and shame. Family rules about who is valued, who is allowed to love and marry whom, who can have children and under what circumstances, and so on, are often tied to broader social beliefs and biases about race, ethnicity, religion, social class, gender, and sexual identity. In many cultural groups, social divisions and inequalities are reinforced by strong prohibitions against romance and procreation that cross racial and social class boundaries, and strictly enforce compulsory relationship patterns based on traditional gender roles. Secrets often develop when members violate these cultural norms. Katharine Hepburn, Margaret Mead, and Eleanor Roosevelt kept their bisexuality hidden, never disclosing it publicly or even to family members.

Langston Hughes
Library of Congress, Prints and Photographs Division, LC-USZ62-43605

African American poet Langston Hughes had a strained relationship with his father, influenced by the father having abandoned him and his mother, and out of his own struggles with racism moved abroad. Probably the tension with his father was heavily shaped also by Langston's homosexuality, although as far as we know, this remained unnamed and unacknowledged between them. Hughes seemed to channel what he could not otherwise express into his writing. His story "Blessed Assurance" explored a father's anger over his son's effeminacy and homosexuality. Many of his poems used homosexual codes, a device often employed by one of his idols, Walt Whitman (McClatchy, 2002). Hughes often had to solicit support from sources that would never have accepted his homosexuality, beginning with his father and including organizations like the Black churches that he often relied upon. His survival literally depended on his keeping his sexuality a secret.

Sometimes family secrets serve to hide how family members may have colluded with various kinds of prejudice and discrimination that are regarded as controversial or immoral by the broader society. Reeve Lindbergh's discovery of the racial prejudices of her national hero father, Charles Lindbergh, forced her to a painful reexamination of who he was (the Lindbergh family will be further discussed with their Genogram in Chapter 4). The process of realizing parental limitations is something most children have to undergo in becoming adults. It was long after Lindbergh's death that his daughter Reeve first heard a tape of a speech he made in 1941 telling the world that one of the greatest dangers to pre-World War II America was the influence of Jews in prominent positions: "I was again transfixed and horrified, again ablaze with shame and fury—'Not you!' I cried out silently to myself and to him—'No! You never said such things! You raised your children never to say, never even to think such things—this must be somebody else talking. It can't be you!' I felt a global anguish—the horror of the Holocaust, the words of my own father ignoring the horror, but surely not condoning the horror, surely not dismissing or diminishing it, surely not. But I also felt a piercingly personal rage. . . . How could you do this to Mother? How could you leave her with this? . . . How could that happen, and what did it mean not just for my own family but for others?" (Lindbergh, 1998, pp. 201–203).

Lindbergh's daughter struggled with who her father was, what he said and did, how to be accountable for it in the present, and how to understand the contradictions in the different messages given. One of the hardest parts is having to make peace with such contradictions, because those who have gone before have left behind a legacy of painful and horrific thoughts and practices that must be modified if we are to create a just and fair world in the future. So, understanding where our families are coming from culturally means understanding the pain reflected in the ways they were oppressed, and how they may have oppressed others through prejudiced attitudes and discriminatory behaviors.

THE PAIN OF RACIAL AND CULTURAL
ISSUES IN OUR HISTORY

On "Finding Your Roots," Henry Louis Gates often shows people surprising facts about their history. Singer and songwriter Roseann Cash, Johnny Cash's daughter, discussed the family's pain at accusations from the KKK in 1965 that her mother was African American, which would have made her marriage to Johnny Cash illegal at that time in their state. Roseann learned through the records that her fourth great grandmother was an enslaved Black woman whose husband freed their nine children and took care of them, although he was not able to free his wife, who was his slave. When Gates asked Cash her response to learning this history she replied: "What's interesting is, there's deep ancestral guilt about my ancestors being slave holders, but it's slightly mitigated by the fact that I also had an ancestor who was enslaved." Gates also discovered that through the probably forced sexual abuse of women of color, the Cash side of the family also had African American roots.

Roseann Cash with her father, Johnny Cash, and her much loved stepmother, June
Ebet Roberts/Getty Images

Pharrell Williams, another well-known musician and songwriter, learned through Gates's research that his first ancestor had been sold into slavery in the 1850s and was not freed until after the Civil War, when he was ten, the same age that Pharrell's son was when he heard this history. Williams also learned from his fourth great aunt's documentation of her family's experiences in slavery that after the Civil War his ancestors had returned to work for their former master who agreed to pay them for their work, but then he reneged on his promise.

Williams was excited to obtain information about his family, and especially appreciative of his aunt's documentation stating, "Her descendants thank her for that." But he was also deeply pained by the details of his family's slave history, saying:

Pharrell Williams
Mike Pont/Getty Images

> When you ask me how do I feel about this, it makes me think about the whole of this country. I love this country, but I want this country to love us in the same way . . . I would love to have a conversation, and it's not about me trying to confront, it's about me having the conversation. . . . How do you enslave children? Who are these people? That's my question. And who are the descendants of these people, that they don't know that the right thing to do is to bring some sense of repair, reparations? . . . I'm not going to ask you to atone for your ancestors' sins, but I'm gonna ask you to get into the conversation. And it's not about me trying to confront, it's just about let's have the conversation. Here's what I do know. As African Americans, we need advocates.

Gates, recognizing his pain, commented, "To me it seemed you were trying to keep from crying, but what's wrong with crying? We have so much to cry about as a people."

COMING HOME: AN AUSTRALIAN PERSPECTIVE ON DEALING WITH OUR ANCESTORS

David Denborough, an Australian community worker, teacher, and author, came to the notion of coming home when he heard a presentation on the topic by an Aboriginal Australian woman, Jane Lester, whose culture is one of the oldest in the world, having developed in Australia over 50,000 years ago. Lester spoke of the impact of the Stolen Generations on her family, talking about the thousands of Indigenous people, including her father and all his siblings, who had been forced to give up their language and customs to serve the white men who had invaded their land. She spoke of the importance for everyone of coming home. Denborough was overcome with sorrow that what she described had been done to her family and to so many others.

David Denborough
Courtesy David Denborough

She then challenged him to find a way to connect with his own ancestors and honor them also. He felt awkward, saying that his family was so different, because no one in his family had been forcibly removed from their siblings, parents, and culture. In fact, one of his great-great grandfathers, Samuel Griffith, was considered to be one of the founding fathers of the Australian Federation, the first Chief Justice, and involved in drafting the Australian Constitution and institutionalizing a system that caused profound harm to the Aboriginal people.

Lester persisted: "Yes, many differences, but some things are the same. Neither of us would be alive if not for the actions of our ancestors." Now, after hundreds of years, this woman was arguing for the importance of "coming home," saying, "We must find ways for everyone to come home. Even if we cannot reconnect with our immediate family, we can still reconnect with our land, still reconnect to our extended family. We can find someone who knows the connections." Aboriginal culture, she said, had from time immemorial been shared through stories. "And because of this it is almost impossible to find someone who has a piece to your puzzle. Even if you've been adopted out and put in another country."

Lester's challenge led Denborough to begin his search to understand his own family history. As he sifted through diaries, clippings, historic correspondence, and memoirs, he could find no record of anyone in his family trying to come to terms with the actions of previous generations. "Nowhere did I find expression of regret or sorrow—only expressions of pride. Nowhere could I find descriptions of how coming to terms with the past would lead to different actions in the present. If future generations of my family come looking for their ancestors, at the very least I want them to know that they are not the first to wrestle with legacies of genocide. Who knows if what I write in 2020 will be of any value for them as they seek to live in an ethical time? But I want them to know they are not alone in seeking" (Denborough, 2020, p. 18).

He decided to write his memoir in the form of a letter to his great-great-grandfather, Samuel Griffith, followed by a letter to his own descendants. He tried to come to terms with "the fact that the so-called golden age of the British Empire was also the golden age of British racism" (Denborough, 2020, 46). "I was born into a country of institutionalized and legalized sexism, heterosexual dominance, and white supremacy. But I was also born into a time when all these things were being challenged and questioned. . . . You were, however, as far as I can tell, completely unaware of the diverse systems of law and the codes that had existed on this land for thousands upon thousands of years. You were completely unaware of how those in the future would view the rules you wrote, or the damage that section 208 would do across the globe" (p. 150).

Denborough tells his great great-grandfather, that through his research he has come to realize many things about going home again. First, that there is no place for a sense of moral superiority toward his ancestors because colonial violence has not ended. There is also, he says, no place for hopelessness, because resistance has never wavered. There is also no time for paralyzing shame, because invitations to partnership are still being offered and there is so much to be done. And finally, what he had not realized before, was that "these partnerships, formed in the hope of redressing harms would bring such meaning, joy, connection, laughter, and yes, even spirituality to his life" (Denborough, 2020, p. 173).

Finally, he writes a letter to those who come after him, asking such questions as whether they will be heartbroken that our generation could go on as usual when we learned that the Earth was warming. Will they ask why our generation didn't do even the simple things to right the wrongs of our ancestors? And then he tells of the many positive things he has loved about Australia and about his family, the inspirations he hopes are remembered.

Denborough's effort to go home is a remarkably inspirational journey to understand our ancestors and see the connections for those who come before us as well as those who come after us.

QUESTIONS ABOUT YOUR FAMILY'S CULTURAL IDENTITY/CONTEXT

- **Ethnicity**: What are the ethnic backgrounds of each branch of your family? How does your family identify itself ethnically? What pride or shame is associated with this identity? Do your family's values and patterns seem consistent with the characteristics of the ethnic groups from which they come? If not, were they attempting to move away from their ethnic roots? Why might they not fit? Were they proud or ashamed of their heritage? Were there clashes of ethnic values or pride/shame issues in intermarriages? If so, how did these influence other family relationships? Did your family grow up with ethnic stories, religious practices, foods, music, holiday rituals? Are these still being carried on with the next generation?
- **Race/Skin Color**: What were the family's messages about race and skin color when you were growing up? How have those messages shaped racial self-identification and relationships? Are there racial truths that no one talks about? Are there differences in complexion and skin tone within the family and if so, how do these shape family dynamics?
- **Migration**: What is the family's migration history? Where did they come from and why did they come? How many came together? Who did they leave behind? How old were they when they came and how did that influence family patterns? What was their experience as new immigrants and how did that influence your family's hopes, dreams, beliefs? Did they dream of returning to the country of origin? Did they try to leave their history behind? How did they deal with language differences? religious customs? the loss of those left behind?
- **Social Location; Social Class**: What were the family's values about class and how were they transmitted? Have family members changed class by "marrying up" or "marrying down"? Have siblings changed class and if so how did it affect their relationships? Have class changes occurred through education, financial success

or failure, marriage into another cultural or class group, professional status, disability? How did this affect sibling patterns, family holidays, get-togethers, and rituals?

- **Money**: What were the attitudes in the family about money (i.e.,
  "the root of all evil" "always pay cash")? What roles have family members played around money: the gambler, the tight wad,
  the compulsive shopper, the bargain hunter, the miser, the spendthrift, the hoarder? Who handles the money? Who controls it?
  Have there been conflicts or cutoffs over wills? How do siblings
  in different financial positions deal with these differences? (This
  is tied to class dynamics.) What are the family's beliefs about children's right to help with education, other financial support, inheritance, buying a home, and so on? How are financial arrangements
  made for the care of disabled family members and how does this
  intersect with emotional caretaking? What have been the gender differences regarding the control, inheritance, or management of money?

- **Religion/Spirituality**: What religions are represented in your family and which orientations have had the greatest power in the family? What is the family's relation to organized religion as well as
  their informal beliefs in what is sacred—music, art, good works,
  community service, spending time in nature? All these beliefs are
  essential to an understanding of what makes your family tick.
  What do family members believe about an afterlife? How are religious and spiritual differences negotiated?

- What kind of training did family members have in spiritual matters? Are there family secrets about religion or spirituality: an
  aunt's years in the convent or the father's aspirations to become a
  rabbi or minister that explain later life choices?

Chapter 3
Transforming Your Family Relationships: The Past as Prologue

We sometimes arrogantly forget that even tragic lives leave a footprint, a legacy. It is tempting to dismiss the lives of Francesco and Elizabetta and people like them as meaningless. They were immigrants who wound up institutionalized for most of their lives, contributing little to society. . . . However, there is a longer arc to every story . . . one that is equally important. The legacy of Francesco and Elizabetta—tragic though their lives were—is one that would have amazed them, 2 sons, 9 grandchildren, 21 great grandchildren, 15 great-great-grandchildren "plus a couple of buns in the oven."

—JOHN MANCINI
Immigrant Secrets

I believe one can never leave home. I believe that one carries the shadows, the dreams, the fears and dragons of home under one's skin, at the extreme corners of one's eyes and possibly in the gristle of the earlobe.

—MAYA ANGELOU
Letter to My Daughter

The focus of this book is on helping you deepen your understanding of yourself and your family and suggesting steps to enhance relationships in your family by changing how you interact with them. This approach is rooted in the work of family therapist Murray Bowen (Bowen, 1978), who encouraged people to apply systems thinking to understanding their own position in their family relationships and to changing their part in the system. At the center of Bowen's approach is a concept called differentiation, which involves relating to others in accordance with our own deepest values rather than out of emotional reactivity to hurt, anger, or other feelings. Increasing your level of differentiation means expanding your capacity to live according to your own values and remaining emotionally connected to others without being dependent on their acceptance and approval. Bowen's concepts are supported by the research of psychiatrist Dan Siegel, whose work affirms the Bowen concept that the greater our level of individual differentiation, or sense of self, the greater our potential for mature, connected relationships, or what Siegel refers to as MWE, or a combination of a mature, differentiated "ME," combined with a connected "WE" (Siegel, 2018).

To be differentiated, or emotionally mature, means being able to relate to others respectfully, appreciating our connection to each other, to our history and to the world of the future. It means having the ability to move freely from emotional closeness in our relationships to working toward our personal life goals, being able to calmly state our beliefs or feelings, or to refrain from this, if such expression would only raise tension for no good purpose. It means having the ability to relate warmly and openly without attacking or gossiping about others, chasing others' approval or defending ourselves, walling ourselves off emotionally, or maneuvering to obtain control from relationships. This doesn't mean we don't defend our right or express ourselves clearly. It simply means that we do not need to justify ourselves to anyone but ourselves.

The pathway to transforming relationships in your family is by focusing on how to change yourself. In this book we will teach you how to deepen your knowledge and understanding of your family system and your role in it, and how to use this information to transform relationships in your family by changing how you think about and relate to others. We encourage you to work on increasing your level of differentiation, or emotional maturity, so you can be simultaneously connected to others while remaining true to yourself. Doing so will not only improve your family relationships, it also will allow you to function more freely in relationships beyond your family.

SEEING YOUR FAMILY AS A SYSTEM AND UNDERSTANDING YOUR OWN ROLE IN IT

Family systems are comprised of many individuals, but your family is also more than the sum of its parts. It is important to understand your family's multigenerational history in terms of its systemic evolution from the past and toward the future. Viewing your family from a systems perspective can illuminate how many so-called individual behaviors or "personality" problems are tied to larger family dynamics. All too often people are not aware of the traits—whether positive or negative—they have absorbed from their families. The qualities we possess, the ways we think and feel about things, our choices and conclusions are often tied to family patterns of which we may not even be conscious.

As you begin to recognize family patterns of conflict and alliance, it gets easier to see how automatic people's responses are to family interactions and events, even when they think they are being objective. For instance, gossip between a mother and her daughters about the "superficial, materialistic, and selfish" daughter-in-law may seem like an objective response to her clearly observed personality traits. But when you step back and look at the genogram, you may realize that the "scapegoating" of the daughter-in-law has been a theme in your family for three generations. Noticing multigenerational patterns will help you recognize how intertwined members of a family can be. Thus, for example, the "hero" brother may be the counterpart to another brother who is "the loser"—one playing out the family dreams and aspirations, the other their fears. Often when family members become polarized around an issue, it is not the issue itself, but the emotional alliances in the family that determine the patterns. In my own family (TL), as I explained in Chapter 1, there was a sibling splitting pattern that occurred over multiple generations whereby in sibling dyads, one was cast in the role of the golden child and the other in the role of the fallen child. Until I realized this pattern, I had bought into the family story that the "fallen siblings" were just dysfunctional personalities. It was only when I recognized this as a pattern that I could see the behaviors of the fallen siblings as part of a broader family dynamic that they could not see and could not break free from. This helped move me from condemnation to compassion.

As you take this journey home you will be learning a lot about your family, and in so doing, you will likely come to realize qualities that have seemed individual are tied to patterns in your family. This is why it is important to gather as much information as possible about your family and to organize it to help you see these patterns.

HOW TO START THE PROCESS OF
LEARNING ABOUT YOUR FAMILY

As you embark on this journey you will need several tools. The primary tool is the genogram—a kind of annotated family tree that organizes information and visually depicts important patterns and themes over time. The main symbols for making a genogram appear on the inside cover of this book and genograms are used throughout the book to illustrate family patterns.

Genograms map out at least the basic three-generational biological, legal, and emotional structure of the family, including key informal kinship connections—who was related to whom, parents, children, siblings, close friends, and godparents. Just as important, genograms can show key facts about the functioning and relationships of family members with each other and with outsiders. The information indicated on the genogram can offer clues about the family's problems and secrets, which the family may have obscured out of shame or embarrassment.

Another key tool to make is a chronology of your family history. Writing a family chronology will give you a timeline of the major family events and stressors that will help you track the evolution of family patterns over time and understand the intersection of each individual's life course within the context of the larger family patterns. This is especially useful because stress and anxiety can easily obscure the connections between major family events and family relationship patterns.

Genograms and chronologies help you track multiple types of family information: from the basic facts and structure of birth, marriage, divorce, moves, illness, and death to information regarding level of functioning of different family members from grandchildren to as far back as you can go. Other information to add includes education, occupation, psychological and physical health and functioning, talents, achievements or struggles, and relationship patterns.

STARTING WITH IMMEDIATE FAMILY: EXPANDING YOUR PERSPECTIVE

People usually begin by drawing a genogram showing the immediate people in the family they grew up with and then the families of their parents, showing basic demographic information and dates (birth, marriage, education, occupation, death, and moves). Once the primary family information is indicated, the next step is to consider the family from the perspectives of different family members. Go through the exercise of telling your family history from the point of view of different family members. If negative feelings about a certain person overwhelm you, try to expand your perspective to include how that person was seen by his or her favorite relative or friend. Always consider relationships and events from multiple perspectives.

The Irish journalist and author Nuala O'Faolain came from a family of nine in which there was a great deal of alcoholism and abuse, which she struggled to understand, writing: "My father was angry nearly all the time and my mother just went around in a silent bubble. I didn't know why they bothered to have children" (2001, p. 5). She struggled especially to understand her mother, with whom she had had a very painful and difficult relationship.

Nuala O'Faolain
© Basso Cannarsa/Opale/Bridgeman Images

She thought of her mother as just sitting in the chair reading and drinking for years. After she published her memoir, *Are You Somebody* (1998), she received a great deal of feedback from people who had known her mother, including a childhood friend who described herself as having been heartbroken when "Caitlin" (O'Faolain had never even known her mother's first name!) had been expelled from her Irish Catholic boarding school for having a crush on another girl. She even received a call from the woman on whom her mother had had the schoolgirl crush.

But the response that surprised her the most was from the local librarian who gave her mother the only praise she had ever heard about her mother. This woman spoke of her mother's great love for reading. She said she was touched by the respect Nuala's mother had given her as a fellow reader. "For me," said the librarian, "your mother was someone who shared my passion for books." To this woman her alcoholic mother was not a failure. She was "a reader." The librarian said she never thought of her as mother, wife, or alcoholic, but as a voracious reader, "a lady," who treated the librarian as an equal, always sharing her insights about the many books she read, suggestions about which books were best and which ones to skip. It somehow opened a door for O'Faolain to expand her view of her mother. She was profoundly moved to realize that this woman saw her mother as a lady and that it was the family who had limited her definition to mother, wife, and alcoholic.

It is worth asking each relative and friend for the facts as well as the myths and stories of your family's history, including asking about their reactions to a given family experience. For example, how did your uncle react when your grandfather cut your father off? And your grandfather's sister? Who actually knew about the conflict that led to the cutoff? How did they handle holidays and family get-togethers after that? Being able to gather information about a person or an event from multiple perspectives is an essential part of the journey to go home.

Sometimes the view we have of another person focuses mostly on the negative, while failing to acknowledge the positive. Allowing ourselves to see what is good in a relationship can help us reshape our connection with the other person. At the same time, we may have idealized a person so much that it is hard to be honest about their inevitable human fragilities and flaws.

We tend to be especially prone to either idealizing or demonizing our parents. As J. K. Rowling put it when she delivered the commencement address at Harvard, "There's an expiration date on blaming your parents" (2008). This work requires learning to see our parents as human beings who had/have strengths and weaknesses. Being able to see both sides is important.

Sometimes a conflictual relationship with a parent has focused onto some specific concrete explosion, such as a falling out over some long-past insult, or some ritual argument over religion or politics. In such cases, we often recommend "letting go of the rope," that is, letting go of the argument to allow the buried emotional issues to emerge. It helps to let go of old and fruitless arguments. The very pause created by such letting go may help you move on to other more emotionally important issues.

It is not uncommon to have "routinized" ways of communicating with certain family members. Breaking from the routine and communicating in novel ways can help you revitalize relationships and create openings for long avoided issues to arise where they can be addressed. For example, if you have been maintaining routine, "dutiful" contact with family members through general letters or emails addressed to both parents, or phone conversations with only your mother, who acts as the switchboard, you might instead decide to develop direct contact with each family member separately. This shift alone might bring long buried issues to the surface. It would certainly make the contacts more personal. If you have routinized relationships with your parents that are not overtly hostile, a first step might be to break off the routine, such as daily phone calls or weekly visits on a certain day and make contacts less ritualized and predictable.

Such initial contact steps might be followed by brief visits, during which your main aim could be to observe and listen to family interaction in a new way. You might then incorporate this information into further planning, during which you could develop tentative hypotheses concerning the role you play and the role you want to take in your family. In thinking what role you would like to have, it may help to predict how others might react to any change you initiate.

Contemplating diverse perspectives will help you develop a richer and more complete understanding of your family. And bear in mind, that whatever the virtues or vices of others, you need to keep coming back to yourself and becoming more conscious of your own behavior and expectations, since that will be the focus of your work.

ENLARGING THE DEFINITION OF FAMILY

To understand your family, you also need to go beyond society's conventional views of family as limited to the biological family of parents, siblings, and children. Most of us have had an informal family system, which is also crucial for our formative development. I (MM), as mentioned earlier, had a nanny, who played a central role in my family life, and a grand aunt Mamie, who was like Santa Claus to us and many others for five generations of our family. There were also family friends who were informal godparents, aunts, uncles, and grandparents. The parents of several of my friends also provided a second home base for me, just as my family provided a home base for others. Every family, of course, includes anyone who belongs, whether biologically linked or not; this includes anyone who was part of your family as you grew up—caretakers, teachers, ministers, friends, neighbors—whoever played a role in your family history. These people are often unsung heroes and "sheroes" of our families.

Maya Angelou
Private Collection, Universal History Archive/UIG/ Bridgeman Images

Maya Angelou (**see Genogram 3.1: Maya Angelou Family**) often talked about the key

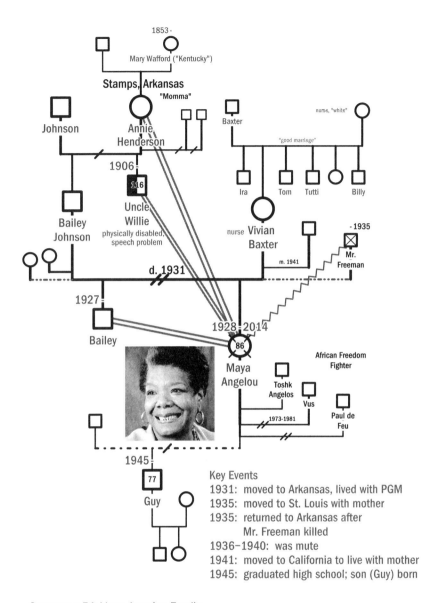

Genogram 3.1: Maya Angelou Family

influence of her Uncle Willie, who played a major mentoring role in her life. He was physically disabled, poor, and severely disabled, but he had a powerful influence on her education and values. He taught her the times tables so well that even late in life she could still say them after a night of partying. Angelou discovered when she went home for her Uncle Willie's funeral in her tiny hometown of Stamps, Arkansas, that her Uncle Willie had had a profound mentoring impact not only her and her brother, but on many others as well. She wrote a poem about him, which is a message to us all about listening to the unsung voices, who have influenced us and who may be "present in the songs that our children sing." They may not make it into history books, or even to greatness in our own families, but their private and personal influence is nonetheless tremendous as was the case with Angelou's Uncle Willie.

Angelou and her much loved older brother were raised mostly by their grandmother and Uncle Willie, returning to their mother only in their teens after many traumatic experiences. Worst of all she had on a childhood visit to her mother been raped by her mother's boyfriend and blamed herself for revealing his name, which apparently led to his murder, a major factor in her refusing to speak for several years.

You might think that Angelou was jeopardized by not having her mother's protection growing up, but in later life she described her mother thus: "We visit often. I have to see about her, and she thinks she has to see about me. . . . I was taken from my Mom to be raised by my grandmother when I was 3 and except for a disastrous bitter visit when I was 7, I didn't see her again until I was 13. I'm often asked how I got over that without holding a grudge. I see her as one of the greatest human beings I've ever met. She's funny and quite outrageous really" (Oliver, 1989, p. 136). Angelou's is an amazing reflection on the possibilities of creating workable relationships—even following very traumatic family experiences. No matter what has happened at one point in your life, change in relationships is possible, as families grow along with each other.

Even family members we have never known may have a powerful impact on our sense of who we are. In his memoir *Immigrant Secrets*, John Mancini describes his multi-year search to find out about his Italian immigrant grandparents, whom he had never even heard his father mention. John's father had died and the mother did not know the father's history. He discovered through diligent research that both his father's immigrant parents had been placed in different mental institutions in the very area where John himself had lived. Both parents were born in Italy in 1900 and had immigrated at age 21 to New York. They married and had three sons, but ten years later, the father was sent to a mental hospital and remained hospitalized for sixty years, dying at age ninety, and buried only a few minutes from where John had been born and lived. John's mother was sent to a mental hospital a few years later and kept institutionalized for sixty-two years, dying at age 102, and buried very near where John had attended Princeton University.

HOW TO GATHER INFORMATION: ASKING QUESTIONS AND HEARING STORIES

To get to know your family in a different way requires becoming an expert at asking questions. It is strange how often we do not ask our families the relevant questions. Some questions occur to us, but we sense they would make others uncomfortable. We may be wrong in these perceptions, but we might be right, too. Other questions never come to mind, because unspoken family rules make it hard to even notice them. Family wisdom may have it that "Uncle Charlie isn't worth talking to because he's a lazy, pompous fool" or "Cousin Betty is an inveterate liar and remembers nothing anyway." Families tend to have rules, assumptions, and stories that members are expected to take at face value. Letting go of such family assumptions is not easy. A person may have been told that Aunt Charlotte "can't handle stress, so don't discuss anything personal with her." She is never asked to help out when problems arise, and no one ever thinks to ask her opinion. But the interesting question is: Who decided Charlotte couldn't handle stress and on what basis? We urge you to question assumptions about family members' functioning, to find out how the conclusion was drawn and by whom. Once you change the mystification into a line of questioning, you may become intrigued about the family myths you have absorbed without realizing it. This can be the beginning of your journey of self-discovery and empowerment, where the aim is for curiosity about family dynamics.

Questions about the facts of birth and death in your family—who, when, where, and how?—may uncover emotionally charged events such as suicide, alcoholism, pregnancy outside of marriage, stillbirths, miscarriages, abortions, or affairs. A person may have forgotten that his grandfather had a twin whose death at age ten left a legacy that is still affecting the family two generations later. A daughter may not have noted that her parents' separation occurred the same year as her grandmother's heart attack. The family may not mention, unless you dig for the facts, that grandma actually had been married before. The excuse given may be that the first marriage didn't really count, because the husband was a scoundrel and left after two months.

LISTEN TO WHAT PEOPLE TELL YOU AND WHAT THEY OMIT: WHAT SECRETS DO FAMILIES KEEP?

The stories people tell about themselves and their family histories must be listened to carefully—both for what they tell and for what they omit. As an example, let's look again at Benjamin Franklin (discussed as a runaway in Chapter 1) and the role that secrets played in organizing his family system across multiple generations (**see Genogram 3.2: Franklin Family**). In Franklin's autobiography, written originally for his son, he admits to many of his youthful follies or "errata," including mistreating his future wife by leaving her, failing to write after promising to marry her, and attempting to seduce his best friend's girlfriend. On the other hand, he passes over the biggest secret in his history: Who William's mother was and when exactly William was born. Obviously, a key rule in the Franklin family was not to mention this subject.

Franklin's wife, Deborah, who apparently raised William from infancy, was not his mother. She and Franklin were never formally married in a church and maintained some secrecy about their marriage. He gives the date, September 30, 1730, in his autobiography. Their silence about their marriage was apparently because Deborah, having been abandoned by Franklin when he left her for England, had eventually married another man, who had disappeared, but who might still have been alive. However, this does not explain the secrecy about William's birth, which was a matter of concern to William through his whole adult life, especially when rumors that he was illegitimate began to affect him politically. Franklin's silence on the matter is all the more

Benjamin Franklin
Library of Congress

remarkable because there was such an obvious need for clarification.

Franklin never disclosed the truth around William's birth and the tradition of secrecy continued into the next generation. Franklin seems to have made a point of missing William's wedding, which was also kept secret, as were the birth and parentage of his son Temple. The story was apparently put out that he was the son of a "poor relation." Temple was often sent greetings by family and friends in their correspondence, but Deborah never once mentioned him in her letters. Perhaps this reflected her resentment of the second generation of fathering a child out of wedlock, but more likely, Deborah was never informed about Temple, since Franklin makes not the slightest allusion to him in any of his letters to her, though he continuously gossips about all other

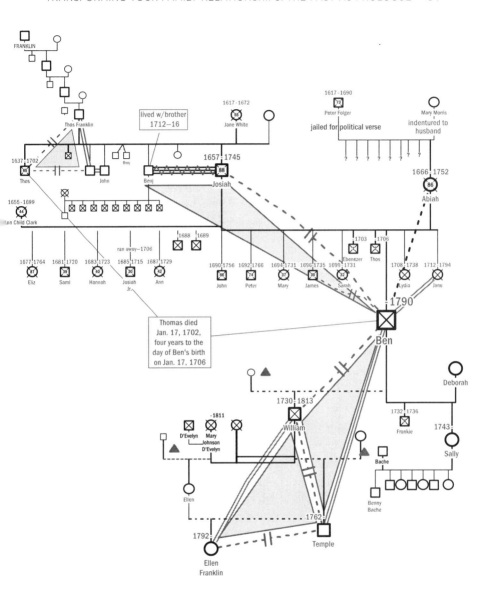

Genogram 3.2: Franklin Family

members of the family. Years later, a family friend referred with amusement to the game the whole family played in pretending they had not guessed the nature of Temple's relationship to the family (Lopez & Herbert, 1975).

Again, in the fourth generation there was secrecy regarding Temple's illegitimate children. In fact, after the cutoff between William and Temple, William even tried to make people believe that Temple's daughter, Ellen, was his own child. The repetition of illegitimacy for three generations in the Franklin family seems almost uncanny. What was the connection between the generations in repeating this so-called secret?

Franklin's biographers commented on the conspicuous omissions in Franklin's writing. One said: Here is a man who talks to us apparently so frankly about himself while increasingly obscuring himself behind the public images, that at intervals we do not know what is fact and what is fiction (Wright, 1988, p. 9). Another biographer about the "private" Franklin, maintained: "His present family is practically nonexistent in the Autobiography: his daughter was not mentioned a single time, his son alluded to quite casually, his wife brought into the picture mainly in the days when they were not yet married—and then not as a personality but as the illustration of a wrong set to right. The focus is exclusively on himself, or rather on a portion of himself. No soul-searching here" (Lopez & Herbert, 1975, pp. 2–3).

If William knew about the negative relationship Franklin had with his own father, he may have resented his father's presentation of the family stories in such a positive light, especially when Franklin was pressuring him to conform in his political views.

It is surprising how often families with an appearance of openness are very closed on certain topics. If this applies to your family, you will want to study how the secrecy works: Who knows the secret? Who doesn't? How do family members learn what questions not to ask? How does conversation get skewed so people do not even realize there is a secret that has been skirted in conversation? A pattern of secrecy in a family tends to breed more secrecy and distortion because it teaches family members that the truth cannot be handled and that some experiences can never be integrated.

GENERATING NEW QUESTIONS

Gathering information and organizing it on your genogram will inevitably lead to more questions. Generating new questions is a vital part of this journey. The more you learn, the more you will have to wonder about. Consider the information we discussed about the Franklin family genogram. This information leads to additional questions:

- Why did Franklin feel he could not survive within the confines of his family?
- Did he feel forced to escape the pressure of their dreams, ambitions, or fears about his performance?

- Were Franklin and his older brother, James, replaying a multi-generational family drama in which the younger brother excels, is forced to submit, and is finally exiled, as seemed to play out in the previous generation between Ben's father, Josiah, and his brother, Uncle Ben?
- For whom were the other brothers named?
- Did anyone else's birth coincide with family losses or important family anniversaries?
- Were there losses in the parental families that led the parents to draw Ben into the role of replacement child?
- In choosing to marry a simple woman with little education, was Franklin repeating the experience not only of his parents, but of his maternal grandparents?
- We know that Franklin's maternal grandfather was also a poet, author, and remarkable public figure, who married his servant. In later years Franklin himself lived more closely with much more educated women and their families rather than with his own wife, whom he abandoned for years at a time. Was this a departure from the traditional Franklin pattern or was there a history of developing intense connections outside the family?

As the Franklin family demonstrates, the more we learn, the more there is to wonder about and explore. As you embark on this journey and listen closely to the stories you hear, more questions are likely to arise. Pursuing these questions is basic to this process.

BEING AN EMPATHETIC DETECTIVE

The process of asking questions requires careful planning and a cool head, so you do not run into reactivity that disheartens you. The important thing is to develop a questioning attitude and a healthy skepticism, never being too sure that any one point of view is the "true truth." Think of yourself as a detective, looking to make connections—between important dates, relationship patterns of your grandparents and your parents, and between current patterns and what your parents were like at the same life-cycle point as you are in now.

The goal is to ask questions because you want to learn about your family's history and experiences. It is essential to approach family members with care and empathy, letting them know that you want to learn about the family to understand yourself better. Try to operate from curiosity rather than jumping to conclusions. All responses are information, even those that are hostile or rejecting.

Be prepared to hear negative feelings and observations and to maintain your cool—for example, if your adored father was perceived by his brothers as a patsy or was a scrooge in business, or if the family views him as arrogant, spoiled, selfish, or succeeding by luck.

Be curious about what factors led to that perception of him, and how that perception has affected their reactions. Even if you don't agree with how others see things, you can't change or control them, so focus on deepening your understanding of multiple perspectives, and only then on deciding what you think. Your ability to maintain your sense of yourself without becoming defensive, regardless of others' perceptions, is essential to this process.

A common error is to go bluntly after information, disrespecting the pain that secrecy reflects for a family, or on the other hand, being too fearful to raise relevant issues. Families often feel security in what is familiar. The fear may be, "If I mention my father's suicide, things might get worse." Proceed gently, approaching any opening of issues with caution and respect, proceeding only when you feel you are ready to handle the fallout and reactivity that may arise. Only raise an issue if you have decided it matters and are willing to deal constructively with the family's possible reactivity.

And don't begin asking questions until you are prepared to handle the answers with respect and equanimity. If you ask your mother about her overall experience with you as a child, you need to be ready to hear how frustrating she found you, without launching into a tirade about *her* motherly inadequacies. Becoming defensive or attacking in reaction to a family member's response to questions is rarely fruitful.

One way to check yourself is to consider your intentions behind the questions you ask. If your goal is self-justification or to prove others in the family wrong, your pursuit will be misguided. The intention underneath your questions needs to be genuine curiosity and compassion. For example, to understand your cold and distant father who was abused by his own father, instead of asking him: "If your father was so abusive, why didn't you tell someone or get out?"—you might start from a more compassionate place with, "It must have been scary never to know when he would go into a rage. Did you ever have warning signs?"

As you gather information through asking questions and hearing stories, work on creating your genogram and a timeline. And as pieces start to come together, be sure to step back to notice patterns. There are many different patterns that occur in families and identifying them is the key to understanding how your family works.

CLOSENESS, CONFLICTS, TRIANGLES, AND CUTOFFS

Triangulating is one of the key mechanisms through which dysfunctional patterns of relating are transmitted over generations in a family. We will be discussing triangles throughout this book, because they are such important patterns in the development of family problems. They involve two people joining against a third who becomes either ostracized, patronized, or treated as too incompetent to be a full participant in the family (see also video *Triangles in Family Therapy: Strategies and Solutions*, available at www.psychotherapy.net).

Benjamin Franklin's family (Genogram 3.2) provides rich examples of how triangles can shape family functioning. The first key triangle while Ben was growing up seems to have involved Ben, his father Josiah, and his uncle Benjamin, after whom Ben was named. The name chosen for a child may in and of itself tell you a lot about a family's "program" or dreams for a child. Franklin himself thought it significant that he was named for his father's favorite brother, who became his godfather. When Ben was six, his Uncle Benjamin, having lost his wife and all but one of his ten children, came from England to live with the family. He and the father had not seen each other for 30 years and they were opposites in personality. Josiah was pragmatic, business minded, and a mechanical genius, but also a fanatical Puritan. Uncle Ben was an ingenious man, a bit fantastic in personality, an inventor, a free-thinker, a poet, a dreamer, a great talker, and given to endless philosophizing, reading, and rhyming, but always hard up for money.

Josiah began a long tug-of-war with his brother for his son Ben's allegiance, forming an intense triangle. As Uncle Benjamin began to inspire his young nephew in the direction of humorous, iconoclastic writing, Josiah became more and more hostile toward his brother. As Franklin later wrote: "Our father . . . used to say nothing was more common than for those who loved one another at a distance to find many causes of dislike when they came together. I saw proof of it in the disgusts between him and his brother Benjamin" (Randall, 1984, p. 32).

The more Uncle Benjamin agreed that young Ben should get the best education possible and go into the ministry, the less enthusiasm Josiah had for his old promise for this, and finally—though Franklin was a brilliant student, Josiah withdrew him altogether from school and humiliated him by insisting he take up a trade.

But the more his father resisted his education, the more Ben loved learning. Although his father terminated schooling for him when he was only eight, he eventually received honorary degrees from Harvard, Yale, St. Andrews, and Oxford. Perhaps in the end, Josiah feared being outstripped by this replica of his own brother more than he wished for his favorite son to be "the tithe of his loins."

Such triangles are common when a particular child becomes the favorite of a grandparent, aunt, uncle, or godparent and triggers the parent's resentment or perhaps old conflicts. When you see a parent negatively focused on one particular child, consider what triangle may be operating in your family.

When you see a cutoff, such as Franklin's brother Josiah running away to sea, Ben disappearing at seventeen, or outsiders moving in, as when Uncle Ben came to live with the family, it is natural to inquire about conflicts or alliances that may have divided the family's loyalties. As we discussed in Chapter 1, there were repeated triangles in the Franklin family, with intense closeness and conflict seeming to complement the cutoffs, leading to further fusion and more predictable cutoffs. Given the triangles in his family growing up, it was perhaps predictable that Franklin and his son William would have a cutoff, after which Ben reached for closeness with William's son, Temple, who had conflict with his father. This was repeated in the next generation where Temple cut off his daughter Ellen, to whom William became extremely attached (see **Genogram 3.3: Franklin Father–Son–Grandchild Triangles**).

As you start to identify dysfunctional triangles in your own family, notice how they tend to exacerbate stress, conflict, and cutoff. While triangles are common in all systems (e.g., our extended family, our work system, with friends, in the community), intense emotional triangles tend to reflect the

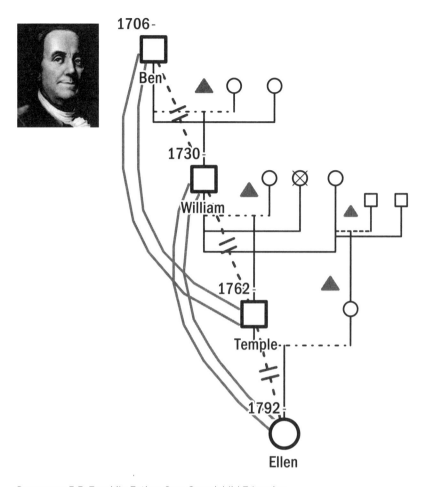

Genogram 3.3: Franklin Father-Son-Grandchild Triangles

original triangles we were caught in with our family of origin. Once you start to see the triangles, try to imagine how relationships might be different if a de-triangulating process could occur. Since triangles are characterized by enmeshment, de-triangulating leads to increased family flexibility.

UNSTATED PRESSURE TO FULFILL A CERTAIN ROLE OR FUNCTION

Families often unconsciously place pressure on a member to fulfill an unstated role, maybe tied to sibling position or past events. We see this, for example, in the Franklin family where, as the youngest son of a youngest son for five generations back, Ben's father identified with him in a special way. We all tend to identify with a child who is in our same sibling position, as with the child who most resembles us physically. If patterns have repeated for many generations, there may be a special legacy and an even greater intensity about our expectation for this child to fulfill a certain role. In Franklin's case, his father's decision that Ben would be "the tithe of his loins" makes sense in relation to his special position as youngest son of a youngest son.

Franklin was also a "replacement child" for no less than three other sons who were lost around the time of his birth. The first, Ebenezer, had drowned. The next, Thomas, named for the paternal grandfather, died a few months after Ben was born. During the same period, the father's twenty-one-year old namesake, Josiah Jr., ran away to sea—returning only once briefly nine years later before disappearing for good. Very likely the family blamed themselves for these losses, especially for the accidental death of Ebenezer, who had drowned unattended in his bath at two years old. They probably hoped that their last son Ben would accomplish enough for four sons (which he did!). Yet they may also have feared becoming too attached to him, as they might lose him as well.

We know from Franklin's autobiography that he dreamed of following his lost brother, Josiah Jr., to sea. Did the family expect him to replace that brother? Had conflicts with Josiah Jr. led to his leaving the family? Were the conflicts Ben had with his parents' part of a legacy of conflict that he inherited once Josiah left? We don't know, but we do know that Franklin remembered all his life the one brief last visit Josiah Jr. made to the family years later. Josiah Jr.'s loss apparently made a deep impression on all of them.

TIMING OF OUR BIRTH AND THE IMPORTANCE OF DATES

The timing of our entry in our family and circumstances surrounding our birth can also significantly influence the role we play in life and how we are seen by others. Each person has a different relationship with parents, siblings, grandparents, aunts, and uncles, so you want to explore those relationships as you study your genogram. Pay close attention to the timing of birth in relation to other family events that may have shaped hidden expectations regarding a person's role in the family.

Looking again at the timing of Franklin's birth, he was born four years to the day after the death of his father's oldest brother, Tom. Anniversary dates can also be important and very much worth tracking. Families often obscure the emotional connections such coincidences can create, which may set up almost mysterious links between events or people. Franklin himself wrote to his son in his autobiography about his resemblance to that uncle: "(Tom) died . . . four years to the day before I was born. The recital which some elderly persons made to us of his character, I remember, struck you as something extraordinary, from its similarity to what you knew of me. 'Had he died,' said you, 'four years later, on the same day, one might have supposed a transmigration'" (Franklin, 1968, pp. 47–48).

This Uncle Tom—whose death ended five generations of Franklins in their home community of Ecton, England—was a very learned man, an ingenious inventor, trained as a smith, but qualified also as a lawyer. He became an important man in his community, and "the chief mover of all public-spirited enterprises" for his county. This sounds remarkably like Ben Franklin, founder of one of the first newspapers in America, the first public library, the first volunteer fire company, the first hospital, the postal service, and the University of Pennsylvania, one of the first universities. What is more, he was President of the Pennsylvania Society for the Abolition of Slavery, Ambassador to England and France, and, of course, a major force in the fashioning of our Declaration of Independence and Constitution.

One's birth may also occur on a date that has an idiosyncratic meaning for a family. For example, Ben Franklin's birth took place on a Sunday, which in that era implied that the parents had had sex on Sunday, which was considered a sin. This made Franklin a child of the Devil—not a small consideration for his staunchly religious father who was "the keeper of the morals" in their church community. The family dealt with this "sin" by maintaining strict secrecy about the exact date of Ben's birth. Similarly, some families might attribute certain meaning to a birth that take place on Friday the 13th, or on the same day as an important family member dies. In such instances, the meaning attached to a person's date of birth may influence the subsequent role they come to play in the family.

COINCIDENTAL EVENTS

In some families, coincidental events can have great power, as occurred in the family of Mahatma Gandhi (see **Genogram 3.4: Gandhi Family**). Gandhi was married at age 13 in a joint wedding with a brother and a cousin because his father and uncle were both older and worrying about getting their sons married before they died. Unfortunately, the father suffered an accident just before the wedding and his health declined from that point forward. Gandhi and his mother became the father's primary caretakers.

Mahatma Gandhi
Ana Maria Tudor/Alamy Stock Photo

He describes in his autobiography (1968): "I was devoted to my father, but no less was I devoted to the passions that the flesh is heir to. I had yet to learn that all happiness and pleasure should be sacrificed in devoted service to my parents. And yet, as though by way of punishment for my desire for pleasures, an incident happened which has ever since rankled in my mind" (p. 9). His wife was pregnant, which he says, "meant a double shame for me. For one thing I did not restrain myself, as I should have done. . . . This carnal desire just got the better of what I regarded as my duty to study and of what was even a greater duty, my devotion to

Gandhi's wife, Kasturbai, and their four surviving sons
Dinodia Photos/Alamy Stock Photo

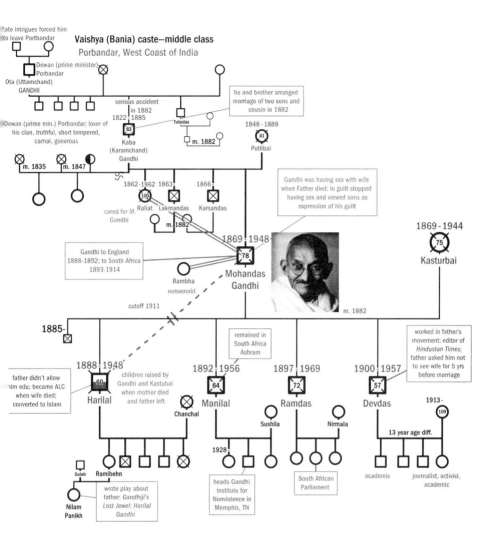

Genogram 3.4: Gandhi Family

my parents" (p. 27). His father died while he was having sex with his wife that night, for which he never forgave himself.

He described the son who was born soon after as "the poor mite that was born to my wife scarcely breathed for three or four days. Nothing else could be expected. Let all those who are married be warned by my example" (p. 29).

Could it be that the very difficult relationship Gandhi had with his oldest surviving son, Halilal, born two years after this trauma, who was always rebellious and then apologetic for his rebellion and died a homeless alcoholic, was bound up in the conflicts of this experience? Gandhi himself was preoccupied the rest of his life with guilt for not having been present when his father died, and the connection seems to have powerfully influenced his belief that one should never give in to human impulses for pleasure. His son's refusal to conform to his ideas was perhaps the biggest disappointment of Gandhi's life.

GENDER PATTERNS

Gender is, of course, another major factor in families. Questions to ask include what were the rules for men and women in your family and to what extent did family members conform to these rules? Gender role constriction in families has played a powerful role over the centuries. Women are typically the carriers of family heritage in certain ways. They often have been socialized to feel more responsible for the family, for those in need, for dealing with the pain of family secrets, and for injustices done to family members. Men may disconnect more easily, given society's support for the "independent" male. Older sisters may be particularly accessible and helpful in promoting family reconnections because they so often feel over-responsible for family well-being. Because of our society's rules for male and female socialization, men may fit into the stereotypes of being less accessible, less willing to acknowledge their vulnerability, and less aware of the emotional process in the family.

Gender norms have not changed as much as many would wish, despite recent dramatic changes for women and in our binary thinking about gender and sexual orientation. Perhaps your grandmother was viewed as a saint because she cooked, cleaned, and took care of all; yet she gets defined as "a bit daffy." And now, perhaps in this generation, your mother is talked about as "a remarkable woman," very successful in her computer business, able to handle a hundred things at once, "but she's a lousy cook!" It is important to notice underlying disqualifying patterns even as patterns are changing.

Be sure to pay attention to how your family has responded to the constrictions of gender roles within their time and society. Did some family members break out of the stringent gender roles of their times? If so, how was this received by others inside and outside the family? Look especially at those who did not conform to the gender norms of their era—the women who were assertive, daring, and did things on their own, and the men who were sweet, nurturing, or did not play "the good provider" or the "macho" role for whatever reason. Be on the lookout for moments when the males in your family became more open, especially during times of transition or loss. As with inequities based on race, and other injustices, it is also impressive when women change oppressive family rules of over-responsibility for others to pursue their own dreams. We can learn a great deal about ourselves and our families by exploring how our families reacted to those who didn't conform to traditional gender roles.

YOUR EVOLVING SELF

An interesting illustration of the power that learning our history has on our self-understanding is the experience of documentary filmmaker and activist Michael Moore, when Henry Louis Gates researched his history. Moore always thought he was 100% Irish Catholic and that his ancestors had come to the U.S. to escape the potato famine of the 1850s. But Gates's research showed that Moore's belief was not accurate. He had Quaker ancestors who were stalwart pacifists in the U.S., dating back 150 years. He also had a Scottish ancestor who had been forcibly brought to the U.S. as a white "slave," and another who had been killed by Native Americans in the 1600s. Clearly his family had roots in the U.S. long before the Irish potato famine. Moore's response to Gates's revelations about his history: "My soul has been touched by this, because who I am, how I feel, and what I believe in didn't just appear. It came through a

Documentary filmmaker and activist Michael Moore
Storm/Splash News/Newscom

shared experience by many, many people, passed down. It's like I'm getting a 2nd birthday here. You've told me something about my formation, about my birth . . . it's a revelation." As Moore demonstrates, obtaining new information about our family almost always shifts how we understand ourselves, which is a critical part of finding ways to change our relationships with others.

The only person you have the power to change is yourself, and this is the goal. If your aim is to make someone else happy, save or change someone, tell them off, get their approval, or justify and explain yourself, the effort will likely fail. In any case, it will probably not be worth the struggle, and may even compound the problem by increasing your frustration that you made an effort, and it didn't work, or even made things worse.

Going home is about developing authentic emotionally engaged relationships with your family while changing your part in repetitive, dysfunctional, emotional patterns. It is not about changing others, but about changing yourself. Since people almost always start out wanting to change others rather than themselves, this is the first hurdle.

When I (MM) began this work, I had the brilliant idea that I would help my mother change her attitude toward her mother and my husband change his relationship with his mother, or even better, change his mother altogether. It was an important turning point when I realized that this was not an appropriate agenda. My husband's relationship with his mother was his business, not mine, and my mother's attitude toward her mother was her business. The part I could work on was my relationship with my mother and to a lesser extent, my relationship with my mother-in-law. To do this I had to focus on my own role in these relationships.

The basic idea is that if you can change the part you play in your family and hold it despite your family's reactivity, while staying in emotional contact with family members, you maximize the likelihood (not a guarantee!) that the family will eventually change to accommodate your change. Most of us do what Murray Bowen called "the two-step" where we attempt to change, but when it doesn't immediately produce the results we want, or if someone says, "change back," we give up. Successful change involves going beyond this and planning how to deal with family members' predictable reactivity to our effort. Any change involves a minimum of three steps: (1) the change; (2) dealing with the family's reaction to the change; and (3) proceeding with your change effort.

A good place to start is by clarifying your role in your family, as well as basic themes and triangles. Anywhere that your role has become stuck, it may help to consider using what we call a "reversal," that is, to change any ingrained pattern of relating by saying or doing something different from what you usually say or do. You may at first think of this as "lying" about your true feelings. If the pattern is stuck, the other person probably knows your feelings already or else isn't listening. The value of a reversal is that it can express the unacknowledged underside of an issue and may break up rigid, predictable, repetitive communication patterns. For example, a wife who ordinarily gets angry when her husband gets sick and calls him a hypochondriac can reverse her pattern by playing Florence Nightingale; a man who usually cannot talk to his father because his father is so dictatorial can reverse the patterns by asking for his father's advice and trying to listen to him attentively without disagreeing, maybe even by responding with, "Thanks, you've given me a lot to think about."

When I was beginning this work, I (MM) was caught in a triangle with my husband and my mother-in-law, who was very critical of me to him. I was coached to "de-triangulate" by using a "reversal" that would hopefully not threaten my mother-in-law. The suggestion was to say to her something like: "Your son has been telling me things you've been saying about me, and I'm so relieved. I had been so worried that you would not like me and would wish your son hadn't married me." This response, while not totally honest did address a deeper truth—my anxiety that my mother-in-law would not like me. She seemed dumbfounded with the first part of the sentence, undoubtedly fearing that her son had been telling me the negative things she was saying about me. But she seemed greatly relieved when she concluded he had apparently not been telling me what she was saying. Indeed, after that she stopped bad-mouthing me to my husband and began reassuring him and me about her positive feelings toward our relationship.

But strategies to reverse the usual pattern of alliances and distance must not be undertaken lightly. Only undertake such a shift if you are totally committed to the value of changing stuck family patterns in a caring manner. It can succeed only if you have the emotional control to edit feelings of hurt, anger, sarcasm, and vengeance from any communication and convey respect for the other. Even then, the family's first reaction will typically be to feel betrayed or suspicious of the new behavior, and you will have to continue to change efforts until you get past their reactivity before they may restabilize in a new pattern. For example, if you usually gossip with your mother about your father and decide to stop doing that, your mother will probably resent your refusal to gossip with her. Moreover, if you start to engage with your father rather than avoiding him, he may experience your approach as a ploy. You will need to ride out the reactivity to get to a different pattern of relating. This takes time and patience. If you and one sibling frequently badmouth another sibling and you are suddenly spending time with the other sibling, the first will likely experience it as a rejection and may become angry or provoked that you are a betrayer. It will take time for the reactivity to diminish, and you will need patience. If you are usually critical of your partner around some issue and now become accommodating and supportive, your partner may get suspicious that you have a trick up your sleeve. Such reactivity is common when relationship patterns have become stuck.

Remember, systems resist change. When you make a change, the first response will typically be resistance. Don't be afraid of this. See it instead as evidence that you are succeeding in changing the only thing you can change, yourself! As Murray Bowen used to say, "If you make a move and no one throws a brick at your head, it probably means they didn't feel your move."

Planning how to respond to family members' reactions to your change effort is extremely important. It helps to keep track of what you already know and what your questions are so far. It also helps to hypothesize about how family members may react, so you are prepared to deal with any reactivity you encounter. Looking at the family broadly can shift the focus from guilt and blame to a more objective "researcher" position about family history. As you begin to observe and listen differently at family gatherings, try to ease into making shifts in your own thinking or relating. And think carefully about whatever you learn from others' responses that can help you in future connections. Above all, bear in mind that encountering resistance and/or reactivity to changes in your ways of behaving is evidence that you are doing the necessary work of taking the journey to go home.

BEGINNING MY PERSONAL
JOURNEY HOME

I (MM) began my genogram journey home after hearing psychiatrist Murray Bowen give a presentation on family systems theory in which he said that if you haven't worked out your relationship with your own mother to the point where you can sit comfortably in the same room with her, you have not really learned how to work systemically. I could hardly listen his presentation because I was so sure he had never met anyone like my mother and had no idea what he was talking about. But in the back of my mind, I was awed to think that I could possibly get to the point of having a relationship with her, having struggled with her all my life.

After Bowen's talk I arranged to begin coaching with one of his students, Phil Guerin. My relationship with my mother had been negative since childhood. As I grew up, we became more distant. Years of individual therapy had confirmed that my mother was difficult, and she also was limited in what she could give. Hence, the best thing I could do was stay away from her and focus instead on my marriage and my friends. In contrast, my coaching encouraged to me look at this relationship in a larger context—first in relation to my very close attachment to my father and to Margaret, the African American caretaker who had raised me. My husband was now the only one in the family who refused to placate my mother, and she did not appreciate it, which put a strain on all our relationships. I fantasized about moving to California and visiting home in the east only once or twice a year. But I did not want to move away.

I tried to gather genogram information, though my mother was very uncooperative, saying that nothing in her miserable childhood had been carried over into our family. She felt her mother, who ranted at everyone and viewed my mother as a nuisance, had ruined her childhood. She categorized her mother as "the vainest woman who ever walked the earth," and said all she ever did was go shopping. When I had asked what she thought her mother thought about while shopping, she assured me her mother thought about absolutely nothing.

Once when I was a teenager and out shopping with my mother, she told me that her mother had had an affair with a local priest right under the nose of my grandfather and she used to tell my mother not to come home from school because Father Egan would be there. My mother became a street kid, smoking from fourth grade.

As I pursued the family history and tried to get genogram information, my mother accused me of trying to destroy her by bringing up painful subjects. I couldn't think how to proceed.

My coach suggested I stop pursuing her entirely and explore how else I could learn about my genogram. I thought that was a ridiculous suggestion. There was no one to ask. It hadn't occurred to me to approach my mother's two sisters. But once I was challenged to question the assumption that they were irrelevant, it was obvious that I was grossly mistaken.

My mother was the youngest of three sisters. Her oldest sister, seven years older, would probably know a lot about their family history. My mother viewed her middle sister, four years older, as her primary supporter in childhood. She had been the closest to my mother's hated mother and would probably have very different stories about my grandmother, if I could get her to share them, but I hadn't seen this aunt in years.

When I called my oldest aunt, she immediately invited me to visit her. The visit was a revelation. Most shocking was that she remembered the night my mother was born! I couldn't imagine my mother had ever been born! I imagined that my mother had risen full-grown out of Zeus's head or something! My aunt offered many memories of my mother as a bratty, whiny kid, for whom my aunt was supposed to babysit.

She went on to tell me that my grandmother didn't have an easy life, never knowing if her policeman husband would be killed on the job, adding, "And don't let anybody tell you different." There was, of course, only one person who would tell me different: my mother.

By the time I got home my mother was calling to say she heard I had been invited to her sister's new house, but she hadn't been. The triangle had been activated!

The next time I visited my parents, my mother had a whole box of family memorabilia for me. She said since I had such an interest in the family history, I might want this. I had asked her so many times for family information and she always said there was none, but now, suddenly, out it came, with the stories to go with it.

A while later I visited my other aunt in Chicago. I asked her to bring any family pictures, but she said she could only find three, including one of Father Egan, the priest my mother felt had ruined her life. I was stupefied and pretended I didn't know who it was. "Oh," she replied, "That was my mother's great friend, don't you know him?" Later in the ladies' room I asked my cousin, who had joined our lunch if she ever heard that that priest ruined my mother's childhood and humiliated our grandfather. She said she hadn't heard that they had an affair. Then she added, "But, you know, our grandmother was one of the early liberated women on Staten Island, the first to drive a car! She was very daring! So an affair wouldn't surprise me." The circuits were definitely being blown on my perspective of my family history.

From here on I proceeded very carefully, trying never to get ahead of my mother's level of comfort and willingness to share what she felt comfortable with. In fits and starts our connection started to grow. With time, and over many years my relationship with my mother grew stronger and more honest until the very day of her death, when I was preparing the first edition of this book, which she had read and commented on in earlier versions.

Because of my journey to learn about our family history, I had come to be a much less judgmental daughter, and with my change, my mother had become a much less judgmental mother. It is for these transformative changes, which have meant so much in my life, that I have dedicated this book to her. She taught me a great deal about courage, even as I learned about her many fears and insecurities. I have worked from that time forward to expand my understanding of my genogram and to go home again.

GUIDELINES FOR WORKING ON FAMILY RELATIONSHIPS

1. To change family relationships, stay focused on changing yourself—connecting to others while remaining true to yourself. The goal is to be our own best self while remaining in a respect-

ful, connected relationship with other family members. The more we can control our reactivity and relate with love, fairness, and respect, the more evolved our relationships will be.

2. The key guidelines for developing respectful, caring relationships are: don't attack, don't defend, don't placate, and don't shut down. We should do everything possible not to put negative energy out into the universe.

3. Keep your own counsel. Working out your family relationships is an individual process, requiring you to act on the basis of your own values. Sharing plans with your spouse or sibling is likely to increase their anxiety, which could lead them to interfere with your efforts.

4. Never underestimate your family's resistance to change, which is likely to be intense and could take you off guard. Anticipate resistance and reactivity to your efforts and plan how you will respond with respect while remaining steadfast in your efforts.

5. Lower your expectations of others in your system. As Murray Bowen used to say, "If you lower your expectations to zero, you'll probably be happily surprised."

6. Serious issues should be addressed with each family member individually, not at a large, ritualized family gathering.

7. Humor may be the best way to detoxify a tense issue, but obviously this does not mean sarcasm or pejorative humor.

8. Be unpredictable by letting go of stubbornly held positions. If you are caught in the same old role or argument, it's time to do something different. Also, if someone seems to always be wrong or right, a villain or victim, try expanding your view of them.

9. Intense anger or hurt are likely to be signals that an important issue is at stake for you. Pause, take slow breaths, and mindfully direct your energy where it needs to go for you to be true to your best intentions and values, and treating others with generosity and respect.

10. When you find yourself being overly eager to work on other people's relationships (especially an in-law or stepfamily member!), look at what you may be avoiding in your own. Refocus your energy on your relationship with your own child, parent, or sibling to get your work back on track.

11. For every piece of critical or negative feedback you give, offer at least four positive or affirming comments. There is science (Gottman, 2007) to suggest humans need this 4 to 1 ratio to be able

to absorb negative feedback. If you offer negative feedback without giving even more positive feedback, the other person is likely not to hear you.

12. Silence and/or distance are not effective strategies. While there are times when it will be more prudent to not respond, and you may need to take some space from intense family turmoil to center yourself and regain some balance and humor, it is important always to re-engage.

13. If someone is blocking your way to another family member, develop a relationship with the blocking person, even if they seem peripheral. It would be futile to try to go around them. If your sister-in-law monitors all your brother's contacts, developing a relationship with her is your best chance to connect with him.

14. Letters that are not attacking or defensive can help to open difficult emotional issues without having to manage your reactivity in real time. In writing letters to a family member, take up only one emotional issue at a time. If you feel intensely reactive to a family member, it may help to write a "tell all letter" where you lay out all your issues (never send this letter!) Next, write a "strategic" letter, staying focused on the key issues you want to express—without attacking or defending.

15. Never stay with your family longer than you can afford to be generous. When you begin to get grouchy, or to shut down, it's time to leave until you can enter again with your sense of humor and equilibrium intact.

Chapter 4
Family Stories and Secrets

Storytelling is fundamental to the human search for meaning.

—MARY CATHERINE BATESON
Composing a Life

I do not see my life as separate from history. In my mind my family secrets mingle with the secrets of statesmen and bombers. Nor is my life divided from the lives of others. I who am a woman, have my father's face, and he, I suspect, has his mother's face. There is a characteristic way my father's eyelids fold, and you can see this in my face and in a photograph I have of him as a little boy. In the same photograph there is a silent sorrow mapped on his face and this sorrow is mine too. All history, including the histories of our families, is part of us, such that when we hear any secret revealed . . . our lives are made suddenly clearer to us. . . . For perhaps we are like stones— our own history and the history of the world embedded in us.

—SUSAN GRIFFIN
A Chorus of Stones

We are born not just into our family, but into our family's stories, which both nourish and sometimes cripple us. And when we die, the story of our lives becomes part of our family's web of meaning (Kotre & Hall, 1990).

Paying careful attention to the stories in your family is a great way to learn about the patterns and values that have traveled down your family over the generations and provide an opportunity to revise your stories by shifting emphasis to other themes that you value. Photos, videos, or writing down the stories of older family members can bring a richness to your search for perspective on your family that cannot be achieved in any other way. Technology now allows us to convey the sound and visual reality of family stories better than has ever previously been possible in human history.

Over time some details recede, and others are highlighted, re-editing memories and stories toward a meaningful narrative. When experiences don't jibe with your family's dominant narrative, you may feel challenged and bewildered. Traumatic family experiences can create myths and superstitions about the dangers of the outside world that flow down the generations, influencing descendants who have no conscious awareness of the origin of the beliefs. Family stories often develop around the facts to reassure, explain, or limit the pain of traumatic family experiences. Family stories and myths give signals about the family's covert values and rules. Families transmit messages that seem to prescribe behavior for generations to come.

Family stories may revolve around the courage of family members against great odds, or about their humorous comeback after humiliation. In families characterized by pessimism, stories may carry a message that "you never win." People may have stereotyped roles in family stories—the hero, the villain, the jokester, or the victim—roles that by identifying the "good guys" and "bad guys" reveal the family's values.

Family stories are often shaped by myths that are transmitted both explicitly and more often, implicitly, which can increase their power to influence the next generation, since the beliefs embedded in them are generally accepted as reality.

We may have to be exposed to values beyond the borders of our family before we can become fully aware of our family's messages and myths and how they influence our perception and behavior. Children learn early what can and cannot be discussed. As we have been discussing, all families convey messages about gender, sexual orientation, social class, race, and ethnicity that are all essential to examine.

Families develop private jokes, routines, and references, transmitted from one generation to the next about how to behave and what to value. For example, my mother (MM), who was about five foot nine had a saying: "Never trust a short woman." My father's mother, at about four foot six, was the only short woman in the family, and my mother despised her. The implications of her imperative were clear. We received other messages as well, such as "Always put a plate under the orange juice, when certain guests visit," which conveyed where she felt we stood in social class in relation to others. We received other messages about never referring to a person's race or cultural background, which also conveyed rules about our place in the social hierarchy.

Children may be drawn into a family expectation to carry out missions left incomplete by an earlier death, or they may be constrained by parental fear of repeating a painful past experience. Family legacies can become a burden for the next generation. In my own family (MM) distancing seemed to be the major strategy for dealing with conflict, although never leaving home was another path chosen by some. Perhaps this was an example of distance and fusion being variations of the same theme. In some families the myth is that leaving home is dangerous, hence family members get strong messages to stay home at all costs. The Brontë family provides a compelling example of this.

THE MYTH THAT LEAVING HOME IS DANGEROUS: THE BRONTË FAMILY

The Brontë family (**see Genogram 4.1: Brontë Family**), whose daughters became famous authors, seems to have developed early the belief that leaving home was dangerous and in the end, no one really left home at all. Yet Emily Brontë, author of *Wuthering Heights*, and Charlotte Brontë, author of *Jane Eyre*, became among the most famous authors of all time and continue to be read around the world almost two centuries later.

The belief that leaving home was dangerous probably developed through early family experiences of illness and death, but the myth itself influenced later reactions when family members did leave. There seems to have been a legacy of emotional conflicts in the family of their father, Patrick, since his father, Hugh Brontë, and grandfather, Welsh Brontë, were both apparently adopted and then mistreated in their adoptive families. This is a story extremely reminiscent of *Wuthering Heights*. The Brontë mother, Maria Branwell Brontë, came from a family in which four children died in infancy or childhood, including the three closest to her in age. There followed many more untimely losses, including both of her parents, before Maria married Patrick in a double wedding with her first cousin, Jane, and Patrick's best friend; and on the same day in a different town Maria's younger sister, Charlotte, married another cousin of theirs, Joseph Branwell!

If we take a systemic view of the "coincidence" of concurrent events in a family, the fact that four members of this family were married on the same day suggests, perhaps, fusion issues in the family, which often follow untimely or traumatic loss.

In the next generation, the family of Patrick and Maria Brontë experienced a further series of tragic losses. These seem to have influenced the future family profoundly, turning them inward on themselves and on one another and finally limiting their ability to leave home.

The six Brontë children were born in a seven-year period. Soon after the youngest was born, their mother, Maria, developed a serious blood disorder. During her painful terminal illness, all six children developed scarlet fever, which must have intensified the family's sense of fragility and trauma. Maria

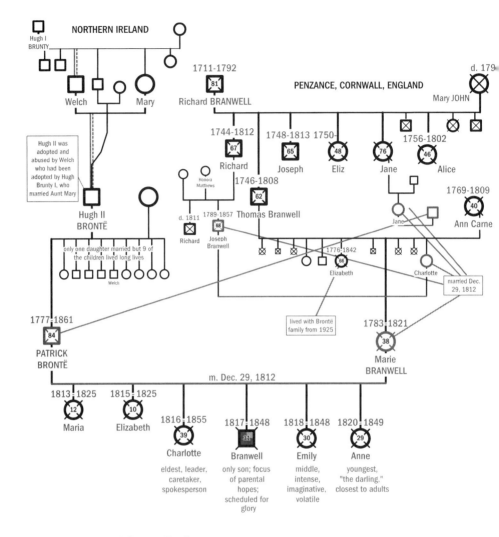

Genogram 4.1: Brontë Family

died an excruciatingly painful death a year later, having rarely seen the children in her final year because of her suffering.

The oldest daughter was only nine when Maria died, after which Patrick found his children's presence a painful reminder of his wife rather than a comfort: "Oppressive grief sometimes lay heavy on me . . . when I missed her at every corner, and when her memory was hourly revived by the innocent, yet distressing prattle of my children" (Frazer, 1988, p. 28). Patrick withdrew into himself and began eating alone, which he continued to do for the rest of his life. His daughter Charlotte later said that "He did not like children . . . and . . . (their) noise made him shut himself up and want no companionship—nay, to be positively annoyed by it" (p. 28). To outsiders, Patrick appeared eccentric, always carrying a loaded pistol, even at prayers. He came to see himself as "a stranger in a strange land," and seems to have conveyed to his children his sense of need to protect oneself from the outside world.

After Maria's death, her unmarried sister, Elizabeth, moved into the household and remained there for the rest of her life. Four years later a family caretaker, Tabby, was added, who also stayed for the rest of her life, dying within a few weeks of the death of the last surviving Brontë child, Charlotte. The six children were left very much on their own throughout their childhood.

From the time of their mother's death, nothing in the Brontë home was changed—no furniture was moved, added, or eliminated—and very few people visited. Such rigidity appears to be a common response in families that have been beset by trauma. But while the externals in their lives remained constricted, the children developed a most extraordinary inner life of imagination and fantasy.

When the oldest daughter, Maria, who was named after their mother, was twelve, she and her sisters were sent to a local boarding school, but further tragedy followed this attempt to leave home. The two oldest daughters developed tuberculosis at the school and died within a few months. Maria's death was especially tragic, because the school authorities were extremely abusive to her in her last days. The other daughters witnessed the torment of their favorite sister, who had become for them their mother's replacement. The morbidity of it all was exaggerated by the fact that the cemetery where mother and sisters lay buried surrounded the family house on two sides. There was no getting away from the eerie sense of death in those gravestones. Probably the stories about children mistreated in school situations and misunderstood by parent substitutes in the writings of the Brontës reflect attempts to work through their painful childhood memories of this time period.

Such early losses must have reinforced the developing Brontë belief that life in the outside world was dangerous. After the oldest daughter's death, the other children were withdrawn from school, and from that point on, when any of the remaining children tried to leave home, they were forced to return, because they or another member became ill or needy. The only son, Branwell, on whom the greatest hopes were placed, was accepted at the Royal College of Art in London and left home to attend, but never actually signed in,

Brontë parsonage surrounded by gravestones
Photo 80318265 © Steve6326 | Dreamstime.com

returning home addicted to drugs and alcohol. Thereafter he left home a few times for jobs he never managed to keep. Branwell's deterioration impinged on the freedom his three sisters felt to enjoy their initial publishing success, which they accomplished under male pseudonyms, telling neither their father nor their brother what they were doing. As Charlotte said: "My unhappy brother . . . was not aware that . . . (we) had published a line. We could not tell him of our efforts for fear of causing him too deep a pang of remorse for his own time misspent and talents misapplied. Now he will never know. I cannot dwell longer on the subject at present—it is too painful" (Frazer, 1988, p. 315). By the time Branwell died three years later, the sisters were renowned under their own names. Branwell painted a portrait of the four of them but then, tellingly, painted himself out of it, although you can still see his shadow. Of the three surviving sisters, Charlotte was the most successful at leaving home, managing at one point to stay away at a school for two years; she was the only one able to develop friendships outside the family, but she too always returned home.

There was something eccentric as well as extraordinary about the Brontë family. Though Patrick Brontë could not tolerate his children leaving him, he rarely spent time with them. Deprived of outside stimulation, the children created the most amazing fantasy world of shared stories, invented and written jointly, in a minuscule, almost indecipherable handwriting and put

Brontë sisters' portrait—their brother, Branwell, erased himself from the center
National Gallery, London, UK © Giancarlo Costa/Bridgeman Images

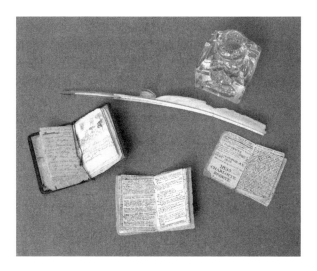

Four of the 800 miniscule manuscripts the Brontës created
*Brontë Parsonage Museum, Haworth, Yorkshire, UK © Brontë Parsonage Museum /
Bridgeman*

together in about 800 tiny manuscript books, about 400 of which still survive. It is almost as if they were fusing in the private world of their imagination. Their minds roamed free in fantasy, creating historical sagas with imaginary characters, as well as historical personages they had heard about.

As Charlotte later wrote, they "wove a web in childhood" (Fraser, 1988, p. 99). As an adult, Charlotte feared their childhood dreams "withered the sod." Even in her youth she looked somehow like a little old woman, though describing herself as "undeveloped," and wore children's chemises all her life. Charlotte's fantasy world remained her "secret joy." When forced to work as a teacher, she struggled to stay at her task—longing for her fantasy life, on which she had become extremely dependent as an escape from her mundane existence: "I carefully avoid any appearance of preoccupation and eccentricity, which might lead those I live amongst to suspect the nature of my pursuits" (p. 111). Whenever she was away, Charlotte tended to have an "indefinite fear" about those at home, worrying unceasingly about her father, as he himself always exaggerated fears about his own health. Though she was the sibling most able to leave home, when away she experienced a variety of symptoms, from a hysterical form of blindness to severe headaches, anxiety, and depression. She wrote: "At home . . . I talk with ease and am never shy—never weighed down by that miserable 'mauvaise honte' which torments and constrains me elsewhere" (p. 128). A friend warned her that staying home would "ruin her," and could never "think without gloomy anger of Charlotte's sacrifices to the selfish old man." And Charlotte herself wrote of her life: "I feel as if we were all buried here—I long to travel—to work, to live a life of action but saw these as my fruitless wishes" (p. 224). To another friend she wrote: "Whenever I consult my Conscience it affirms that I am doing right in staying at home—and bitter are its upbraidings when I yield to an eager desire for release" (p. 183).

The other Brontë siblings were even less able to leave the family. Emily, after a few unsuccessful forays, gave up completely. She became ill at the time of Branwell's funeral, and never left the house again, dying three months later. Anne became ill at this time as well, and died five months after Emily, leaving only Charlotte of the six siblings. Charlotte feared that the shadow of her brother and sisters' last days conveyed how the legacy of trauma can shut a family down, locking them into myth, secrecy, and avoidance of any experience that reminds them of what they cannot bear to face: "I must not look forward, nor must I look backwards. Too often I feel like one crossing an abyss on a narrow plank—a glance round might quite unnerve." She buried herself in her work, clinging to her faculty of imagination to save her from sinking.

Several years later her father's curate, Arthur Nicholls, persuaded Charlotte to marry him. Her father went into a rage and fired him. A year later, unable to put up with Nicholls' replacement, Patrick Brontë relented and agreed that Nicholls could marry Charlotte, if they would both agree never to leave him. They agreed. Charlotte was not really in love with Nicholls, as we know from her letters to two close friends, but shortly after the marriage she accompanied him to his home in Ireland and began to see him in a different light. She saw his humor and found him more interesting in the context of his family. She began to fall in love with him. She became pregnant. However, out of anxiety about her father's health, she returned early from her honeymoon. While the father's health improved, hers deteriorated and she died shortly after, losing the baby as well.

The cause of Charlotte's death is unclear. Many have speculated about a possible psychological component. Her beloved caretaker, Tabby, died just before her. Charlotte was thirty-eight, the same age her mother had been when she died. The specter of family rules and myths in the Brontë family seems uncanny. Only Patrick lived on, dying at the ripe age of eighty-six.

Thus ended a most creative family. One might almost think they were "doomed" psychologically by the narratives they had created in response to their many losses, even while the narratives they themselves created in their writings will last as long as our culture.

THE MYTH THAT ANYTHING LESS THAN SUCCESS WAS FAILURE: THE ADAMS FAMILY

The Adams family tells a story that centers around the myth that it was imperative to succeed in exceptional ways and anything less was tantamount to failure (**see Genogram 4.2: Adams Family**). Across four generations the family produced two American presidents, a famous diplomat, accomplished essayists, historians, and wealthy businessmen. But over those four generations they were also a family of catastrophic failures. There were illiterates, alcoholics, and ne'er-do-wells, failed marriages, and suicides. Their biographer Paul Nagel pointed out, "No Adams, success or failure, made a comfortable accommodation to life" (Nagel, 1983, p. 6). They seemed to accept a myth that there were only two options: you were either a great success or you were a great failure. In fact, even the most successful family members were often depressed, full of self-doubt, and rarely satisfied with their efforts. Charles Francis Adams, the most successful member of the third generation observed about their family: "The history of my family is not a pleasant one to remember. It is one of great triumphs in the world but of deep groans

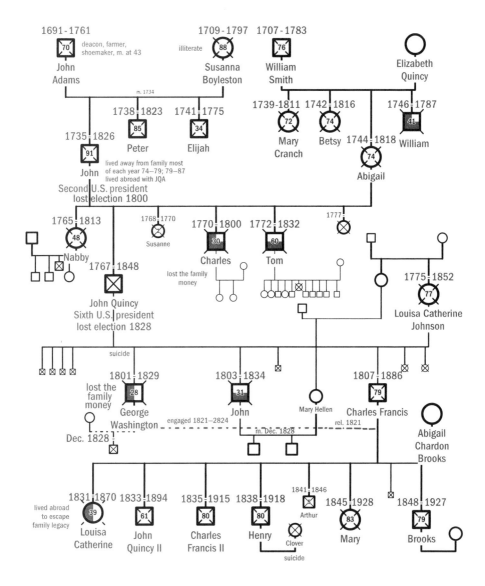

Genogram 4.2: Adams Family

within, one of extraordinary brilliancy and deep corroding mortification"
(Nagel, 1983, p. 3).

   The Adams family had a sense of being different from the common
crowd. This is not surprising, given their accomplishments. They saw themselves as having a unique independence of mind, devotion to public service,
and freedom from impulses of greed or political ambition. Along with this

sense of specialness and expectation of greatness came serious self-criticism. They were hard in their demands of others, but even harder on themselves and held themselves up to impossible standards.

John Adams, our second president, was his own greatest critic, full of self-doubt, questioning of his own motives and extremely sensitive to the criticism of others. He was equally quick to criticize his children hoping it would help them avoid succumbing to weakness. As Abigail once said to her husband: "Sometimes . . . I think you too severe. You do not make so many allowances as Human Nature requires" (Nagel, 1983, p. 21).

John Adams
National Gallery of Art, Washington, D.C. Gift of Mrs. Robert Homans.

John's letters to Abigail are marked by the self-criticism that continued to characterize the family for generations. Despite his extreme diligence as a lawyer and patriot, he repeatedly castigated himself as a lazy wastrel. The family's intolerance for human frailty joined with a pessimistic view of human nature.

John Adams and his wife Abigail were from families steeped in a Puritanism that emphasized original sin and human fallibility and as they grew in eminence, they developed a sense of mission as the moral conscience of the nation.

Both John and Abigail were deeply committed to raising their children correctly although when Adams became involved in politics, he spent more and more time away from his New England home and hence he often had to be satisfied with giving advice and admonitions by mail. His absence meant that Abigail was left to run the farm and rear the children largely on her own. Thus, his project became starting a new nation and hers became the raising of a new generation that would lead that nation.

Perhaps because the dissipation of Abigail's brother William had devastated her family of origin, to the point they would not speak his name, she was obsessed with her children's good behavior and achievement. Indeed, her brother's own son died of alcoholism at the same age as his father, and the multigenerational pattern was evident in the family. Abigail's response was: "God grant that we may never mourn a similar situation" (Nagel, 1983, p.

John Quincy Adams
Courtesy U.S. National Park Service

33). She pondered the sins of her brother, knowing that, despite the most earnest parental efforts, vice and viciousness could take early root and, as she put it, "tho often crop'd, will spring again." She told her oldest son, John Quincy, when he was only ten: "I had much rather you should have found your Grave in the ocean you have crossed, or any untimely death crop you in your infant years, than see you an immoral profligate or a Graceless child" (Nagel, 1983, p. 30).

As much as they tried to get their children on the right track, John and Abigail's entire lives were marred by problems with their children. They never realized that their anxiety, high standards, harsh criticism, pessimistic expectations, and the suffocating togetherness of the family might contribute to their children's difficulties. To a considerable extent their worst parental fears were fulfilled. Their oldest daughter Abigail (Nabby), partly in response to her parents' intrusions, ended up marrying an uncaring, irresponsible husband, who eventually went to prison for fraud and debt. The third child, Charles, became an alcoholic, lost the family investments, and became cut off from his parents and family. He died of his alcoholism at the age of thirty, just as his father was leaving office as U.S. president. John Adams wrote to Thomas Jefferson about the loss: "It is not possible that anything of the kind should happened to you, and I sincerely wish you may never experience anything in any degree resembling it" (Meacham, 2013, p. 350). The fourth child, Thomas, also an alcoholic and a failed lawyer, was described negatively by everyone as an embittered and difficult bully; he too made a disaster of his and his family's lives. Thomas was apparently reminded through his life that he was responsible for his maternal grandmother becoming ill and dying while caring for him, when he had cholera at three. The grandparents, John and Abigail, ended up having to support and raise the wives and children of both Charles and Thomas.

The one exception seemed to be the eldest son, John Quincy. At the age of fourteen he accompanied his father to Europe on a diplomatic mission. He returned to go to Harvard and eventually started his own law practice. At the age of twenty-seven, he was sent to his own diplomatic post in Holland and began a career in public service. Eventually, he became the sixth President of the United States. He shared not only his father's dedication as a statesman, but also his outlook on life. He took it even further in harshness and severity. The expectations for him had been great. His father had said to him: "You come into life with advantages, which will disgrace you if your success is mediocre. And if you do not rise to the head not only of your Profession, but of your country, it will be owing to your own Laziness, Slovenliness, and Obstinacy" (Nagel, 1997, p. 76).

Unlike his brothers, John Quincy was partly able to fulfill these expectations, but at great personal cost. Despite his achievements, his life was even more overshadowed by self-doubt and depression than his father's. He never felt he was living up to the standards handed down to him by his parents. Like his father, he was defeated after a single term as President and saw the world of politics as crass, devoid of ideals, and unappreciative of what the Adams family had done for the nation. Remarkably, years later he returned to Washington as the only president ever to then serve as a congressman. He also became the major spokesman for the anti-slavery movement and deserves great credit for his accomplishments.

John Quincy's marriage was difficult. His wife, Louisa Johnson, was an extraordinarily capable woman and a joyous and affection-craving spirit. She wondered in later life whether, if she had been more mature, she might have recognized that her husband's "unnecessary harshness and severity of character" would make the marriage a perpetual trial. Not surprisingly, she had problems with the outlook of the Adams family that took itself so seriously and saw the world as so prone to evil. Her father's bankruptcy, at the time of her marriage had humiliated her, and left her painfully dependent on her critical and distant husband, who ignored her in bouts of depression and focused on his career. Her husband could not or would not respond to her emotional needs. She had four miscarriages before her first child survived. Many more losses followed. In all she bore ten children, only three of whom lived to adulthood.

John Quincy took up the family escutcheon of public service, family greatness, and intense anxiety about childrearing and passed it on to the next generation. He taught his children that much was expected of an Adams in the constant struggle against an unappreciative world. He once wrote to his son:

Your father and grandfather have fought their way through the world against hosts of adversaries, open and close, disguised and masked . . . and more than one or two perfidious friends. The world is and will continue to be prolific with such characters. Live in peace with them; never upbraid, never trust them. But—"don't give up the ship!" Fortify your mind against disappointments. (Shepherd, 1975, p. xxi)

He also taught that the family must stay together and recognize its special place in history. However, long separations again had their impact on the next generation. Because of his diplomatic duties, John Quincy and Louisa spent many years abroad, leaving the older children behind with their grandparents. Their absences were especially hard on their oldest son George Washington Adams, who felt these separations left him unprepared for life. George was the oldest son of the oldest son of John Adams, who was the oldest son of another John Adams. As if this positioning wasn't enough pressure, George's birth followed

George Washington Adams
Courtesy U.S. National Park Service

four miscarriages, which must have intensified the parents' expectations and fears for the first surviving son. A lot was expected of this unfortunate young man, who was born just after his grandfather lost a bitter election for a second term as president.

Further conflict was embedded in his very name. Instead of being named John for his father, grandfather, and great grandfather, he was named for our first President, which wounded John Adams (McCullough, 2001), who believed that Washington owed his career to Adams himself (Adams, 1976). Surely there must have been family meaning to this naming.

Sadly, George Washington Adams failed to live up to the expectations of the family. Unruly and difficult from childhood, he did poorly at everything he tried. Having spent few of his early years with his parents, he blamed his parents' long absences for his difficulties and lack of self-discipline, though he also seemed relieved to have them gone when his father moved to Washington to become president.

Just before entering college at sixteen, George had a dream in which he was showing interest in a young woman, when his father appeared, "his eyes fixed upon me" (Nagel, 1983, p. 268). Under his father's gaze, George lost interest. He said he was always trying to escape that gaze. He once said he could not remember a day when he didn't think about becoming the president. Years earlier, his grandfather had written to him: "I fear that too many of my hopes are built upon you" (Musto, 1981, p. 57). Indeed, his life was a series of disappointments. George's engagement to a flirtatious first cousin, Mary Catherine Hellen, was broken when she married his younger brother, John, which must have been very painful for him (she also had a romance with the third brother, Charles Francis). Additionally, he made a mess of the family's finances, and then, just after his father was defeated in re-election, the maid he impregnated gave birth. His parents requested that he come to Washington to accompany them home to Boston. On the boat to meet them, he became very disturbed, and jumped overboard and drowned, probably in anticipation of having to live again in the shadow of his father.

George was born at the moment when his grandfather was defeated for his second-term election as president and when his dissipated, alcoholic uncle, Charles, who had lost the family savings, killed himself. Then, at the similar moment of his father's failure to win a second term as President, he took his own life, leaving a painful and humiliating legacy, like that left by his uncle.

John Quincy's second son, John, also became an alcoholic failure and died from a mysterious disease at the age of thirty-one. As in the earlier generation, only one son, the third, Charles Francis, survived to carry on the Adams legacy. As a youngest son he was probably freer of the family constraints. He was indeed very different from his father. He was also the only child who had accompanied his parents on their travels. Perhaps because of his mother's connection to him, she was able to soften for him the negative aspects of the Adams family legacy. Louisa later warned him: "Go on and do not suffer yourself to be intimidated or brow beaten as your brother was, but pursue your course steadily and respectably" (Musto, 1981, p. 44).

Charles Francis was more relaxed, less self-critical, and better able to face

Charles Francis Adams
Courtesy U.S. National Park Service

differences with his father squarely without letting his father dominate him. He still had the strong sense of the Adams legacy and special place in history. It was he who began editing the family papers, which would demonstrate to the world the uniqueness of his parents and grandparents. At first, he did not follow the same path to public duty, but was content to manage the family finances and be a "family man" for his children. He even used the pessimistic Adams views about the corruptibility of his countrymen as an argument against entering the dirty business of politics. He did eventually become a congressman at age fifty-six, and later even ambassador to Great Britain (like his father and grandfather before him), where he used his remarkable diplomatic skill to keep England out of the Civil War. His success at this made him the most noted American diplomat of his time. Indeed, Charles Francis found considerable satisfaction in fulfilling the family tradition of public service. But, perhaps luckily for him, when his name was submitted as a candidate for the presidency in 1872, he lost!

Charles Francis married Abby Brooks, the favorite daughter of a wealthy Boston businessman. Abby was not a strong personality in the mold of Abigail and Louisa. She depended on her husband for constant reassurance and allowed him to think for her in all areas except the social. She loved to entertain and successfully resisted the Adams tendency toward social isolation.

It was in the area of childrearing that Charles Francis departed most from the generations before him. Perhaps aware of the fate of his brothers and uncles, he was determined to be an easier, less demanding, and more available father. He considered parenthood the most serious of all his duties. Although he still focused on his children's development, he was determined to raise them differently. He said of his mission: "I hardly dare to look at my children with the hope that I can do for them what I ought in order to save them from the dangers which I barely escaped myself without shipwreck" (Nagel, 1983, p. 186). He believed in offering sympathetic encouragement and nourishing independence and he recognized the limitations of parental influence. Most of all, he spent a good deal of time with his children when they were young.

Charles Francis partially succeeded in shifting the Adams legacy. Among the sons of the fourth generation. The only early deaths were the women. The oldest daughter, Louisa Catherine, considered the most brilliant of all the children, was difficult and resentful from an early age, feeling she could have become president had she been male. The family was indeed dismayed that their first child was a girl (Nagel, 1987, p. 264). She rebelled against the family and attempted to escape the legacy by living and marrying in Europe, where, however, she led a hedonistic, almost suicidal existence. She died in an accident at the age of thirty-nine. The other tragic woman of this generation was the wife of Henry Adams, Clover, a gifted photographer, who committed suicide at the age of forty-two, having also apparently struggled much with the gender constraints of her time. The youngest sister, Mary, disobedient and stubborn as a child, became the most conventional of the fourth generation of Adams, submitted to family ways, though in later life she became addicted to morphine.

John Quincy II, Charles Francis's oldest son, felt the burden of the family legacy acutely, considering: "John Adams a grievous heavy name to bear" (Nagel, 1983, p. 239). He felt overwhelmed by the expectations others had of him. "What can a man say when he is thus absolutely beaten over the head with ancestry?" His relationship with his father was never easy, between the son's self-doubt and the father's encouragement mixed with impatience.

It might have been easier if others had left John Quincy II alone, but because of his position, the family heaped counsel and then criticism on him. He later burned his diary and his letters, believing, "the less weight you carry the better." He wanted to be left alone—a dream shared by all the generations of the Adams family, but this could not be. In response to his father's continuous prodding, he replied: "I am afraid you, like most parents, overestimate your children. I am no consequence here under heaven except to my home" (Nagel, 1983, p. 243).

John Quincy Adams II
Courtesy U.S. National Park Service

John Quincy II blundered in the face of his father's pressure to become a family leader. He viewed himself as his father's errand boy: "I should be grateful once (but I know it is useless) if I might in any one thing be considered as an individual and not a Son or Grandson" (Nagel, 1983, p. 239). As a consequence, he retreated from responsibility, handing over even the management of the family finances to his younger brother. He was put up to run for election several times, as state representative, governor, and once even as vice president; but he only enjoyed his candidacy when he was sure he would not win. He shrank from the unpleasant grind of politics, which would come with victory. He wanted to lose. He once confessed to his father: "Politics, except just at election time, had not much attraction for so lazy a devil as I am" (p. 242). Even in the personal arena John's life was doomed to misery, when two of his beloved children died of diphtheria, an experience from which he never recovered. He became a sad, quiet, retiring figure, who carefully destroyed all his papers, as if to make sure that the legacy would stop with him.

The three younger sons of the fourth generation all became accomplished in their fields, though they too had their problems. While John resolved to obliterate all traces of his life, Charles Francis Jr. determined to leave a huge written record about himself (carefully edited, of course!). Charles also determined from his earliest years to succeed in areas beyond the traditional Adams role of statesmanship. He became a successful entrepreneur and president of the Union Pacific Railroad, although he eventually lost it to Jay Gould. He said of his failure: "There being nothing more for me to do, I got up to go. . . . My ideas were right, but I did not hold to them. I was weak of will" (Shepherd, 1975, p. 419).

We can see here again the underside of the Adams's success—their lack of self-assurance, evident even for those who achieved greatness as Charles Fran-

Charles Francis Adams Jr.
Courtesy U.S. National Park Service

cis Jr. did. He was continually disabled from digestive ills and, after losing much of the family fortune in 1893, cut off from his brothers and sister, as the earlier Charles (John Quincy's brother) had become cut off two generations earlier.

Henry Adams, the most famous of the fourth generation, was an eminent historian and Brooks, also a historian, was one of America's earliest geopoliticians. There was still a sense of specialness and commitment to public service, but this fourth generation consisted more of thinkers than doers. Rather than entering politics, they wrote about it. This fourth generation were all philosophically interested in the family outlook they had inherited from earlier generations. They edited the family papers and speculated on the fate of humankind. With them the traditional Adams ability to view the world with derision and pessimism was harsher than ever. Henry and Brooks wrote cynical historical essays with emphasis on the poor prognosis for the social ailments of their times. They saw little hope in modern trends.

Brooks was in everything argumentative and misanthropic, while Henry, in particular, felt he was being left behind by the Industrial Age.

Psychiatrist and family historian, David Musto, has written a penetrating analysis of the patterns in the Adams family patterns:

> The middle generations of the Adams family had an unusual disparity in life-spans between the successful and the less successful. Not all the shorter lives can be attributed to failing the family's imperatives, but the contrast is suggestive. The successful: John, John Quincy, and Charles Francis Adams, lived an average of 80 years, while the remainder: Charles, Thomas Boylston, Nabby, George Washington, and John 2nd

Henry Adams
Courtesy U.S. National Park Service

> lived an average of 40 years. The fittest survived. The imperatives of excellence and achievement which developed in the Adams family during the first years of our national life were a burden as well as a spur to subsequent generations. (Musto, 1981, pp. 57–58)

By the fourth generation, there was no longer the unifying shared family outlook to keep the Adams family together. Rather, each of the Adamses in this generation was strongly individualistic, brilliant, but often eccentric. Each strove to escape the Adams legacy and to find his or her own way. The estate was eventually divided. Ironically, Charles Francis's sympathetic encouragement of independence and individual development did not lead to stronger family ties as he had wished. Perhaps, the anxiety and fear of the world was no longer there to keep the family together. In any case, the loss was not mourned by the children. As Brooks, the last member of the fourth generation

Brooks Adams
Courtesy U.S. National Park Service

argued: "It is now full four generations since John Adams wrote the constitution of Massachusetts. It is time we perished. The world is tired of us" (Musto, 1981, p. 44).

The high expectations of achievement in the Adams family did not apply to the daughters. Abigail Smith Adams (wife of the second president) and her sisters were given a certain latitude to distinguish themselves, perhaps because their only brother was a failure. In the next generation, John Quincy Adams's older sister, Nabby, took considerable responsibility, particularly when her father and brother were in Europe, but in terms of achievement, she was expected only to marry well and be a good wife. Her husband, like her mother's brother, turned out to be an alcoholic failure, and she ended up spending time in prison with him for debt. John Quincy's wife, Louisa, was, like her mother-in-law, a very gifted woman. But she seems to have lived a life of quiet desperation. In the third generation

no daughters survived infancy. Charles Francis's wife, Abby Chardon Brooks, was a lighthearted, spontaneous, and sociable woman. After a few years of marriage into this demanding, self-critical family, however, and with the arrival of babies, public life, and other distresses, she found that "the poetry of life has fallen into prose" (Nagel, 1999, p. 260). However, through the tragedy of the early death of one of their sons, Arthur, Charles fell into a collapse of depression and self-reproach, for having punished the boy just before his fatal illness. In Charles's time of trouble, Abby's strength emerged, and over their many years together she and her husband evolved a strong closeness and ability to enrich each other.

Abigail Adams
Library of Congress, Prints and Photographs Division, photograph by Harris and Ewing, LC-DIG-hec-13515

THEMES FROM THE ADAMS FAMILY HISTORY THAT YOU MIGHT CONSIDER IN YOUR OWN FAMILY

The Adams family provides a useful illustration of various family themes and dynamics. We outline some of these in Table 4.1 to help you to identify similar themes and dynamics in your own family.

Table 4.1: Family Themes/Dynamics with Examples from the Adams Family

Themes/Dynamics	Examples from the Adams Family
The Role of Naming	Naming sons "John" with the implied pressure of high expectations Problem of naming George Washington Adams for a man his grandfather resented
The Role of Sibling Position	Younger-born sons having more freedom from expectations, as in the case of Charles Francis as a third son, as well as Henry and Brooks, who were younger sons
The Role of Gender	As women, neither Nabby nor Louisa Catherine, despite their talent and ambitions, had any chance to shine in their role as firstborns
Parental Expectations	Harsh, high expectations for sons Low expectations for daughters
The Role of Legacies	Dramatic extremes between being either a super-achiever or severely dysfunctional (e.g., alcoholic, debtor, unreliable)
The Role of Loss	Parental distance for George Washington Adams, who felt wounded by the distance his parents kept, as well as feeling the pressure of being the "replacement child" after four previous siblings died in infancy Infant loss for Louisa Catherine, who lost seven babies
Implications of Cutoffs	Abigail's brother William Smith III Nabby's husband William Stephens Smith Charles Adams Thomas Boyleston Adams George Washington Adams Louisa Catherine, who chose to live abroad
Family Members Who Overcame Others' Expectations of Them	John Quincy via "lower status" of congressman Nabby, Brooks, and Charles Francis by shifting away from politics to focus on recording the family history
Addictions	First generation: William Smith (brother-in-law) Second generation: William Smith (Nabby's husband), Charles Adams, and Thomas Boyleston Adams Third generation: George Washington Adams and John Adams Fourth generation: Mary (in later life)

FAMILY SECRETS

Family stories and myths are profoundly influenced by the secrets families keep. All families have secrets and these may have far-ranging influence, at times undermining the family for generations. Secrets may remind family members of their boundaries. Other times it is the content of the secret itself that is powerful: a suicide, a pregnancy that occurs outside of a marriage, or a sexual liaison. In other cases, it is the boundary established by the secret that gives it its power, as when one family member is excluded from knowledge of a certain family experience. A secret is also often a source of power, binding together those who share it, though it may also create shame, guilt, and isolation because of its rule of silence. Because they create covert bonds and splits in a family, secrets also have a mystifying power. Imagine, for example, the power of a parent naming a child for a secret lover. The spouse may not know the meaning of the child's name. The child, siblings, and the other parent may evolve experiencing a distance that none of them understands. This could ripple down to that child's experience of being a parent to his own children. Winston Churchill's mother, Jenny Jerome, seems to have been named for her father's lover, Jenny Lind. Jenny Jerome named her younger son John Strange Spencer for her lover, John Strange Jocelyn. One can only guess at how these secrets influenced family relationships under the surface.

Secrets may exist also to protect a person or a family from shame. Some secrets are kept because of society's disapproval of behaviors, as has often been the case with sexual orientation, such as for the lesbian relationships of Margaret Mead, Eleanor Roosevelt, and Katharine Hepburn. But society also plays into distortions and secrecy that support the dominant values of the culture. For example, until very recently the media have generally participated in keeping the extramarital secrets of male politicians, while our legal system denied the actual origins of children, creating official documents to attest to their being born to their adoptive parents.

Secrecy is often maintained about money—sometimes to hide wealth, other times to hide poverty. Even today men still may keep their finances secret from their wives, considering this to be "none of their business," protecting their male power. But such secrecy also reflects the economic pressure our society still places on men by attaching their value to their money.

Women keep money secrets too, about what they spend for clothes or presents or to help a friend or relative for fear of their husband's disapproval, or they may hold back a certain amount of the household money in a separate fund to create financial security. Because my (TL) paternal grandfather had a predilection for gambling away money that was needed for living expenses, my grandmother used to siphon off a little from whatever household monies he gave her. She kept this money hidden in a jar that my grandfather did not know about. After saving this way for many years, she finally had enough for a down payment on a house, which is when she revealed her secret. After years of living in rented apartments and dreaming about a home of her own, she took the money she had secretly been squirreling away and purchased a home on a tree-lined street in Queens. It was her dream come true, but my grandfather was enraged by her secrecy, referring to her as "a cunning woman who can't be trusted." Of course, as much as he resented her secrecy, he was pleased about their spacious new home and not having to pay monthly rent anymore. Obviously, because money influences power, money secrets have different meanings in different contexts. To understand money secrets, you will need to assess who is protected by or excluded from the secret.

Men's secrets pertain mostly to their main areas of vulnerability: perceived financial, work, status, sexual, or emotional problems. Women keep secrets to protect men's vulnerabilities, sexuality, and their alliances with other women, which might threaten the men in their lives. Women are more often the confidantes of other women, as well as of men. They also keep secrets to protect children from their father's rage or about their age or looks, generally a response to the societal values favoring youth and beauty. The culture generally tells men to be strong, all-knowing, and capable of handling anything, so they are pressed to keep secret any fears and attitudes that would give the opposite impression. Most of all, men keep their private selves secret from other men. It is worth figuring out who has kept which secrets from whom in your family and how that may have influenced relationships.

Secrets tend to beget other secrets. If your parents married because your mother was pregnant and this has become a family secret, the entire family history may end up being distorted out of anxiety about that one secret. The whole family story may then become mystified for fear that that one question could lead to exposing the secret.

In one family we saw the mother confessed to her oldest daughter as a late teenager that her fourth child, born when the oldest was seven, was the son of the mother's lover. The mother swore her daughter to secrecy about this. The daughter then began to struggle with that brother and other siblings, leading her to seek therapy. She was plagued by the secret, feeling it explained why that brother had always been treated differently by all the other children and was still the most isolated. In therapy she decided to tell her mother she could not keep the secret, because it was alienating her from her siblings as well as from her father. Through a long process of realignment, the family began to repair their relationships, coming to adjust to the reality of their history and strengthening their connections to each other. The hardest relationship was not the father's adjustment to recognizing his son had another biological father, nor the son's dealing with that fact himself, but the daughter's repair of the sense of betrayal by her mother who had tried to draw her into the secret instead of facing the truth of their history.

SECRETS RELATED TO ADOPTION

In 1966, Deann Borshay traveled from Korea to become part of the Borshay family in Fresno, California, where, with her new family, the memory of her birth family was nearly obliterated, along with her Korean language. The Borshays had begun sending money to a Korean orphanage to support an only child named Cha Jung Hee, whose parents were both thought to have died. In that era in the U.S. an enormous number of children who had been orphaned by the Korean War were adopted in the U.S. and elsewhere.

Deann Borshay Liem
Courtesy Helga Ingibjörg Sigvaldadóttir

But Deann had a specific compounding issue. She was a last-minute replacement for Cha Jung Hee, whom the Borshays thought they were adopting, but who had been taken away from the orphanage by her father before she was to be sent to the U.S. As the orphanage sent Deann on her way to the U.S., they gave her the name Cha Jung Hee and told her never to talk with her adoptive family about her true history.

The Borshays thought she was the same Cha Jung Hee they had been corresponding with in Korea. But Deann had memories of her mother and siblings. While she had been warned never to mention her real history, she eventually told her adoptive mother, Alveen, about her memories. Her mother challenged her, showing her immigration papers and telling her that her memories were just fantasies. Deann thought her mother's response indicated that she wasn't interested in Korea or in her history. She learned to push her memories of her birth family, of Korea, and even of her language, out of her mind.

But once she grew up and moved away from her adoptive family, she began having recurring dreams and nightmares about her Korean family that led her to investigate her past. She discovered that her Korean mother and siblings were very much alive, and she traveled to Korea to find her birth family. She was amazed to look at faces that resembled her own. "For so many years I had looked into blue eyes, blond hair, and all of a sudden there were people in the room and when I looked at them, I could see parts of myself in them. There's sort of a physical closeness, as if my body remembers something, but my mind is resistant." She could not communicate with her birth family. She tried to relearn Korean but had difficulty with the language. She felt she was supposed to choose one family over the other, and one language over the other. She was feeling she didn't have room in her mind for two mothers. She said she couldn't talk to her adoptive mother about her birth mother. When she finally got the courage to ask Alveen, her mother, why she never asked her any questions about her birth mother, she replied that perhaps she had been afraid to know.

Deann realized that to solidify her identity she needed to bring her biological and adoptive families together. She invited her adoptive parents to go with her to Korea to meet her birth family. She felt that seeing both families together would help her integrate the different aspects of herself. While visiting

Korea, many members of Deann's Korean family came to meet her and her adoptive parents. Deann gave her birth mother a book her daughter had made of her life from the earliest picture she had from Korea through her life in the U.S. Her Korean mother very movingly thanked her family for taking such good care of her.

Having become a documentary film maker, Deann created an exploration of her family history in *First Person Plural* (2000), where she explored the power of the secrets kept by her adoptive family and those secrets that had been kept from them about her history.

Deann Borshay Liem with both of her mothers
Courtesy Deann Borshay Liem

SECRETS RELATED TO INTERRACIAL ADOPTION: ANGELA TUCKER

Another remarkable example of reconnection and unpacking secrets is Angela Tucker, an African American woman who was born in 1985 in Chattanooga, Tennessee. After a year spent in foster care, she was adopted by a white family in Bellingham, Washington, that eventually had eight children, with all but the oldest being adopted. Angela had been diagnosed with spastic quadriplegia at birth and her adoptive parents were told she might never walk. As it turned out, the foster family she had lived with had given her physical therapy every day, and Angela became not only an academic star but a sports star from childhood on.

As she grew up, Angela became increasingly interested in learning about her birth family. She married and began studying psychology, but the impulse to find her family only became stronger. Her older sister felt this was

Angela Tucker
Courtesy Emily Thornton

a betrayal to their parents who had done so much for them all. The mother too felt uneasy, but the family came around to supporting Angela in her search. However, she had no luck, until her husband suggested they try looking for her father instead, since his name was very unusual: Oterious. They eventually found someone who could possibly be her father and when they found his picture Angela was sure that he was the one. She convinced her whole family to go with her to try to find him. He did turn out to be her father, though his mother told Angela that her son had fallen when he was young and could never have children! This seemed one of those stories families often tell themselves when they do not want to deal with possibilities. Angela found him and he agreed to do a DNA test, which was positive. He then agreed to take her to where her birth mother, Deborah, lived. Deborah had had four other children, three of whom she raised with the help of her family.

But when Angela came to meet Deborah, Deborah told her she was not her mother. Angela was devastated. But her family were very supportive. She had at least found her father and his family.

She and her adoptive family went back to Bellingham, and she continued to try to see if she could find any of her birth siblings or aunts or uncles who might be willing to talk with her. She found an aunt Belinda who had just joined Facebook and an uncle Mike who was keen to talk to her. Then she connected with her oldest aunt, Mamie, whose first words when she answered the phone were: "Hello Sweet Pea, I just thank God that you were inquisitive and found your folks, and found me before I left this earth. I'm just really thankful. From my perspective you got the best of the deal. In my family there's not a lot of material things. I'm rich in spirit and knowledge." Angela then asked her aunt Mamie about her mother, Deborah, and about the family. Mamie thought their sister Belinda would be the one who could get through to Deborah about meeting Angela. Finally, Angela dared to ask directly: "Do you think she'll talk to us when we come?" Mamie's answer: "Angela, I'm gonna say this, and if you tell, I'm gonna lie like a mug. If that bitch don't talk to you, then I want you to just ignore the hell out of her. Don't kiss her ass, you don't owe her nothing." Angela's response was: "I don't know her and all I want is, I don't know what I want, but . . ."

Mamie then laid it out: "I'm so glad you said that, psychology major, because you don't know what you want. What has happened to my sister is, it's like the old people used to say, what you do in the dark will come to the light. And so she probably figured it would never come to light and so . . . she needs to get over it and get on with it. She will never be your mother. Teresa is your mother. She needs to forgive herself. Once she forgives herself then the lines of communication will be open. I just pray to God that the fool don't die before she do it." Angela decided to make one more visit to Chattanooga to see if she could connect with her mother in spite of her mother's reluctance to connect.

She then managed to get Deborah on the phone and their reconnection began. Deborah said: "Off the board I have to apologize to you." She said she would have known immediately when she saw Angela's picture that she was her daughter because of her great resemblance to her other daughter Na-Na.

Angela's family then took another trip to Chattanooga to visit all the family, as well as a side trip to the foster family that had cared for Angela so well during her first year of life. Reconnections were made all round, including going to collect all the letters and pictures Angela and her family had written to Deborah from the time of her adoption onward. Then Deborah came out to Bellingham to see where her daughter had grown up. Angela and her husband Bryan Tucker made a profoundly moving documentary, *Closure* (2013), which conveys her remarkable journey. The video conveys her extraordinary commitment to learning her history, and the systemic support of many others who traveled the journey with her.

SECRECY ROOTED IN THE LEGACY OF WHITE SUPREMACY: THE JEFFERSON–HEMINGS FAMILY

Many families in the U.S. are shaped by secrecy that emanates from the legacy of white supremacy. Many have become known in recent years because of DNA. Thomas Jefferson, one of the most well-known of our government founders, kept many secrets about the family he fathered with his slave, Sally Hemings. It is interesting that Jefferson named all of the children with Hemings after people in his life, hinting at their connection to him, yet he never admitted he was their father. As Shelby Steele conveys of Jefferson in the documentary *Jefferson's Blood* (2013):

> He cannot sell these children because they might talk. He can't free them because that special treatment might give him away to his enemies in the press. He can't acknowledge them as his own without ending his career and disgracing his white family. He is circled now by the terms of America's racial primitivism. And now this man of the Enlightenment must know himself as primitive. This is the sort of untenable self-knowledge that lives within people in racist societies.

This denial of the truth has extended over many generations. Jefferson's biographers colluded with the secrecy for more than 200 years by creating

every rationalization they could not to acknowledge Jefferson's slave children, and many family members have tried to hide their interracial ancestry. Those who have dared to acknowledge the truth have often been subject to harsh censure and cutoff. The cutoffs related to descendants of Jefferson-

Thomas Jefferson
National Gallery of Art, Washington, D.C. Gift of Thomas Jefferson Coolidge IV in memory of his great-grandfather, Thomas Jefferson Coolidge, his grandfather, Thomas Jefferson Coolidge II, and his father, Thomas Jefferson Coolidge III.

Hemmings are continuing into the twenty-first century. *Jefferson's Blood* tells the story of several families descended of Jefferson and Hemings, five and six generations later. In one family, three daughters made the decision to get a DNA test to be certain, but also to participate in a film about Jefferson's descendants. Their father, who had cut off from his African American family as a young adult, was angry with his daughters for exposing the secret he had tried to keep buried for so long. He considered their actions to be a betrayal and as a result, he cut off from anyone who dared to acknowledge the truth of the family's interracial ancestry.

Amalia Cooper, a sixth-generation descendent, wonders how it could possibly make any difference if people knew her ancestry, but, she says, "If they look at me differently, they just do." The influence of white supremacy was so intense that when their father married their mother, who was white, her family disowned her completely and threw everything of hers away.

Decades later when the daughters participated in the documentary, it was because they wanted their lives and their children's lives to be free of secrecy. Upon receiving the negative reaction to her willingness to address the family secret, Amalia was very clear: "I feel like an outsider now. And I'm pissed off about that, because there's nothing to split us apart." The cutoffs caused by race secrets go right back to Jefferson's children. When three of them, Harriet, Beverly, and Eston passed into the white world, all ties to their siblings were cut off.

The remarkable part in this story is that those who dare to break the secrecy and work toward repair of the multigenerational cutoffs often risk further cutoffs in the present through their openness. The efforts of Amalia Cooper and her sisters toward reconnection and openness are powerful signs of transformation and healing for a family, even when the reactivity of others leads to perpetuation of their cutoff.

OTHER SECRETS INVOLVING DENIAL OF RACE: ANATOLE BROYARD

The life of Anatole Broyard, a writer, literary critic, and longtime book review editor for *The New York Times*, was defined by his denial of his Black identity for his whole adult life. Broyard was born in New Orleans to parents of Louisiana Creole mixed-race ancestry. When he was a young child his parents moved the family to Bedford-Stuyvesant, Brooklyn, New York, where, because they were light-skinned, the parents passed as white for their employment.

As a young adult Broyard came to adopt whiteness as a new and total identity, distancing himself entirely from his African American family of origin. He never told his children that he was Black, and they only began to learn his secret and their own history as young adults from their white mother as he was dying. They met their only surviving Aunt, Shirley, their father's sister for the first time at his funeral. She had long been married to a well-known Black Civil Rights attorney and activist and was able to tell them a good deal about their family background and history.

After growing up in Brooklyn, Anatole Broyard had attended Brooklyn College for a time before enlisting the segregated U.S. army in World War II as a white man. Then, as a young adult, he basically cut himself off from his family. He did a version of what many young adults do, hoping to reinvent themselves without all the problems they might otherwise inherit from their parents and other ancestors:

Anatole Broyard
Fred W. McDarrah/Getty Images

Eventually, I ran away to Greenwich Village, where no one had been born of a mother and father, where the people I met had sprung from their own brows, or from the pages of a bad novel. We buried our families in the common grave of the generation gap, silenced them with the so-called failure of communication. . . . Orphans of the avant-garde, we outdistanced our history and our humanity. (Broyard, 1979 as cited in Gates, 1996)

Problems in our families of origin are often repeated in the families we create ourselves, however much we may wish it were not so. Even people with remarkable abilities in other areas, such as Broyard himself, are often blind to new ways of perceiving their families and may lose all objectivity when they return to their childhood homes. It is especially difficult to see how our own thinking and behavior can perpetuate problems that already have a long history. Decades after Broyard left his family in Brooklyn and "ran away" to Greenwich Village he wrote:

My family had to die before I could understand how much I missed them and what they meant to me. . . . Now that I have a wife and family of my own, I've begun to feel what it is. When we go out together, I do my own share of strutting and I wonder how my children feel about it. . . . Do they understand that after all those years of running away from home, I am still trying to get back? (Broyard, 1979, p. C6)

Sadly, Broyard never managed to end his family cutoff. He believed he could reinvent himself as a white person who would be seen and accepted as a writer and not a "Black writer" in Greenwich Village. He married a Puerto Rican woman and had a daughter, but he separated from her soon after and he cut off permanently from his daughter.

He then married a white social worker of Scandinavian background and proceeded to live his life as a white man. His children had no idea of their father's racial identity until, when he was dying in 1990, their mother finally told them the truth, because he continued to refuse to do so himself.

In 2007, Broyard's daughter, Bliss, wrote an extraordinary memoir, *One Drop: My Father's Hidden Life—A Story of Race and Family Secret*. In it, she remembered her father's terrible anger on Mother's Day of 1979, when she was twelve. Her father had bought her mother very special earrings, which he brought in for the meal. His wife was cooking, perhaps a bit resentful that she had to do all the meal preparation even on Mother's Day. Anatole wanted her to stop what she was doing at the stove and come over to the table, where he had brought his present. She said she was busy, but he kept pressing. Finally, she turned around to explain that she couldn't just stop cooking in the middle of the preparations. At that point her husband yelled "Fine, Happy Mother's Day" and flung the earrings across the kitchen. Bliss made an angry comment to her father about ruining the day and left the room.

Late that night, her mother woke Bliss up, asking if she knew where the bologna was, since her father always ate bologna before he went to bed. She felt irritated with her mother for pursuing the father's needs and tried to go back to sleep, but she could not. Finally, she went downstairs herself, only to see that her father had pulled every drawer from the refrigerator onto the floor and made a mess of

Bliss Broyard
Erin Patrice O'Brien

broken glass, jelly and mayonnaise on the floor. Bliss had never known her father to lose himself to this extent. Her mother was trying to clean up, saying the bologna had been right in the drawer where it always was, but he hadn't looked. As Bliss and her mother talked about what had gone wrong, especially when the father had meant to give his wife such a special present, her mother told her that perhaps he was upset because it was Mother's Day and his own mother had recently died. Bliss had no idea he even had a mother or that she had died, since her father never even mentioned this family.

Only years later did she learn that her father had left his family behind. He had never told his children anything about his family or his history. What looked like an irrational rage on Mother's Day when she was twelve, turned out to be something with deep resonances to her father's inner problems in cutting off his family, and then feeling guilty about it, the pain of which he then took out on his wife.

Interestingly, the year after Broyard's mother died, his father having died almost 30 years earlier, he wrote an article for *The New York Times* called "The Advantage of Growing Up Irrational" in which it almost seems as if he wanted to reveal his secret.

While making fun of his wife for calling him irrational, he sees her as an "irrational" person, who digs in the backyard while he, the rational one, stays inside to brood on the modern family. His article goes on to talk about how he had to escape his family as a young man.

He refers to his father's "unruly hair" and "brown-and-white wing-tip shoes, saying that his parents "were too folksy for me, too colorful. . . . Anyone who saw me with my family knew too much about me. . . . My mother, who was mildly stout, might as well have been the Venus of Willendorf, a primitive fertility figure. My father was a rogue male, a creature of such reckless masculinity that I always thought of him as breaking the law. While I loved them, I was uneasy about our relationship."

He says he wanted desperately to run away from home. His love for "these two misfits, these character actors, was too heavy to bare." And then, he says, he became "an amnesiac."

Broyard had spent his adult life trying to escape both his family of origin and his Blackness that was a reflection of them. Even with all the racial suggestions in his piece, he refused to acknowledge his racial truth. When it came out after his death that he had denied his racial origins, people of color who had known him said they could always tell he was not white. It was white people who were surprised. But it is interesting how much a part of him seems to have been wanting to tell the truth himself. His wife knew his history of passing and ignoring his family continued to pain him. It was on her that he took out the rage and pain of his denial that Mother's Day after his mother had died.

He said his family had to die before he could understand how much he missed them and what they meant to him. But he did not acknowledge them even after they were dead. He still did not become open with his wife or children about his family nor include his extended family in his life.

So his children had to figure out for themselves how to make sense of their father's life of secrecy. Bliss experienced her father's secret that turned her world upside down: "Overnight my father's secret turned my normal young adult existential musing of *Who am I?* into a concrete question: *What am I?* My old identification no longer worked. I was determined that unlike my father I wouldn't keep my African ancestry hidden. My mother had said that his secret caused him more pain than the cancer in his bones. I didn't want any shame clouding up my life. Besides, I wasn't any good at keeping secrets. When people asked me what I was, I would tell them. But the question was, 'What exactly would I say?'" (Broyard, 200, p. 67).

Bliss had also come to realize that Black identity had its own surprises. As she learned about her extended Broyard family, she says, "In a few short hours I'd gone from believing that my great-grandmother was born a slave to discovering that she'd grown up in a family of Black slave owners!" (Broyard 2007, as cited in Maslin, 2007). It wasn't what she had expected. And there were many more layers to unpack as she met white Broyards and Black Broyards and came to see herself in more complex ways.

Her remarkable memoir demonstrates the power that secrets have over our families, and the efforts we need to make to unpack them and free ourselves from them. They keep everyone mystified, and it is only in the search to know oneself and to contemplate what keeping the secret meant for those who kept it that we can begin to free ourselves from the consequences—the other secrets that become bound up in keeping the first one, and the cutoffs and mystification in relationships that secrets cause, preventing us from being ourselves.

SECRETS RELATED TO SUICIDE

Secrets often reveal a family's vulnerabilities. The playwright A. R. Gurney described the legacy of his great-grandfather's suicide, never mentioned in his own lifetime: "My great-grandfather hung up his clothes one day and walked into the Niagara River and no one understood why. He was a distinguished man in Buffalo. My father could never mention it, and it affected the family well into the fourth generation as a dark and unexplainable gesture. It made my father and his father desperate to be accepted, to be conventional, and comfortable. It made them commit themselves to an ostensibly easy bourgeois world. They saw it so precariously, but the reason was never mentioned" (Witchel, 1989, p. 103).

Four generations later, the pattern set in motion by this death was still operating. Gurney was forty-eight when he first learned of the suicide from his father-in-law, a genealogist. This was at the time when Gurney's own father died, and, in an interesting continuation of the pattern, Gurney himself refused to talk about his own father's death. Without realizing it, we may follow patterns set up by the secrets of earlier generations of our families unless we make a conscious effort to change the pattern.

A. R. Gurney
Oliver Morris/Getty Images

THE COLLUSION OF OTHERS IN SECRECY: THE FONDA FAMILY

Secrets are especially important in families, because of the potential trauma their revelation may cause for those not prepared for the knowledge. When Peter and Jane Fonda's mother, Frances, committed suicide in April 1950 (**see Genogram 4.3: Fonda Family**), the entire community colluded to keep the facts from them. Henry Fonda, who was starring on Broadway at the time, had apparently told his wife a few months earlier that he wanted a divorce to marry Susan Blanchard, a twenty-two-year-old step-daughter of Oscar Hammerstein. Frances went into a tailspin, was hospitalized, and she killed herself. Henry went onstage that very night as if nothing had occurred. The family removed all access to news from Peter and Jane, and Jane read about her mother's death in a movie magazine the following year, surely a horrendous way to learn such a secret.

Henry Fonda remarried before the end of the year. While he was on his next honeymoon, Peter "accidentally" shot himself in the stomach. You can't help wondering whether the dreadful secret around the mother's suicide and the conspiracy of silence wasn't already showing its power. For the rest of his long life, Henry Fonda apparently never once discussed his wife's suicide with his children. A further element to the secret is probably the fact that Fonda's new wife, Susan, had just "adopted" a baby who shortly afterward was

Fonda family picnic—Frances at center, Henry behind, Jane on the left
Genevieve Naylor/Getty Images

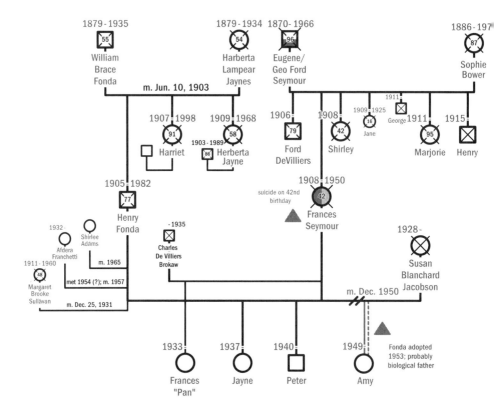

Genogram 4.3: Fonda Family

adopted by Henry. This seems to have been another secret, which would add layers of complexity to the conspiracy secrecy. Why would Susan Blanchard, a very young woman from such a prominent family involved with a famous actor, adopt a baby before she married and when she was involved already with a famous star? And why would Fonda soon after adopt her child?

Peter Fonda later wrote movingly about the pain of not being able to learn the truth of his family history, which had been "sanitized" over the generations, but which he felt sure would, if he could learn it, help him make sense of the mystifying experiences he had growing up.

"My father's autobiography, as told to someone else, was full of so much sanitation that it had little base in reality.... Dad was ... too intensely private, to truly expose the part of his history that mattered to him" (Fonda, 1998, p. 116).

He said that already at age twenty he "wanted to say good-bye to the dark, silent, booby-trapped thing that had been my 'family'" (Fonda, 1998,

Fonda family with Peter, Jane, Henry's new wife Susan, and her "adopted" baby, Amy
Bettmann/Getty Images

p. 133). Of his father's inaccessibility he said, "Things happened to him that we will never know. He was never beaten. But something happened to him that made him very quiet, very shy, and he let those qualities define his personality. They were the makeup and costume that he wore in real life. Somewhere, he found it was easier to say nothing. Easier on his heart, I mean. . . . The deeper the emotion, the deeper he hid it. I say more about our father, because I know more about him. But I'll never know enough" (p. 496).

Peter, Jane, and Henry Fonda
ZUMA Press, Inc./Alamy Stock Photo

Discussing his inability to unravel the secrets of his mother's family history he says: "I doubt I would believe a story told me by any remaining elder from either side. Too much time has passed, with too much opportunity to revise and sanitize the truth" (p. 116).

MULTIGENERATIONAL SECRECY ABOUT INCEST: NATHANIEL HAWTHORNE'S FAMILY

Perhaps no writer has shown more preoccupation with the multigenerational power of secrets than Nathaniel Hawthorne (**see Genogram 4.4: Hawthorne Family**). His stories reflect an obsession with both anguished confession and concealment of potentially ruinous ancestral secrets, along with an eerie, mystifying, multigenerational legacy of guilt for the misdeeds of long-dead ancestors.

In his preface to his book, *The Scarlet Letter*, Hawthorne alludes to misdeeds in his family generations earlier. He says his hometown of Salem, Massachusetts possessed a mysterious hold over him, and that his earliest immigrant ancestor had haunted him since childhood; he wondered if his ancestors ever repented the sins they had committed, "which have been written up in various histories."

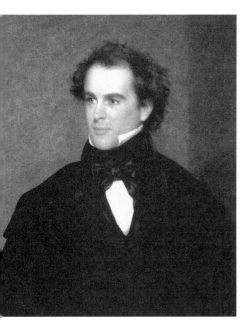

Nathaniel Hawthorne
Peabody Essex Museum, Salem, Massachusetts, USA © Peabody Essex Museum/Bridgeman Images

He then apologized on behalf of his ancestors: "At all events, I . . . as their representative, hereby take shame upon myself for their sakes, and pray that any curse incurred by them . . . may be now and henceforth removed. . . . Such are the compliments bandied between my great-grandsires and myself across the gulf of time! . . . Strong traits of their nature have intertwined themselves with mine" (Hawthorne, 1969, p. 300).

This is the theme of his other most famous novel, *The House of Seven Gables*, in which the ghosts of the Salem Witch Trials, who are held responsible for ominous misdeeds, overshadow the lives of those living more than 100 years later. *The Scarlet Letter* is also about the damage caused by secret sins, and the mystification created by secrecy in relationships.

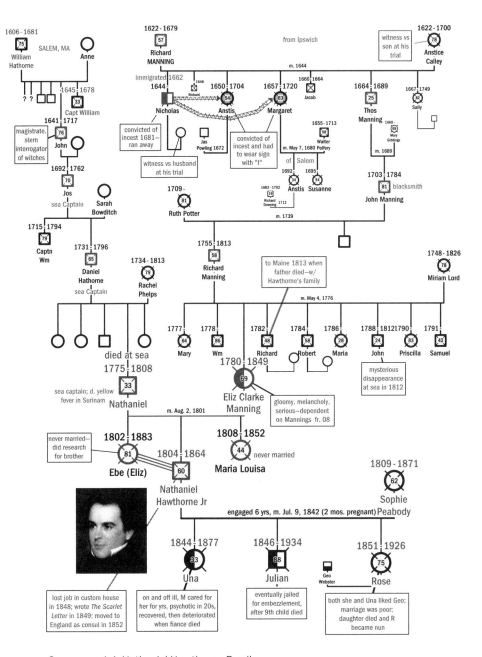

Genogram 4.4: Nathaniel Hawthorne Family

Hawthorne's friend, Herman Melville, believed there was a dark secret in Hawthorne's own life, which would perhaps explain all the mysteries of his career. Others who knew Hawthorne had the same suspicion. His lawyer wrote: "I should fancy from your books you were burdened by secret sorrow; that you had some blue chamber in your soul into which you hardly dared enter yourself" (Young, 1984, p. 99).

Hawthorne lived for years as a recluse, rarely leaving his house except at twilight: "I have made a captive of myself and put me into a dungeon and now I cannot find the key to let myself out—and if the door were open, I should be almost afraid to come out" (cited in Cowley, 1983, p. 4). For years he isolated himself, studying the old records of Salem, just like the novel's narrator. He apparently discovered in the town's public records the details of the sins of his own earliest maternal ancestor, Nicholas Manning, who had come to America in 1662. He was put on trial for incest with two of his sisters, and both his wife and mother testified against him at the trial. The Judge in the case was William Hawthorne (1607–681), very possibly Hawthorne's ancestor on his father's side. Hawthorne spoke of revealing secrets in his tales yet keeping "the inmost Me behind its veil" (Hawthorne, 1969, p. 294).

The theme of sibling incest seemed to preoccupy Hawthorne throughout his life, and there are strong suggestions that he himself had an incestuous relationship with his sister, Ebe.

At his death, Hawthorne left two unfinished manuscripts on the theme of incest. He wrote an early story about sibling incest, which he published at his own expense. He then tried to retract it by destroying the copies. He never mentioned this story again. Nor was it included in his collections of his works. Yet, fifty years later his sister, Ebe, referred to this early hidden story as a good example of her brother's special genius. The story involves a brother and sister in the early days of Salem, who have lived in fervent affection and "lonely sufficiency to each other" since they alone of their family survived an Indian attack. The brother realizes that it is through the death of his parents that his sister becomes his. Hers was "the love which had been gathered to me from the many graves of our household." The story mirrors events of Hawthorne's own life. His seafaring father died when he was four, and the family was forced thereafter to live amid "uncongenial" relatives. His mother became a recluse, which left Nathaniel alone much of the time with his favorite older sister, Ebe. The four-year younger sister, Marie, born shortly before the father died, was too young to experience the loss and grew up in a very different position from her two older siblings. Years later Ebe resisted Hawthorne's betrothal, and though the couple lived together with Ebe for many years, she and Hawthorne's wife rarely even spoke to each other.

From what we know of Hawthorne's experience, he always had a sense of deep secrets in his family even before his intense study of the records confirmed the shameful secrets of their history. How this history may have been connected to a secret relationship with his sister Ebe we will never know. But certainly, the more we know about our own family's history, the better we can navigate our lives and make informed choices about our own behavior. Try to understand how family secrets may have distorted relationships and influenced your family even generations later, as seems to have happened in the Hawthorne family.

As appears to have happened with Hawthorne, family members born at pivotal moments in a family's history may have a sense of something beyond what is said, even though they have never been told anything directly. One gets the sense that Hawthorne's preoccupation with the early history of his family in America came from a sense of the traumatic secrets buried there, long before he learned what his family's history was.

CONFRONTING THE BETRAYAL STEMMING FROM SECRETS: CHARLES LINDBERGH'S THREE SECRET FAMILIES

All secrets involve betrayal and when that betrayal is exposed, it is painful. Family members, and others, inevitably struggle to reformulate their understanding of themselves and their family in light of the new information tied to the secret. Depending on the nature and extent of secrecy, it can take years, or even generations as in Hawthorne's case, for some to be revealed, processed and eventually, hopefully, reconciled.

Charles Lindbergh illustrates the incredible power of building a life of secrets, and the magnificent creative potential of a child's effort to undo the legacy. Lindbergh was viewed by many as a hero for being the first to complete a solo and nonstop transatlantic flight in 1927 in his plane "The Spirit of St. Louis." The world learned a lot about his six children and his distinguished writer wife Ann Morrow Lindbergh, including the kidnapping of their baby in 1932 (**see Genogram 4.5: Lindbergh Family**). Lindbergh was a handsome aviator who played a major role in promoting aviation in the U.S., for which he was treated as a national hero. Over time his reputation became tarnished through indications of his Nazi sympathies. Within his family Lindbergh acted as a stern, moralistic father with his five surviving children.

In 1974, thirty years after Lindbergh's death and two years after his wife's death, his youngest daughter Reeve found out that, while raising his first set

Charles Lindbergh
Library of Congress,
Prints and
Photographs Division,
LC-USZ62-115128

of children in the U.S., he had had seven other children from three other secret families in different countries of Europe, "I had brothers and sisters I had never known about: two girls and five boys, living in several different countries on another continent."

As Reeve describes: "During all the years when he was the stern arbiter of moral and ethical conduct in our family, he had been leading another life . . . according to a whole different set of standards from those he had taught us. . . . I became furiously angry. . . . I was not angry with my 'new,' living relatives, no more to blame for the circumstances of their birth than I am, but with my long-dead father. I raged against his duplicitous character, his personal conduct, the years of deception and hypocrisy. . . . What really drove me crazy . . . was (the) chastising letter (he had written) to my sister when she was at college. It was . . . a searing page of paternal moralizing, telling her that she had too many boyfriends and doing it in a cruel way hinting at her potential "'promiscuity,' a

Reeve Lindbergh
Caleb Kenna/The
New York Times

Three other children of Charles Lindbergh
Ken Liu/picture-alliance/dpa/AP Images

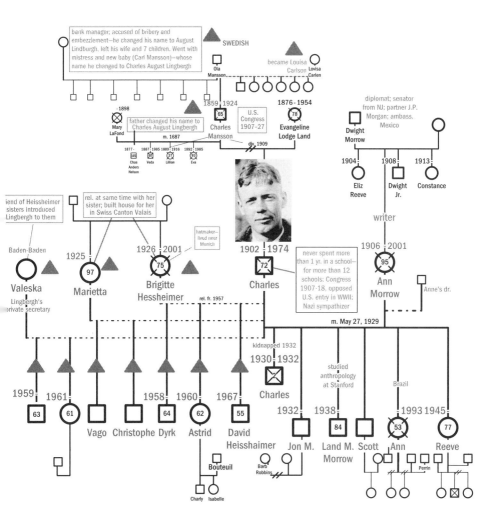

Genogram 4.5: Lindbergh Family

strange word for a father to use. . . . Ann had saved it for thirty years. . . . She died before she knew about his own behavior" (Lindbergh, 2003, pp. 201–202). Reeve was pained to see what her sister had had to absorb over all the years of their father's rigid moralistic judgments, when his whole life and behavior involved phenomenal duplicity.

Reeve tried to understand what had happened, overwhelmed by the "absolutely Byzantine layers of deception on the part of our shared father. These children did not even know who he was. He used a pseudonym with them (to protect them, perhaps? To protect himself, absolutely!)" (Lindbergh, 2003, p. 203).

She concluded: "Every intimate human connection my father had during his later years was fractured by secrecy. He could not be completely open with anybody who loved him anywhere on earth. . . . What remains with me is a sense of his unutterable loneliness" (Lindbergh, 2003, p. 218).

From his death bed in Hawaii, Lindbergh wrote to all three mistresses pressing each to keep her segment of the family secret. At some point over the years his daughter Astrid, who had learned to call her father "Careu Kent," saw a picture of Charles Lindbergh and recognized it as the man she knew as her father. She then found his love letters to her mother over many years. It was not until both her own mother and Ann Morrow Lindbergh died in 2001 that she revealed the truth and contacted her siblings in the U.S.

Reeve concludes:

> I'm hoping that as I get older I'll get braver, and someday I may even be brave enough to . . . let the family history go, let it be. Gently, so as not to disturb anybody, I may open a door and just walk through it. I may tiptoe away from the closed rooms of the past with all their stories and move quietly into the present I love so well, and then even further out into the open future, forward from here. (Lindbergh, p. 220)

Reeve's brilliant perception of the bravery required to free oneself from the power of the secrets in order to gain an open future is an inspiration for anyone seeking to go home again. Her sensitivity about the complexities and pain of unraveling and dealing with such powerful secrets, acknowledges the dilemma of addressing what it may mean in exposing others, who may not have the same readiness for exposure; care must always be taken for other family members' experience.

DEALING WITH FAMILY SECRETS AS AN ESSENTIAL PART OF GOING HOME

Going home again is about making the effort to connect with any sources of understanding about our family's history and legacies, maybe especially about the secrets. Yet we must be extremely thoughtful of others' fear and pain about sharing traumatic experiences. As Barbara Krasner expressed it in her memoir, "The close-up realization of how easy it would be to destroy others and ourselves haunts me" (Krasner et al., 2020). We must convey our sensitivity and respect for our legacies, both positive and the negative. There are many layers to secrets, the pain of those involved, the shame of those on the sidelines, and the anxieties of those who fear provoking pain or rage if they raise the issues. We need courage so we can ask graciously and generously about those pieces of history that do not seem to fit together. As a multigenerational legacy in the Lindbergh family, it turns out that Lindbergh's grandfather, a banker in Sweden, was accused of embezzling. He had seven children with his wife and had just had a son with his mistress. He decided to leave his wife and seven children, change his name and that of his new son and girlfriend and move to Minnesota, which he did. So one can begin to imagine how his grandson taught himself two generations later to make the same transformation, employing the lying and secrecy and drawing other family members into his lies.

Asking our relatives to tell us their experiences, including the painful things that occurred in the past is not to hurt them, but to help us figure out the best way to learn where people got stuck in the past so we can avoid these pitfalls in the future. My own mother (MM) found many things in her childhood too painful to talk about, but at some point she decided to talk slightly about what had happened. I was most fortunate that later when she refused to talk more about those things, instead of raging at her secrecy and failure to communicate, I let her know that I was okay, and that I appreciated what she had shared already.

Another issue to consider is when to share the secrets you learn. Family gatherings are generally not the time to reveal secrets, as such events themselves are likely to increase families' tension. Probably a quiet moment on a more private occasion when there is time to deal with the emotional process would be a better time, after much preparation for the reactivity of others to the news.

There is also the issue of who knows others' secrets. One of my (MM) mother's closest friends as a young adult, who had married a friend of our father, so the couples knew each other for many decades, was generous enough to share with us several family "secrets" that helped my sisters and me better understand our parents' young adult lives, including some painful misjudgments. As another example, my grandparents were long dead when I began researching our family history, but one of my grandmother's best friends was still alive. She welcomed me when I asked to visit and was more than generous in sharing what she knew from my grandmother about our family, which was a great deal, including history that was before her time and secrets about our great grandparents' history that no one else had told me (see

video: *The McGoldrick History Mystery*, available at multiculturalfamily.org).
Perhaps her knowing secrets that had been hidden in our family was not surprising. We often tell friends secrets about our family and couple relationships
that we do not share with family members.

At some point it seems that the purpose of our lives is to "pay it forward."
We owe it to ourselves to make life better for those who come after us. This
requires gaining our best understanding of what came before, so we can find
ways to break destructive cycles and offer our children—and not just our
own children but all the next generations—a better world. Asking our relatives to tell us their experiences, including the painful things that occurred
in the past is not to hurt them, but to help us figure out the best way to move
forward—to learn where people got stuck in the past so we can avoid these
pitfalls in the future.

QUESTIONS ABOUT FAMILY STORIES AND SECRETS

- Have family members tended to conform to typical American
  middle-class family life-cycle norms? If not, are there "off time"
  events on your genogram? May–December marriages? Families
  leaving home, marrying, or having children very early or very late
  or not at all? Living in unconventional groupings, etc.? What values might these patterns reflect?
- Are there coincidences of life-cycle events—births, deaths, marriages, leaving home, onset of illness—that may have intensified
  the stress of particular events in your family?
- What kinds of rituals does the family have for dinnertime, holidays, leisure time, vacations, and family get-togethers? What
  values do these rituals strengthen? What cultural patterns are
  strengthened or minimized? Also, who does the work to make the
  rituals happen? And who cleans up?
- What customs are there for celebrating weddings? Funerals?
  Births? Birthdays? Anniversaries? What happens when someone
  breaks the pattern?
- What are the basic family rules (e.g., "Don't trust small men," or
  "Don't eat ice cream more than once a day" or "Don't raise your
  voice when you argue" or "Men shouldn't cry" or "Only marry
  within your race")?

- How are various family members characterized in family stories told: As heroes? Harsh? Super smart? Fun? Full of quirks? Are there cautionary tales? Do the stories seem to reflect the family's underlying beliefs, myths and values in any decipherable way?
- Are stories told about particular issues (e.g., migration, death, dealing with the outside world, race, education, money, sexuality, holidays, betrayal, survival, good guys and bad guys)?
- What legacies were there in the family about strength, vulnerability, anxiety, mental illness, resilience, success, hope in the face of despair?
- In what areas does the family keep secrets (e.g., about money, death, pregnancy, sexual behavior, marriage, divorce, affairs, mental illness, addiction, parentage, school, or work failure)?
- What impact have secrets had on the relationships in the family and how are secrets maintained? Who conveys messages about dealing with secrets and how?
- Might there be "outsiders" who know some family secrets (e.g., friends who were privy to a lot about the family because of their long connection to family members)?

Chapter 5
Family Ties and Binds

Anyone can become angry. That is easy. But to be angry with the right person, to the right degree, at the right time, for the right purpose and in the right way—this is not easy.

—DANIEL GOLEMAN
Social Intelligence

Because families do not always communicate optimally, relationships often go awry. In fact, some researchers have suggested that communication is often used more to obscure than to clarify meaning. As the saying goes, often attributed to Maya Angelou: "People will forget what you said. People will forget what you did. But people will not forget how you made them feel." It is very often the emotional feelings people have that determine how relationships go in a family. It seems that the more family members depend upon the approval of others for their self-esteem, the more likely their communication is to be distorted, avoiding clear meaning to preserve the relationship.

To understand your family, you need to explore the way emotional relationships work in terms of closeness and distance. Cultures differ in the amount of closeness expected, but ideally, families can balance closeness and individuation so that the more they can be themselves, the more they can be connected. However, if there is only room for "togetherness" and not for each person to express individual needs and beliefs, the system will likely get out of balance, just as it will if each person attends to their own interests and not to the needs of the group. Similarly, if there are high caretaking needs but not enough caretakers, the family will be stressed. How a family communicates and cooperates will play a key role in how imbalances are managed especially as needs change over the life cycle.

FAMILY COMMUNICATION PATTERNS

Communication is the vehicle through which families maintain their relationship closeness or distance. In a healthy system, people communicate openly, clearly, empathetically, harmoniously, and with tolerance for difference, which balances closeness and distance. Conversely, disordered communication is indirect and unclear. The challenge is to decipher how the communication patterns operate in your family. What patterns might members of our family have become caught in without realizing it, and how might we change our part in the system to improve communication? One of the best ways to do this is to ask yourself a few questions such as: Who speaks to whom and who does not? Who tends to relieve tension with humor or a diversion? What family issues get avoided? What are the basic alliances and conflictual relationships? Are relationship patterns repeats of patterns in previous generations: Triangles? Cutoffs? Sibling conflicts? Are siblings being drawn into parental conflict? Patterns of over-functioning or under-functioning, where one person always takes the role of helper or caretaker while another acts oblivious, needy, or incompetent? Have certain life-cycle transitions seemed especially difficult in your family's history? Adolescence? Launching? Older family members' caretaking?

FAMILY COMMUNICATION PATTERNS REGULATE CLOSENESS AND DISTANCE

Families generally maintain a stable level of closeness and distance, however much their emotional relationships may seem to fluctuate. We all know that families can do a lot of talking without communicating much or even connecting. Some families use humor to maintain distance, others use fighting. Some families appear very warm and friendly to outsiders, but insiders know that it's all "form" and that if you disobey the rules of "appropriate" behavior, you will be shut out.

High-conflict families may also have a high degree of intimacy. Some families share a private language, full of obscure jokes and references. Others communicate through rituals passed from generation to generation. At times it can seem as if family members are connected by an invisible web, operating as one organism, even when separated by thousands of miles.

Generally speaking, if something changes the comfortable level of closeness and distance established for relationships, the family unit will try to bring things back to the familiar level. If one family member becomes sick, another may come closer to decrease anxiety, or they may begin fighting to preserve the familiar distance and avoid too much closeness. In times of anxiety and change, families generally try to stabilize themselves by regulating the closeness and distance in their relationships. They may not talk at all, they may blame themselves, or someone else, or they may distract the conversation with humor or by changing the subject.

The level of communication distortion is a good measure of the overall anxiety and rigidity of family relationships. If two family members always agree, this is probably more a reaction to anxiety than because they are soulmates. Conversely, if two family members are always in disagreement, the subject of their conflict is probably not the real issue. They will end up on opposite sides no matter what the content of their discussion.

Dysfunctional communication most often develops in times of stress, as when people stop speaking to each other after a death or a financial crisis. If many stresses occur at the same time, the family probably won't communicate very effectively, at least for a while. Chronically maladaptive ways of relating tend to ripple out and down the generations in a system.

THE WRIGHT BROTHERS: AN EXAMPLE OF FAMILY COMMUNICATION PATTERNS

The family of the Wright brothers (see Genogram 5.1: Wright Brothers Family) illustrates many interesting issues in family communication. Wilbur and Orville, though four years apart in age and seeming opposites, were actually described by their father as "inseparable as twins." Wilbur once wrote: "From the time we were little children, my brother Orville and myself lived

Wilbur Wright
Library of Congress, Prints and Photographs Division, Wright Brothers Negatives, LC-DIG-ppprs-00683

Orville Wright
Library of Congress, Prints and Photographs Division, Wright Brothers Negatives, LC-DIG-ppprs-00680

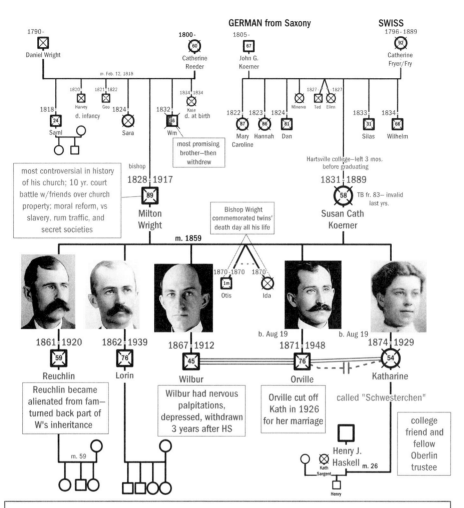

Genogram 5.1: Wright Brothers Family

together, played together, worked together, and in fact, thought together. We
usually owned all of our toys in common, talked over our thoughts and aspirations so that nearly everything that was done in our lives has been the result
of conversations, suggestions, and discussions between us" (as cited in Crouch,
1989, pp. 49–50).

The two brothers were so like twins that they could complete each other's sentences. Their collaboration on the development of the airplane was

Reuchlin Wright
Library of Congress, Prints and
Photographs Division, Wright Brothers
Negatives, LC-DIG-ppprs-00482

Lorin Wright
Courtesy of Wright State University
Libraries' Special Collections and
Archives

one of the most productive partnerships in history, a relationship more binding than most marriages, to the point where each could use their joint bank account without consulting the other. They often began whistling the same tune, while at work in their bicycle shop, as if there was a psychic bond between them. And their voices were so alike a listener often could not tell them apart except by seeing them. They attributed this "twinship" to an association of ideas stored in a common memory (Howard, 1987). Though both were mechanically minded and intelligent, it was their combined abilities and efforts that allowed them to succeed at man-made flight. Only together did they experience genius.

On the surface their "twinship" appears surprising. Other sibling pairings in the family would have seemed more natural. Wilbur and Orville were more than four years apart in age, while their two older brothers, Reuchlin and Lorin, whom most people have never heard of, were only a year apart. The two youngest siblings, Orville and Katharine, might also have been thought of as "like twins" for sharing a birthday. Yet it was Wilbur and Orville who shared this remarkable twin-like connection. Why is that?

It turns out that between them a pair of twins, Otis and Ida, had died. Their "twinship" was likely powerfully influenced by their book-end connection to their lost twin siblings. Their father apparently commemorated the twins' birthday for the rest of his life (Crouch, 1989). Though we know nothing of earlier twins in the Wright family, except that the mother had twin siblings who had also died early. But it's hard not to wonder if the Wright family's need for twins reflected some earlier traumas involving twins in previous generations.

Families that lose children often form a special attachment to the surviving children, especially those closest to the lost children, who may become emotional replacements and have difficulty leaving home. The Wright brothers' father, Milton Wright, actually boasted that neither Orville nor Wilbur ever married or left their parental home. The reasons for this remain obscure, leaving us to wonder whether there was some covert message to them not to leave.

Katharine Wright
Courtesy of Wright State University Libraries' Special Collections and Archives

But there may have been other forces as well. In his senior year of high school, Wilbur sustained a sports injury and withdrew to his home, where he nursed his mother who was dying of tuberculosis. Indeed, he seemed solidly embedded at home even after his mother died—unable to mobilize himself to leave and seek out his own life, leaving several family members wondering if he was malingering or depressed. That same year the father lost his position as a bishop, due to political conflicts, which put him in difficult circumstances financially and in his community. As it turned out, neither Wilbur nor Orville completed high school, both dropping out for unclear reasons.

But then the brothers began their intense collaboration directed at developing a flying machine. As their work on inventing the airplane developed, the charge in their already close relationship apparently heated up. For six or seven weeks they worked together day and night, arguing all the way. One has to wonder if their arguing didn't help them regulate the intensity of their emotional closeness. According to others who were around them, whenever the brothers were in the same room, the shouting would start, resounding through the house.

As their assistant recalled, one morning after the worst argument he had ever overheard between them: "Orv came in and said he guessed he'd been wrong, and they ought to do it Will's way. A few minutes later Will came in and said he'd been thinking it over and perhaps Orv was right. The first thing I knew, they were arguing it all over again, only this time they had

Wilbur, Katharine, and Orville Wright
Bettmann/Getty Images

switched ideas" (cited in Walsh, 1975, p. 115). This is a great illustration of the
way that distance can be regulated in an intense relationship.

We might hypothesize that this family somehow "needed" twins. Consider that after Wilbur died in 1912 at the age of only forty-five, Orville and
Katharine lived on together as a pair with their father until he died five years
later and for years after that. It almost seems that the lost twins were replaced
by Wilbur and Orville, and then when Orville no longer had Wilbur, he and
Katharine became like replacement twins, living on as a kind of couple for
many years.

Then, however, at fifty-one Katharine reconnected with an Oberlin student, now widowed, who asked her to marry him. She didn't tell Orville for
over a year, fearing his wrath. When she did tell him, he stopped talking to

her for the rest of his life. As one of the Wright biographers put it: "Katharine violated a sacred pact. In admitting another man into her life, she had rejected her brother. Katharine of all people had shaken his faith in the inviolability of the family ties that provided his emotional security" (Crouch, 1989, p. 483).

This reflects a common family pattern: fusion leads to cutoff, as cutoff leads to fusion. In other words, if you cut off feelings about one relationship (say, the loss of the twins in the Wright family), you may intensify feelings in another (Wilbur and Orville), which might, if the first fusion is broken (by Wilbur's death), get transferred to an even more intense fusion (Orville and Katharine), which led eventually to another cutoff (Orville rejecting his sister because he could not tolerate her having an intimate relationship with anyone other than him).

The Wright family illustrates how unresolved traumatic experiences can lead to intensely rigid patterns that constrict growth and freedom. Once families shut down in response to experiences that feel too overwhelming to handle, something needs to release the pressure to set the system free again. The act of cutoff is in this sense the equivalent of death, and that becomes the final act of rigidity in a system that is in trouble. It seems especially interesting that in the end, when Katharine was dying several years later, it was Lorin, one of the forgotten brothers, who at the last minute convinced Orville to visit Katharine before she died.

We might also look at the specific positions and gender of siblings. Katherine had already been put in a special position in their family by age fifteen, when her mother died. Her father wrote to her, his youngest child and only daughter: "You have a good mind and good heart, and being my only daughter, you are my hope of love and care, if I live to be old. . . . But for you, we should feel like we had no home" (Crouch, 1989, p. 87).

Katharine Wright was even called "Schwesterchen" (little sister), defining her primary role by her position from childhood, even in her nickname. Consider that both parents and the two oldest brothers attended college, though none of them graduated, and both Wilbur and Orville were high school dropouts. But Katharine graduated from Oberlin College, years later becoming an active member of their board of trustees as well as an activist in the suffrage movement. But after college she obediently returned home and took on the role of caretaker for her father and brothers, in addition to becoming a teacher. Then, as Wilbur and Orville developed their aviation collaboration, she began managing the financing of their bicycle shop, which was funding their efforts. Despite her obvious intellect and ability, she spent much of her adulthood being the "good daughter/good sister" by caring for her family and putting her own aspirations aside. We can only wonder about the price the Wright family, and other families, have paid in the lost talents of their daughters.

In the Wright family, we see the creativity and imagination that "twin-ship" produced, but also the deadening effect of the lack of flexibility brought on by unresolved traumatic loss over the generations. We might say that the Wright brothers taught us all how to fly yet, like the Brontës, they were never able to leave home themselves.

RESPONSES TO STRESS

All life involves change and there is no change without disruption. Even posi-tive change is stressful because it disrupts the status quo. In families that lean heavily toward closeness, times of change may lead them to cling to "the way things were," as if they could prevent the pain and disturbance of change. To a degree, resistance to change is necessary and healthy. It is a natural prop-erty of all systems. But, beyond a certain point, a family that resists change becomes rigid and unable to adapt. Extreme resistance to change leads to dis-torted communication that will weaken the family.

We learn ways of coping with stress in our families growing up and tend to continue doing things the way our families did them, or if we are unhappy about how our family has done things, we may try to do the opposite. Our families probably handled things the way their own families did them, or they reacted and tried to do the opposite.

When under stress, families tend to fall into blaming others or blaming themselves for what is going wrong. Sometimes they become placaters, deny-ing their own experience to appease others out of fear or anxiety; they may become rigidly authoritarian, irrelevant, illogical, or silent altogether, to cope with their own or the other's distress.

Some families pull together under stress, closing the doors to keep out-siders out and insiders in—demanding a sameness in feelings and behavior, which family therapists often call "enmeshment." Disagreement gets seen as disloyalty. Other families under stress fall into a mode of "everyone for them-selves." Such families cannot organize to handle problems. Outside regula-tory systems such as the police or the social service systems may become overly involved with them in an effort to impose organization on them.

Sometimes a family's coping patterns seem to reverse themselves over each generation. If the grandfather was an alcoholic and handled his stress by going to the pub, and the grandmother berated him when he came home, the next generation may swear off alcohol and develop rigid rules for censuring others by silence and avoidance of all emotional issues—drink as well as other problems. The third generation, responding to the second generation's rigidity, may again turn to drinking or drugs and acting out to deal with stress. If we look more closely at the patterns of relating in such families, we may find a stable pattern of emotional avoidance and a cycle of shame, guilt, and repentance that remains the same right down the generations, although superficially the behavior of each generation may look different.

As families move through the life cycle, they experience anxiety in response to the many stressors they face, both internal and external. The flow of anxiety through a family can be vertical (from issues coming down the family tree from the past) or horizontal (influenced by current experiences), from developmental changes (e.g., leaving home, getting married, separated or divorced, having a child, launching young adults, retirement, illness or death) and unpredictable pressures (e.g., economic reversals, illness, premature death, migration, natural disasters). With enough stress on the horizontal or developmental axis, any family is likely to break down.

For example, if a young mother has unresolved issues with her own parents (vertical anxiety), she may have particular difficulty dealing with the normal vicissitudes of parenthood (horizontal anxieties), which are hard enough in themselves. Explore your family's evolution to understand their patterns, paying attention to the impact of current stresses, along with the previous events and stresses that may be influencing current patterns of response.

THEODORE ROOSEVELT'S FAMILY AROUND LAUNCHING OF HIS DAUGHTER ALICE

To explore these issues, let us look at the family of President Theodore Roosevelt at the time when he was launching his twenty-one-year-old daughter, Alice, which was around 1905 (**see Genogram 5.2: Roosevelt Family**). While launching children creates some stress for all families, concurrent and prior stressors seem to have intensified this particular transition for the Roosevelts. For one thing,

Theodore Roosevelt
Library of Congress, Prints and Photographs Division, LC-DIG-ppmsca-37558

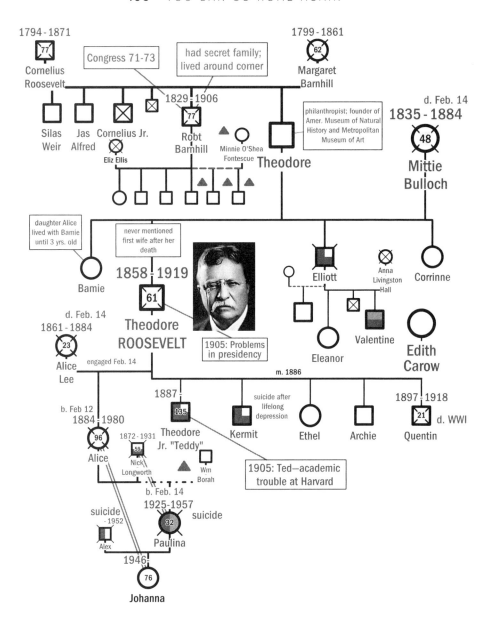

Genogram 5.2: Roosevelt Family

TR was going through a difficult period as president. Secondly, his favorite son, Teddy, who had had serious physical and emotional problems over the years, was in academic trouble at Harvard. Furthermore, there had been a painful history of family losses around Alice's birth: Her mother (also named Alice), had died on Valentine's Day, February 14, 1884, giving birth to Alice.

The death occurred coincidentally on the fourth anniversary of the couple's engagement and, tragically, on the very same night that Roosevelt's mother died upstairs in the same house. After those losses, TR decided to leave for a year-long trip out west, leaving his baby daughter Alice with his older sister, Bamie. During that time Roosevelt became secretly engaged to Edith Carow, whom he had known since childhood, though he wrote to his sister, who disapproved:

> I utterly disbelieve in second marriages; I have always considered that they argued weakness in a man's character. You could not reproach me one half as bitterly for my inconstancy and unfaithfulness as I reproach myself. Were I sure there were a heaven, my one prayer would be I might never go there, lest I should meet those I love on earth who are dead. (Miller, 1994, p. 281)

This letter was, interestingly, suppressed by the family for almost a century, an indication of the power of families to keep embarrassing information secret. Roosevelt had regarded his daughter Alice as a kind of peace offering to his sister, Bamie, who raised Alice from the time of her birth until she was three, and was greatly pained to have to give her back. Roosevelt remarried in 1886 and fathered five more children. He never mentioned his first wife's name again and there is not a word in his autobiography to indicate her existence. His daughter Alice grew up to bear a remarkable resemblance to her mother, to whom she, also, learned not to refer.

Within the family, Alice also became invisible. TR hardly counted her among the family members. Starved for attention, she became increasingly flamboyant in her behavior by late adolescence, in spite of a deep shyness. By the time she was twenty, she was continuously making the newspapers for her outrageous drinking, smoking, racing cars, and betting on horses. One might imagine she was forcing her father to pay attention to her. On February 17, 1906, at age twenty-two, the same age at which her mother had died, Alice decided to marry and leave home. Both the concurrent (horizontal) stresses in the present and the coincidental experiences of the past (vertical) undoubtedly contributed to Roosevelt's difficulty in letting his daughter go, and to her difficulty in leaving him.

We offer a partial chronology to show the connection of key events in the Roosevelt family during that time. Creating such a chronology for your own family can be extremely useful for exploring events, which often get obscured by family anxiety.

Alice made a poor choice of a husband with a hard drinking, sexually promiscuous Congressman, Nicholas Longworth, twelve years her senior. As she departed, her stepmother, Edith, is reputed to have said: "I want you to know that I'm glad to see you go. You've never been anything but trouble" (Cordery, 2007, p. 159). The launching was not successful and within a year Alice was spending more time with her father than with her husband, which was probably what she had been seeking all her life.

Table 5.1: Partial Roosevelt Chronology

1880, Feb 14	TR proposes to Alice Lee
1884, Feb 12	Alice gives birth to baby, also named Alice
1884, Feb 14	Alice Lee Roosevelt dies at age 22 Mittie Bulloch Roosevelt, TR's mother, dies in same house the same night
1884, Feb 16	Double funeral for Alice Lee Roosevelt and Mittie Bulloch Roosevelt
1884	Baby Alice is given to TR's sister Bamie to raise
1884, Summer	TR submerges grief in adventures out west and presidential politics
1886	TR remarries to a childhood friend, Edith
1887	Alice has to leave Bamie and comes to live with her newly remarried father
1887	TR and Edith have the first of their five children
. . . .	
1905	TR having difficult time dealing with Alice, now 21, and her wild behavior
1906	TR having problems as president
1906, Jan	TR's favorite son, Teddy, failing at Harvard
1906, Feb 17	Alice, age 22, marries hard-drinking, sexually promiscuous congressman Nick Longworth, age 34
1907	Marriage unhappy; Alice and Nick are mostly apart and Alice spends more time with her father
1925, Feb 14	Alice has daughter on the anniversary both of her mother's and grandmother's deaths and of her parents' engagement. The baby is the child of her lover William Borah; she wanted to name the child Deborah, but her husband refused

Alice Roosevelt with daughter Paulina, whom she wanted to name Deborah after her paramour William Borah
Library of Congress, Prints and Photographs Division, photograph by Harris and Ewing, LC-H25-110077-XFC

Twelve years later, Alice had one child, coincidentally born on February 14, apparently fathered by William Borah, a much older married Senator, with whom she had been having an affair. Alice's daughter, Paulina, led a miserable and neglected life, first attempting suicide when she was in college.

After college, Paulina married someone of whom her mother disapproved, who drank heavily and killed himself when their daughter, Johanna, was six. Paulina, after further depression, suicide attempts, and hospitalizations, finally took her own life when Johanna was ten. It might seem that Paulina was "doomed" as the stand-in for the stand-in, the second-generation daughter of loss and neglect, whose life was marked by such eerie coincidence of birth, death, and anniversaries—for three generations. Her birth was connected not just to unfortunate coincidence, but to the secrets of a failed marriage and an affair. Interestingly, Paulina's legal father, Nick Longworth, adored her, though he died when she was only six, just as Joanna's father died when she, too, was six.

A most interesting aspect of the family history is the loving and generative relationship that evolved between Paulina's neglected daughter, Johanna, and Paulina's neglectful mother, Alice Roosevelt. Alice won custody of her granddaughter, Johanna, after Paulina's death, and raised her from then on, demonstrating powerfully that patterns do not doom a family. One can turn family dynamics around. This instance of the family's resilience is the kind of illustration we always look for in efforts to transform a system toward connection and away from cutoff. Alice decided to make up for her past neglect of her daughter by developing a close relationship with her granddaughter, Johanna, which she did. They had a happy relationship until Alice died at age ninety-six in 1980. This example illustrates how important it is to track relationships as they continue down the family tree, tracking patterns of resilience as well as patterns of dysfunction in your family.

FAMILIES HANDLING CONFLICT

Conflict is inevitable in families. The question is *how* it is handled. In many cases families repress and side-step conflicts, which doesn't make them go away. Such families may become masters of covering up their disagreements, changing the subject, or stifling their feelings while pretending to agree, leaving underlying pain to escalate as time goes along. Families that prioritize togetherness tend to avoid discussion of their differences. They cover them over, change the subject, or stifle their feelings and pretend to agree, perhaps leaving underlying pain to escalate as time goes along.

Alternatively, some families engage their conflicts directly, but if they do so in ways that are attacking and defensive, it can create hurts and resentments that escalate over time. In families that tend to erupt repeatedly in response to anxiety, disagreements may lead to unresolved family conflicts or cutoffs. Turmoil may become the basic style in families with continual argument without resolution. At a certain point, unable to resolve their conflict, they may switch to a different disagreement. The husband says the wife "always" interrupts and the wife says he "never" listens. The son may then distract the parents by picking a fight with his sister. At this point the parents join together to stop the children fighting. This continual shifting can keep the anxiety level of the family within certain bounds, but even if a stable balance results, it may be quite unsatisfying for the participants.

Sometimes family members, particularly couples, get into cycles of fighting and making up, the intensity of the reconciliations may make the conflict almost worthwhile. A partner may even pick a fight to experience the close-ness of making up.

Other families live in a "cold war"—no battles, just chronic tension. A cold, contemptuous glance can be the emotional equivalent of a devastating verbal attack. Typically, conflicts between any two family members will affect others in the family. As anxiety rises, conflicts have a ripple effect. Family members become polarized. It is hard to avoid taking sides. Even those who try to remain neutral and above the fray will be seen as having chosen a side by their very silence.

For example, when Kathleen Kennedy, child of Joseph and Rose Ken-nedy, married a Protestant in England, against her parents' wishes and their religion, Rose retreated to her room. Joe, torn between his wife and his daughter, had his wife admitted to a hospital to protect her from publicity and, perhaps, from having to commit herself publicly to a reaction; Kathleen had to read about the family's response to her marriage in the newspaper and draw her own conclusions. Joe Jr., the oldest son and the closest to Kathleen, finally cabled his parents on his sister's behalf: "The power of silence is great" (Kearns Goodwin, 1987, p. 679). Such responses may temporarily stabilize the family, but they create a situation in which the family may be less equipped to handle future problems and anxiety. Pay close attention to how your family has dealt with conflict.

THE POWER OF SILENCE

An extreme example of the power of silence is the family of Jennifer Teege, who was thirty-eight before she learned anything about her traumatic fam-ily history. She was born in Germany in 1970 to a German mother and a Nigerian father. Her mother soon put her in an orphanage because of her father's addiction and abuse. By age three, Jennifer was in a foster family who eventually adopted her. She grew up knowing nothing about her own family history, although she had had visits with her mother and maternal grandmother until she was adopted.

At thirty-eight, as a wife and mother of two, Jennifer by chance came across a book in a library entitled *I Have to Love*

Jennifer Teege
Sven Hoppe/picture-alliance/dpa/AP Image

my Father, Don't I? (2002). Jennifer recognized the name Monika Goeth as her biological mother's name. As she read the book, she also recognized various pictures, especially her grandmother, Ruth Goeth.

She later realized that fate must have led her to that book, of all the books in that library. She came to see her life as divided into two parts, the time before she knew her history and the time after. She had been plagued by depression for years. Her mother's book was the key she had been looking for to understand herself. As she began to learn about her grandfather's cruel behavior, she began to think her depression might have been caused by her origins (interestingly, her grandfather's extremely vicious role was played by Ralph Fiennes in the movie Schindler's List) **(see Genogram 5.3: Jennifer Teege Family)**. Jennifer now had to rethink whatever she knew about German history.

In her youth, she had spent several years studying in Israel. Now she had to worry that her very close Jewish friends there had relatives who might have been killed by her grandfather. She read books about the era, trying to understand her history. One author who had studied grandchildren of the Nazis described them as sugarcoating the role their ancestors had played. As she says in her memoir: "So many innocent grandfathers, so many suppressed family secrets" (Teege, 2015, p. 13). Another psychologist who treated grandchildren of Nazis wrote: "Violence and brutalization have a deep impact on the generations that follow. What makes them ill, however, is not the crimes themselves, but the silence that surrounds them. There is an unholy conspiracy of silence in perpetrator families, often spanning generations" (p. 17). Jennifer remembered that her adoptive father had been unable to stop disputing the number of Jews killed in the war. His children could not understand his preoccupation with the number.

Jennifer became obsessed with figuring out the details of her history, struggling to imagine how her much loved grandmother, Ruth, could have loved this brutal man. She had kept his picture by her bed all her life. When Ruth had died, Jennifer's adoptive parents had given her the obituary, but it didn't include the fact she had killed herself on the day after she was interviewed about her history with Goeth. Though Jennifer had loved her grandmother, who had visited her until her adoption was finalized when she was seven, she felt anger and rejection about her mother, who had not even mentioned Jennifer in her memoir. It would take her two years to be ready to reconnect with her mother.

She eventually went to the house where Amon Goeth had lived with her grandmother, Ruth, speaking with a guide who mentioned that she had once met Jennifer's mother, Monika Goeth who had visited the house. She asked

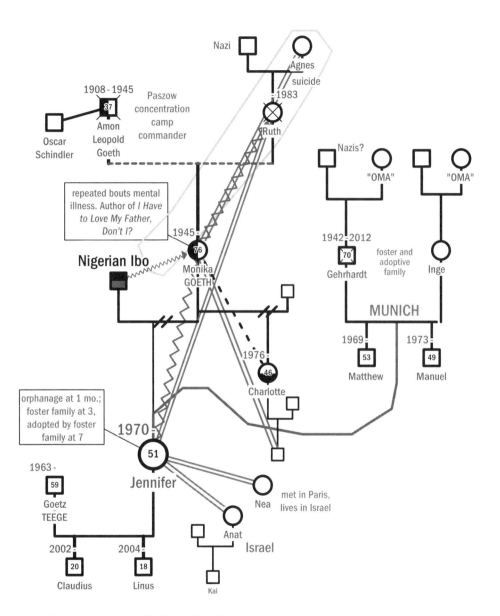

Genogram 5.3: Jennifer Teege Family

the woman what her mother was like and was told she thought she was a bit strange and sad, and that as she left she touched the doorpost and said she had loved her father (Teege, 2015, p. 42).

Finally, after going to the site of the Plaszow concentration camp, where her mother had also gone to trace the steps of her parents, Jennifer felt ready to meet her mother. It had been almost twenty years since they had last seen each other. She wanted to see her, not for a reckoning, but to answer all the questions that were going around in her head. She remembered that Ruth had been abusive to her mother, striking her because she had asked too many questions. Jennifer, too, now needed to ask questions.

Once she met her mother, she no longer saw her as a mother who abandoned her child, but as the daughter of Amon Goeth, who had shaped her identity and her life. And though very disappointed that her mother did not seem to want to include her in her life, Jennifer now began to understand her mother in a different way. Monika had grown up with her abusive mother, Ruth, and a beloved grandmother, Agnes, whom Monika had adored. Jennifer felt she had lived the same pattern: her mother was distant, while she and her grandmother Ruth had loved each other much more easily. She learned that Monika had also not been close to her daughter from her second marriage, whose life was as troubled as Jennifer's, but had developed very close relationships with her grandchildren, whom she was now raising.

It remained for Jennifer to reconnect with her Israeli friends, with whom she had not dared talk to until now. When she finally visited them to repair her relationships, she felt a great release. Her friend Anat then suggested that her thirteen-year-old son would be coming to Germany with a student group to visit concentration camps and asked Jennifer to meet with them.

Jennifer was petrified, but could not say no. The last time she had gone to Plaszow she had not had the courage to admit her identity to a Jewish tourist she had met, as she had not been able to tell her Israeli friends who she really was for two years! Now she realized she had to talk openly with these students.

Just before the meeting, Jennifer's adoptive father died. He had been absorbed by the topic of the Nazis, getting into heated discussions with his friends, to the point of destroying some of his friendships. But he would not apologize, which Jennifer and her brothers could not understand. Finally, as he was dying, he began to talk about his parents, asking questions about whether humanity was evil. As his son put it: "My father carried around this unresolved conflict with his parents. He grappled with the Holocaust without realizing that what he really wanted was to understand his parents" (Teege, 2015, p. 210). Jennifer and her brothers realized that their father's rigidity was about his never-ending pain that his parents supported the Nazis.

Regarding Jennifer's presentation at the memorial, her friend Anat was reassuring, saying she worried that the students would end up hating the Germans and seeing themselves only as victims of persecution. She felt it was extremely important for Jennifer to tell them her story. "It is too easy to hate Amon Goeth. If the Germans and their allies can turn into murderers then we, too, can become murderers. If the Germans could turn a blind eye, it can happen to us. I hope that my sons will always remember that. I hope that they will always see the Palestinians as human beings, not as enemies" (Teege, 2015, p. 206).

When the day came, the children were deeply moved as Jennifer told her story and answered their questions. As they moved on to their own memorial service, for which they had prepared sayings and prayers, they invited her to join them, even asking her to be the one to lay the flowers at the memorial. When she had come the first time to Plaszow, she had put down her flowers in private, which had freed her enough to contact her mother for the first time. But this time, she said, "It is better. I am not alone."

Jennifer's courage in facing her history and encouraging others to do so as well is a powerful example of "going home" to face even the most painful aspects of our history in order to free ourselves and our children for the future.

FUSION AND CUT OFF

When families are under stress, there is often pressure to think and act alike—to sacrifice their own identity for family loyalty. Individuals are forced to give up a part of themselves for the group. Differences must be ignored or minimized. We call this kind of connection *fusion*. The boundaries of each person are lost and people conform to the needs and feelings of others.

Closeness and fusion are not to be confused. Closeness is defined by genuine intimacy, sharing, and warmth, but this requires respecting each person's individual differences. Fusion, on the other hand, is a state of all-consuming closeness that does not allow each person to retain their autonomy. Fused families are threatened by the individuality of its members and have difficulty allowing a diversity of ideas and feelings in relationships. Fused families often take a stance of "us-against-the-world" that limits further a family's ability to cope with stressors and change. If family members must always follow the "party line" it is difficult to adjust to change. Closed to outside influences and ideas, family members may come to see each other as opponents rather than potential resources. Moreover, if something threatens the illusion of unanimity, it often results in devastating cutoffs.

THE O'NEILL FAMILY: AN EXAMPLE OF FUSION AND CUTOFF

Eugene O'Neill never really resolved the fusion in his family of origin (**see Genogram 5.4: O'Neill Family**). He sought closeness and ran from it at the same time. He fled from his first marriage, totally abdicating his responsibilities for his wife and his son, Eugene Jr., whom he did not even meet until he was eleven. Following a tortured affair with the wife of a close friend, O'Neill married for a second time, to Agnes Boulton, with whom he was extremely possessive, wanting her exclusively for himself, not distracted by children,

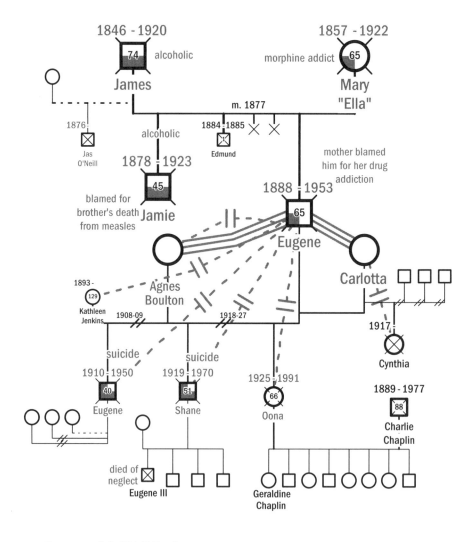

Genogram 5.4: O'Neill Family

family, or friends. Agnes left a daughter behind when she married O'Neill, just as he had left his son. He was insanely jealous, telling her: "I want it to be not you and me, but us . . . in an aloneness broken by nothing. Not even by children of our own" (Sheaffer, 1968, p. 65).

The couple did, however, have two more children, Shane and Oona O'Neill. But O'Neill ignored them and when this second marriage broke up, he made Agnes the villain. Fusion, when it disintegrates, typically leads to disillusionment and cutoff. After the divorce, O'Neill not only cut off Agnes, but his children as well, refusing even to mention their names.

Eugene O'Neill and wife Carlotta
Library of Congress, Prints and Photographs Division, Carl Van Vechten Collection, LC-USZ62-42540

O'Neill's pattern of fusion and cut off intensified in his third marriage to Carlotta Monterey. They had met while he was still married to Agnes, only weeks after his mother's death. Of their first meeting, Carlotta said: "He began to talk about his boyhood. He talked and talked, as though he'd known me all his life, but he paid no more attention to me than if I had been a chair. He talked about how he'd had no home, no mother . . . (or) father in the real sense, and how deprived his childhood had been. Well, that's what got me into trouble with O'Neill; my maternal instinct came out—this man must be looked after, I thought. He broke my heart" (Gelb & Gelb, 1987, p. 62).

It is interesting that Carlotta recognized their mutual projections so early. She was an "object" to fill his emptiness and he was a "child" she could take care of. They both had a desperate need to belong. Her previous marriage had foundered because of her husband's continual infidelities.

To justify abandoning his family for someone who would devote herself wholly to him, O'Neill convinced himself that Agnes's resentment of his divorcing her was unjustified. But once he and Carlotta were off by themselves, she having also left behind her daughter, O'Neill was tormented by guilt over having abandoned his family. As time went on, O'Neill and Carlotta built up a two-against-the-world stance. They isolated themselves further by living abroad. Even after they returned to the United States, Carlotta tried to minimize O'Neill's contact with his children. For twenty-six years they developed a romantic legend of the handsome, remote, chateau-dwelling O'Neill, secluded in work and in love with his devoted Carlotta.

In later years because of a Parkinson's-like illness, O'Neill was unable to write, and Carlotta's protectiveness intensified. O'Neill, cut off all three of his children, and never saw his grandchildren. Both of his sons eventually committed suicide. He cut off his daughter Oona entirely after her marriage at age eighteen to Charlie Chaplin, who was fifty-four and O'Neill's contemporary. In later years both O'Neill and Carlotta were seriously depressed; and after he died, she went on alone, trying to preserve the legend herself as long as she lived.

Unlocking a family that has become closed down such as this one would require acknowledgment of the pain that led them to view fusion and cutoff as solutions rather than as the deadly perpetuator of the very losses they were struggling with in the first place. O'Neill, so pained by loss of his own parents, proceeded to lose all his children and to require his spouses to do the same thing. An alternative way to change the system would be if the children themselves formed a sufficient coalition to reconnect with each other and then with their parents.

THE SYMPTOM BEARER

In times of stress one family member may become identified as the patient or symptom bearer. This person, whom therapists often call the IP or "Identified Patient," may actually serve as a distress signal for the whole family. The symptomatic person can provide a focus for the family's emotional energy and distract them from their anxiety. There may even be an unconscious arrangement among family members for one to be symptomatic, so the others have someone to take care of. Family members may even take turns being the symptom bearer, one person rallying to take care of another. But in rigid families the positions are likely to remain fixed, as in the case of O'Neill and Carlotta. In their case, even when Carlotta herself had to be hospitalized and the roles should have reversed, O'Neill managed to get himself hospitalized in the same hospital, not to be outdone in his role as patient.

Headaches, depression, anxiety attacks, children's school failure or behavior problems may all provide clues to family problems in which the symptom bearer is peripheral to the primary issue. Often it is the least powerful family members who develop symptoms. When parents are having marital problems, children are likely to become the symptom bearers, particularly if the parents cannot deal with their issues themselves. Women are often the ones who become symptomatic in families, usually having less power to change a system than do men, who are generally socialized not to acknowledge their needs or vulnerability, nor to ask for help.

What this suggests is that responding only to the symptom, without exploring the overall context in which it occurs, may lead to misunderstanding about what is happening. For example, when a child's stomachaches are responded to only with medication, or school failure only with punishment and remedial help, such responses may miss the real issue, which may be the child's distress over family problems.

Symptoms of illness often tell us more about anxiety in a family as a whole than about the symptomatic individual alone. Studies have actually indicated that the time of seeking medical help for a child often has more to do with changes in the parents' anxiety than with changes in the child's state of health, just as symptoms often reflect the burnout of the caretaker rather than an exacerbation of the problem for the caretakee.

In the O'Neill family, Eugene was diagnosed with tuberculosis in 1912, which was a time of dysfunction for the entire family. Being miserably alcoholic with no money and no career after his first humiliating divorce, he had attempted suicide earlier in that year. His mother had a severe morphine addiction, his brother Jamie was a serious alcoholic, and his father was profoundly frustrated about his own career. The family had become increasingly isolated. While the tuberculosis obviously had a biological cause, we also know that people are more vulnerable to illness when their immune system is stressed.

O'Neill's TB symptoms finally forced him to enter a sanatorium, where he found supports, which helped him transform his life. By the time he returned home a few months later, he had developed the goal to become a writer, and was soon on his way. Within a year his mother had transformed her life as well. She entered a convent, where she finally overcame her twenty-eight-year morphine addiction.

While we know from the later O'Neill history that such transformations did not extend through the whole family, a new creativity can evolve when a closed system is sufficiently disturbed to be opened up to new outside influence. Such infusion of new energy and resources can be the very hope for healing a closed, dysfunctional system.

TRIANGLES

Generally, two-person relationships tend to be inherently unstable and under stress will seek to draw in a third person to form a triangle. Triangulating is a process by which two people lower tension in their relationship by drawing in a third. In some cases, a person may feel threatened by another who disagrees with them and will seek someone else who will validate their view of things and form an alliance against the person who disagrees. Together these two oversimplify the situation by thinking of themselves as "good guys" in relation to the "bad guy," that is, the outsider who gets labeled as wrong, bad, sick, or helpless. There are a number of common types of triangles that may occur in families.

- Marital triangles typically involve a child, an in-law, an affair, a job, or a friend who becomes the focus of the couple's attention, diverting focus away from the tension in the couple relationship. A child may unify parents by being "sick" or bad or forming an alliance with one parent to the exclusion of the other.
- Three generational triangles (more common in single-parent families living in three-generational households) predictably involve grandparent and grandchild siding together against a parent who is in the outside position, labeled incompetent, "sick," "mean," "wrong," or "bad."
- Sibling triangles tend to occur when parents regard one child as "the good seed" and another as "the bad seed," or one as the caretaker and another as incompetent.

Triangles occur not only in families, but in all human relationship systems: including work, friendship networks, communities, business, politics, and, of course, also in international politics. They are more dysfunctional when they become rigidified and when they are not overtly acknowledged. Triangulation is problematic because you give up some of your integrity to form the alliance. In other words, each time we get into a triangle we give up a little of ourselves to create stability in the relationship and to lower anxiety. Triangulation is also problematic because whatever we have avoided dealing with in the original relationship by forming the triangle gets pushed underground, creating a more closed system that is less open to new information. This contributes to fear and anxiety about openness in future relationships. (See video *Triangles and Family Therapy: Strategies and Solutions*. Available from www.psychotherapy.net.)

When two people are in the alliance against a third, they tend to become less able to disagree with each other for fear the partner might move toward the "enemy." In this way, triangles get rigidified and the initial difficulties between people do not get worked out.

Triangles tend to expand out into interlocking triangles, extending dysfunction throughout the system. Many times, given the patriarchal and other structural arrangements in which family relationships have been embedded, triangles reflect prejudices and inequities along lines of social class, gender, race or culture, disability, sexual orientation, and other dimensions in the larger system as well.

In family relationships, triangles often become particularly painful because members are dependent on each other for support and self-validation throughout their lives, and because, unlike other systems, families are entered only by birth, marriage, or adoption and can be left only by death, if even then.

BEETHOVEN FAMILY TRIANGLES

The family of the composer Ludwig von Beethoven was dominated throughout by triangles, which may help us understand the process of triangulation and thus figure out how to de-triangulate in our own families (**see Genogram 5.5: Beethoven Family**).

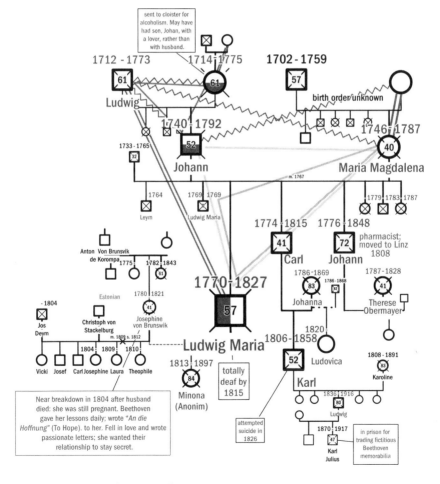

Genogram 5.5: Beethoven Family

Ludwig von Beethoven
GL Archive/Alamy Stock Photo

Beethoven's father, Johann, the only surviving son in his own family, was held close by his powerful, successful father, also named Ludwig, excluding Johann's mother, Maria, who had been sent away to a cloister for her struggles with alcoholism (**see Figure 5.1: Triangles of Beethoven's Parents with Their Parents**). Beethoven's mother, Maria, had an alliance with her mother after the premature death of her father. Maria had married at sixteen, but her first husband and an infant son died soon after. Undoubtedly those losses of her father, her first child, and her first husband played into what happened in her second marriage and with her later children, as did her mother's attitude toward her second husband, Johann Beethoven. Both of Beethoven's parents were thus tied to their own same-sexed parent, who feared losing them and strenuously disapproved of their marriage, on the notion that their partners were unworthy. So their marriage occurred in the context of two primary triangles with their families of origin. (In fact, recent DNA of Beethoven's hair suggests that Beethoven's father may have been a product of an affair his mother had, and not part of the Beethoven line, thus adding one more triangle to the Beethoven family. This paternal grandfather had a difficult relationship with Beethoven's father, and died when Beethoven was three. But Beethoven revered this grandfather all his life and had his portrait with him until the day he died! (*The New York Times*, 2023).

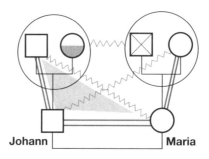

Johann   Maria

Figure 5.1: Triangles of Beethoven's Parents with Their Parents

In any case, Maria and Johann von Beethoven had seven children, of whom only three survived. The first child, Ludwig Maria, died six days after birth in 1769. The second, Ludwig Maria von Beethoven, the great composer, was born on December 16, 1770, and was given the same name as the baby who had died. Perhaps not surprisingly, he grew up confusing his birthdate with that of his dead brother and namesake. From birth he seems to have been part of a sibling triangle with his parents and his lost brother, with whom he felt he could never compare (**see Figure 5.2: Triangle of Beethoven, Parents, and Dead Brother**). Beethoven was also involved in a three-generational triangle with his father and paternal grandfather, also named Ludwig (**see Figure 5.3: Triangle of Beethoven with Father and Grandfather**). His grandfather was a successful wine merchant, talented singer, and choirmaster of Bonn. Though he died when Ludwig was only three, his grandson continued to idolize him

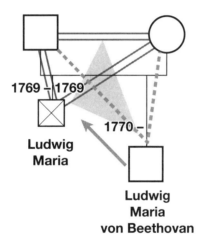

Figure 5.2: Triangle of Beethoven, Parents, and Dead Brother

with something bordering on hero worship. The grandfather had indeed been talented and successful, but also domineering and intrusive toward his only son, Johann, who was amiable and submissive in his youth, but lacked talent and initiative. To make matters worse, the grandfather repeatedly broadcast his contemptuous view that his son would amount to nothing, calling him "Johann the Loafer." Johann fulfilled his father's prophecy, becoming an abusive drunkard, cruel and arbitrary in his demands on young Ludwig to practice, and an embarrassment to the whole family. (It is especially interesting to read about these patterns in light of the likelihood that Johann was not actually the father of Ludwig the composer.)

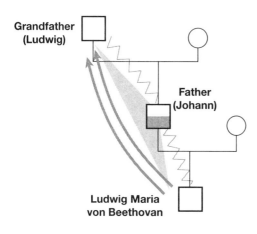

Figure 5.3: Triangle of Beethoven with Father and Grandfather

In the nuclear family, Beethoven, as the oldest of three surviving children out of seven, ended up in a painful triangle with his parents **(see Figure 5.4: Triangle of Beethoven with His Parents)**. Although he defended his father fiercely against outsiders and intervened desperately when the police came to arrest the father for drunkenness, Beethoven could hardly have avoided being drawn into a triangle with his parents on the side of his sad, gentle, long-suffering mother, a triangle from which he tried to escape as a child by isolating himself. His mother's death of tuberculosis, when he was only seventeen, placed him in charge of the family. At this point his father largely gave in to his alcoholism. Ludwig had to become the father's guardian, even being paid the father's pension, which embarrassed him and greatly humiliated the father. Nowhere in his extensive correspondence does Beethoven refer to his father by name, and when his father was dying, Beethoven left home.

The relationships of Beethoven's adult life were also characterized by triangles. Early on he became involved with a series of unattainable women (either married or otherwise attached), with whom, not surprisingly, he was always the outsider. Sometimes being the outsider in a triangle is preferable,

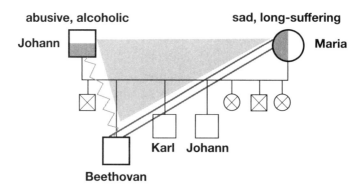

Figure 5.4: Triangle of Beethoven with His Parents

because one can play the role of romantic hero without actually having to make a commitment, and this may have been true for Beethoven.

This pattern continued for years. Then he fell totally in love with a woman known to history only as his "immortal beloved," and there has been speculation ever since about her identity, but recent research seems to clarify that she was Josephine von Brunsvik, whom Beethoven had met in 1799 when she came to Vienna, and he gave her piano lessons. She then married. But her husband died suddenly while she was pregnant with her fourth child. Soon afterward, Josephine, in a distraught state, reconnected with Beethoven, who resumed almost daily piano lessons with her and seems to have fallen in love with her. He wrote a song for her—"An Die Hoffnung" ("To Hope")—but she wanted their relationship to remain secret, apparently thinking it would be difficult for him to take on the role of father to her four children. In February 1810 Josephine was pressured by her family to marry again, this time to a man she did not love, with whom she had two more daughters. The birth-date of the first daughter was kept secret for years, apparently because she was conceived before her parents' marriage. After finding out her husband was involved in an embezzlement scandal, Josephine left him shortly thereafter. In early June 1812, she and Beethoven met again, possibly by chance. But his hopes for their relationship were reignited.

Beethoven's letter to his "immortal beloved" was written with a pencil she had given him the night before and in the hope that their love would bring them together. "My angel, my very self . . . can our love endure without . . . our demanding everything from one another; can you alter the fact that you are not wholly mine, that I am not wholly yours. . . . However much you love me—my love for you is even greater. . . . My thoughts rush to you, my immortal beloved . . . waiting to know whether Fate will hear our prayer—To face life I must live altogether with you or never see you. . . . Oh, do continue to love me—never misjudge your lover's most faithful heart."

She, however, did not follow through with committing herself to him, and instead soon went back to her husband. Beethoven's rejection in this relationship with her and her husband led him finally to give up on having a love relationship altogether (**see Figure 5.5: Triangle of Beethoven with His "Immortal Beloved"**). It is interesting that Josephine had a baby daughter born nine months exactly after her July 3 encounter with Beethoven. She named this child Minona, which spelled backward is "Anonim!"

Beethoven's letter to his "immortal beloved" was found among his belongings when he died. It is unclear whether he ever sent it to her. He never again had a serious involvement with a woman. Instead, he turned back to his

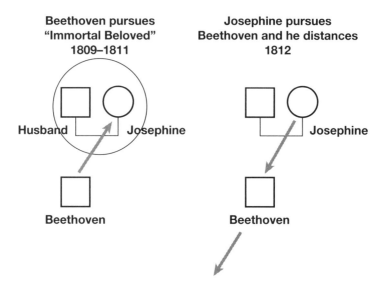

Figure 5.5: Triangle of Beethoven with His "Immortal Beloved"

family of origin and became embroiled in several destructive and intrusive triangles with his brothers' families. His relationships with his two younger brothers had been intense for years, having reached the point of violence more than once, always followed by emotional scenes of reconciliation.

He almost never spoke of his youngest brother, Johann, by name, usually referring to him by leaving a blank space or using an epithet such as "pseudo-brother," "brain-eater," "my ass of a brother," or "brother Cain." When he learned his brother was living unmarried with his partner, Theresa, he was enraged and tried to break up their union (**Figure 5.6: Triangle with Beethoven, Brother Johann, and Theresa**). Years before, he had tried unsuccessfully, but in a similar manner, to prevent his older brother Karl from marrying his wife Johanna (**see Figure 5.7: Triangle with Beethoven, Brother Karl, and Johanna**), although at times he also played the role of protector to Johanna against Karl's violence. Like their father, Karl often beat his son, Karl, to make him obey, and Johanna was not spared either. In 1811 Karl had denounced his wife, charging that she had stolen money from him. She was convicted and sentenced to a month of house arrest, even though any "stolen" money would have been her own, because of the large dowry and inheritance she had brought into the marriage.

Beethoven would listen to nothing negative about this brother, though some of his friends believed that Karl was taking advantage of him and even being dishonest. When one friend finally took it upon himself to speak directly about the brother's mistreatment of Beethoven, the latter closed his ears and refused to speak to his friend for ten years.

In 1815, the day before Karl died, he wrote a will providing for Johanna and

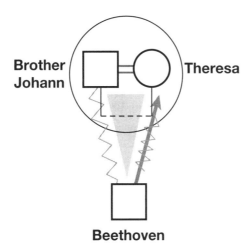

Figure 5.6: Triangle with Beethoven, Brother Johann, and Theresa

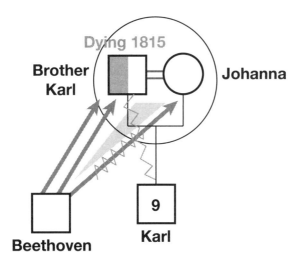

Figure 5.7: Triangle with Beethoven, Brother Karl, and Johanna

Ludwig to be co-guardians for his son, Karl. Beethoven, learning about this, intervened and compelled his brother to change the will, leaving him as sole guardian. Realizing that Ludwig wanted to exclude Johanna from joint guardianship, Karl added another paragraph to his will later that day, which read:

Having learned that my brother . . . desires after my death to take wholly to himself my son Karl. . . . I have found it necessary to add to my will that I by no means desire that my son be taken from his mother, but that he shall always . . . remain with his mother, to which end his guardianship is to be exercised by her as well as by my brother. (Solomon, 1977, p. 234)

In spite of this, Beethoven moved immediately after Karl's death to attain sole custody of his nephew and to have Johanna declared unfit even to have visiting privileges (see **Figure 5.8: Triangle with Beethoven's Nephew**). The struggle went on for years, with the nephew trapped between his loyalty and affection for his mother and his dutiful respect for his strange but famous and seemingly well-meaning uncle. Beethoven was at this time an unkempt, eccentric bachelor of forty-five, preoccupied with composing, though he had alienated most of his patrons by then. He was totally deaf, often in pain and in very poor health, not the best situation to take responsibility for a nine-year-old. Over the course of various court battles, Johanna won back custody from Beethoven, though he continued his pursuit and retrieved the nephew again. He was intrusive, abusive, inconsistent, and extremely overprotective of his nephew. He used his brother's earlier unjustified accusation of Johanna's embezzlement as justification for obtaining custody. He saw himself as a divinely authorized and heroic rescuer of his poor, unhappy nephew and became convinced that Johanna had destructive powers. He applauded his nephew whenever he repudiated his mother. If one did not know the history of triangles in this family, his behavior would have seemed mystifying indeed.

Beethoven's nephew Karl
INTERFOTO/Alamy Stock Photo

Perhaps it was predictable that, when on several occasions Beethoven moved toward a rapprochement with Johanna, Karl reacted negatively (see **Figure 5.9: Triangle with Nephew When Beethoven Moved Closer to Johanna**). Such is the nature of triangles that even though they may be hurtful and destructive for all involved, systems tend to resist change. Painful as it must have been for Karl to be pulled between his mother and uncle, he was also threatened when they seemed to draw together. In 1822, when Johanna became ill and was unable to pay for her medicines, Beethoven took over a portion of a debt she owed and soon determined to help her financially.

Karl, by then sixteen years old, protested vigorously against his uncle's proposed generosity to his mother, maligning her in an attempt to forestall a rapprochement between her and his uncle. His fear of closeness between them is understandable from the perspective of triangles. As long as they were

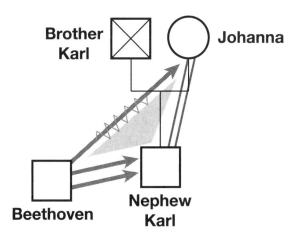

Figure 5.8: Triangle with Beethoven's Nephew

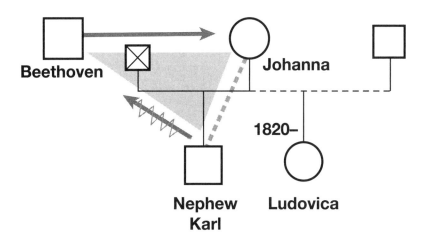

Figure 5.9: Triangle with Nephew When Beethoven Moved Closer to Johanna

fighting over him, his role was pivotal. But if they joined forces, he might end up the outsider.

Karl and his mother had become estranged after she gave birth out of wedlock in 1820 to a daughter conceived with a well-to-do man. The child was named Ludovica, an interesting choice of name, given her long conflicts with Ludwig! Very possibly the intense hostilities between Ludwig and Johanna reflected an underlying attraction. As Beethoven continued to move toward her, Karl's feeling of threat seems to have diminished, and for some time they appeared to reconnect. This reconciliation coincided precisely with Beethoven's composing the "Ode to Joy" for his Ninth Symphony. This was the most harmonious period in Beethoven's relationship with his nephew who worked as his secretary and spent weekends and summers with him.

However, by 1825 Beethoven again became suspicious of Karl and fearful that he had again been seeing his mother. A number of factors may have intensified the triangle at this time. Perhaps Beethoven, who seems to have been petrified of closeness, was uneasy in a good relationship with his nephew, as much as he coveted it. Perhaps Karl's emergence into young adulthood was threatening to Beethoven, or perhaps Beethoven's deafness along with his heavy drinking were increasing his sense of isolation and powerlessness. There may also have been changes in Johanna's life that we do not know about.

The conflicts between uncle and nephew reached a climax when Beethoven began stalking his nephew and withholding money from him. Karl then began sneaking visits to his mother, exacerbating Beethoven's worst fears. He would not leave Karl alone. Finally, despairing of any other solution, Karl tried to shoot himself in the head. He survived but was hospitalized and his feelings of being tormented by Beethoven were made public. The crisis seems to have relieved pressure on the system. Beethoven's dream of somehow fusing with his nephew and becoming his father—was broken. The suicide attempt brought in outside influence from doctors, who confronted Beethoven about his nephew's feelings. Though Beethoven sought other explanations for the suicide attempt, Karl's explanation was "weariness of imprisonment." After this Karl became better able to insist on his right to have his own relationship with his mother: "I do not want to hear anything that is derogatory to her; it is not for me to be her judge. . . . In no event shall I treat her with greater coldness than has been the case heretofore . . . (seeing my mother) will not prevent you and me from seeing each other as often as you wish" (Solomon, 1988, p. 284).

Karl decided to enter the military, which Beethoven helped him to do. During the last period of his life, Beethoven finally agreed to visit his surviving brother, Johann, from whom he had been cut off because of prior conflicts and he did so with his nephew (see **Figure 5.10: De-Triangulating with Nephew and Brother Johann**).

Perhaps anticipating his own mortality, he wanted to put his life in slightly better perspective during his last months. He ended on good terms with Karl, who became his sole inheritor. He reconciled also with Johanna, who, in the end was the only family member present at his death. Three days before he died, he wrote a codicil to his will, specifying that she would inherit his entire estate if Karl died unmarried, as appeared possible, since he was in

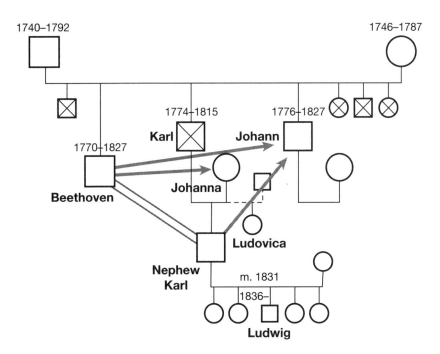

Figure 5.10: De-Triangulating with Nephew and Brother Johann

the military.

Beethoven's life reflects two classic patterns of triangulation. In his romantic relationships he played the role of outsider with women, the "other" lover—a peripheral, safe role, which protected him from the responsibility and dangerous power of his childhood triangles, in which he had been forced to take far too much responsibility as a child.

After he gave up the dream of having a family of his own, he intruded himself aggressively into other people's relationships, attempting fusion and creating conflict and cutoff all around him in the families of his two brothers, even though he was intending to create a loving family. In the end, possibly through the remedial efforts of Johanna and Karl, he seems to have achieved, for the first time, some sense of connection without fusion or triangulating. Without knowing the history of triangles in the Beethoven family it would be extremely difficult to fathom his stormy relationship with his sisters-in-law, nephew Karl, or Karl's suicide attempt.

Tracking the patterns of communication, fusion, cutoff, and symptom development in your own family can open up new perspectives on your family's patterns of communication as well as on your own family triangles. You may be surprised to learn that, as with the Beethoven family, the fusion, conflicts, and cutoffs are not always what they seem.

TOWARD DE-TRIANGULATING

Working to de-triangulate relationships in your family is a key part of the journey to go home again in a new way. It involves paying attention to the patterns you have been drawn into and disentangling yourself from them to develop a personal relationship with each person in your family (Bowen, 1978). Tracking the triangles and learning to de-triangulate are among the most important tasks to free yourself in order to go home again and have it be a different experience.

De-triangulating oneself is no simple task. It's a complex undertaking that offers a deep and enriching reward. But it takes a lot of hard work. The first step is to understand that you have a triangulated relationship involving yourself and two others. Then you have to see the triangle and understand the purposes that is serves.

Consider the case of Molly Haskell, a New York journalist, who displayed great insight and awareness about a triangle that developed between herself, her mother—who wanted fusion with her—and her husband, with whom her mother developed a deep sense of rivalry. Even though in her head Haskell knew that mother-in-law triangles are so commonplace as to be material for cartoons and jokes, she could not keep herself from getting hooked into the "ferocity" of the triangle. "It was a tragedy for me that the two people I loved most couldn't get along, yet it was a situation that I, in my own dividedness, had created. Only children . . . expect those they love to love each other, and the child in me persisted long after the adult should have taken over and accepted the inevitable. And yet, beloved of triangles, creators of triangles by our very birth, how is it possible not to keep recreating them, and reinserting our mediating and trouble-making selves into their midst?" (Haskell, 1990, p. 25).

Haskell describes how difficult it is to be the third player when two others are alienated—how hard it is not to get caught up in the pattern yourself. "Basically, their pained looks and noises would pass each other by and hit me, like magnetized arrows, and settle in my stomach. The cocktail hour was our Armageddon. . . . Andrew, who was partially deaf anyway and whose voice had a tendency to rise with the least

Molly Haskell
ZUMA Press, Inc./Alamy Stock Photo

emotion, would unwittingly interrupt Mother. Mother would wince; I would feel her wince and cringe; I would be angry with her for her fastidiousness, angry with Andrew for his boorishness as we turned into a Tennessee Williams parody of ourselves. Andrew the elemental brute; Mother the impossibly refined hostess, and me, rigid with the sense of my two halves breaking apart, feeling vaguely responsible" (Haskell, 1990, p. 25).

As Haskell describes so well, it is exceedingly difficult to be friends with two people who are at war with each other, because each wants to be your best friend. The sides of the triangle generally have more to do with the emotional needs of the system than with the characteristics of the players. It was not really Andrew's "boorishness" that was the problem, but rather the threat he represented to Haskell's mother's fantasy of fusion with her daughter. As Haskell describes it, Andrew represented the antithesis of what her mother had raised her to be: "The ladylike daughter of the Old Confederacy, who would . . . join the Garden Club and settle down and raise a family nearby. Andrew was my rejection of that dream staring her in the face" (Haskell, 1990, p. 26).

A person caught between two others might indeed become symptomatic, shifting the triangle so that the two "enemies" are forced to join together to care for him or her. Or a healthier approach would be for a person in Haskell's role to de-triangulate by getting out of the way and leaving the other two to relate to each other directly.

We conclude this chapter by offering questions you can use to guide you on your journey to learn about your family's patterns of communication, emotional closeness, distance, and triangulation so you can ultimately free yourself to go home again, but have it be a different and more rewarding experience.

QUESTIONS ABOUT COMMUNICATION, RELATIONSHIPS, AND TRIANGLES IN YOUR FAMILY

- What were the rules of communication in your family? For example, what topics were discussed and what topics were avoided? Who spoke to whom about what? What were the rules around emotional expression? What were the rules around how to handle conflict?
- How were the rules of communication transmitted? Were the rules overt or covert? Who conveyed them?
- How did family rules influence how life-cycle events were experienced (e.g., births, deaths, leaving home, marriage, divorce, child-rearing practices, illness, retirement)?
- Which family members were extremely close?
- Who was always in conflict? Who didn't speak to whom? How did others react when two were in conflict or cutoff?
- Who were the most frequent symptom bearers? What symptoms did they show? How did the family respond to the symptoms?
- What were the rules for each gender in the family? What did they view as the ideal male and the ideal female? Were there family members who broke out of the traditional gender stereotypes? Were there women or men whose symptoms might have reflected their difficulty accepting gender constraints (e.g., a poetic, gentle man, who became alcoholic or a feisty, brilliant woman worn down by having no outlet beyond childcare and housekeeping)?
- What were the splits and alliances in the family? Who had a caretaker/caretakee relationship? a pursuer/distancer relationship? An intense love/hate relationship?
- How did family members react to change? By silence? Rigidity? Shutting down? Trying to hold on to the past? Escaping into pipedreams of the future? Blaming others? Blaming themselves?
- What labels did each family member have: battle-ax, sad sack, miser, weirdo, success story?

- How did the family react to stress? Drawing together? Becoming more separate? Did certain family members have strong reactions such as silence, constant talking, changing the subject, or becoming authoritarian?
- What were the major family triangles? Were there particular types of triangles in the family that repeated over the generations: husband/wife/mother-in-law; husband/wife/affair; father/mother/sick-bad-special child; two close siblings and a third outsider sibling?

Chapter 6
Death and Other Losses

The single most important thing to know about Americans . . . is
that . . . (they) think death is optional.

—JANE WALMSLEY
Brit-Think; Ameri-Think

If I do not connect myself with my own past. . . . I will remain adrift from
it. Those whom I have loved in the past cannot catch hold of me, for they
are dead. It is I who must catch them.

—AUDRE LORDE
Sister Outsider

Death ends a life, but not a relationship, which struggles on in the survivors'
minds, seeking some resolution which it may never find.

—ROBERT ANDERSON PLAY
I Never Sang for My Father

Coming to terms with death and other traumatic losses is the most difficult experience we face in life. In fact, if you could explore only one issue to
understand your family history, we would suggest the issue of loss. More than
any other human experience, loss puts us in touch with what matters in our
lives. Loss may strengthen survivors, bringing out their creativity and spur-
ring them on to accomplishment, or it may leave behind a destructive legacy,
all the more powerful if it is not dealt with. Families may also follow patterns
set up by losses in earlier generations that they know nothing about. By examining our family's multigenerational responses to loss, we can learn a great
deal about how our family operates, what happens when they get stuck, and
possibilities for changing these patterns.

Facing death, especially of a family member, can be a life-changing experience, making us question the meaning and purpose of our own lives and
stimulating us to clarify our priorities and savor our lives more fully.

We all hope that death will occur at a point when family members are at peace with each other and when there is a sense of completion about relationships. But we know this frequently doesn't happen. Untimely deaths are especially difficult to integrate. Regrets about an unfinished relationship can haunt a person throughout life, and when accounts are left unsettled, a great vacuum may remain.

All families are marked by their losses, which generally require family members to deal with each other in an intimate way at a vulnerable time. This can be particularly difficult for families that are not close. Siblings who have had little to do with each other for years may suddenly be forced to share wrenching experiences. This has the potential to bring a family together, but it can also cause old conflicts to resurface. As with other pivotal family experiences, if things do not get better, they will likely get worse.

All change in life requires loss. Death, of course, is not the only loss. Marital separation or divorce, chronic illness, addiction, lack of a job or home, or becoming disabled also involve loss—the loss of our dreams and expectations, as well as real physical and emotional losses. All losses require mourning, acknowledging the giving up of the relationship, and allowing people to move on in life. When families do not adequately mourn their losses and their feelings go underground, they cannot get on with life. They may blame themselves or each other for a death or try to mold others into replacements for their lost person or keep themselves from experiencing closeness again. The avoidance of the pain of loss is what tends to become most problematic.

Reorganizing a family system to function without the dead person is a complex and often painful process, entailing perhaps a shift in caretaking roles, leadership functions, the social network, or the family's focus, as when an only child dies, or an emotional reorganization of the generational hierarchy, as when the last grandparent dies. Surviving family members, strengthened by the shared experience of loss, can focus more clearly on what they want to do with the rest of their lives and with their remaining relationships. Ultimately, moving beyond loss involves a reinvestment in other relationships and life pursuits.

JAMES BALDWIN'S REFLECTIONS ON THE DEATH OF HIS ABUSIVE STEPFATHER

James Baldwin often looked to the past to make sense of the future. When he was nineteen, and his stepfather died, Baldwin experienced a profound learning process and came to a very different understanding of himself and his life. Never having known who his own biological father was, he had grown up searching

James Baldwin
© SZ Photo/Brigitte Friedrich/
Bridgeman Images

James Baldwin and his youngest
sister, Paula, born the day their father
died
Collection of the Smithsonian National
Museum of African American History and
Culture, Gift of The Baldwin Family

for a father figure. He had an almost obsessive negative preoccupation with his stepfather, a minister from New Orleans, who his mother had married when he was two, and with whom she had eight more children, the last one, Paula, born on the day the stepfather died. The stepfather had struggled in his last years financially and emotionally, before dying at sixty-one in 1943.

Baldwin put off visiting him in the hospital because, he told his mother, he hated him. But he later realized: "This was not true . . . I *had* hated him, and I wanted to hold on to this hatred. I did not want to look at him as a ruin . . . once hate is gone, you will be forced to deal with the pain" (Baldwin, p. 75).

Finally, he went to the hospital with his stepfather's older sister, whom he and his siblings had grown up imagining they lived with to escape their abusive father. She quarreled all her life with her brother but she was one of the few people in the world who had loved him. Now she gave her nephew a hard time for smoking, but he knew it was because she couldn't bear her brother's dying. "Neither could I endure the reality of her despair, her unstated bafflement as to what had happened to her brother's life, and her own" (p. 75).

The father's funeral took place on Baldwin's nineteenth birthday. As he saw it, the only other person whose relationship with his father rivaled his aunt's was his mother, who was not there because she had just given birth. Baldwin thought the preacher's eulogy was praising a man no one in their family had ever met. Then he began to think about his siblings, changing their diapers, feeding them, scolding them. Then suddenly someone was singing one of the father's favorite songs and it brought him way back to his early relationship with his father: "Sitting on his knee, in the hot, enormous, crowded church . . . I had forgotten, in the rage of my growing up, how proud my father had been of me when I was little. Apparently, I had had a voice and my father had liked to show me off before the members of the church. I had forgotten what he had looked like when he was pleased, but now I remembered that he had always been grinning with pleasure when my solos ended. I even remembered certain expressions on his face when he teased my mother—had he loved her? I would never know" (p. 77).

He wondered when it had all begun to change. His father had not always been cruel. He remembered his father's face as he soothed his crying when Baldwin scraped his knee. He found himself trying to realize that his father had once been kind and nurturing, until for unknown reasons that kindness had disappeared. He then remembered their fights, which were made worse by Baldwin's handling his emotions with silence, which, he realized in retrospect, was the worst possible response.

Then he recalled the one time in all their lives together when he and his father had really spoken to each other. It was shortly before he left home and his father asked him abruptly: "You'd rather write than preach, wouldn't you?" Baldwin was astonished, "Because it was a real question." And he answered "Yes." That was all they said. "It was awful to remember that this was all we had *ever* said" (pp. 79–80). Baldwin was confronted with layers of loss in his relationship with his father: the loss because he and his father had never really spoken, and then the realization that there had been a moment when his father did actually speak to him and conveyed a real understanding of his needs, but Baldwin had failed to seize the opportunity and the moment was lost.

Baldwin's realizations at the funeral helped him re-examine his own past and his relationship to his father, but also his father's life, and connections to the others—his father's sister, his siblings, and his mother, wondering about her love for the father, but also imagining her at the very moment of the funeral up the street holding her newborn child. "Life and death so close together, and love and hatred, and right and wrong, said something to me which I did not want to hear . . . concerning the life of the man" (p. 81).

Baldwin realized that the charge that day was to keep his own heart free of hatred and despair. . . . "This intimation made my heart heavy and, now that my father was irrecoverable, I wished that he had been beside me so that I could have searched his face for the answers which only the future would give me now" (p 84).

Years later Baldwin addressed his book, *The Fire Next Time* (1962), to his nephew and namesake, focusing on many of the very insights he had learned at the time of his father's death. He imparted some of the wisdom he had gained when his father died to help his nephew make connections: "Dear James, . . . I keep seeing your face, which is also the face of your father, my brother. Like him you are tough, dark, vulnerable, moody—with a very definite tendency to sound truculent, because you want no one to think you are soft. He adds that in these dark tendencies his nephew may be also like the grandfather he never got a chance to meet, who, Baldwin tells him, had a terrible life and was defeated long before he died because he had come to believe what racist whites said about him.

Baldwin tells his nephew: "I have known both you and your father all your lives, have carried your Daddy in my arms and on my shoulders, kissed and spanked him and watched him learn to walk. . . . Other people cannot see what I see whenever I look into your father's face, for behind your father's face . . . are all those other faces which were his. Let him laugh . . . and I hear . . . his laughter as a child. Let him curse and I remember him falling down the cellar steps and howling. I remember with pain his tears, which my hand and your grandmother's so easily wiped away. But no one's hand can wipe away those tears he sheds invisibly today, which one hears in his laughter and in his speech and in his songs. I know what the world has done to my brother and how narrowly he has survived it."

Then Baldwin tries to advise his nephew how to handle resentments that have hurt his ancestors, remembering when his nephew was born: "Though your father and mother and grandmother . . . had every reason to be heavy-hearted, they were not. . . . For here you were, Big James, named for me . . . to be loved, baby, hard, at once and forever. To strengthen you against the loveless world. Remember that . . . if we had not loved each other, none of us would have survived. And now you must survive because we love you and for the sake of your children and your children's children" (p. 6).

Baldwin powerfully illustrates how the death of a family member can shed light on how a family can foster a deeper understanding of the relationships the deceased had with various family members. He used his understanding of the past to deepen his connections with other family members and to act in ways to support and protect future generations. Baldwin dared to see the present, even loss, in light of the hopes and dreams that came before and our need to carry our lives forward to those who will come after us. He used his awareness of his missed opportunity with his father to inspire the next generation to reevaluate their relationships with other family members and see loss always in the context of what has come before and what we need to protect for the future.

RESPONSES TO DEATH

Our society's widespread denial of death often means that people do not discuss how they want to die and how they want to be memorialized. A great many people make no will at all, in spite of the extreme hardship this can cause survivors. The quality of dying is often ignored in the service of prolonging life by whatever medical means necessary. In spite of the very positive care provided by hospice, which has been an extremely helpful development for many families dealing with the end of life, death still often occurs in a cold, sterile medical setting that allows little consideration for the family's personal experience. Families are often physically separated, leaving them even more vulnerable to disruption and isolation in the aftermath of loss, which complicates mourning.

Some people avoid contacts that remind them of the dead person. Men in particular often try to keep themselves from "breaking down." The emotional and physical burdens that follow death are still too often considered "women's work." Women typically handle the social and emotional tasks of bereavement, from the expression of grief and caretaking of the terminally ill to meeting the needs of surviving family members for support and nurturance, while men more typically manage the finances, arrange for the funeral, choose the coffin, and in general handle the "administrative" tasks of death, except for providing the food. While women are free to weep openly, men may deny, withdraw, and avoid their grief, fearing a loss of control. The reactions of each often make the other uncomfortable. Men generally take refuge in their work and distance from their wives' open mourning, while women experience their husbands' pulling away as a double loss. As one woman put it referring to the pain of the loss of one of her three sons: "Through my eyes flow the tears for our whole family." When a family member must grieve alone, the pain is that much worse. Men in our society are often deprived of sharing these key life experiences that are seen as women's responsibility. Society's denial of male vulnerability and the sanctions against men's emotional expressiveness undoubtedly contribute to marital distress after the loss of a family member and to the high rate of serious illness and suicide for men following the death of a spouse. When our society allows the full range of human experiences in bereavement as in other areas of family life, we will all surely benefit.

The death of a child seems to be the most devastating loss a family can experience. It can have a cataclysmic effect on the parents' health and marriage and leave lifelong scars for the siblings. Guilt feelings tend to be especially strong in the survivors. It is said that when your parent dies, you have lost your past, but when your child dies, you have lost your future. Because children are the receptacle of parents' hopes and dreams, families may often create an idealized image of a lost child, which is difficult for surviving children to live up to.

Death in the "prime of life" also brings special hardships. For the spouse, there is the loss of a helpmate and companion; for the children, there is the loss of a parent, perhaps the breadwinner or the caretaker; for the siblings and friends there is the loss of an age-mate with whom they expected to grow old; for the parents there is the wrenching of the death being "off time."

The manner of death also affects the family's response. When we are prepared as much as we can be, when the deceased has lived a long and fruitful life, and when it is a peaceful death with minimal pain, recriminations, or unfinished business, families generally come more easily to acceptance. Sudden death provides no opportunity to prepare or say goodbye. A murder, a suicide, or an accident, where others feel responsible, may leave especially deep scars. Suicides tend to be particularly toxic. The true circumstances of the death are frequently kept secret, which compounds the emotions families already feel when a life is ended intentionally and is likely to isolate them further.

At the other extreme are the deaths that come after a protracted period of illness or disability that may have drained family caretaking resources and required the family to live in a state of prolonged uncertainty. In such cases, the family may come to wish the person dead, to see an end to the pain and agony as well as relief from their burdens. The strain on the caretakers can take energy away from all other relationships and may leave a residue of guilt and ambivalence.

THE TIMING AND CIRCUMSTANCES
AROUND WHEN A DEATH OCCURS

To understand how losses in your family have been dealt with, you will want to explore the context in which the deaths have occurred, including the state of family relationships at the time of death and other stress factors associated in time, which are likely to have influenced your family's response to the loss. When there is guilt or shame about the loss or where there has been family conflict or estrangement at the time of death, the family may have been left with a bitter legacy, which is hard to undo.

Historical circumstances may also be important. For example, both JFK and Robert Kennedy experienced sudden, violent, premature deaths that devastated the nation and their families. But Robert's death in 1968 came at a time of great social upheaval and disorganization in our country, which intensified the resulting sense of disruption and loss, especially for his children. When JFK was assassinated, tragic as that was, his children were quite young. Conversely, many of Robert's children and their cousins were then in their adolescence, a time when their vulnerability to drugs and other reckless behavior put them at much greater risk than was experienced at the time of his brother's death. And many of them had serious problems in the aftermath of Robert Kennedy's death.

A loss that occurs on a holiday or anniversary can also be more traumatic. Sometimes such coincidental anniversary events seem to point up almost mystical connections. Both Thomas Jefferson and John Adams died on the fiftieth anniversary of the Declaration of Independence, July 4th, 1826. John Kennedy was shot on November 22, the same day that both his paternal great-grandfathers had died. Anthropologist Gregory Bateson's middle brother committed suicide on the birthday of the oldest brother, who had died a hero in World War I. Such coincidences are likely to intensify a sense of loss and the legacy of family anxiety around the anniversary. As individuals, we may also fear that we will die at the same age or same time of year as a same sex parent or a sibling with whom we have been identified. If deaths have occurred around Christmas or another important family holiday, they may also amplify the pain of that day for years to come.

Among the most difficult of all losses are those that are ambiguous. For example, when a family member disappears, there is some hope that the person may still be alive, and their psychological presence may remain in the family for years. Fantasies develop about the lost person's survival and return. A similar situation is created in the case of Alzheimer's disease or other catastrophic, degenerative illnesses or brain injury, where the person may be physically present but psychologically absent for years before death. Such ambiguous losses are extremely difficult to mourn and integrate.

THE IMPACT OF DEATH ON FAMILY ROLES AND RELATIONSHIPS

The role and function of the deceased person in the family and the resources available to fill in for the loss will also influence the family's ability to integrate the death. A person who has been a scapegoat may be hard to mourn. An alcoholic father who dies in a car crash may leave a legacy of guilt and resentment in which the death is compounded by the painful years that the family lived through with him. On the other hand, it is also generally difficult for the survivors to compete with the ghost of a dead hero—a supermother, a successful son—or anyone who has been a central figure in the family.

The loss of a parent or primary caretaker presents a most difficult challenge. Central caretaking and economic and emotional functions must be assumed by others. Sometimes uncles or aunts or grandparents can help to fill in the gap. But if practical or emotional resources are unavailable, the loss may be greatly compounded.

Consider again the death of Robert Kennedy. His loss not only came at a more difficult social era of our history than that of his older brothers, Joe in World War II and John in 1963, but it left a much greater leadership vacuum in the Kennedy family than did the other deaths. After John's death, Robert had taken over the caretaking role for their parents, for John's wife and children, and for many others in the family. But when Robert himself died five years later, his wife Ethel was pregnant with their eleventh child. There was no one who could fill in for him with his children, for his sister Pat, who had separated from her husband the very day his brother John was shot, or for the other members of the family who needed support.

Ted Kennedy, the only surviving brother, had always been the baby. Although he did eventually grow into a family leader, he was not prepared to do so at the time, and the tragedy left a huge vacuum for the entire extended family. What followed for the Kennedys were years of turmoil and problems for the next generation. In the end, fortunately, Ted Kennedy did transform his role, especially after his remarriage, becoming a tremendous resource to his own children, his nieces and nephews, and many of the next generation.

MOURNING

If myth, secrecy, and taboo surround a death and family members cannot talk about the loss, they may become more vulnerable to future losses. When families communicate openly about the death (no matter what the circumstances), and when they participate together in rituals that have meaning for them (e.g., funeral rites and visits to the grave), the loss becomes easier to integrate. Attempts to protect children or "vulnerable" members from the experience are likely to make mourning even more difficult.

Sharing the experience of a loss and finding some way to put it in context are important. A part of this sharing is joint storytelling about the life and death of the dead person, which can help the family integrate the loss by promoting their sense of familial, cultural, and human connectedness, empowering them to regain a sense of themselves as moving on in time from the past with the lost person into the future without the person. Family stories are an important facilitator and enhancer of the integration of loss. It seems important for families to be free to remember as well as to let go of memories.

Most funeral rituals incorporate traditions that link family members to previous generations, which, as with James Baldwin, can provide them a sense of belonging, even while they are experiencing the pain of loss. Rituals allow the person to see family history in the making, as the family stories of the life and death get told and retold.

Cultures differ greatly in their patterns of mourning—their rituals and the length of time considered appropriate to "complete" the mourning process. Within the dominant U.S. culture, which reflects Anglocentric values, the trend has been increasingly toward minimizing death rituals and expressions of mourning. Considerable social control is exercised over the process through legislation, custom, and public health and work regulations. Funeral rituals have been commercialized by the funeral industry. The allowable leave for bereavement in the workplace (usually one to three days) severely constrains families whose cultural values contrast with Anglocentric values. The failure to carry out death rituals can contribute to a family's experience of unresolved loss, a danger to both personal health and family relationships.

DYSFUNCTIONAL ADAPTATION TO LOSS

The process of mourning generally lasts for years, with each new season, holiday, and anniversary re-evoking the old sense of loss. When families cannot mourn, they may become locked in time—either in dreams of the past, the emotions of the present, or dread of the future. They may become unable to engage in the relationships they do have, fearing that to love again will mean further loss. Others focus exclusively on their dreams of the future, trying to fill in the gap left by the loss with new relationships formed on fantasy and escape from the pain. Usually those who cut short their mourning by rushing into the future find that the pain comes back to haunt them when the dreams give way to the realities of a new relationship. Problems that families have in managing other developmental transitions, such as marriage or, having or launching children, often reflect this inability to deal with previous loss.

In some families, the myths, secrets, and expectations that develop around a critical loss may be incorporated and passed down from parents to children. Some families, as we saw with Teddy Roosevelt, and will see with the Hepburns, and Fondas, stop all mention of the deceased, as if they could thus banish the pain. Some families even make the dead person's room into a memorial or mausoleum, as Queen Victoria did. The mythmaking entailed in such delusional responses may bind family members to each other in pathological ways or create psychological rifts among them. Such myths can naturally affect children, who may become replacements for family members who have died, even when they have no knowledge of the lost person they are replacing. Many of the rigid patterns we routinely observe in families—affairs, continuous unresolved conflict, alienation, isolation, fear of outsiders, repeated divorce, depression, severe anxiety, workaholism, escapism into TV, sports, or soap operas—may actually be compensations for people's inability to deal with loss.

Family psychiatrist Norman Paul grew up knowing nothing of his family's traumatic past and of his aunt, who had tragically killed her lover and then herself, leading his family a year later to change their name and move to the U.S. They never mentioned the trauma again. Paul became a psychiatrist preoccupied with issues of trauma and loss, with no awareness that he was in profound ways attempting to address his own family's unacknowledged traumatic loss until an aunt came and told him the history he had never known (see video about his theories and work on loss and his own family story: *Freeing Ourselves from the Ghosts of Our Past* at: www.psychotherapy.net). Often, as in this case, people are totally unaware of their family's loss history and are mystified by the forces influencing them.

THE HEPBURN FAMILY

Katharine Hepburn's family (**see Genogram 6.1: Hepburn Family**) provides a striking example of a family's ability to develop creative responses after the most stigmatizing of all deaths, suicide, even as such tragedies constricted their functioning. Members of the family had founded Corning glass and Houghton Mifflin publishers. They were among the most successful and independent thinking families in New England and Virginia.

When Katharine was thirteen, her sixteen-year-old brother Tom hung himself, while the two of them were visiting family friends on their Easter

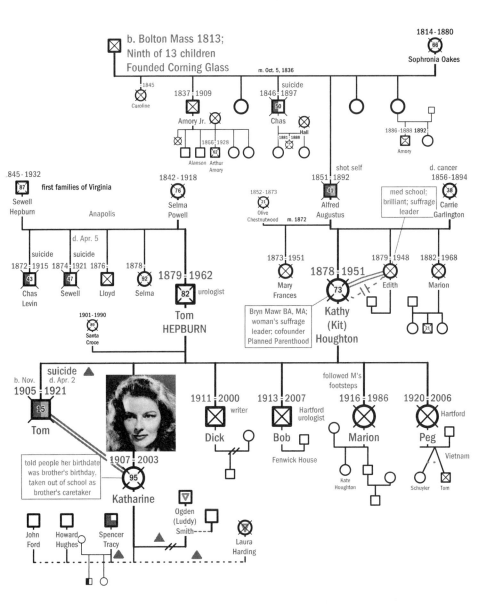

Genogram 6.1: Hepburn Family

Katharine Hepburn
Archive PL/Alamy Stock Photo

vacation. Katharine was the one who found his body. Tom had made a rope strong enough to hang himself out of his bedsheet. Their father, a successful urologist, told reporters: "My son was normal in mind and body. The taking of his own life can be accounted for only from a medical point, that he was suddenly afflicted with adolescent insanity" (Anderson, 1988, p. 182).

Katharine became obsessed with absolving her brother, reminding her father that her brother had been intrigued with the story of a Black

Hepburn children with their mother. Tom stands behind, Katharine is sitting on the left
Katharine Houghton Collection

man who could constrict his neck muscles to avoid dying at the hands of a lynch mob and had tried to hang himself once before. Dr. Hepburn then made a new announcement to reporters, explaining away the suicide as the result of a foolish schoolboy stunt: "I had entirely forgotten that (Tom) considered himself an expert in hanging by the neck in such a way as to look as if he were dying, to the entertainment of his brothers and sisters" (quoted in Anderson, 1988, pp. 185–186).

Katharine Hepburn's father, a Hartford urologist
Johns Hopkins Chesney Medical Archives

He went on to say that his son must have been "rehearsing" for a performance that night, though the death occurred about 4 a.m., showing the incredible lengths a family may go to avoid facing a painful reality. In her autobiography, written seventy years later, Kate maintained her brother died "under strange circumstances" and that his death was unexplained. She acknowledged that Tom's death must have tortured their parents. Neither parent ever mentioned his death again. Hepburn said death seemed to separate her from the world as she had known it until then (Hepburn, 1991).

Tom's suicide drew the family into itself. Tom had always been the family's great hope, but also vulnerable.

Katharine Hepburn's mother Kit, who became well known for women's rights activism
Alpha Stock/Alamy Stock Photo

Katharine Hepburn's aunt, Edith Hepburn Hooker, a well-known social worker, who cut off her sister after Tom's suicide
Alpha Stock/Alamy Stock Photo

His father had been pressuring him to follow in his own footsteps and enter Yale Medical School that fall, but Tom had been hesitant about that. Since childhood he had suffered various physical and emotional problems, including bouts of confusion and depression.

The parents had withdrawn Tom from school to protect him and they withdrew Katharine to be his companion. Since she was younger, this set her up as the caretaker of her older brother. After his suicide, all the children were withdrawn from school and tutored at home.

Hepburn did not mention in her autobiography that four other family members had died by suicide in her family, two on each side. Her maternal grandfather shot himself in the head at the age of forty-one when her mother was fourteen and her younger sisters were twelve and nine. Five years later this grandfather's brother Charles shot himself as well.

Her father's brother (also named Charles) killed himself at the age of forty-three by jumping out the window of his New York City home six years before her brother's suicide. Then, only three days after Tom's suicide, and even before the funeral, her father's brother, Sewell Hepburn, killed himself with carbon monoxide in the middle of the night in his garage. Again, the family made up a story that he "had a heart attack while working on his car." The fact that it was the middle of the night was omitted from the narrative. And from the time of Tom's suicide, Katharine began using her brother's birthday as her own, never revealing the truth until her autobiography seventy years later.

Katharine's mother, Kit, had been extremely close to her sister Edith since childhood. Their bond intensified when they were orphaned through their father's suicide and their mother's death of cancer two years later. Both sisters had married men who had gone to Johns Hopkins Medical School with Edith. Both sisters became suffrage leaders and activists. The two families spent summers together for many years. But Edith cut herself off from their family after Tom's suicide, apparently blaming the father's overbearing attitude toward his son and his physical punishment of his children for the son's suicide.

When Edith and her sister Kit were growing up, their father had felt humiliated at Corning glass by his oldest brother, Amory, who had inherited the business, which led to his suicide. After his death, Kit tried to arrange for her daughters to attend Bryn Mawr, to ensure that as women they would never be left helpless and dependent, as she had been. When the mother died, Kit, as older sister had to become mother to her two younger sisters, the three of them orphaned by the loss of both parents and left under the financial control of their uncle Amory, who despised them, especially Kit, and refused to support their education. Kit, then sixteen, became a fighter and went to court for the right to control her own money, a lifelong concern of her mother. She won the right to hire a lawyer to be her guardian. She then moved herself and her sisters to Bryn Mawr and went to college while caring for her sisters in defiance of her uncle. She went on to become a leader in the women's suffrage movement and with Margaret Sanger, became one of the founders of Planned Parenthood. The uncle's ongoing hostility toward Kit is illustrated in a letter he wrote to her when she married Tom Hepburn:

> Dear Katharine . . . My opinion of you is the same as it always has been—that you are an extravagant, deceitful, dishonest, worthless person. You have squandered thousands of dollars and left your honest debts unpaid. When you see Tom, please tell him I do not think he could do worse . . . Disgusted, Your affectionate Uncle A. Houghton, Jr. (Hepburn, 1991, p. 13)

Katharine said her father's favorite saying was "The truth will make you free." Indeed, the family was viewed with outrage in their neighborhood because the parents were so open

Katharine Hepburn's maternal uncle Amory, who controlled the nieces' money
CMGL 134305. Courtesy of the Rakow Research Library, Corning Museum of Glass, Corning, NY.

about sex, allowing Katharine, for example, to watch the childbirth of one of her younger siblings. But one topic could never be mentioned: the names of any of those who had died by suicide.

After Tom's death, the other Hepburn children became a self-contained system, with Katharine, now the eldest, taking responsibility for her younger siblings. She said that her brother's death "threw my mother and father and me very close together, very close." Shortly after the suicide she went through a period of serious behavior problems (vandalism, breaking and entering), symptoms that are not too surprising when we think about the extraordinary ordeal the family had been through and the pressure on her as the oldest surviving child. However, perhaps because of the legacy of her grandmother, who had elicited a deathbed promise that her daughters go to college, Kate went off to Bryn Mawr, her mother's alma mater and began to turn her life around. In the end she more than fulfilled her distinguished family's demands for high achievement, at the same time that she seems to have responded (as did her siblings) to the need of the family to remain close and in a certain emotional sense, to never leave home. One brother continued to live in the family's summer home. The other followed the father into the practice of urology at Hartford Hospital, living within blocks of the original family home. One sister followed closely in the mother's footsteps as a non-conformist, first in politics, and then author of books on Connecticut history. The other, a librarian, remained within ten minutes of the family home in West Hartford.

Even though Katharine married briefly and lived 3,000 miles away from her family for much of her adult life, she always sent her money home to her father, who supported her with an allowance for as long as he lived (Anderson, 1988). One close friend and biographer says that he could not recall a single conversation in which Hepburn did not mention her parents and the impact they had on her life. In her autobiography she wrote: "We were a happy family. We are a happy family. Mother and Dad were perfect parents." (Hepburn, 1991, p. 27). Of their impact she said: "The single most important thing anyone needs to know about me is that I am totally, completely the product of two damn fascinating individuals, who happened to be my parents" (Anderson, 1988, p. 14).

Her loyalty to her parents seems to have elicited a price in her personal life. As she said herself, "I never really left home—not really" (Anderson, 1988, p. 25). She kept dolls and stuffed animals on her bed well into adulthood. And even at the age of eighty, she spoke of the family home (then owned by her brother) as her home and thought of herself as the dutiful daughter.

There were complex reasons for this, not the least of which was another family secret, Katharine's gender fluidity. A tomboy from childhood, Katharine shaved her head from age nine to thirteen and called herself "Jimmy" (Anderson, 1988, p. 140). She had relationships short and long throughout her life with both men and women. There were obvious societal reasons for secrecy, which reinforced the family's personal dynamics. Her sudden and brief marriage to Luddy (Ogden) Smith, appears to have been a cover for both of them. He took his lover, and she took hers, Laura Harding, with them on their honeymoon. Smith remained a close friend of the Hepburn family for the rest of his life.

Hepburn's twenty-five-year relationship with Spencer Tracy seems to have fit well with patterns evolved in her earlier life. He was an alcoholic, seventeen years her senior, who already had liver and kidney damage when they met. One might say he was a doomed man, and very moody, reminiscent of her brother. In addition, although separated from his wife for many years, he was resolved never to divorce her, an attitude that was attributed in part to his guilt about abandoning her and their deaf son, and in part to his Irish

Katharine Hepburn with her long-term partner, Laura Harding
New York Daily News Archive/Getty Images

Catholicism. The combination of Tracy's tough masculinity and his vulnerability seemed irresistible.

Hepburn's career took second place to his throughout their relationship, and he always got first billing. Between 1942 and 1950 she made ten films— four alone and six with Tracy. The four she made alone were compromises to stay close to him. Indeed, he was reported to have frequently been abusive to her, although in private she had certain power over him (Porter, 2004). One senses a repeat of the caring younger sister, who became a functional oldest. She was forced to spend a lot of her time caretaking Tracy, who was like a replacement for her brother. But perhaps it allowed her to hold onto her brother, and to have more privacy because their relationship had to remain more clandestine than is usually available to stars; she could maintain her own residence and loyalty to her family of origin, as well as to her other relationships with her longtime partner, heiress Laura Harding, and other partners, including Claudette Colbert.

But the original losses seem never to have been dealt with. Hepburn pondered about her brother's death: "Did it push me further into make-believe? Who knows? I would think it must have" (Anderson, 1988, p. 187). The family seems to have made conflicting requests of their children: "Be independent, successful, and fight for what you want." But also: "Never leave home." This required another rule: "Let's pretend." As often happens in families stressed by tragedy, Katharine and her siblings seem to have found ways to be successful and independent. Katharine became one of the most successful American screen actresses of all time, and yet, in a certain sense, she never left home.

Considering the Hepburn family legacies, you may want to think about secrets kept in your own family and what they perhaps cost family members. To what extent did certain children play out legacies reflecting struggles of earlier generations as with the painful suicides and disruptions in the Hepburn–Houghton families? But also, what resiliencies may have developed, as in the Hepburn family, through the strength of women to be independent and successful, and to fight for what they wanted in life?

THE KENNEDY FAMILY

The Kennedy family, to whom we have already been referring, is another in which multigenerational patterns of dealing with untimely loss appears to have had a profound impact, right up to the present day (**see Genogram 6.2: Kennedy Family**). The image of three-year-old John Kennedy Jr., born on Thanksgiving Day two weeks after his father's election to the presidency, saluting his father's casket on that cold November day, was heartbreaking and reminded everyone who saw it of the fragility of our lives. Then five years later Robert Kennedy's funeral, his ten children in mourning and Ethel pregnant with the last, Ted's voice cracking in his eulogy for yet another brother.

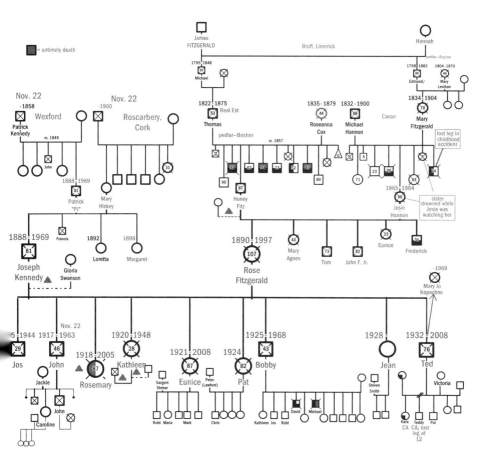

Genogram 6.2: Kennedy Family

John Kennedy himself had been a stand-in for his older brother, Joe Jr., who had died in World War II. The oldest sister, Kit Kennedy, had lost her first husband in the war as well, and then died herself a few years later at twenty-eight in a plane crash with her fiancé.

A year after the mantle of leadership was passed to Ted came his confused explanation of his role in the death of Mary Jo Kopechne in a baiting accident at Chappaquiddick. In the next generation there followed the ter-

John Fitzgerald Kennedy
Courtesy of the National Archives and Records Administration. Series: Cecil Stoughton's White House Photographs.

John Kennedy Jr. at his father's funeral
UPI/Alamy Stock Photo

rible inglorious death of David Kennedy whose drug overdose seemed so much the fallout of previous losses. Then Michael Kennedy died at thirty-nine in a dangerous family skiing game. John Kennedy Jr. died at the same age, with his wife and sister-in-law in a plane crash on a dangerous flight in 1999. Kara Kennedy, who like her brother Teddy Jr. had survived cancer, died at 51 after a workout; Mary Kennedy, ex-wife of Robert Kennedy Jr., died by suicide in 2010; Bobby Kennedy's granddaughter Saorise Kennedy died at twenty-two of an accidental drug overdose in 2019, and another granddaughter Maeve Kennedy McKean, daughter of Kathleen Kennedy Townsend, former lieutenant governor of Maryland, drowned with her three-year-old son in the Chesapeake Bay in 2020.

We tend to be fairly familiar with the losses in our own families within our lifetime. Usually, we know less about the losses that have come before—losses that may have very much shaped our family's myths and attitudes. Our families' traumatic losses go way back, just as does the Kennedys' history of tragic loss.

Joe Kennedy's own father, Patrick Joseph (P. J.), had been the only surviving male in his own family. An older brother, John, had died as a baby, and then P. J.'s father died before he turned one. One would guess these losses left his mother with special feelings for her only son, and a heightened sense of the fragility of life—especially male life.

Having come up the hard way—with no father and serving as a replacement for his dead brother—P. J. became a hardworking but cautious man, who "married up" to a clever woman from a successful family. He too was clever, but his insecurities made it hard for him to say no to anyone. He started a liquor business, and like so many of the Irish of his time, moved into politics. Having grown up as a fatherless child in desperate need himself, he seems to have identified with those in need. He was a caretaker for the families in his ward, serving eight terms in the state legislature. His first child, Joseph P. Kennedy, became again the only surviving son when his younger brother

P. J. Kennedy, Joe Kennedy's father
The History Collection/Alamy Stock Photo

Joseph Kennedy with his oldest sons Joe (left) and Jack (right)
Everett Collection Historical/Alamy Stock Photo

died at two. Though there were also two surviving younger sisters, Joe became the focus of attention for the whole family. Perhaps it was this legacy of special-ness of the male survivor, intensifying the general cultural bias in favor of sons that led Joe to focus his expectations so strongly on his own oldest son in the next generation.

In the end, P. J. was defeated by the Boston political machine, very likely double-crossed by his son Joe's future father-in-law Honey Fitz himself. Though P. J. accepted his defeat with dignity, underneath he grieved like a child who had been unjustly punished. The lesson his son Joe took from this was that political loyalty and generosity were mere commodities. Joe grew up to emulate his mother, who believed in putting family first, and saw his father's support for others as weakness. Joe apparently decided to trust no one but himself, developing a will of steel and a calculating, manipulative approach to dealing with others.

He seemed to want to escape the embarrassing identification with his softhearted father, who had identified with those who experienced loss and was repaid with exploitation and rejection. A clue to Joe's relationship with his father is that he did not even attend his funeral, remaining in Cali-fornia with his paramour, Gloria Swanson. As much as P. J. longed for a close relationship with his son, he did not achieve it. Just as P. J., having no father at all, had gravitated to his mother, Joe's special closeness was to his mother.

Joe Kennedy's wife Rose Fitzgerald Kennedy's family had also experi-enced overwhelming traumatic losses in their history. Her father, John Fran-cis, called "Honey Fitz," the one who probably betrayed Joe Kennedy's father, P. J., was the fourth of twelve children. The three oldest children died in infancy. Five other sons had lives destroyed by alcoholism. The ninth brother, Joseph, had brain damage from malaria and barely functioned. Thus, of the twelve children, only three survived in good health, including Honey Fitz, who became the favorite. After his mother's death, when he was 16, his father developed a special ambition for him to become a doctor, since illness had caused such painful losses in their family. However, after one year at Harvard Medical School, the father died and Honey Fitz switched his ambitions to politics, which offered immediate income and an opportunity to provide jobs for his brothers. When he became mayor of Boston, many said that the whole brotherhood of Fitzgeralds actually ran the government. He considered it his responsibility to provide for his brothers, and he did. Later his grandsons would, of course, do the same.

Honey Fitz met his future wife, Josie Hannon, who was his painfully shy second cousin, only a few months before the death of his mother. Many said that his bond to her was based on their mutual losses. Josie was the fifth of nine children, only four of whom survived. One brother died at age six, while the mother was pregnant with Josie. Another had died four years earlier. Two other sons died early of alcoholism. The only surviving son had his leg crushed by a train at age 13. But the family's most tragic loss was the youngest sister, who drowned with her best friend, while Josie was taking caring of them. The devastating loss any family would feel about the death of a child was compounded by a complex web of guilt that they and Josie had contributed to the death by failing to protect the children. The family never recovered. Those who knew the three surviving sisters said that sorrow hung over them for the rest of their lives.

John "Honey Fitz" Fitzgerald, father of Rose Kennedy

Library of Congress, Prints and Photographs Division, George Grantham Bain Collection, LC-B2-5704-13

It is easy to understand what attracted Josie to the confident, forceful, adventuresome, and enthusiastic Honey Fitz, whose very name reflected his ability to charm with his words. His long courtship of Josie was indeed an effort to bring her out of herself with his humor, magnetism, and sociability. Like so many generations of the family that followed him, he dealt with loss by mobilizing into frantic activity and trying not to look back. Once the challenge of winning Josie was complete, the difference in their natures was overwhelmingly apparent. Or perhaps the very sadness in Josie, which had drawn him to her, now became toxic and he fled from it. As the years went by Honey Fitz expanded outward, while Josie turned further inward. It was his beloved firstborn daughter Rose who seemed to replace his mother and sisters. She grew up as his companion in the exciting political arena of his colorful life—she went everywhere with him.

She led a charmed life until adolescence, when suddenly it all changed. Her father's manipulative ambition, perhaps a reflection of his many early losses, led him to betray her. Rose's dream was to go to Wellesley College, where she was accepted at age sixteen. She was a brilliant student, as well as a passionate, untamed spirit, but her father sacrificed her dreams for his personal political aims. His political wheeling and dealing had led to fraud charges and to his being ousted as mayor of Boston. The deal he made with the leaders of the Catholic church to save himself required that Rose go to a Catholic school rather than Wellesley. Perhaps he also had a compulsion to repeat his own experience at sixteen of having to give up his plans for medical school.

Rose was forced to go to a convent school abroad. She was totally cut off from her exciting social life and from her family and put in a rigid environment, which demanded silence and denied all spontaneous attachments. Typical of the parochial school repression of the era, there was even a rule against girls' forming "particular friendships." Rose's response was one she would show again and again in her long life: she smothered her feelings of resistance, bowed to her father's will, and forced herself to channel her energies into prayer, leading to a kind of detachment from human relationships, which was to characterize all her later life. What she lost was her belief in having a special relationship with her father, as well as the sense of power to determine her own life. She had to bend to the will of a stronger male. Religion helped her swallow that pill and many bitter pills to follow.

Rose and Joe Kennedy's losses of their children by death are familiar. But the first loss was not a death. It was the dysfunction of Rosemary, their oldest daughter, who was institutionalized far from the family and cut off from everyone (except Eunice) for decades. By the time she was in her early twenties she had developed severe behavior problems. Such a tragedy represents a loss of dreams, an embarrassment, and a pain that never goes away. Wishing to keep Rosemary within the family, the Kennedys kept her psychological problems and limitations a secret for many years and made every effort to maintain her in as normal a fashion as possible.

Then, in 1940 Joe decided, while Rose was away, that Rosemary, then twenty-two, should have a lobotomy. The operation, which was kept totally secret, worsened her condition disastrously. Joe then arranged to have her sent to an institution in the Midwest and never told Rose—not then or afterward—about the lobotomy. Rose was told only that it would be better if she didn't visit "for some time." According to friends and relatives, it was only twenty years later, after Joe's stroke in 1961, that Rose began to piece the story together for herself (Kearns Goodwin, 1987). Why didn't she insist on visiting this daughter to whom she had devoted herself for so many years? How could

Rose Kennedy with her two oldest daughters, Kit (left) and Rosemary (right)
Keystone Press/Alamy Stock Photo

she never ask? How could it be that others never asked or questioned the disappearance of one of their members? Did Joe blame himself for what had happened? Did others blame him or themselves for ignoring her for so many years? All we know is that in her memoirs, written thirty-three years after the operation, Rose still maintained that she had participated in the decision for the lobotomy and failed to mention that she had not visited or asked about Rosemary for those twenty years.

The Kennedy family never talked about Rosemary's problems; the first public mention of it was not until 1960. The shame and guilt leading to the secrecy and mystification that surrounded Rosemary's disability, lobotomy, and disappearance gave this loss a lingering power. In such circumstances, other family members may be left with the "If she could disappear, I could disappear." It seems that years later a grandson, David Kennedy, who eventually died of a drug overdose, found a magazine story about lobotomies that included a picture of his aunt Rosemary and while in the midst of his own troubles he is quoted as saying:

Kennedy Family (Pat, Jack, Rosemary, Jean, Joe Sr., Ted, Rose, Joe Jr., Kathleen, Robert, and Eunice)
Everett Collection Inc./Alamy Stock Photo

The thought crossed my mind that if my grandfather was alive the same thing could have happened to me that happened to her. She was an embarrassment; I am an embarrassment. She was a hindrance; I am a hindrance. As I looked at this picture, I began to hate my grandfather and all of them for having done the thing they had done to her and for the thing they were doing to me. (Collier & Horowitz, 1984, p. 441)

The ambiguity of Rosemary's loss must have been particularly distressing because it could not be mourned like a death. She remained alive, but not physically or mentally present. Rose said in her memoirs that Rosemary remained pleased to see them and recognized them, and that she was "perfectly happy in her environment and would be confused and disturbed to be anywhere else" (Kennedy, 1974, p. 286). Yet surely other family members, like David, must have wondered whether this was true and questioned her extrusion from the family.

A most positive sign of resilience and transformation under these painful circumstances, was that Eunice, who was the one person to retain contact with Rosemary, convinced John Kennedy to sign the Mental Health Center legislation, which he did the very week before his assassination. This had a tremendous positive impact for decades on mental health services in this country.

Unfortunately, Rosemary was only the first of many children lost in the Kennedy family. In each instance there was a similar tendency toward secrecy about any facts that did not fit with a positive image. Joe Jr., the "Golden Boy," programmed by his father to become president, was shot down in an unnecessarily reckless flying mission in June 1944. Only his heroism was mentioned, not his exaggerated risk-taking nor the fact that he had received a warning that day from his electronics officer that

Rosemary Kennedy
SuperStock/Alamy Stock Photo

his plane could not possibly make it (Davis, 1984). The Kennedys also never mentioned that he was living with a married woman, Pat Wilson, at the time of his death. When Wilson wrote a letter of sympathy to his mother, Rose did not respond.

It is hard to escape the sense of repeated mingling of tragedy, accident, and tempting fate in the Kennedy family. Joe Kennedy Jr. had been repeatedly carrying out hazardous bombing missions, where he was told his chances of survival were less than 50 percent. He had already completed his tour of duty but was looking for a mission from which he would return a hero, perhaps because his younger brother, John, had just received a military medal for his performance in the Pacific. (In that instance, John had initially been reported missing in action, and a funeral had been held by the surviving crew members. Joe Sr. was told this news but kept it from his wife and children for a week, after which he learned that John had, in fact, survived.)

In this incident and in numerous examples that followed, we see examples of the Kennedys' avoidance in dealing with loss. When Joe Jr. died, his father announced the fact to the children, warned them all to be "particularly good to your mother," and then retreated to his room. Rose retreated to her separate room turning to religion, repeating the rosary over and over, leaving it up to her husband to handle arrangements and to respond to correspondence. She was initially consumed by her grief, while he immediately mobilized into action—the usual response of the Kennedy men to loss, and consonant with our culture's gender rules.

The second daughter, Kathleen, who had been cut off by Rose for marrying a British Protestant peer in May of 1944, lost her husband in the war that September. When the news of his death came, she was in the United States with her family, because of her brother Joe's death shortly before. She was out shopping, and her sister Eunice went to meet her. In typical Kennedy form, Eunice complimented her on her purchases and said nothing until they were finished shopping, at which point she suggested Kathleen call their father before they went to lunch. Joe then gave her the news of her husband's death. That night the family was solicitous of Kathleen, while diligently avoiding any mention of her husband's death! A friend who came to stay with her was appalled by the family's frenetic need to carry on as if nothing had happened (McTaggart, 1983).

Kathleen once told another friend that she had been taught that "Kennedys don't cry." When her brother Joe had died and his roommate called her to give condolences, she had broken into sobs. Later she wrote him a letter of apology saying: "I'm sorry I broke down tonight. It never makes things easier" (Kearns Goodwin, 1987, p. 690). Following her husband's death, she left her parents' home and returned to England, where she did allow herself to go through months of overt mourning, staying in her in-laws' home for comfort and support.

Four years later Kathleen fell in love with another Protestant, this time a married British peer, Peter Fitzwilliam, who had a reputation for high living, gambling, and affairs. This time her mother said that if Kathleen married, she would not only disown her, but would see that Joe cut off her allowance. Rose vowed she would leave Joe, if he refused. Kathleen decided she could not break off the relationship in spite of her mother's threat. In hopes of appealing to her father, she arranged to meet him while on a weekend trip with Fitzwilliam to the Riviera. In an eerily familiar scenario, Fitzwilliam insisted on flying in a small plane, although weather reports were so bad that all commercial flights had been canceled and his pilot strongly urged a delay. Their plane crashed in the storm and both Kathleen and Fitzwilliam were killed.

Her father, who was the one to identify the body, said Kathleen looked beautiful and as if asleep, though she had been horribly disfigured by the crash. The circumstances of her death with Fitzwilliam were concealed and she was buried as the widow of her first husband. Her father was the only family member to attend her funeral. Even then he took no role in the funeral arrangements, which were handled by her former mother-in-law, who even wrote her epitaph: "Joy she gave, Joy she has found." The Kennedys and their in-laws joined in a conspiracy of silence about the circumstances of the death.

Friends were appalled that Rose Kennedy sent a mass card with a prayer for those who had not gone to heaven. John and Bobby Kennedy visited Kathleen's housekeeper, drew out all her recollections, and then said: "We will not mention her again." They seem to have kept their word, though Bobby named his oldest daughter for her. Twenty-four years later Rose wrote in her memoirs: "In 1948 (Kathleen) had taken a spring holiday on the Riviera and was flying in a private plane with a few friends to Paris, where her father was waiting to meet her. On the way—a route threading the edges of the French Alps—the weather went bad, navigation equipment was not adequate, and the plane crashed into a mountainside, killing all on board. Joe was notified and hurried to the scene. He watched as the body of his daughter was brought down the mountainside. We lost our beloved Kathleen on May 13, 1948" (Kennedy, 1974, p. 332). All reference to the fiancé was eliminated as if he never existed, along with all reference to the fact that Rose had disowned her daughter.

The Kennedys experienced many other deaths and near deaths after those traumatic losses. Three times John Kennedy was given up for dead and was administered the last rites. Twice Ted almost died, a year after John's death, when he broke his back in a plane crash, and a year after Robert's death, when he almost drowned (and his companion Mary Jo Kopechne did drown at Chappaquiddick). Was it just coincidence that his near fatal accidents followed so closely the tragic deaths of his brothers, or is this an example of something that has been documented repeatedly in the research on stress: that such experiences increase our vulnerability to emotional distress, illness, and accidents?

What leads a family into such reckless and self-destructive behavior? Was the reckless risk-taking behavior of Kathleen and Joe Jr., the extremely promiscuous sexual behavior and politically dangerous liaisons of Joe and especially John Kennedy in particular, somehow a response to their fear of death—living on the edge and, as it were, "tempting fate" to prove to themselves that they were still alive?

Robert, Ted, and John Kennedy
NARA/Alamy Stock Photo

When the news came that John Kennedy had been shot, Rose decided to operate on a principle that she and Joe had adopted years before: bad news should only be given in the morning, not late in the day, because it would then upset your sleep. She therefore arranged for a "conspiracy of kindness" to keep Joe, who had by then suffered a stroke, from learning about the death until the next day. All TVs were unplugged, different stories were told about the relatives and friends who began to appear, and everyone kept up a charade of conversation with him for the whole afternoon and evening. He was told the next morning.

Rose believed that Jackie's composure at the time of John Kennedy's death was an example for the whole world of how to behave. The following week, Rose says, the family "had the Thanksgiving celebration, with every one of us hiding the grief that gnawed at us and doing our best to make it a day of peace, optimism, and thanks for the blessings that were still left to us." Rose quotes Jackie's praise for how the Kennedy family dealt with tragedy: "You can be sitting down to dinner with them and so many sad things have happened to each, and—God—maybe even some sad thing has happened that day, and you can see that each one is aware of the other's suffering. And so, they can sit down at the table in a rather sad frame of mind. Then each one will begin to make this conscious effort to be gay or funny or to lift each other's spirits, and you find that it's infectious, that everybody's doing it . . . (they) bounce off each other. They all have a humor. . . . It's a little bit irrelevant, a little bit self-mocking, a little sense of the ridiculous, and in times of sadness of wildly wicked humor of irreverence. . . . They bring out the best. No one sits and wallows in self-pity" (Kennedy, 1974, p. 448).

Commenting on the death of her third son, Robert, five years after Jack's, People said that the grim reality of the second assassination was so incredible, it would seem beyond fiction to imagine her self-possession at the funeral. Rose responded: "As for my being composed, I had to be. If I had broken down in grief, I would only have added to the misery of the others and possibly could have set off a chain reaction of tearfulness. But, in fact, it was not just I who set an example of fortitude. They all set it for one another" (Kennedy, 1974, p. 477).

Grief is a personal matter. Every family must find its own ways of handling it. The Kennedys showed many strengths in their handling of an incredible series of tragedies, and they also showed glaring vulnerabilities, particularly in facing up to losses that were embarrassing and not heroic. The remarkable thing about this family is their ability to persevere even after the most devastating losses.

Families like the Kennedys that have experienced so many traumatic, untimely deaths may develop a feeling of being "cursed" and unable to rise above the experience, or they may come to see themselves as survivors, who can be struck down but never beaten. For all their difficulties in handling feelings, the Kennedys showed an amazing life force and courage in overcoming tragedies. It was almost as if their sense of the family mission carried them through. The dignified death of Ted Kennedy, and moving as well as honest tributes after his long life, perhaps illustrate the transformation he brought about over many years of reassessment of his family's legacy.

The value of exploring the history of losses in your own family is that it may similarly give you a sense of your family's resilience as well as their difficulties in dealing with traumatic losses. It is extremely important to take the long view of how people have adapted and what they and their descendants did eventually to transform their lives and relationships.

THE FREUD FAMILY

The Freud family (**see Genogram 6.3: Freud Family**) provides another interesting example of patterns of repetition, which appear to have been legacies of loss. Sigmund, the oldest of his mother's eight children, was born in 1856 in Freiburg, Moravia. In addition to being the oldest, he was also the only son for many years. He had an intense relationship with his mother, Amalia, who always referred to him as her "Golden Sigi." By all accounts, he was the center of the household. He was followed by a brother who died, then five sisters, and finally by another brother ten years later.

For his father, Sigmund's specialness was probably intensified by the death of the paternal grandfather three months before his birth. This grandfather, Schlomo, was a rabbi, and Sigmund, in his fervency for his new belief system, psychoanalysis, has been compared to a religious leader and thus, in his own way following in this grandfather's footsteps. Sigmund's father, Jacob, had also lost two children in his first marriage. We know no details about those losses, but we know such loss is always difficult.

Sigmund's next brother, Julius lived for only seven months. Sigmund's closeness to his mother may have become even more important after the death of her second son, intensified by the fact that Amalia's youngest brother, also named Julius, died at the age of twenty exactly one month before this second son's death. She had probably known that her brother was dying when she named her son for him seven months earlier, since it is against the Jewish custom to name a child for a living family member. We might then speculate that the emotion connecting her dying brother to her new child was more powerful than the Jewish rule to name a child for someone who has already died. In later life Sigmund said that he had welcomed this brother with "ill wishes and real infantile jealousy, and his death left the germ of guilt in me" (Krull, 1990, p. 135). At the same time, Sigmund's nursemaid was dismissed from the household, apparently accused by his half-brother Philip of stealing, so Freud lost another caretaker as well. In addition, the family had to move twice, because of financial difficulties. Shortly afterward, both half-brothers were like uncles, and Freud's nephew, John, who was like a brother to him, emigrated to England.

Soon there was a new baby, Anna, with whom Freud had to share his parents' affections. He never got along with this sister. His sense of his own specialness and special treatment in the family were undoubtedly influenced by this pileup of losses around his birth.

Another critical period occurred when Freud was forty and his father died, just after the birth of his last child, Anna (named not for his sister, but for the daughter of his mentor, Samuel Hammerschlag) (Gay, 1990). Perhaps it is not surprising that this last child, Anna, became his primary follower, and by far the most emotionally linked to him of all his children.

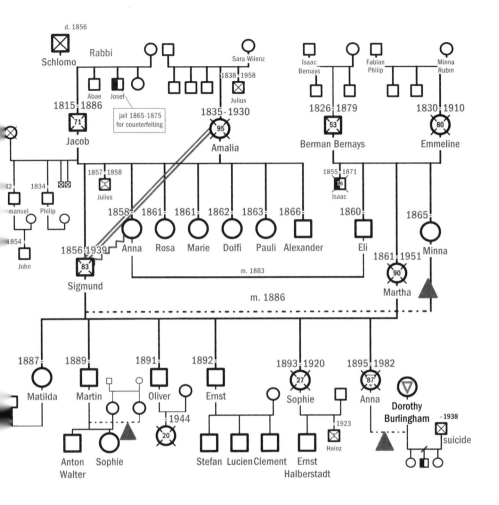

Genogram 6.3: Freud Family

He also drew closer to his sister-in-law, Minna, who moved into the household just at this time and became Freud's intellectual and emotional companion for many years. Freud describes Minna during these years to his closest friend Wilhelm Fleiss as "otherwise my closest confidante" (Masson, 1985, p. 73). He apparently took at least seventeen vacations with her, while his wife stayed with the children. He became sexually involved with her, a pattern which seems quite common following a loss, even though the connection between a death and an affair frequently remains out of awareness. Freud's oldest son repeated this pattern of having an affair with his wife's sister in the next generation (Freud, 1988).

Sigmund and Martha Freud
Chronicle/Alamy Stock Photo

Sigmund Freud's daughter, Anna Freud
Album/Alamy Stock Photo

Jacob Freud, like his son Sigmund, was forty when his father died. Freud seems to have had a special identification with his father. He called his father's death "the most important event, the most poignant loss, in a man's life" (cited in Shur, 1972, p. 108). When his father died in 1896, Freud wrote: "By one of those obscure paths behind official consciousness the death of the old man has affected me profoundly. I valued him highly, understood him very well, and with that combination of deep wisdom and romantic light-heartedness peculiar to him, he had meant a great deal to me. His life had been over a long time before he died, but his death seems to have aroused in me memories of all the early days. I now feel quite uprooted" (Masson, 1985, letter of 11/2/1896, p. 202).

We might contrast this reaction to his father's death with his description of his reaction to his mother's death at the age of ninety-five in 1930: "No pain, no grief, which is probably to be explained by the circumstances, the great age and the end of the pity we had felt at her helplessness. With that a feeling of liberation, of release . . . I was not allowed to die as long as she was alive, and now I may" (Jones, 1955, pp. 152–153).

Freud himself had already been suffering with cancer for seven years, and was spared the dread that he would die before she did. He did suggest there might have been other effects on him "in deeper layers" of his consciousness. For example, he did not attend his mother's funeral, but rather sent his daughter, Anna, as "the family representative," suggesting an avoidance of his feelings.

But it is also true that when his mother died, he was seventy-five and basically dying, himself. When his father died, Freud was only forty and went through a major life crisis with depression and other physical and emotional symptoms. He began his famous self-analysis, and constructed the edifice of his new theory, which led to the publication of *The Interpretation of Dreams*. It was also at this time that he both formulated and then recanted his seduction theory, that the sexual abuse many women reported having experienced was not just their fantasy but had actually occurred and patients should be

Minna Freud
Chronicle/Alamy Stock Photo

believed when they report it. Many have viewed his recanting his daring and pro-feminine theory as reflecting a sense of guilt over his fear that his theory of seduction might apply to his father, whom he thought might have sexually abused his sister Anna.

Consider how different members of your own family reacted to losses, depending on the circumstances, the age of the deceased and of the mourner, and the relationships in the family at the time. But look also for the resilience that sometimes emerges from dealing with loss, as it did with Freud when his father died.

RESILIENCE IN THE FACE OF LOSS

Families' resilience (Walsh, 2006, 2023) in the face of loss, trauma, and dysfunction enables us to survive. It is important to explore such resourcefulness in your family and to underline it when you find it. Mexican artist Frida Kahlo (see Genogram 2.2), whom we discussed in Chapter 2, is a remarkable example of such resilience. Though neither of her parents seems to have come to terms with their early traumatic losses, she showed amazing resilience in her ability to transform her losses into transcendent strength, creative energy, productivity, and hope in her art, in spite of her severe disabilities. She had held hopes of becoming a scholar and physician, but instead, became an artist, like her father and her maternal grandfather before her. Her mother was

Freud with his mother, Amalia
akg-images/Newscom

extremely religious and apparently high strung, but both parents were so distraught by her accident that neither managed to attend to her. Her sister Mati
was the only family member to visit her during the entire year she was in the
hospital her after the terrible accident when she was impaled by a pipe. As
discussed in Chapter 2, Kahlo's art seems to have touchingly incorporated
many of the unmourned losses in her family. She wished, she said, to be "worthy, with my paintings, of the people to whom I belong and to the ideas which

strengthen me" (Helland, 1990–1991, p. 12). She created pictures depicting the most traumatic experiences of her life including the bus accident in which she was impaled, the loss of her pregnancies that did not survive. In all these works she seems to be saying we are a part of all that has come before, conveying that we can dare to acknowledge our traumatic losses and still feel hope. She never avoided the pain of loss in her own or her family's experience, but was inclusive, as if to give us the message that we can dare to face the pain that has come before and draw from it to move ourselves forward in our lives.

LOOKING AT LOSS IN YOUR OWN FAMILY

Given the disconnection of our society, the very experience of sharing a loss can help families expand the context in which they see themselves. It can help them experience continuity from the past to the future and see their connection to each other, to their culture, and to others. Family rituals are excellent ways to promote healing and transformation. A toast made at a wedding, or an anniversary party, or even a eulogy at another family member's death, may help to hold the memory of a lost person in the context of ongoing family relationships. One young man, making the family toast at Thanksgiving, gave thanks for the happy memories they all had of his brother's wife, who had died two years before in an automobile accident. In another case a woman held a memorial service twenty-five years later for her brother, who had died by suicide on his birthday. She began a process of reconciliation around a loss

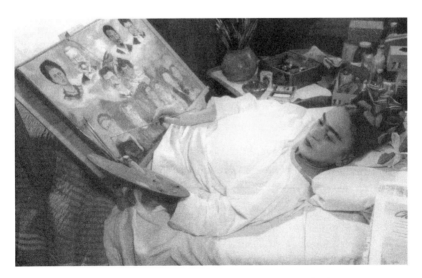

Frida Kahlo painting her family portrait (genogram!) from her bed
© *The Granger Collection Ltd d/b/a GRANGER Historical Picture Archive*

that had gone unacknowledged for a quarter of a century. Such evocations to integrate loss may occur even long after the death. The healing process can benefit the family in profound ways. Questions, again, are a most powerful tool for gaining a new understanding of losses.

QUESTIONS ABOUT LOSSES

- Are dates of death remembered or barely honored? How comfortable are family members in talking about the deceased and the circumstances of the death? Are both good and bad memories accessible? What mythology has been created in the family about the dead person? Was the deceased made into a saint, or ignored?
- Who spoke at the funeral and who did not? How did various family members express their reactions to death? Tears? Withdrawal? Illness? Depression? Frantic activity? Did they talk to each other about the loss?
- Who was present at the death? Who was not present who "should have been"?
- Who arranged the funeral? Who defined the character of the service?
- Who attended? Who didn't? Who gave the eulogy?
- Was the body cremated or buried? If cremated, what happened to the ashes? Is there a marker at the grave? Do family members visit the grave? How are the dead remembered and with what frequency? What happened to the belongings of the dead person?
- Other than funeral services, what kinds of mourning rituals did family members engage in?
- Did family conflicts or cutoffs occur around the time of death?
- Did family members have unresolved issues with the person who died?
- Was there a will? Were there family rifts because of provisions in the will? Were any members cut out of the will?
- Was there secrecy about the cause or circumstances of the death? Were facts kept from anyone inside or outside the family?
- How would the history of the family have been different if the dead person had survived longer or died earlier?
- Do family members feel stigmatized by the death (e.g., a suicide, a death from AIDS)?

- How have the survivors' lives been influenced by their relationships with the person? What do they carry with them from this person?
- What are the family's beliefs about afterlife and how have these beliefs influenced their understanding of the loss? What other beliefs do family members have that may help sustain them in the face of loss?
- In addition to death, what other kinds of losses occurred in your family?
- How did various losses affect the way life-cycle events were experienced (e.g., births, leaving home, decisions to marry/divorce, child-rearing practices, illness, retirement)?

Chapter 7
Where We Come From: Parents and Children

If we had not loved each other, none of us would have survived. And now you must survive because we love you, and for the sake of your children and your children's children.

—JAMES BALDWIN
The Fire Next Time

If you can lower your expectations to zero, you'll probably be happily surprised.

—MURRAY BOWEN

No one can ever replace our parents. Hopefully they provided for us when we were infants and helpless, and throughout our lives, we have been able to rely on them in one way or another. We may feel a debt we can never repay or a pain we will always struggle to move beyond. In the complex web of the family, many people feel little joy in their connection to their parents. Whatever their virtues and vices, few of us ever really get to know our parents as people. We may be too busy "fending off" parental demands, expectations, neglect, or abuse. But by seeing parents in the context of their own lives—as children, as siblings, lovers, workers, and friends, and by exploring family patterns of parent–child relationships, we may come to a different understanding.

For some people, relationships with their parents are the most difficult ones they will know. Experiencing themselves as victims, they may feel misunderstood, mistreated, or abandoned in dangerous places, required to perform adult tasks at too young an age, like Snow White, Cinderella, or Hansel and Gretel. They may fantasize that they were adopted, once belonging to some saner, kinder, more "normal" father or mother. And some people find it impossible to mature beyond these childhood experiences of intimidation and powerlessness.

Later parent–child roles may also reverse. As parents age and become dependent, children's responsibility may increase. This can be a gratifying time of human connectedness or, if earlier resentments persist, a time when problems intensify. It is often difficult for children, even as adults, to develop a clear sense of their parents that goes beyond their early larger-than-life expectations of "mother" and "father." Children also have a tremendous power to hurt parents. Maya Angelou's son chided her: "Mother, I know I'm your only child, but you must remember this is my life, not yours." Her response: "The thorn from the buds one has planted, nourished, and pruned pricks most deeply and draws more blood" (Angelou, 1991, p. 7).

We must remember that what we say to our parents taps into their profoundest feelings about themselves and about what we mean to them. The gender and sexual orientation of each child, as well as that of each parent, influences how they relate, even as we try to create a world with more flexibility in the roles parents play in our families. Traditionally, fathers have more often been unknown and unknowable, while mothers, more present in children's lives, have tended to get the brunt of children's anger as well as more of the affection and love. Mothers are indeed often perceived to be overly present, offering too much advice and wanting too much intimacy. To understand our parents, it is useful to consider the gender role expectations that may have shaped decisions about how actively to be involved as parents, the degree of closeness and distance with children especially in terms of issues like a child's gender or sibling position. Part of expanding our view of men beyond the idea of the dominant male and the selfless or over-intrusive female involves appreciating the homebody fathers who have been able to admit their doubts and inadequacies and become nurturers, while also celebrating the businesswomen mothers who have dared to defy conventions by expressing their strengths directly in the world outside the family.

The ideal would be for everyone to have a comfortable, trusting person-to-person relationship with each parent. But this ideal is rarely achieved. Because it takes two adults to create a child, everyone starts out as part of a three-person system (at least), and this threesome generally becomes the central triangle in life, even where it includes an absent parent, an adoption, or in more recent times, a sperm or egg donor.

If everyone gets along, things are fine, but if there are conflicts, this triadic pattern is likely to become problematic. In fact, the basic triad often fails to remain in place. Current estimates are that more than one third of this generation's children will live in a single parent household before the age of eighteen, while many others will be raised by grandparents, nannies, foster or adoptive families, and in many other types of households.

The classic parent–child triangle involves the child or children siding with one parent, while the other becomes the outsider. Whether in heterosexual or same-sex-couple families, children often feel closer and more aligned with one parent than the other, for whatever reasons, and this can cause tensions and conflicts.

Such a classic good guy/bad guy triangle can be seen in Eleanor Roosevelt's family (**see Genogram 7.1: Eleanor Roosevelt Family**). Her relationship to her father, Elliott, was very close. She was his first child, "a miracle from heaven," he had said (Lash, 1971), born eight months after the family's double tragedy, discussed in Chapter 5, when her uncle Theodore Roosevelt lost both mother and wife on the same night. Perhaps Eleanor was a consolation for her father's grief. He certainly identified with her, giving her the same nickname, "Nell," that he had been called as a child; and she, in turn, adored him. Though he died when Eleanor was only ten, she carried his letters around with her for the rest of her life. In her autobiography, written when she was seventy-four years old, she wrote: "He dominated my life as long as he lived and was the love of my life for many years after he died. With my father I was perfectly happy. . . . He was the center of my world. . . . With his death went for me all the realities

of companionship which he had suggested for the future, but . . . he lived in my dreams and does to this day" (Roosevelt, 1984, p. 5).

In contrast to the intense bond with her father, Eleanor saw her mother as distant and unsympathetic. She saw herself as homely and was sure that her mother concurred in this assessment. She recalled in her autobiography: "My mother was one of the most beautiful women I have ever seen. I felt a curious barrier between myself and . . . (her) . . . I can still remember standing in the door, often with my finger in my mouth, and I can see the look in her eyes and hear the tone of her voice as she said: 'Come in Granny.' If a visitor was there, she might turn and say, 'She is such a funny child, so old-fashioned

Eleanor Roosevelt
Everett Collection Historical/Alamy Stock Photo

that we always call her "Granny."' I wanted to sink through the floor in shame" (Roosevelt, 1984, pp. 3, 8–9).

Even when parents may be deeply flawed, a child who loves them will go to great lengths to hold onto their idealization of their parent. In Eleanor's case, while she adored her father, he was an alcoholic who often acted erratically. Despite his amiability, social position, good looks, and reputation as an adventurer, which had led to his marriage to a highly sought-after debutante, Anna Hall, Elliott never lived up to his potential and background of wealth and success, dropping out of school in his teens. For the first few years of the marriage, his charm, intelligence, and inherited wealth kept him going, although he did not provide much income for his family. Then, after an injury

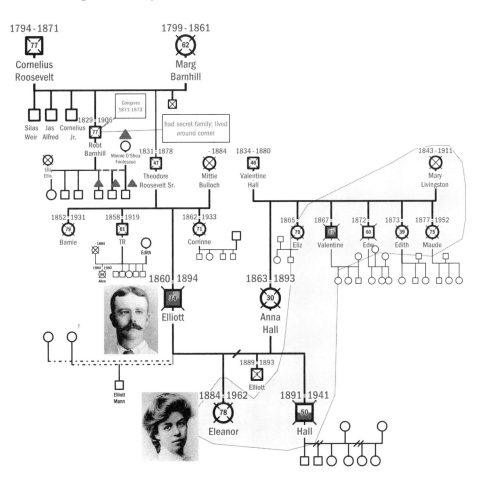

Genogram 7.1: Eleanor Roosevelt Family

Anna Hall Roosevelt
Franklin D. Roosevelt Presidential Library

to his ankle, he transformed rather quickly into a depressed addict and alcoholic. Sometimes hostile and even suicidal, he would disappear, leaving his wife and small children alone and unsure of his whereabouts. When he would finally reappear, there were drunken sprees and bouts of violence. Even then, Eleanor favored her father. In describing one of his returns, she remembered almost guiltily: "My father had come home . . . and I am sorry to say he was causing a great deal of anxiety, but he was the only person who did not treat me as a criminal" (Roosevelt, 1984, p. 7).

The extended family made various efforts to help their wayward son, persuading him to undergo several sanitorium stays. Finally, to protect

Elliott Roosevelt with his three children. Eleanor is standing in the middle.
Courtesy of the National Archives and Records Administration. Series: Franklin D. Roosevelt Library Public Domain Photographs.

his estate, they moved to have him judged insane. He was not allowed to live with his wife and children. For a time, he made a partial recovery, working in a small southern factory town as part of his rehabilitation. During this period, he lived with different women and his family did not know where he was. He had at least one son in 1891 with a German housekeeper named Katy Mann.

An interesting parallel in the previous generation of this family was his uncle Robert, who maintained a secret second family almost around the corner from his first family and had two sets of children. When his wife died, he moved the second family in, pretending it was a stepfamily.

In the midst of Elliott's problems, Eleanor's mother died of diphtheria. To Eleanor's relief, her father reemerged in her life. But there was no storybook ending. Elliott continued to drink and could not care for his two small surviving children, who ended up living with their kind but stern grandmother Hall, who disapproved of him. Elliott wrote Eleanor letters full of promise and hope, but rarely visited. Once when he did visit, he took her to his club, but abandoned her in the vestibule. Hours later she had the humiliating experience of watching him be carried out drunk. Despite such painful experiences, Eleanor continued to feel that one day he and she would go off blissfully together. She remembered his reassurances: "He began . . . to explain to me that . . . he and I must keep close together. Someday I would make a home for him again; we would travel together and do many things. Somehow it was always he and I. I did not understand whether my brothers were to be our children or whether he felt that they would be at school and college and later independent" (Roosevelt, 1984, pp. 9–10).

He wrote Eleanor letters, raising her hopes that he would return, only to disappoint her when he did not. When he moved back to New York, he lived under an assumed name and out of touch with the family. In 1894 when Eleanor was ten years old, and only two years after his wife's death, he died of his alcoholism. Later Eleanor wrote about her childhood: "I acquired a strange and garbled idea of the troubles around me. Something was wrong with my father, but from my point of view nothing could be wrong with him. If people only realized what a war goes on in a child's mind and heart in a situation of this kind, I think they would try to explain more than they do, but nobody told me anything" (Roosevelt, 1984, p. 8).

Eleanor Roosevelt's suggestion about how to help children of dysfunctional parents is extremely important. Of course, children become mystified and have distorted thinking when their parents cannot function appropriately, and it is an important part of maturity to find ways to understand parents' limitations maturely.

When Eleanor was a teenager, an aunt, in an argument, told her the truth about her father's drinking and affairs, but her love for her father remained unshaken. It seems especially unfortunate to tell a child a painful truth in anger. In fact, it seems even to have strengthened Eleanor's belief that she and her father had needed each other and that he had been as vulnerable as she was.

Eleanor's one-sided loyalty is a good example of how an unrealistic view of a parent can be imprinted early, and can last a lifetime if the need to preserve it is intense. In Eleanor's case, it was as if she allowed her imagination to fill in his absences with the father she wished she had had. By doing that, she never really knew the father she did have.

Nor did she ever gain a clear view of her mother, whose judgmental attitude probably seemed to Eleanor the cause of her father's problems. Young children often see things this way. The more rejected she felt by her mother, the more loyal she felt to her father, and the more she valued her special relationship with him. In the end, she was not able to see either parent for who they really were.

For many years Eleanor's daughter Anna, named for her grandmother, was caught in a similar triangle in which she saw her father, Franklin, as the hero and her mother, Eleanor, as the villain. Anna wrote about her parents: "It is no wonder that my Father was my childhood hero. . . . He talked about all sorts of things I liked to hear about—books I was reading, a cruise we might . . . take . . . (Mother) felt a tremendous sense of duty to us . . . but she did not understand or satisfy the need of a child for primary closeness to a parent" (Asbell, 1982, p. 19).

Her brother James said of their mother: "Having gained no useful knowledge on the subject from her own unhappy years as a child . . . was absolutely terrified to find herself a parent. . . . (Her) fear of failure as a mother in turn hurt her as a mother. For many years—until it was too late for her to become a real mother—she let our grandmother act as our mother" (Roosevelt, 1976, p. 24).

Eleanor herself seems to have agreed about her difficulties as a mother, which is not surprising, given her own wretched childhood: "It did not come naturally to me to understand little children or to enjoy them . . . because play had not been an important part of my own childhood" (Asbell, 1982, p. 19).

There was also Eleanor's sense of betrayal that Anna colluded in FDR's intimate relationship with Lucy Mercer. Anna herself wrote regarding both parents' difficulty with intimacy: "It has always seemed to me that the greatest contradiction in my parents was, on the one hand their supreme ability to 'relate' to either groups of people or individuals who had problems, and on the other hand, their apparent lack of ability to 'relate' with the same consistent warmth and interest to an individual who was their child" (Feldman, 2003).

Three of the children testified to their father's charisma and elusiveness and their mother's coolness and confusing inconsistency. Further, although parents are not responsible for their children's choices, the five Roosevelt children married a total of nineteen times, reflecting perhaps that intimacy was not something they had learned at home. Anna's husband said she used to tell him that her mother was unpredictable and inconsistent—sweet and lovely one hour, critical and demanding the next. Many people continue to seek parental approval or try to get others to make up for what they did not get from their parents. They are, of course, likely to be disappointed, and might better focus on their own approval for their behavior than anyone else's. Luckily for both Eleanor and her daughter, they lived long enough and worked hard enough to move past their conflicts and problems. Eleanor was to write later: "Today no one could ask for a better friend than I have in Anna, or she has in me. Perhaps because it grew slowly, the bond between us is all the stronger. No one can tell either of us anything about the other, and though we might not always think alike or act alike, we always respect each other's motives, and there is a type of sympathetic understanding between us, which would make a real misunderstanding quite impossible" (Asbell, 1982, p. 31). Both Eleanor and her daughter Anna seem to have evolved a relationship where they could maintain their own values while appreciating each other.

THE FAMILY OF FRANZ KAFKA

Some people, like the Jewish Czech writer Franz Kafka, never get past their preoccupation with whatever didn't work out in their relationships with their parents. All his life he was obsessed with his difficult relationship with his father. He wrote about people caught in terrifying situations, where they were the victims of a senseless, impersonal, all powerful, persecuting world.

He saw his father as a terrifying, loud, overpowering, hot-tempered, self centered, hypocritical man, incapable of providing emotional support, yet sabotaging his children's efforts to break away, blaming him for his lack of confidence and sense of guilt, and for trying to intimidate him into being less timid and unmanly, a tactic that, of course, never worked.

Kafka at one point said of his parents: "Enclosed in my own four walls, I found myself like an immigrant imprisoned in a foreign country.... I saw

Franz Kafka
IanDagnall Computing/Alamy Stock Photo

Franz Kafka's parents
Historic Collection/Alamy Stock Photo

my family as strange aliens whose foreign customs, rites, and very language defied comprehension. . . . Though I did not want it, they forced me to participate in their bizarre rituals. . . . I could not resist." Kafka was the oldest of six children, but his two next brothers died in infancy, which perhaps left him, like so many other children, as the replacement for the other lost sons. In any case, he was the only surviving son, with three much younger sisters.

In typical triangular fashion, Kafka viewed his mother as everything good: a kind and considerate peacemaker who buffered the tensions between him and his father. But in the end, he felt she failed to protect him and sided with his father, saying that she could not act as an independent force on her son's behalf, because she loved her husband too much. Kafka viewed his father as the villain and his mother the unwitting, if well-intentioned accomplice; he had only fleeting awareness of his own provocations in the triangle—always turning to his mother as intermediary and never dealing with his father directly.

At thirty-six he wrote a letter to his father in an attempt to reconcile with him. He was trying to free both of them of any blame in their strained relationship, suggesting they just had a mismatch of natures. Unfortunately, he went on to list numerous incidents of his father's insensitivity, blaming his stammering on his father for not allowing himself to be contradicted. He said his father expected him to do poorly and sure enough, in his nervous-

Franz Kafka with two of his three surviving sisters. Two brothers died in infancy.
PVDE/Bridgeman Images

ness, he fumbled. The father expected him to marry yet insisted that no one he wanted to marry was good enough. Kafka even predicted that his father would dismiss his letter with "Is that all you're so worked up about?"

Kafka's letter provides an astute analysis of the role played by the "good" parent, in this case his mother, in perpetuating parental triangles:

> Mother unconsciously played the role of a beater in a hunt. Even if in some unlikely event your upbringing could somehow have set me on my own feet by producing spite, aversion, or even hatred in me, mother balanced it out again by her kindness, her sensible talk (she was in the chaos of childhood the archetype of good sense!) by interceding for me, and I was again driven back into your orbit, from which I might otherwise have broken free, to both your advantage and mine. No real reconciliation came about . . . (because) mother . . . secretly protected me from you. (Kafka, 1953, pp. 31–32)

He realized that his mother's efforts to keep the peace actually kept him and his father from resolving their conflict. Her failure to confront the father made him feel justified. Kafka blocked his own efforts to deal with his father by relating only through his mother, never managing to see him as other than a tyrant and a bully.

Both Kafka's parents had come from poor and struggling families and were extremely ambitious to survive. They looked to each other for the love and caring they had each missed in their childhoods. They seem to have had a devoted marriage, working together in their dry-goods business and socializing in the evening. As Kafka saw it, he and his sisters were left out, raised by caretakers, while the parents worked to establish the business. Looking at his genogram we can't help wondering if he didn't also feel powerless and that he had to make up to his parents for their loss of their other two sons, as children so often do when young siblings close in age are lost. The father's main worry was for family's survival and economic security, and in the end he was right to be fearful as the family later died in the Holocaust.

Franz Kafka, who died in 1924 at forty-one, could never bring himself to marry. He feared marriage and parenthood might make him more like his father. Even worse, he feared he might have children who would resent him as much as he resented his father. In his letter to his father, he admitted that he was a difficult, obstinate son who tended to be oversensitive and that there were times when he deliberately provoked his father by taking contrary opinions.

Kafka was sure his father would mistrust his letter, seeing it as full of veiled recriminations, and would chide him for continuing to accept money while criticizing him. Thus, anticipating his father's criticisms, he offered a detailed rebuttal of all his arguments to close his letter. But, despite his professed desire for reconciliation, his tone in the letter was bitter. By itself it would probably not have improved his relationship with his father, though it would have been the most honest communication he had ever had with him.

However, true to the family triangle, instead of giving the letter to his father directly, Kafka gave it to his mother to deliver! And she, instead of giving it to the father, returned it to her son, so the letter was never delivered. Family therapists often refer to this pattern as the "Two Step"—a dance in which even an effort toward change is followed by a backing down and falling back into line. We can only wonder what potential was lost by Kafka never giving his letter to his father directly. How often do we fail to even try to work out issues with our parents because, like Kafka, we feel intimidated, resentful, or hopeless about changing a troubled relationship?

The opposite side of the "parent as villain" is the "parent as saint." Whether a parent is vilified or idealized, it is necessary to go through a transformative process to understand your parent's story in context, since there are few real villains or real saints in our families. Going home again requires our accepting the good and bad of our probably imperfect parents and families of origin.

GENDER INEQUITIES IN PARENTING ROLES

As you consider your family tree, be sure to consider the prevailing cultural constraints of their historical era and cultural context. Traditionally women were evaluated primarily for their beauty, their mothering, and their housekeeping skills. Their creative work often had to be accomplished in scraps of time and space that has rarely been appreciated, although these patterns are hopefully changing in our times.

Sophia Tolstoy, wife of Leo Tolstoy, bore thirteen children, eight of whom lived to adulthood. She also copied and edited her husband's 1,500-page novel *War and Peace* seven times from beginning to end by candlelight at night after her children had gone to bed! She wrote after forty years of catering to her "genius" husband: "Geniuses must create in peaceful, enjoyable, comfortable conditions; a genius must eat, wash, dress, he must rewrite his work countless times; one must love him, give him no cause for jealousy so that he has peace, one must raise and educate the innumerable children who are born to a genius, but for whom he has no time" (Smoluchowski, 1987, p. 217).

Providing such an atmosphere for genius was a constant struggle for Sophia, since she, like her husband, was brilliant, passionate, volatile, sensitive, easily jealous, and prone to self-analysis. She asked ironically: "But for what would I, an insignificant woman, need an intellectual and artistic life?" Because women have been valued mainly for their caretaking roles, we must rewrite the narratives of our families to understand them in context. In the Tolstoy family it was many years before Sophia's son was able to appreciate his mother's importance: "I understand better than I did then the importance of my mother in our family life and the great value of her care for us and for my father. At the time, it seemed to me that everything in our life went on of its own accord. We accepted mother's care as a matter of course. I did not notice that beginning with our food and clothes to our studies and the copying for father, everything was managed by her" (Smoluchoowski, 1987, pp. 124–125).

A woman who was not able to be a good caretaker never had an easy time. If she wanted to have a life of her own, with its own adventures, she often, as author Carolyn Heilbrun long ago suggested, had to develop an "eccentric story," to free herself from the strictures of marriage and family (Heilbrun, 1988). George Eliot, for example, removed herself from conventional expectations by her decision to live with a man who could not divorce his legal wife. By one act that was considered outrageous she escaped social demands and made up for her despair at being considered unattractive. Katharine Hepburn, whom we have already discussed, similarly married a gay man who was her friend, which allowed them both to conduct their personal lives and relationships with more flexibility than is usually allowed to women. Illness, even to the point of invalidism, has sometimes been the only way women could see out of the burden of traditional roles.

THE COST OF MARITAL DISRUPTION ON CHILDREN: THE DICKENS FAMILY

After twenty-two years of marriage, Charles Dickens suddenly declared that he had never loved his wife Catherine Hogarth Dickens and was leaving her. The Dickenses' relationship involved triangles from the start, since Dickens was an impoverished writer, supported by his future father-in-law's journal. Over the years Dickens became successful and felt entitled to include other women in his marriage. Twice when Catherine suspected his affairs, he gaslighted her, accusing her of pathological jealousy and making her apologize to his mistress. In time he convinced himself that his wife was boring and useless, writing: "I believe my marriage has been for years and years as miserable a one as ever was made. I believe that no two people were ever created with such an impossibility of interest, sympathy, confidence, sentiment, tender union of any kind between them, as there is between my wife and me" (Rose, 1984, p. 180).

Over the course of their marriage Catherine had twelve pregnancies and raised the ten children who survived, while being a writer, an actress, and a cook, as well as an involved mother. But Dickens, who had begun as a struggling writer supported by his wife's journalist father, George Hogarth, had become so famous and successful that even the queen read his work, and, not surprisingly, his views of his own importance escalated.

After deciding to leave his wife for his mistress, Ellen Ternan, Dickens's first act was to wall up the connection between the marital bedroom and his dressing room, which he now took as his own bedroom. As unfortunately happens sometimes when parents become preoccupied primarily with themselves, he ignored his children's ongoing needs, and he seems to have had no regard for their well-being in this negativity toward his wife. He cast his wife in the role of villain to justify himself, claiming that if her sister Georgina had not lived with them and become the energetic, intelligent, inventive, and attractive "mother," his children would have had no mother. He declared that his wife was the only human being he had ever known with whom he could not get along or find common interest. He claimed no one could get along with her, not even her own mother.

Dickens's affair and sudden separation from his wife triggered disruptions with his children, friends, colleagues, and other relatives. He tried to blame everything on his wife and took elaborate efforts to protect the secrecy of his affair. He never again had a single residence, but always multiple abodes, so no one would know when he was with Ternan.

But his actions had a profound impact on his children who ranged in age from six to twenty-one at the time of the separation. As often happens when parents separate, children feel as if they must choose sides. In the Dickens family most of the children sided with their father, whom they adored, as he was fun, magical, famous, entertaining, and funny. Only the oldest son, Charlie, remained with the mother and stopped talking to his father, defiantly announcing his engagement to the daughter of Dickens's now estranged publisher.

As their mother was not very responsive, undoubtedly because she was seriously depressed, was used to blame her for losing their father's love.

Charles Dickens
The Picture Art Collection/Alamy Stock Photo

Catherine Hogarth, Charles Dickens's wife
Smith Archive/Alamy Stock Photo

Dickens was given custody of all the other children. Moving them in with his wife's sister Georgina, who became the family caretaker, he showed no consideration for his children and soon sent his eight-year-old son away to boarding school with his three older brothers, leaving them there for the Christmas holidays, which is one of the saddest memories he evokes in his famous story *A Christmas Carol*. The oldest daughter ended up as his caretaker and never left him.

Years later, Catherine gave one of the daughters the love letters he had written her, hoping she would see how wronged she had been as mother and wife. The daughter consulted George Bernard Shaw, who predicted that history would sympathize more with Dickens's wife, who had sacrificed her life, bearing twelve children in fifteen years, and that her only real sin was that she was not a female Charles Dickens. The daughter did eventually participate in publishing the story from her mother's point of view and dedicated it to her (Storey, 1939).

Dickens, whose father had lived in a debtors' prison, had married "up" in marrying Catherine Hogarth, daughter of a well-known journalist who employed him. In the early years Dickens appears to have been extremely happy with her. He wrote of the early days of his marriage, "I shall never be so happy again . . . never if I roll in wealth and fame" (Rose, 1984, p. 149).

It is also important to take the long view in relationships. Most of us go through many different phases as we move through life depending on our connections to others, our health, our resources, and many other circumstances. Remember as you assess your family's functioning and relationships over the life span, to take into account what else is going on in the broader context. In Dickens's case, he seems to have changed his views as he became involved in other relationships and as his own fame as a writer grew. There was also the aspect that, while he could tell a great story, the one he lived showed much less consideration for the needs of others. Be sure as you think about your family to take account of the different stories that get told, along with your own assessment of what was going on at both the high and low points of your family's history.

FINDING YOUR PARENTS AS YOU LOSE THEM

In the normal course of events, we know that our parents will most likely die within our lifetime. Yet knowing this and fully realizing it are two different things. If the relationship with a parent has been estranged or stormy and much is left unsaid or unresolved, their loss is likely to be more complex. But in the experience of a parent's dying, intergenerational understanding may be achieved.

For most of her life Simone de Beauvoir had devalued her mother as critical, unsophisticated, bourgeois, and guilt-inducing. She dealt with her by avoidance. But as her mother was dying, Simone began to reevaluate her, realizing that a full-bodied, spirited woman lived inside her mother, but was a stranger to her. Her mother had spent all her strength in repressing her desires, squeezing the armor of principles and prohibitions over her heart and mind, as she had been taught to pull the laces tight around her body.

De Beauvoir shows remarkable insight into the ways in which this construction developed in her mother. Her husband had studied law, but spent much of his time as a dandy, improving his status through his marriage. Shortly after the marriage, her mother's father, who had been a wealthy banker, was sent to jail for fraud and the family experienced a very public and humiliating bankruptcy.

As De Beauvoir thought about her mother's life, she realized that her concern for convention and her desire to please were compensation for the shame she felt about her father. Her mother also felt guilty all her life that her husband had never received the dowry he expected and considered him noble for not blaming her for her family's poverty after the bankruptcy, though the husband was not much of a provider, and the family struggled for many years just to survive. As De Beauvoir thought about her father's extramarital affairs, she began to appreciate just how difficult life had been for her mother and how strong her mother had actually been. She also came to appreciate her mother's strength in how she had recovered after her husband's death, which had left her penniless at the age of fifty-one. Her mother

Simone de Beauvoir
Hulton Archive/Getty Images

did not let herself be trapped by her past, but instead took advantage of her late-life freedom to take courses, receiving a certificate to work as a Red Cross librarian, learning to ride a bicycle, studying German and Italian, reestablishing ties with friends and relatives who had been driven away by her husband's surliness, and was able to satisfy one of her earliest longings—to travel.

As De Beauvoir reevaluated her mother, she perceived with touching clarity the tragedy of her mother's limited options: "It is a pity that out-of-date ideas should have prevented her from adopting the solution that she came round to 20 years later—that of working away from home—She would have risen in her own esteem instead of feeling that she was losing face. She would have had connections of her own. She would have escaped from a state of dependence that tradition made her think natural but that did not in the least agree with her nature. And no doubt she would then have been better equipped to bear the frustration that she had to put up with" (De Beauvoir, 1973, p. 25).

Simone de Beauvoir with her mother and younger sister
© Tallandier/Bridgeman Images

De Beauvoir had been very close to her mother as a child, but her adolescence had become a stormy battle for independence, the conflict continuing into her adult life. However, when she learned that her mother had contracted terminal cancer, she was shocked, stating, "It's one of those things we know, but imagine will take place in some other 'legendary' time." As she began to face her mother's impending death, she decided to attempt a reconciliation. As Simone sat and talked with her mother and really contemplated her life, she achieved more perspective and began to see her mother as a person. "She was capable of selfless devotion for my father and for us. But it is impossible for anyone to say 'I am sacrificing myself' without feeling bitterness. . . . She was continually rebelling against the restraints and the privations that she inflicted upon herself. . . . She flung herself into the only other course that was available to her—that of feeding upon the young lives that were in her care. 'At least I have never been self-centered; I have lived for others,' she said to me later. Yes, but also by means of others. She was possessive; she was overbearing; she would have liked to have us completely in her power" (Beauvoir, 1973, pp. 35, 38).

Gradually Simone saw her own part in her earlier alienation from her mother, though she had difficulty overcoming her negative reactions. She would promise herself to find common ground with her mother, but then become irritated by her mother's clumsy use of language. Even so, as she sat with her mother in the hospital, she gradually developed the patience to listen to her mother's story for the first time and to admire her courage. De Beauvoir wrote, quoting her mother: " 'I would not admit that I was old. But one must face up to things; in a few days I shall be 78, and that is a great age. I must arrange my life accordingly. I am going to start a fresh chapter.' I gazed at her with admiration" (Beauvoir, 1973, p. 17).

In absorbing her mother's story, Simone realized what an unhappy childhood her mother had had. She was also the older sister in her family and had grown up feeling that her own mother was cold and that her father favored her younger sister. Realizing that her mother had wanted from her children what she did not receive from her parents, Simone began to comprehend the intensity of her mother's investment in her as the intellectual oldest sister.

In the end, she managed to retrieve her relationship with her mother, which had been short-circuited so long before: "I had grown very fond of this dying woman. As we talked in the half-darkness, I assuaged an old unhappiness; I was renewing the old dialogue that had been broken off during my adolescence and that our differences and our likenesses had never allowed us to take up again. And the early tenderness that I had thought dead forever came to life again" (Beauvoir, 1973, p. 76).

Unfortunately, too many people wait until it is too late before achieving such understanding. It is, of course, much easier to reconcile with your parents if they are still alive. But, even if they are not, you can better understand yourself and your family by trying to discover as much as you can about them.

The goal of reconnecting is to share with family, not just to find out about their lives. Family members may resist one-way questions, if they feel they are being "investigated." They are more likely to respond if you express interest in family stories. Self-disclosure, along with nonthreatening, specific questions will encourage them to flesh out the details that help you see them as human beings, trying to get by as best they can.

You may think, "Not my father, he's too intimidating," or "I could never talk to my mother; she's too domineering and intrusive." From this perspective, whatever the parents' behavior, it is a challenge to understand how they got to be that way. Parents who act controlling got that way somehow. Such behavior typically reflects a sense of insecurity or inadequacy rather than a willful attempt to harm a child. Once parents feel they still have something to offer, such as information about their own lives and experiences, the need to be so controlling may lessen.

Accepting parents means giving up efforts to change them. It will help you improve your relationship with a parent if, as Murray Bowen suggested, you lower your expectations to zero. This isn't to say that you don't keep working to understand your parents and try to communicate more effectively. But instead of building the relationship on the basis of an expected "payback" from the parent, the emphasis is on understanding and connecting with them.

QUESTIONS ABOUT PARENTS

- What kind of relationship did each of your parents have with each of their parents? Their siblings? Their grandparents? Their aunts and uncles? How did they like school? Did they do well? Did they have friends? How did they spend their time? How did the family spend holidays and vacations?
- Were there critical life experiences that changed things for them—a death, an illness, a move, a change in financial circumstances? What do they remember of those experiences?
- What do/did they remember of their experiences growing up? How did they experience adolescence? Did their parents approve of their friends? What were their dreams? Did they get in trouble or keep secrets from their parents?
- When your parents met each other, how did their parents react? Were there conflicts over the wedding? Did their parents disapprove of their partner or their childrearing practices?
- What was it like for them to become parents? What do you think they perhaps wanted to do differently from their own parents? What do you think was most difficult for them about childrearing? Were you and your siblings hard to discipline? What were the good memories? What did they find most difficult about parenting? How did they manage when any of their children had problems? Were there times when parenting was particularly difficult for them? Adolescence? Early childhood? Were there hard times financially? Migration?
- Were there ways that any women in the family did not conform to the stereotypes of mother or woman? Did women work outside the home? Did they want to? What about aunts and grandmothers? What do you think were their dreams? How did they manage or react to the socially approved women's roles in their time? How did others react to them?

- Did any men in the family not conform to the stereotypes of man or father? Were they affectionate? Caretakers? Talkers or story-tellers? Emotionally involved with other family members? Able to show their vulnerabilities? How did they manage against the constrictions of men's roles in their time?
- What were the best parent–child relationships in the family? What were the typical parent–child relationships for each gender? What were the rules for parent–child relationships at each phase of the life cycle: infancy, childhood, adolescence, launching, young adult, maturity? Are parents and children expected to be physically affectionate? To spend leisure time or holidays together? To share intimate thoughts?
- Could family members tell parents what they appreciated about what they gave and forgive them for what they were not able to give? What would they have to let go of?

Chapter 8
Sisters and Brothers

My dearest friend and bitterest rival, my mirror and opposite, my confidante
and betrayer, my student and teacher, my reference point and counterpoint,
my support and dependent, my daughter and mother, my subordinate, my
superior and scariest still, my equal.

—ELIZABETH FISHEL
Sisters

I don't believe that the accident of birth makes people sisters and brothers.
It makes them siblings. Gives them mutuality of parentage. Sisterhood and
brotherhood is a condition people have to work at. It's a serious matter. You
compromise, you give, you take, you stand firm, and you're relentless. . . .
And it is an investment. Sisterhood means if you happen to be in Burma
and I happen to be in San Diego and I'm married to someone who's very
jealous and you're married to somebody who's very possessive, if you call me
in the middle of the night, I have to come.

—MAYA ANGELOU
The Heart of a Woman

Elizabeth Fishel and Maya Angelou convey the profundity of sibling connections, even though many people do not live up to these obligations. As
a society we are having ever fewer siblings, as couple relationships and parenting patterns are changing, especially in the twentieth century. But sibling
relationships remain a key factor in family patterns and functioning. Even
now when families are having fewer children, more than 82 percent of children grow up with at least one sibling, a higher percentage than grow up in
a household with a father figure (McHale, Undegraff, & Whiteman, 2012).

Indeed, our sibling relationships are generally the longest relationships we
have in life, and they can be an incredible protection for well-being as we age.
While parents are our first caretakers, from whom we learn about trust and
independence, it is our siblings with whom we first learn to collaborate and to

relate as partners and equals. In some ways, we have more in common with our brothers and sisters—beginning with the fact that we shared our parents and our family history—than we will ever have with others. Our parents usually die a generation before we do, and our children live on for a generation after us. Thus, our siblings tend to share more of our lives genetically and contextually than anyone else, and sisters even more, since they tend to be emotionally more connected and to live longer than brothers. In fact, we can divorce a spouse much more finally than a sibling. Luckily it is rare for siblings to break off their relationship or to lose complete touch with each other.

In some families, siblings are among the closest relationships people have throughout their lifetime. In others, sibling rivalry and conflict cause families to break apart. Siblings often serve as the model for future relationships with friends, lovers, work partners, and other contemporaries. In our modern world, spouses may come and go, parents die, children grow up and leave, but siblings, we hope, are always there.

Unfortunately, the importance of siblings has been overlooked in much of the psychological literature. Freud viewed the defection of his colleague Adler (who viewed siblings as among our most important relationships) as the act of an ungrateful younger brother. Although Freud himself had five sisters, a brother, and two half-brothers, he wrote a whole autobiography without mentioning that he even had any siblings! He completely ignored sibling relationships and his ideas won out over Adler's.

Unfortunately, parents sometimes make things worse. This is particularly true when siblings only see each other at the parental home, or when adult siblings only hear about one another through their parents, especially the mother, who often becomes the family "switchboard." Whether deliberately or inadvertently, parents can perpetuate problematic sibling patterns, comparing one child with another, perhaps chiding one for not calling as often as the other does or talking repeatedly about how proud he is of his son, not realizing he is ignoring his daughter. A parent may praise one sibling in an effort to give the other a message to "shape up."

Sibling experiences vary greatly. An important factor is the amount of time they spend together in childhood. Two children who are close in age, particularly if they are of the same gender, generally spend a lot of time together and must share their parents' attention. Siblings born farther apart generally spend less time together and grow up in a different family in many ways, because they develop at very different points in the family's life cycle.

In today's world of frequent divorce and remarriage, there may be a combination of siblings, stepsiblings, and half-siblings who live in different households and only come together on special occasions. In only-child families, their closest sibling-like relationships will typically be with playmates. In two-child families their relationship tends to be more intense if they are close in age because they only have each other. Clearly, the more time siblings have with each other, the more intense their relationships are likely to be.

SISTERS AND BROTHERS OVER THE LIFE SPAN

Sibling relationships can be our most important connections in adult life, especially in the later years. According to what is probably the most comprehensive longitudinal study of men over their entire life span (which included six Harvard classes from 1938–44), the single best predictor of emotional health at age 65 was having had a close relationship with one's sibling during one's college years. This was more predictive of well-being than even childhood closeness to parents, emotional problems in childhood, or parental divorce. Indeed, it was more predictive even than having had a successful marriage or career, which says something about the importance of family connections in general, but sibling connections in particular (Valliant, 1977).

Sibling connections, especially the ties between sisters, tend to be a great resource in later life. Sibling relationships can have a profound role on our lives from beginning to end. But we must consider gender, abilities and disabilities, and distance apart in age, as well as the life span to understand the sibling patterns in our families. Sisters and brothers often have very different roles in a family. As Gloria Steinem has put it, "A boy and a girl can come out of the exact same household with two very different cultures." There is, of course a very long history in most cultures of privileging sons over daughters and siblings may be treated very differently and may play very different roles from earliest childhood. As the old adage goes: "A son is a son till he takes a wife; a daughter's a daughter for all of her life."

Meanwhile, though research indicates that the preference for sons is diminishing there is still a greater likelihood that a family with only female children will continue to try for a boy and families are also more likely to divorce if they have only daughters. Divorced fathers are more likely to lose contact with their children if they are daughters (Dahl & Moretti, 2008; Rawat, Yadav, Bhate, 2021). On the other hand, recent research has shown that parenting daughters increases feminist sympathies. A study of fathers in the legislature showed that fathers of daughters voted significantly more liberally than fathers who had only sons, and the more daughters they had, the higher their propensity to vote liberally, particularly on reproductive rights issues (Washington, 2007). Although daughters have traditionally been expected to become the caretakers of aging parents and cheerleaders of their brothers rather than the stars themselves, in the current generation more daughters than sons are going to college and participating in most aspects of our society's work, though, obviously we still have a long way to go for equality between the sexes.

If the brother is older, he is often idolized and catered to. If he is younger, he may be envied and resented by the sister for his special status. Sons have been expected to continue the family legacy, while their sisters were more often expected to become part of their husband's family.

In any family where negative sibling feelings have persisted into adulthood, the care of an aging parent may create particular difficulty, likely influenced by gender. When parents need caretaking, siblings who have been apart for years may have to work together in unfamiliar ways. The child who has remained closest to the parents, usually a daughter, will still often get most of these caretaking responsibilities, which may cause long-buried jealousies and resentments to surface.

Once both parents have died, sibling relationships become independent for the first time. From here on, whether they see each other will be their choice. This is the time when estrangement can become complete, particularly if old rivalries continue. This can be an important time to work toward reconciliation with your siblings, to get beyond conflicts over who did more for an ailing parent or who was more loved. Throughout life, as Valliant's research showed, even for the most privileged of our society, having a close sibling is a huge benefit. Sibling bonds are very protective throughout life.

Much of our literature has ignored the role of sister relationships. They typically get less glory than brothers. A woman who wanted to avoid a move made necessary by her husband's job in order to remain near her sister has often been viewed as "enmeshed" or "undifferentiated." And yet, it is the sister who was there at the beginning, before the husband, and who will most likely be there at the end, after he is gone.

There is a concept of a brotherhood being the perfect relationship, as in the phrase brotherhood of man or Henry V's band of brothers. However, in Western culture, we have tended to emphasize the inherent conflict in brotherly relationships ever since Cain and Abel—a story that ends, strikingly, in brutal murder, for which there is even a word: fratricide. There is no similar word for sister killing sister. This less idealized version of brothers reappears elsewhere in the Bible—most notably in the stories of the Prodigal Son, Jacob and Esau, and Joseph and his brothers (Lott, 2012). Relationships between brothers in literature are often defined both by deep and enduring fraternal bonds, as well as by competition and rivalry. According to researcher Deborah Gold (1989), sibling rivalry is highest between brothers. She says this phenomenon is rooted in the fact that parents and society are more likely to compare boys to each other in terms of achievement, power, and dominance. This idea of rivalry is one laid out by Frank Sulloway's research on birth order in his book *Born to Rebel* (1997), which suggests that firstborns tend be traditional and conservative and grow up taking on the role of parental surrogates, historically being the ones likely to inherit the farm or business, while latter born sons are "born to rebel," becoming the inventors and creators of new methods. Younger sons in European tradition had to leave the family, for the priesthood, the military, the crusades, or for other adventure, because if they stayed at home, their presence would create family conflict.

Jackie Robinson
Alpha Stock/Alamy Stock Photo

In any case, your parents and grandparents even with the best intentions may have conveyed very different messages to their sons than to their daughters, and thus you will want to explore carefully the sibling patterns in your family.

Consider the family of Jackie Robinson. Both he and his wife Rachel grew up in families with the same sibling constellation: a middle daughter between brothers. Jackie was the youngest with an older sister, Willa May, who cared for him, while none of their three oldest brothers did any caretaking. Jackie and Rachel Robinson had three children who formed the same sibling constellation consisting of a middle caretaker daughter between brothers (**see Genogram 8.1: Jackie Robinson Family**). In his autobiography Robinson revealed his awareness later in life of how the pattern had unwittingly been reproduced with his own children. Regarding his middle daughter, he says: "She was just such an ideal and perfect child in our eyes and in the opinion of virtually everyone who came in touch with her that she sometimes seemed a little too good to be true. While fathers may be crazy about their sons, there is

Jackie Robinson, the youngest, with his mother and four older siblings

Hulton Archive/Getty Images

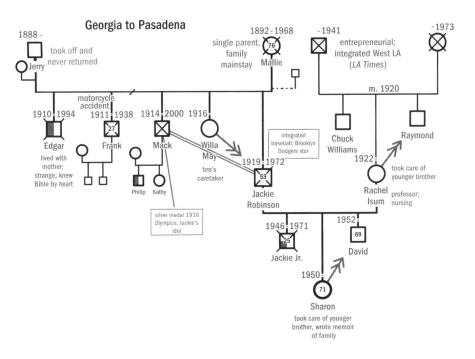

Genogram 8.1: Jackie Robinson Family

something extraordinarily special about a daughter. It's still the same—our relationship—perhaps even deeper. . . . Rachel had been brought up with the same family pattern: a girl in the middle of two boys. She was the busy, loving, but not necessarily always happy, mainstay of her family, who took care of her younger brother. With a kind of grim amusement, I recall our assumption that Sharon was strong enough to cope well with whatever she was confronted with. We took her development for granted for many years. She rarely signaled distress or called attention to her problems by being dramatic" (Robinson, 1972, p. 124).

In some families daughters are more likely to be raised to take care of others, including brothers. Some cultural groups, such as Irish American and African American families have had a long pattern of tending to overprotect sons, and underprotect their daughters for various historical reasons. Other groups have less specific expectations. Anglos, for example, are more likely to

Jackie Robinson with his wife, Rachel, and children, Jackie Jr., David, and Sharon
AP Photo

believe in brothers and sisters having equal chores. The point is to notice how gender roles have influenced sibling patterns in your family.

TWINS

The ultimate shared sibling experience is between identical twins. Twins have been known to develop their own language and maintain an uncanny, almost telepathic sense of each other. Even fraternal twins often have remarkable similarities, because of their shared life experiences. The major challenge for twins is to develop individual identities. Since they do not have their own unique sibling position, there is a tendency to lump twins together. This becomes a problem especially in adolescence, when young people are trying to develop their separate identities. Sometimes twins have to go to extremes to distinguish themselves. Other times they may continue to be each other's closest friend. They are more likely than others to even marry other twins!

BIRTH ORDER

By virtue of your unique location in the birth order of your family, every sibling actually grows up in a different family. Parents in general have no prior experience when they have their first child and have to invent their approach as they go along. Their approach to their second child will be influenced by their experiences with the first. Hence each child has different parents and experiences their family differently. It is not uncommon in large families for older children to report that their parents were much more rule-bound with them than with their younger siblings. This makes sense, given that by the time parents have been though the childrearing process multiple times, they are more confident and more tired, and their approach to parenting is probably more free flowing.

While birth order can profoundly influence later experiences with spouses, friends, and colleagues, a particular place in the birth order obviously does not guarantee a particular type of person. Many other factors influence sibling roles, such as temperament, abilities and disabilities, looks, intelligence, talent, gender, sexual orientation, and the timing of each birth in the family history in relation to deaths, moves, illnesses, cultural background, changes in financial status, and so on.

Additionally, parents may have a particular agenda for a specific child, maybe expecting them to be the responsible one or the "baby," regardless of their position in the family. Or a child may be expected to be like a certain family member they resemble. A child's temperament may also be at odds with their sibling position. This can explain why some children struggle so valiantly against family expectations—the oldest who refuses to take on the responsibility of the caretaker or standard bearer or the youngest who strives to be a leader. In some families, it will be the child most comfortable with responsibility, not necessarily the oldest child, who becomes the leader. Parents' own sibling experiences also affect their children, but certain patterns often occur that reflect a child's birth order.

THE OLDEST

In general, oldest children are likely to be tradition-bound, conscientious, and over-responsible. They typically make good leaders, since they have experienced authority and responsibility for younger siblings. Often serious, they may feel they have a mission in life. In identifying with their parents and perhaps being favored by them, they tend to be conservative even while leading others into new worlds, and while they may be self-critical, they do not necessarily handle criticism from others well.

We have already noted in Chapter 6 that there were various factors contributing to Sigmund Freud's special status in his family (see Genogram 6.3: Freud Family). As the oldest and a son, the household was generally organized around his needs. He was the only one of the children who had a special space set aside for him to work. The family story even goes that when his sister Anna wanted to play the piano their mother bought one, but immediately got rid of it when Sigmund complained that the noise bothered him. That was the end of Anna's music education! The family even gave him the privilege at the age of ten of naming his younger brother, whom he named after his hero Alexander the Great. Freud apparently did not think much of his siblings, particularly his sisters. He once said to his brother Alexander: "Our family is like a book. You and I are the first and last of the children, so, we are like the strong covers that have to support and protect the weak girls who were born after me and before you" (Eissler, 1978, p. 59). More significantly, he did not mention his siblings once in his autobiographical writings about his own development, so it is not surprising that sibling patterns play no role in his psychological theories. He does, however, mention his two-year-older nephew, John, who for the first few years of his life was like a big brother: "Until the end of my third year we had been inseparable; we had loved each other and fought each other and . . . this childish relationship has determined all my later feelings of intercourse with persons my own age. . . . John, has since had many incarnations, which have revived first one and then another aspect of character and is ineradicably fixed in my conscious memory. At times he must have treated me very badly and I must have opposed my tyrant courageously" (Jones, 1975, p. 8).

Freud was never to have a true equal. In later life he became a powerful leader, but as is so often the case with firstborns, he had difficulty sharing the stage with colleagues who would not accept his leadership in every idea, bringing about a falling out with most of his followers (Adler, Jung, Stekel, Ferenczi, and others) as soon as they challenged him.

George Washington, our first President, is an outstanding example of an oldest, becoming commander in chief of all Virginia military forces by the age of twenty-three. He had a seemingly miraculous ability to lead his men into battle and emerge unscathed. A brilliant leader, he kept a single-minded focus on his objectives and his obligation to duty, regardless of the sacrifices involved. Washington's leadership skill, determination, and sense of responsibility were undoubtedly intensified by his father's sudden death when he was only eleven, which left him responsible for his mother as well as his four younger siblings. His fourteen-year-older half-brother, Lawrence, then returned from abroad and became George's guardian and mentor, but unfortunately died six years later, which left George even more alone as the family leader. Though he could never have children of his own, he became a devoted stepfather to his wife Martha's two children and to numerous other relatives,

George Washington, an oldest
National Portrait Gallery,
Smithsonian Institution; acquired
as a gift to the nation through
the generosity of the Donald W.
Reynolds Foundation.

whom he supported, mentored, or even raised. As a brother, he was caring and responsible. He wrote of his younger brother John late in life: "I have just buried a brother who was the intimate companion of my youth, and the friend of my ripened age" (Bourne, 1982, p. 111).

Being the firstborn can be a mixed blessing. As the answer to parents' dreams and as a beginning of a new family, the firstborn may receive an intensity of interest and devotion denied to the children that follow. But the burden may be heavy. When firstborns explicitly reject family expectations, uneasiness and guilt may plague them for not living up to their appointed role.

TAMMY DUCKWORTH: AN OLDEST

Like George Washington, Senator Tammy Duckworth is an oldest who has demonstrated leadership skills from a very young age. She is the older of two children (though her father, like Washington's and Freud's father, had had several other children many years earlier, whom she and her brother did not know).

Senator Tammy Duckworth, an oldest

Abaca Press/Alamy Stock Photo

She was the only woman in her class training to become a helicopter pilot and one of the first women to fly in Blackhawk helicopter combat missions for the U.S. military. She lost both legs and partial use of her right arm when her helicopter was shot down in 2004, for which she received a Purple Heart for her bravery.

Tammy's mother, Lamai, was from China and Thailand. She had been raised by her aunts and grandmother in China and struggled growing up, migrating to Bangkok, Thailand, where she met her husband, who was serving in the military.

For Tammy's father's family, military service had been a cornerstone going back to the 1600s, when his first ancestors came to this country as indentured servants to British colonists. At least one of his four great-grandfathers served in the Revolution, and ancestors served on both sides in the Civil War. Tammy's father lied about his age to join the Marines at fifteen. He served in World War II, receiving a Purple Heart himself for wounds in Okinawa, and suffered disabilities from his war experience for the rest of his life. After the war he was sent to France and then to Thailand, where he fell in love with both his future wife and with Southeast Asia, having been left by his American wife for another man while he was away.

As Tammy grew up, she experienced that her younger brother was the prized child, while she had to do chores and housework as the oldest. But by 1984, when she was a teenager, her father had lost his job and things had become so desperate that the parents decided the father and children would move to Hawaii and the mother would stay and work because she didn't have the proper paperwork to immigrate to the U.S. She also did not speak English well and she and Tammy usually conversed in Thai. As things deteriorated in Hawaii with her father and brother, Tammy, as the oldest, felt she had to act. Her mother had told her, as Tammy describes it in her memoir, *Every Day Is a Gift* (2021), she, as the oldest, was to be in charge. "As the eldest child and only daughter that was my job. And I understood even then that it would remain my job into the years when my parents got older and my mom needed care herself. My sense of responsibility was always strong, and this would be my first real test of it" (p. 40).

Tammy had realized early that she had to become a leader for the family. She took it upon herself to get jobs from her early teens after school and at night, so the family would at least have food and she studied hard to skip a year ahead so she could begin college early. Though her father had been seriously disabled in the military, he was always unable to ask for or accept help. So Tammy wrote secretly to her mother about their desperation, begging her to rejoin them, which the mother managed to do. Tammy would later address this issue of men not being able to ask for help, when she became the assistant secretary of Veterans Affairs in the Obama administration, realizing it was a common problem of military men.

By the next year, Tammy had begun college at the University of Hawaii and the rest of the family was able to move back to Virginia, where her father man-

Tammy Duckworth hurrying along in the Senate hallway with her baby daughter
AP Photo/J. Scott Applewhite

aged to get at least a low-paying job. He then became interested in genealogy, inspiring his family to learn about their long family history of military service and strengthening Tammy's dedication to veterans, which became especially important after her horrific injuries and experiences as a double amputee.

After Tammy recovered from her injuries, Obama appointed her as assistant secretary of Veterans Affairs. She worked hard to support veterans like her father, who could not easily ask for the support they needed. In 2012 she was elected to the House of Representatives and then on to the Senate in 2016. She received her PhD at age forty-eight that same year. She was the first woman to give birth while serving in Congress and had her second child at age fifty, becoming the first person to bring her baby to the senate floor. She is the first woman amputee senator and has become a powerful and outspoken political leader on issues of race, immigration, the military, disabilities, and safety for the poor.

The oldest daughter often has the same sense of responsibility, conscientiousness, and ability to care for and lead others as her male counterpart. However, daughters generally do not receive the same privileges, opportunities, or expectations in the wider world to excel. Thus, they may be saddled with the responsibilities of the oldest child without the privileges or enhanced self-esteem.

Tammy Duckworth describes in her memoir: "[I] always worked my tail off trying to get good grades. I wanted so badly to make my Dad proud, but no matter how hard I worked, he never seemed to notice. Tom, (her younger brother) never angled for Dad's attention the way I did—because he didn't have to. He always had it, just by virtue of being a boy" (p. 21). When siblings are all female, oldest sisters may have certain privileges and expectations urged on them that would otherwise go to sons.

Che Guevara, an oldest
Emiliano Rodriguez/Alamy Stock Photo

CHE GUEVARA: ANOTHER OLDEST

Another typical oldest was Che Guevara, the responsible oldest of five children (**see Genogram 8.2: Che Guevara Family**). Che was another natural leader. It is perhaps no wonder that he became a hero of the guerilla revolutions in Cuba and South America. He was following in his family's footsteps in becoming a rebel. He grew up surrounded by people emotionally involved with the Spanish Republican cause. He had a passion for justice, and as a classmate said of him, Che was always mature for his age, "incredibly sure of himself and totally independent in his opinions" (Sinclair, 1970, p. 2). He took difficulties as challenges, never complaining; though he had serious asthma all his life, he became an athlete and a tireless and dar-

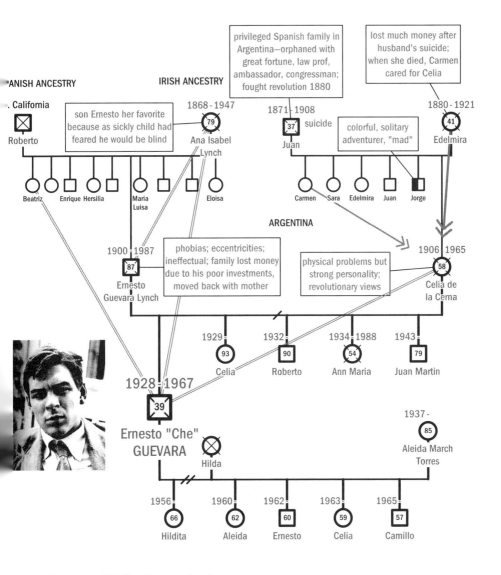

Genogram 8.2: Che Guevara Family

Che Guevara, at left, with his parents and three younger siblings
Historic Images/Alamy Stock Photo

ing traveler as well as a doctor and a revolutionary. He finished his six-year medical program in three years. One biographer described him as seeming "to feel responsible for all the world's injustices." All these are typical characteristics of an oldest: mature for his age, super-responsible, uncomplaining, and a striver. In a way very similar to George Washington at the battle of Trenton, Che drew strength from his early failure in Guatemala to prepare and rise again for his next effort. This confidence too is typical of an oldest, who can lead others against all odds, but with great and disciplined effort, not just bravado.

THE YOUNGEST

The youngest child often has a sense of specialness, which allows for self-indulgence without the overburdening feeling of responsibility of firstborns. This pattern may be more intense the more siblings there are in a family. The younger of two probably has more a sense of "pairing" and twinship—unless there is a considerable age differential—than the youngest of ten. Freed from convention and determined to do things his or her own way, the youngest child can sometimes make remarkable creative leaps leading to inventions and innovations, as in the examples of Benjamin Franklin, Marie Curie, Jackie Robinson, Paul Robeson, and Thomas Edison.

Edison invented the phonograph, the microphone, the motion picture camera and projector, the typewriter, the light bulb, made the telephone practical, and had more than 1,100 other inventions. He followed very much his own path in life. Like Ben Franklin, his special position may have been reinforced by the early death of the three next older siblings. Besides being a youngest child, Edison came from a long line of independent, stubborn, ambitious, determined individualists (**see Genogram 8.3: Edison Family**). His great-grandfather, John Edison, was forced into exile at the time of the Revolutionary War because of his Tory allegiance. His grandfather had also been voted out of the Baptist church for ridiculing and refusing to obey its rules. His father had to flee back to the United States after participating in a rebellion against the Canadian government. Edison too was an individualist, but an amazing innovator as well, despite (or some have argued, because of) only having six months of formal education.

Thomas Alva Edison
Library of Congress, Prints and Photographs Division, LC-DIG-ds-00179

In adult life he was eccentric. He dressed in baggy, shabby clothes, although eventually he was a multimillionaire. He slept little, worked incessantly, and was curious about everything. He developed into an extraordinarily good businessman, rewarding ingenuity and hard work but caring little for bureaucratic regularity. His concern about money was purely for the freedom it allowed him, a typical attitude among youngest sons.

Since youngest children have older siblings who have often served as caretakers, they tend to be more used to being a follower than a leader. They may remain the "baby," a focus of attention for all who came before, expecting others to be helpful and supportive. Youngest children may feel freer to deviate from convention. Youngests may have a rebellious attitude and feel compelled to escape from the "baby" role, as did Edison and Franklin, who both ran away in adolescence.

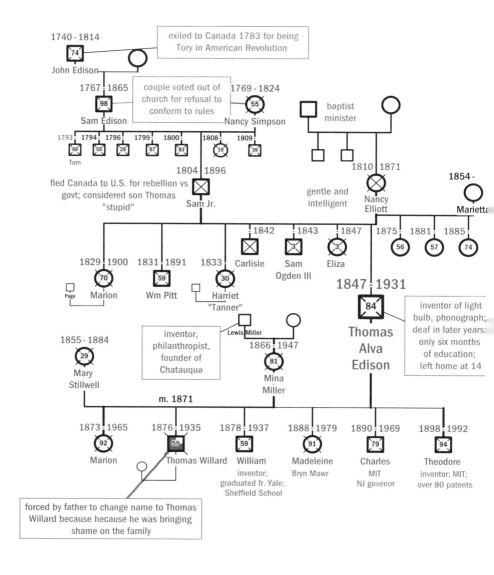

Genogram 8.3: Edison Family

Given their special position as the center of attention, youngest children may think they can accomplish anything. They may feel more carefree and content to have fun rather than to achieve. Less plagued by self-doubt, they are willing to try what others would not even consider, and thus their creativity. They can also be spoiled and self-absorbed, and their sense of entitlement may lead at times to frustration and disappointment. In addition, youngests often have a period after the older siblings have left home where can enjoy the

Thomas Edison with his phonograph
Dennis MacDonald/Alamy Stock Photo

sole attention of parents, but it can also lead to feelings of abandonment by their siblings.

Often the youngest child would rather be liked than right. John Adams, a good and typical oldest son, saw Benjamin Franklin as too much amused by frivolous pleasures and remaining noncommittal, so that everyone would like him: "Although he has as determined a soul as any man, it is his constant policy never to say yes or no decidedly, but when he cannot avoid it" (Van Doren, 1938, p. 600). Franklin was indeed self-indulgent and rather under-responsible, particularly when it came to his family. He left his fiancée (who later became his wife) to go to England, writing to her only once in a whole year and later he was extremely negligent of her feelings and of his daughter, leaving them for years at a time for his social life of diplomacy abroad.

Another extraordinarily creative youngest was Marie Curie (**see Genogram 8.4: Marie Curie Family**). Born Marie Sklodowski in 1867, last of five children in her Polish family, she had one brother and three sisters, the oldest of whom died in childhood. Marie was a brilliant scientist and received two Nobel prizes, for Physics in 1903 and for Chemistry in 1911. She showed an independence and lack of concern for convention from childhood onward. Determined to follow her own path, she was perhaps the extreme non-caretaker, a common characteristic of youngest children. Like Edison, she paid no attention whatever to her clothing or surroundings as she pursued her interest in science to the extreme. Shortly after she went to France to study, she was found unconscious on the street, weak from starvation, because she was too preoccupied with her work to bother with food.

Marie then married Pierre Curie, a marriage of two youngests. The story goes that when they were first married, Marie, in an effort to develop domestic skills—which did not interest her at all—asked her sister's advice about cooking chops. Later, when Marie asked her husband how he enjoyed his lamb chop, he gave an astonished look: "But I haven't tasted it yet," not noticing his empty plate (Pflaum, 1989, p. 56). Marie pursued science with

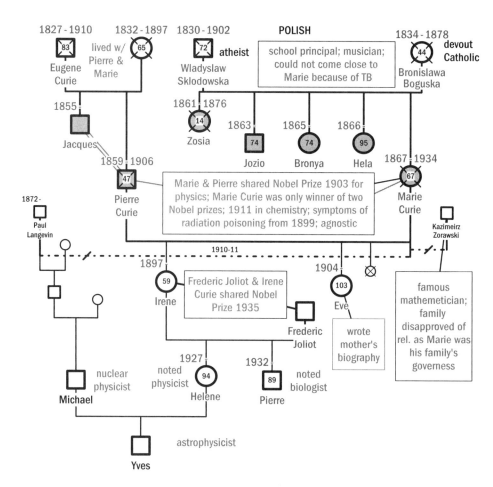

Genogram 8.4: Marie Curie Family

Pierre and Marie Curie—both youngests—
with their daughter, Irene
World History Archive/Alamy Stock Photo

no ambition for success or honor, much
less to lead others, but only to answer her
inner questions. Einstein once said of her
that she was "of all celebrated beings, the
only one whom fame has not corrupted."
Her younger daughter, Eve, who wrote her
biography, described her as remaining to
her last day "just as gentle, stubborn, timid
and curious about all things as in the days
of her obscure beginnings" (Curie, 1939, p.
xi). Interestingly, her older daughter Irene
Joliot-Curie won a Nobel Prize with her
husband Frederic Joliot as well.

Paul Robeson (**see Genogram 8.5: Paul
Robeson Family**), another brilliant and
creative youngest, was the multitalented
star in his family. Outstanding athlete in
every sport, Phi Beta Kappa in college, law-

Irene Curie Joliot, daughter of
Marie and Pierre, who also won
a Nobel Prize with her husband
Frederic
*Everett Collection Historical/Alamy
Stock Photo*

yer turned world famous singer and actor and then political speaker, Robeson was deeply aware of the importance to him of each of his siblings in his life. He said everyone lavished an extra measure of affection on him and saw him as some kind of "child of destiny . . . linked to the longed-for better days to come" (Robeson, 1988, p. 16). This is a common role for a youngest, especially where the family has experienced hard times. The oldest Robeson brother, William Drew, was named after their father, a minister who was born into slavery in North Carolina and escaped to Pennsylvania at age fifteen. After studying for the ministry at Lincoln University, their father became a minister in Princeton, New Jersey. As the oldest son and as his father's namesake, William Drew Jr. also attended Lincoln University, and then went to medical school. Robeson thought this brother was the most brilliant in the family and the one who taught him to study. William never reached his potential, largely because of racism. The next brother, Reed, was also brilliant, but too overtly angry to survive easily as an African American in the community. He became the "lost" middle child, though Paul felt he learned toughness from this brother. The third son, Ben, a successful minister like the father, was an outstanding athlete and role model for Paul, while the fourth child Marion, became a teacher, like the mother, and was noted for her warm spirit. The

three middle children all played out variations of the middle child role: Reed as the rebel, Ben and Marion as team players, willing to do without the limelight and to facilitate the relationships of others, "reserved in speech, strong in character, living up to their principles—and . . . selflessly devoted to their younger brother" (Robeson, 1988, p. 13). This support was all the more important because their mother died tragically in a fire when Paul was only five.

There were different lessons from Reed, his "rough" older brother, who carried a little bag of stones for self-protection. Robeson admired Reed and learned from

Paul Robeson, a most creative youngest
Library of Congress, Prints and Photographs Division, FSA/OWI Collection, LC-USF34-013362-C

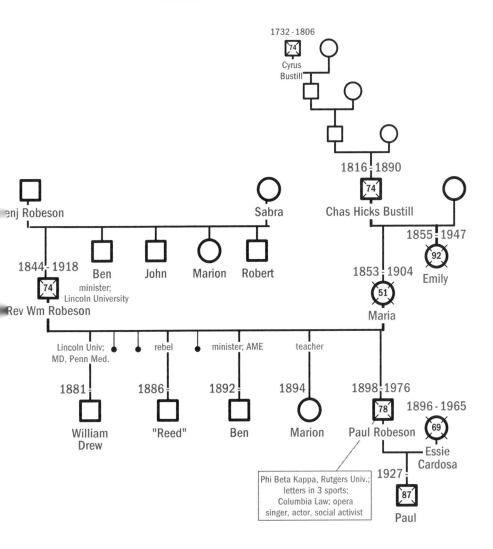

1732-1806
Cyrus Bustill

Benj Robeson

Sabra

Chas Hicks Bustill

1816-1890

Emily
1855-1947

1844-1918
Rev Wm Robeson

Ben
minister;
Lincoln University

John

Marion

Robert

Maria
1853-1904

1881-
William Drew

Lincoln Univ;
MD, Penn Med.

1886-
"Reed"

rebel

1892-
Ben

minister; AME

1894
Marion

teacher

1898-1976
Paul Robeson

Essie Cardosa
1896-1965

Phi Beta Kappa, Rutgers Univ.;
letters in 3 sports;
Columbia Law; opera
singer, actor, social activist

1927-
Paul

Genogram 8.5: Paul Robeson Family

him a quick response to racial insults and abuse. Robeson had a special feeling for this middle brother, who did not live up to the father's high expectations of his children. Robeson later wrote about Reed: "He won no honors in classroom, pulpit or platform. Yet I remember him with love. Restless, rebellious, scoffing at conventions, defiant of the white man's law. I've known many Negroes like Reed. I see them every day. Blindly, in their own reckless manner, they seek a way out for themselves; alone, they pound with their fists and fury against walls that only the shoulders of many can topple. . . .

When . . . everything will be different . . . the fiery ones like Reed will be able to live out their lives in peace and no one will have cause to frown upon them" (Robeson, 1988, p. 14).

Although Reverend Robeson eventually turned Reed out for his scrapes with the law, Reed, like many middle children, was surely expressing feelings that others did not have the courage to express, in his case the rage against racism. Paul saw Reed as having taught him to stand up for himself. In the famous biographical play written about Robeson, he says there was one conversation he and his father could never finish. Remembering the night his father turned Reed out, fearing he would set a bad example for his younger brother, Paul imagined getting together with his father and brother Ben to go looking for Reed and bring him home. He imagined defending Reed to his father.

> Aw Pop, don't change the subject. . . . Reed was not a bad influence. Only horrible thing he said to me was, "Kid, you talk too much." All he ever told me to do was to stand up and be a man. Don't take low from anybody, and if they hit you, hit 'em back harder." I know what the Bible says, Pop, but Reed was your son too! You always said you saw yourself in me. Pop, you were in all your sons. (Dean, 1989, p. 298)

This dramatization eloquently expresses the importance of the underlying connectedness of siblings and how much it matters if one is cut off, even if others in the family do not realize it. It also conveys the way middle children may dare to take rebel positions others in the family do not dare to express.

MIDDLE CHILDREN

Follower to the oldest, and leader to the youngest, middle children are less likely to show extremes. Middle children are "in between," having neither the status of the first as the standard bearer, nor the latitude given to the last as the "baby." Without the rights and prerogatives of the oldest or the privileges and benefits of the youngest, they often feel somewhat lost and unappreciated. On the positive side, in intense, highly fused families, the somewhat removed middle child may become the mediators, the one who avoids getting pulled into the family vortex.

While middle children run the risk of getting lost, especially if all the siblings are of the same gender, they may develop into the best negotiators, more even-tempered and mellow than their more driven older siblings and less self-indulgent than the youngest. They may even relish their invisibility, though they may also become rebels, like Reed Robeson. Henry Adams liked to say he had the good fortune to be born a fourth of seven children, which gave him a status so trifling he could fritter away his life and "never be missed" (O'Toole, 1990, pp. 3–4). Middle children are under less pressure than oldests to take responsibility, but they often have to try harder to get out of the oldest's shadow to make their own mark. Especially among same-sex siblings, middle children often find themselves feeling like they are scrambling to catch up with the older one while running frantically from the younger one who threatens to overtake them (Fishel, 1979). In short, unless the middle child is the only girl or only boy, they often have to struggle for a role in the family. Often this role involves being the compromiser, or the go-between, who tends to be gregarious, and a good mediator who tries to find a middle path between extremes.

Martin Luther King is an example of the best a middle child can be in terms of the ability to play multiple roles and bring others together. His brilliant ability to practice the tactics of nonviolent group resistance are a

Martin Luther King, a middle child mediator
Archive PL/Alamy Stock Photo

Martin Luther King with his wife and children
AP Photo/Atlanta Journal-Constitution

good fit with his middle-sibling position, since siblings in the middle do not have might on their side, but the power of joining forces comes naturally to them. Unlike the youngest, who would be unlikely to make a good leader, middle children may become outstanding collaborative leaders because they can draw together multiple factions through collaboration and mediation.

While middle children may escape certain intensities directed at the oldest or the youngest, they often struggle to be noticed. Mary Todd Lincoln (**see Genogram 8.6: Todd–Lincoln Family**), the wife of Abraham Lincoln, was a middle child and a daughter of two middle children!), who sought recognition all her life. She was the third daughter in a large family of thirteen surviving children out of seventeen in a remarried family. Mary was weaned at eleven months and lost her place as youngest to a son, Robert, who died the next year. The following year she lost her middle name, Ann, to a new sister Ann Marie. Then her mother died when Mary was only seven, giving birth to a third brother. By the time Mary was seven, a new wife absorbed her father's attention. Her father had been the third son "lost" among twelve children, who became a reckless and often absent parent. Interestingly he named three of his sons Robert, each sadly dying as a baby.

Ten more children were born to Mary's restless father and his second wife. All Mary's siblings may have felt disoriented in this family drama, but she seems to have been the most affected. Her two oldest sisters had already formed a strong alliance with each other. Ann, the youngest sister, in the first family, was the namesake and favorite child of the aunt who took over after their mother died until the father remarried. And the two surviving sons held a special place in their father's and uncles' affections.

Thus, Mary was the neglected middle child, whose response was a pervasive sense of insecurity. She was extremely vulnerable to slights, rejections,

Mary Todd Lincoln
Library of Congress, Prints and Photographs
Division, LC-DIG-ppmsca-19221

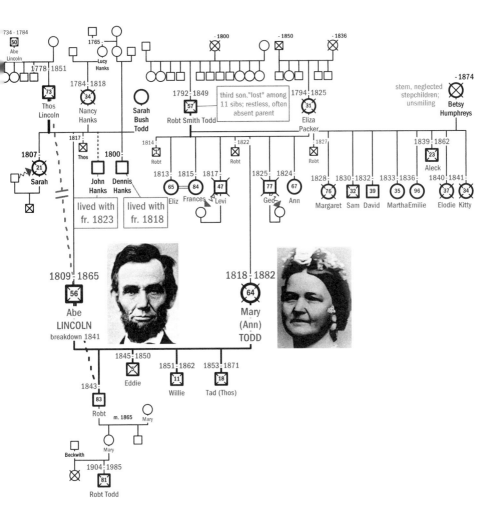

Genogram 8.6: Todd–Lincoln Family

and to the sense of being ignored. Not surprisingly, having felt invisible as a child, she developed a great determination to be recognized. She was a highly intelligent student, much better educated and socially sophisticated than Lincoln, a superb horsewoman, and an outstanding hostess. She was very ambitious for her husband and played the role of "the woman behind the man." Her husband referred to her as his "child wife" and "mother," suggesting, perhaps, that she vacillated between both roles. Lincoln's opponents criticized Mary for her extravagance, flamboyance, "interference" in politics, and unwillingness to accept the passive womanly role, all characteristics of a middle child who seeks attention. Later, when she was institutionalized in a mental hospital against her will, she managed to engineer her own release through great efforts to bring others to her cause. This was perhaps the supreme example of the resourcefulness of a middle child.

ONLY CHILDREN

Like middle children, only children show characteristics of both oldests and youngests. They may even show the extremes of both at the same time. They may have the seriousness and sense of responsibility of the oldest and the conviction of specialness and entitlement of the youngest. Not having siblings, only children tend to be more oriented toward adults, seeking their love and approval, and in return expecting their undivided attention. The major challenge for only children is to learn how to get along with others their own age. They often maintain close attachments to their parents throughout their lives but may have more difficulty relating to friends and spouses.

Indira Gandhi, Prime Minister of India—an only child
Keystone Press/Alamy Stock Photo

Young Indira with her father, Jawaharlal Nehru
Keystone Press/Newscom

Indira Gandhi, the second prime minister of India, is an example of an only child (see Genogram 2.4) who grew up quite isolated and primarily in the presence of older people, early becoming her father's confidante. She clearly had the sense of mission and responsibility of an oldest, but as a leader she was autocratic and led a rather isolated existence, keeping her own counsel. Both her father and paternal grandfather were functional only children as well. Her father, Jawaharlal Nehru, was eleven years older than his next sibling and the grandfather, Motilal Nehru, also a leader of India, was sixteen years younger than his next sibling. He was raised in the home of his adult

brother, because their father had died before Motilal was born. The illnesses of both Jawaharlal's mother and Indira's mother undoubtedly compounded their independent roles as only children and their connections to each other as father and daughter.

The French philosopher Jean-Paul Sartre is another interesting only child. His father died when he was just over a year old, and he spent his early childhood with his mother and her parents. All the adult attention of this household became focused on him. By his own account, he was a spoiled and pampered child: "My mother was mine; no one challenged my peaceful possession of her. I knew nothing of violence and hatred. Not having been bruised by its sharp angles, I knew reality only by its bright unsubstantiality. Against whom, against what, would I have rebelled? Never had someone else's whim claimed to be my law" (Sartre, 1964, p. 20).

Philosopher Jean-Paul Sartre, an only child
© René Saint-Paul/Bridgeman Images

Trouble began for Sartre at the age of twelve when his mother remarried and he was sent off to school. "He was an irascible, cantankerous, quarrelsome boy, most unpleasant toward his peers," remembered one of his classmates (Cohen-Solal, 1987, p. 45). Sartre's classmates felt only contempt for this pompous, affected child, who was always trying to be the center of attention. At times, he would try to buy friends or impress them by lying or a spectacular misdeed. He was often beaten up and rarely asked to join the different teenage groups. He would spend much of his time alone, creating his own world through his reading and writing. Eventually, Sartre did adapt to his new situation and found a kindred soul in a

Jean-Paul Sartre
Album/sfgp/Newscom

friend who was also an only child who liked literature and writing stories. He never did lose his sense of self-importance or confidence in his ability to do great things. It is perhaps not surprising that he was one of the founders of a philosophy that focuses on the importance of individual consciousness, the basic existential solitude of humanity, the absurdity of life, and the necessity for each individual to create his or her own reality.

SIBLING POSITION AND MARRIAGE

Sibling relationships often pave the way for couple relationships—for sharing, interdependence, and mutuality, just as they can predispose partners to jealousy, power struggles, and rivalry. Since siblings are generally a person's earliest peer relationships, intimate relationships are likely to reproduce the familiar sibling relationship patterns. Generally speaking, marriage seems easiest for partners who repeat their original sibling pattern, as when an oldest marries a youngest, rather than two oldests marrying each other. If a wife has grown up as the oldest of many siblings and the caretaker, she might be attracted to a dominant oldest, who offers to take over management of responsibilities. But as time goes along, she may come to resent his assertion of authority, because by experience she is more comfortable making decisions herself.

All things being equal (though they seldom are in life!), the ideal marriage based on sibling position would be a complementary one where the husband was the older brother of a younger sister and the wife the younger sister of an older brother.

In addition to complementary birth order, it seems to help in marriage if one has had siblings of the opposite sex. Most difficult might be the youngest sister of many sisters who marries the youngest brother of many brothers, since neither would have much experience of the opposite sex in a close way, and they might both play "the spoiled child" role, waiting for a caretaker. But all these patterns may just indicate hurdles that couples need to overcome to develop a working relationship, not that it is impossible to overcome such limitations of our history to make accommodations that work.

ELEANOR AND FRANKLIN

Eleanor Roosevelt, an oldest, and her cousin Franklin, an only (**see Genogram 8.7: Franklin and Eleanor Roosevelt Family**), are a good example of two strong-willed spouses whose marriage seems to have survived only because each evolved separate spheres. Leaders in their own separate worlds, they came to live apart except for holidays. Early in the marriage, Eleanor generally subordinated herself to Franklin and to his powerful mother, Sara

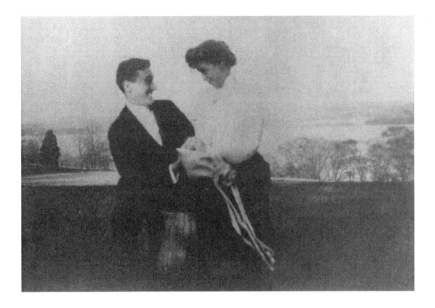

Franklin and Eleanor Roosevelt
Alpha Stock/Alamy Stock Photo

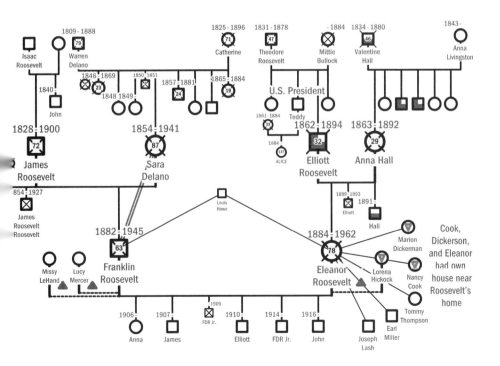

Genogram 8.7: Franklin and Eleanor Roosevelt Family

Lucy Mercer
© The Granger Collection Ltd
d/b/a GRANGER Historical
Picture Archive

Sara Delano Roosevelt and her
son, Franklin, in his teens
nsf/Alamy Stock Photo

Delano, who played a major role in their lives. However, as she became more self-confident and developed interests of her own, she began to show the determination of an oldest. The crisis came when Eleanor discovered letters revealing Franklin's affair with Lucy Mercer. Franklin's mother told her son he would never receive a penny from her if he divorced. Then Eleanor offered him his freedom, and he supposedly said, "Don't be a goose" (Michaelis, 2020, p. 165).

Since oldests and only children are oriented to parents, Sara may have been the only one who could have kept him from separating and she did.

The Roosevelts remained married, but began to live separate lives, with politics as their common ground. After Franklin's paralysis from polio, three years later in 1921, Eleanor became especially essential to his political career. But she had her own political views and activities, her own house near Hyde Park, which she shared with her friends, and her own intimate relationships with Lorena Hickok and others. She had an amazing ability to master the most horrendous experiences of her childhood and managed to live a remarkably generative and creative life. But she realized the price she was paying. She later wrote about learning her husband had been elected president: "I am sure that I was glad for my husband, but . . . I felt detached and objective, as though I were looking at someone else's life. This seems to have remained with me down to the present day. I cannot quite describe it, but it is as though you lived two lives, one of your own and the other which belonged to the circumstances that surround you" (Asbell, 1982, p. 29).

Eleanor Roosevelt (right) and longtime partner
Lorena Hickok (left)
Bettmann/Getty Images

Sara Delano, FDR, and Eleanor
Bettmann/Getty Images

Eleanor's description of this experience reflects not only the gender bias, which has for so long required women to give up their own lives for their husbands; it also suggests the creative solution she and Franklin worked out to their difficult dilemma in marriage, probably based in part on their childhood sibling roles. The remarkable thing about Eleanor is how effective she was in creating a life of her own (Michaelis, 2020). Not only did she have intense political activities in large part for her husband, and intense friendship and love relationships, including her long relationship with Lorena Hickok, but after Franklin's death in 1945, her career flourished even more, including her assignment as Ambassador to the United Nations.

There are, of course, many other possible sibling pairings in marriage. The marriage of two only children might be difficult unless they have separate spheres as the Roosevelts did, since neither has the experience of intimate sharing that one does with a sibling. Middle children may be the most flexible, since they have experiences with a number of different roles.

Those who have struggled in their sibling position while growing up, may over-identify with a child of their same gender and sibling position. Consider a father who was an oldest of five who felt that he had been burdened with too much responsibility, while his younger brothers and sister "got away with murder." When his own children came along, he spoiled the oldest and tried to make the younger ones tow the line. Or, consider a mother who finds it difficult to sympathize with her youngest daughter, because she had always felt envious of her younger sister. This was how Simone de Beauvoir described her mother, who had been the older of two sisters: "Until I began to reach adolescence, Maman ascribed to me the loftiest intellectual and moral qualities: she identified herself with me and she humiliated and slighted my sister. Poupette was the younger sister, pink and fair, and without realizing it, Maman was taking her revenge upon her" (de Beauvoir, 1959, p. 33).

Parents may also identify with one particular child because of a resemblance to another family member. Whether these identifications are conscious or unconscious, they are normal. It is a myth that parents can feel the same toward all their children. Feelings will depend on each child's characteristics and unique position in the whole family constellation, as well as on the parents' own histories and experiences.

Problems arise when the identification is so strong that parents perpetuate their old family patterns or when their own experience is so different that they misread their children. A parent who was an only child may tend to assume that normal sibling fights are an indication of serious problems.

SIBLING CONNECTIONS WHEN THERE ARE DYSFUNCTIONAL OR ABSENT PARENTS

Siblings with dysfunctional, absent, or unavailable parents may become each other's refuge (see also Nathanial Hawthorne, who appears to have had a secret sexual relationship with his sister) or become completely disconnected from each other. Charlie Chaplin and his half-brother Sydney (four years older) developed an unusually close, lifelong bond, while Chaplin and his younger brother, who became the actor Wheeler Dryden, never even met until well into adulthood.

Charlie Chaplin
Pictorial Press Ltd/Alamy Stock Photo

Sydney was less than three months old when his mother married Charles Chaplin senior, who became responsible for his support, though he did a very poor job of it. Chaplin Sr. separated early from the boys' mother, became an alcoholic, and more or less abandoned them. Their mother suffered repeated mental breakdowns throughout their childhood and had to be institutionalized. Their aunt once said of the boys' relationship: "It seems strange to me that anyone can write about Charlie Chaplin without mentioning his brother Sydney. They have been inseparable all their lives, except when fate intervened at intervals. Syd, of quiet manner, clever brain and steady nerve, has been father and mother to Charlie. Charlie always looked up to Syd, and Sydney would suffer anything to spare Charlie" (Robinson, 1985, p. 2).

At one point in childhood, when the brothers were separated, Sydney became concerned that Charlie was not responding to his letters, which, as it turned out, was partly because Charlie could not spell

Charlie Chaplin's mother
VTR/Alamy Stock Photo

Charlie Chaplin with
his brother Sydney
RGR Collection/
Alamy Stock Photo

well. Sydney reproached him and touchingly recalled the misery they had endured together: "Since Mother's illness, all we have in the world is each other. So, you must write regularly and let me know that I have a brother" (Chaplin, 1964, p. 82).

From early childhood they had to fend for themselves and move about from place to place—to the workhouse, to an orphanage, and to a series of apartments, having at times to help their mother receive care. Sydney, who had performed with his brother and then became his manager, late in life wrote to Charlie: "It has always been my unfortunate predicament, or should I say fortunate predicament, to concern myself with your protection. This is the result of my fraternal or rather paternal instinct" (Robinson, 1985, p. 22).

Chaplin's younger half-brother, Wheeler Dryden, was abducted away to Canada by his father as an infant, and never met Chaplin until they were in their late twenties, at which point Wheeler had to make many efforts to reconnect before Chaplin would even speak to him. Chaplin eventually persuaded him to agree not to acknowledge their brotherhood and never mentioned Dryden in either of his autobiographies. But later Dryden worked for him and became a more than devoted follower, who totally revered his brother. Probably Chaplin's refusal to connect with this brother related to the shame that their mother could not care for him, because of her mental illness or because of having each child with a different partner. Such painful disconnections are not uncommon among siblings in these situations, as is the intense bonding of Chaplin with his older brother, who became a kind of "filler" parent for the missing caretakers of his life.

In your own family it is important to explore the specifics of sibling patterns, not just along the obvious dimensions of gender, distance apart in age, talents and disabilities, resemblance to each parent and to extended family members, but also in terms of how relationships played out in your family. Who was the leader, the mediator, the creative thinker, the one who dared and the one who followed, the joker, the caretaker? We should especially be on the lookout for siblings taking complimentary roles: leader/follower; over-functioner/under-functioner, or taking symmetrical roles, where they are continuously in competition for accomplishments, jokes, parental appreciation, etc.

Charlie Chaplin with his brother Wheeler
Dryden
Popperfoto/Getty Images

QUESTIONS ABOUT SIBLING PATTERNS IN YOUR FAMILY

- Do members of the family conform to the generalized characteristics described for birth order? If not, have mitigating circumstances influenced sibling patterns, such as a child with special needs or characteristics or other family changes around the birth of a child?
- How were siblings in the family expected to behave: pals, "blood brothers," rivals, partners, opposites?
- Have family legacies influenced sibling roles and relationships?
- Have any siblings been especially close? In business together? Estranged? If so, what were the issues involved? Caretaking of a parent? Rivalries about careers, money, spouses, who was the preferred child or whose children were more special? Do any specific sibling patterns run throughout the family?
- Did parents tend to identify with the child of the same sex and sibling position as their own?
- Which sibling was the most "triangled"? Do you have any hypotheses about why this child was "it"?
- Can you tell anything about the family values and patterns by the labels different siblings had? The star and the loser? The angel and the villain? The strong one and the weak one? The good seed and the bad seed? Why might such labels have been given, beyond the obvious?

Chapter 9
Couple Relationships

> Every marriage is a mystery, of course, which no outsider can ever truly understand.
>
> —TIM EGAN
> *Scenes from a Mogul's Marriage*

The institution of marriage,* in some form, exists in all societies, although cultures vary in who may marry and under what circumstances, what purpose marriage serves, and the roles and responsibilities of each partner. Some cultures have no expectation that marriages will be intimate, as they are contracted between fathers for the economic and social stability or betterment of the family. In the United States, marriage is generally thought to be a matter of individual partner choice for spiritual, emotional, and physical intimacy. This creates many problems, since the main need society has for marriage is for the production and nurturing of children. Thus, there are many potentially conflicting goals at work in any family when it comes to the place of marriage in the family as a whole.

A particular difficulty regarding marriage is that it is the only family relationship in which exclusivity is expected. We can love more than one child, sibling, or parent. But we are not supposed to love more than one partner (at least not at one time!). Also, while marriage is the weakest relationship in the family, as our current divorce rate of 50 percent attests, it is the only one we swear is for-

---

* The term marriage refers to a legally or formally recognized union between two people that reflects a lifelong commitment entered into for various purposes that may include having and raising children, companionship and sexual and emotional intimacy, and economic security. We acknowledge however that some couples, either by choice or because of social prejudice, may not be married and yet may be joined in a long-term committed relationship that, while not legally or religiously sanctioned, is no less valid. Hence our use of the term marriage, unless otherwise noted, includes these unions as well.

ever. Indeed, it would probably be a good idea if we made that promise for our parents, siblings, and children. Maybe the very fragility of the marriage bond is the reason we have to swear that our marriage vows are till death do us part.

Indeed, the most powerful experiences human beings have of intimacy are probably in couple relationships, along with the most common sense of disillusionment. Being "in love" is more disorienting than any other relationship. It is the most mysterious of emotions, as well as the one that most often fools us. Women traditionally even lost their names, not to mention their identities, and in many cultures even their families of origin in marrying. People have often been willing to give up everything for a love, who is presumably a hoped-for marriage partner, although people are often less generous to a long-term marital partner than to a new one. Our confusion between lust, love, companionship, loyalty, friendship, and sexual intimacy runs deep, and no other relationship is so linked with our very sense of who we are.

Indeed, some marriages are so full of intensity that they become intolerable. But marriages lacking in intensity also have their problems. Eugene O'Neill, whose difficulties with marriage and other relationships we have already discussed, had the following dream for the perfect marriage: "My wife and I will live on a barge. I'll live at one end and she'll live at the other, and we'll never see each other except when the urge strikes us" (Gelb & Gelb, 1987, p. 256).

But the conflicting goals, intensity, and difficulties of gender arrangements are not the only reasons marriage is so complex. It is often said that what distinguishes human beings from other animals is the fact of having in-laws. Human beings are the only animals who tend to develop intense relationships with their in-laws. The joke that there are six in the marital bed is really a gross understatement. Marriage places no small stress on a family to open itself to in-laws—outsiders who now become official members of the family—often the first new members in years.

Naturally it is often hard to enter a family, because of its long-shared history of which the new spouse is not a part. It is hard to incorporate a new person, who does not share your memories, private jokes, code words, and family traditions. Marriage shifts the relationship of a couple from a private twosome to a formal joining of two families. Issues that the partners have not resolved with their own families tend to be factors in marital choice and inevitably influence couple relationships, but they also change the extended family relationships moving forward. The intensity of romantic love is, of course, also influenced by patterns of the family of origin.

From this perspective, Romeo and Juliet might have felt intensely attracted to each other precisely *because* their families were enemies. In idealizing the forbidden person, they, like many other romantic couples, including Tristan and Isolde, were spared any broader perspective on their relationship. In addition, their untimely deaths saved them from possible later conflicts over who would pick up the socks and how to handle the mother-in-law. In everyday life the outcome of such forbidden love affairs is not always so romantic. If couples marry expecting the other to solve their problems, they are likely soon to be disappointed.

Marriage is indeed a difficult proposition. Yet our culture's mythology portrays marriage, along with parenthood to which it has long been the symbolic precursor, as the easiest and most joyous life-cycle transition. Our society's myths about marriage probably add to its difficulty. Marriage, more than any other rite of passage, is viewed as the solution to loneliness or turmoil: the fairy tale ending: "And they lived happily ever after." On the contrary, in the context of the multigenerational family life cycle, marriage comes in the middle of a complex evolving process of two families, as they are transformed by new roles and relationships.

Part of the journey to understand yourself better through studying your family entails focusing on the patterns that were passed down through the generations related to marriage and couple relationships in your family. It will require you to identify the forces that supported and discouraged various relationships, and to be curious about why some relationships were strained and others successful. A good starting point is finding out how and when your parents, grandparents, and other couples in your family met, the story of what attracted them to each other, and how they decided to marry. The answers to these questions will tell you something about how marriage takes place in your family.

TO MARRY OR NOT TO MARRY: THE INFLUENCE OF SOCIOCULTURAL ISSUES

In the U.S. we like to think that individual rights and freedom of choice are what determine our life course, and to some extent they do. But our lives are also shaped by the broader sociocultural context in which we are embedded. Regarding whether or not one marries, gay and lesbian couples did not even have the option to choose marriage until 2015. With respect to race, the U.S. had laws prohibiting people of different races from marrying until 1967. Even when no legal restrictions exist, barriers based on religion, social class, ethnicity, and race influence who is considered an acceptable spouse. Barack Obama shared in his memoir his experience of cross-racial dating someone white for almost a year. Alone together they could fall into their own private world. But then one weekend she invited him to go with her to her family's country house, which had been inherited from her great-grandfather. The family library was elaborately full of material about the famous people her grandfather had known, and it left Obama feeling clear that they were from vastly different worlds and if they remained a couple, he would eventually live in her world, because he had already mastered the craft of living as an outsider and accommodating to try and fit in for most of his life.

When Obama's sister asked him what happened, he said when he thought about the future, it pressed in on "our warm little world." He took her to see a play by a Black playwright: an angry, funny play, of "typical black American humor." Afterward she asked why Black people were so angry all the time and he responded that no one asks why Jews remember the Holocaust. She said that was different and that Black anger was just a dead end. Though they had been close in their private relationship, they could not put their worlds together and the relationship broke up.

Despite the prohibitions that may exist against marrying across religious, social-class, ethnic, and/or racial lines, people do make decisions to marry across these boundaries, and the result is often tension, in part because familial and societal prejudices do not diminish once a couple has formed. At the same time, marriage is one of the primary ways that we human beings have for learning to cross cultural boundaries.

Weddings, because they are innately stressful, often become the site where these tensions become particularly charged. The new spouse may be subtly rejected as "Not our class, Darling" (N.O.C.D.), or of the "wrong" cultural or religious background. Parents may see their child's involvement with a partner who is "not our type" as a personal rejection. The tears that are so frequently shed on the wedding day may reflect the profound stress of the changes taking place in the family, rather than distress over the photographer's ineptitude, the guest list, the seating arrangements, the bridal gown, or the usher's cummerbund. Family conflicts around weddings are often fascinating indicators of underlying family values, alliances, and fears. And, of course, eloping or having a wedding without key family members present may indicate problematic family relationships just as clearly.

Traditional gender norms have exerted pressure on women to marry and locate their identity with the confines of the marriage, while men have been raised to see intimacy as a threat to their autonomy. Thus, men more often maintain a pseudo-independent stance in marriage. While implicitly depending on their wives to take care of them, they tend to deny their dependence, admitting no needs, doubts, or mistakes. Women, on the other hand, are generally expected to maintain a pseudo-intimacy, while actually being able to function almost entirely without spousal reassurance or support for their needs. In particular, our culture has promoted the myth that marriage is like Cinderella being found by Prince Charming and then sacrificing her identity to his. Moreover, until recently, societal heterosexism and homophobia prohibited gay and lesbian couples from having the choice to marry, and many LGBTQ couples have had to negotiate their relationships against the backdrop of intense prejudice and persecution, even from their own families.

TO MARRY OR NOT TO MARRY: THE INFLUENCE OF FAMILY BELIEFS AND MESSAGES

All families have beliefs about marriage that influence their thoughts and feelings about it. Some families transmit the message that marriage is an institution created by God and it is our sacred responsibility to enter into this union. Or a family might view marriage as a hopeful beginning of a great love story. Conversely, families may view marriage as a doomed enterprise, warning members against the institution. This was certainly the case in the remarkable Blackwell family (**see Genogram 9.1: Blackwell Family**) where several unmarried aunts apparently warned the Blackwell children repeatedly against marriage. In their grandparents' generation, their maternal grandfather disgraced the family, first with his promiscuity, and then with his arrest and deportation to Australia for forgery. Their paternal grandfather was a quarrelsome ne'er-do-well. He was said to have "crushed the life out of his wife," who said of him, "How careful girls ought to be before they listen to the flatteries of a man, seeing that all that ceased when they'd got a woman to marry them, and then the poor girl found what a dreadful master marriage had given her, what a slave she was, and what a world of care, labor, and worry she had got into, adding that those were wise who did not marry and if it were to do over again, most certainly she would not marry Grandpapa" (Nimura, 2021, p. 10).

In the next generation, their father died relatively young, leaving his wife and nine children unprovided for, as had both his father and his father-in-law. The family stories in the wake of such experiences may create powerful messages about the role and meaning of marriage. They do not, of course, doom the next generation to repeat the pattern. Instead, such marriages may inspire the next generation to creativity in their life choices.

All five of the Blackwell daughters chose to remain unmarried, though four of them adopted children. One, Elizabeth, became the first woman phy-

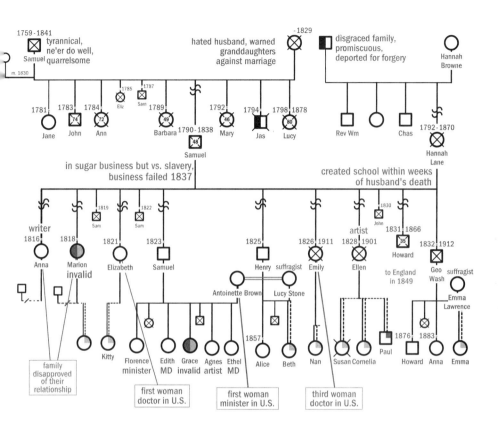

Genogram 9.1: Blackwell Family

sician in the U.S.; another, Emily, soon became the
third U.S. woman physician. Their sisters, Anna,
became a journalist, and Ellen, an artist. The fifth
sister, Marion, was an invalid, though she, like
three of her sisters, adopted a child to raise.

The three sons were also amazing men in
what they did with the family messages about
marriage. Henry Blackwell fell in love with the
famous suffragist Lucy Stone. He was attracted
by her fiery speeches on the abolition of slavery and the rights of women, including impas-
sioned pleas against traditional marriage. Lucy
Stone said: "How soon the character of the race
would change if pure and equal real marriages

Elizabeth Blackwell, first woman
physician in the U.S.
*Schlesinger Library, Harvard
Radcliffe Institute*

Emily Blackwell, third woman
physician in the U.S.
*Schlesinger Library, Harvard Radcliffe
Institute*

Henry Blackwell
*Schlesinger Library, Harvard Radcliffe
Institute*

could take the place of the horrible relations that now bear that sacred name" (Lucy Stone expressed to her husband, Henry Blackwell, July 27, 1853). Henry Blackwell and Lucy Stone wrote their own marriage vows, which deliberately omitted the promise for the wife to obey, followed by an eloquent protest Henry had prepared against a woman's legal subservience to her husband in marriage: "I wish, as a husband, to renounce all the privileges which the law confers upon me, which are not strictly mutual" (Wheeler, 1961, pp. 276–277). Henry's protest became the model for generations of couples who wanted to transcend the traditional gender inequality of marriage. The couple kept separate names and bank accounts and Henry encouraged Lucy wholeheartedly in her career as in everything else.

Lucy's family had also given her negative messages and stories about marriage. She had anguished over her mother's "bondage" and self-denial in relation to her father's abuse and dominance. Her father was "ugly" to his wife about money, and Lucy felt pained by her mother's lack of freedom and that of all other women in marriage. She wrote a friend: "It will take more than my lifetime for the obstacles to be removed which are in the way of a married woman

having any being of her own"
(Wheeler, 1961, p. 277).

Lucy had grown up determined
never to marry, and changed her
mind with great reluctance, becoming severely symptomatic having
a near breakdown at the prospect.
Her symptoms were so severe that
her marriage had to be postponed
several times. Shortly before she
"succumbed" she joked to her closest friend and future sister-in-law,
Antoinette Brown: "If the ceremony is in New York, we want
you to harden your heart enough
to help in so cruel an operation as
putting Lucy Stone to death. But it
will be all according to law, so you
need fear no punishment. I expect,

Lucy Stone
Library of Congress, Manuscript Division,
Blackwell Family Papers

Henry Blackwell and Lucy Stone Blackwell in later years, smiling and surrounded
by their relatives
Schlesinger Library, Harvard Radcliffe Institute

however, to go to Cincinnati to have the ruin complete there" (Wheeler, 1961, p. 128). Henry himself wrote with similar humor to one of his good friends: "I have just entangled myself beyond the possibility of release. . . . I lose no time in conveying information of the frightful casualty." Despite their fears, the marriage was a long and happy one for both of them.

As you think about the couple relationships in your family, did any family members defy family rules and messages around what was considered "appropriate" gender? If so, how were they viewed by the family? For example, if you had an aunt who never got married, was she viewed pitifully as a spinster, or admired for being an independent woman who didn't need a marriage to establish her identity and worth? Was there a man in your family who, though not successful in the business world, was a beloved nurturer of his children and grandchildren? Did the family value or devalue him for being an affectionate stay-at-home man?

THE INFLUENCE OF LOSS

The stories families have about the reasons for marriage—love at first sight, the wish to have and raise children, the need for security, prospects of money and prestige, or anxiety about growing old alone, may obscure the influence that family events, especially experiences with loss, may have on the decision to marry. This certainly was the case in the Antoinette Brown's family, where she was the sixth of ten children. She lost five siblings in the years before she met Samuel Blackwell. She was perhaps impelled toward Oberlin and the ministry out of a need to come to terms with the early deaths of four of her siblings. Then the death of a fifth, her sister Augusta, who had followed her to Oberlin, and who succumbed after a five-year struggle with tuberculosis, appears to have symbolized for Antoinette the end of her family.

Antoinette, like the Blackwells, was remarkably farsighted in her views about women's roles. She asserted that human knowledge would be enriched by adding to the traditions of logic and scientific inquiry the traditional "female" ways of knowing: intuition and personal experience. Antoinette and Lucy Stone had met years before at Oberlin College, where they formed a deep attachment and vowed never to marry. Both felt that marriage would be a severe hindrance to their work. Antoinette advocated that men's obligations should extend to family and home—a view that would take other feminists a full century more to espouse. No other writer publicly proposed that men should share childcare and homemaking as well as work for pay.

Perhaps it was the loss of her sister Augusta that led Antoinette to reverse her decision never to marry. In the long marriage that ensued, Samuel was extraordinary for the untraditional caring role he played within his family, living out his wife's ideas wholeheartedly. He readily shared in the work of the home and was viewed as a saint by the entire Blackwell family. Antoinette later said of him: "This fellow spirit has been so woven into mine that nothing could quite tear us asunder."

Supported by Samuel, Antoinette had a full life as the first woman minister in the U.S., a speaker and author of poems, novels, and philosophical tracts until her death at age ninety-six. She lived long enough to vote and receive an honorary doctorate of divinity from Oberlin, which had earlier refused to grant her a ministerial degree, even after she completed her studies there.

Samuel and Antoinette had five daughters, four successful, and one an invalid, just as had the previous generation. Again, as in the previous generation, there were five unmarried aunts who played a critical role in the children's development. Of their daughters' marriages, Antoinette said all were more than satisfactory. Interestingly, at least one of these daughters, Flo, rebelled against the prescription for women to have an independent career. She married a storekeeper, to the family's great disapproval, though they eventually realized that he was excellent, much in the model of his father-in-law. Flo herself eventually followed in her mother's footsteps, becoming a lay minister.

Beyond family stories of love and marriage, it is worth exploring your genogram for family events that may have influenced decisions to marry or not to marry as well as decisions to divorce. You may be surprised how often couples falling in love and deciding to marry has

Samuel Blackwell
Schlesinger Library on the History of Women in America, Radcliffe Institute, Harvard University. MC411-1017-6.

Antoinette Brown Blackwell
Schlesinger Library, Harvard Radcliffe Institute

been connected to other events in your family. From a systems perspective, we might hypothesize that Romeo and Juliet falling in love might have been a way to lower their anxiety about conflicts between their warring families.

MARITAL PATTERNS OVER TIME

To understand your family, track marital patterns over time and across generations, looking at periods of high tension and thinking about how couples handled conflict. Pay special attention to situations involving triangulating with a child, a mother-in-law, or with other outsiders and notice whether these events happened at the time of other family stresses in the family. Be sure to consider how couples balanced the forces of connection and autonomy. Were couple dynamics organized more intensely around similarities or differences?

HOW CONFLICT IS HANDLED

Conflict is inevitable in all relationships. Some couples engage in conflict directly, either hashing things out, using constructive communication to resolve disagreements, or escalating into aggressive confrontations that do not usually lead to resolution but inflict instead relational injuries and resentments. Other couples avoid conflict altogether. Couples who find it threatening to have direct conflict often lower their anxiety by focusing on a child, who obliges them by becoming "the problem," allowing the parents to subvert their conflict and form a united front.

TRIANGLES

When couples cannot resolve issues, a number of triangles commonly develop. They may come together around a mischievous or sick child. Or they may focus on their in-laws as the source of the problem: "If it weren't for your mother's intrusiveness, we'd be alright." Men have traditionally moved outside the family when they had marital problems, to work or an affair, or focusing their energies on "male" activities—socializing with buddies at the pub, sports, etc. Addictions are surely the most destructive of the common male responses to marital tension. Women, while also turning to drugs and alcohol, are likely to turn their marital frustrations into anxiety, depression, social withdrawal, rigid housekeeping, or overinvestment in their children. More recently, women have also turned to work or affairs, and couples commonly struggle over in-laws, but as we have been saying, accepting one's in-laws is extremely important for family well-being.

Author Amy Tan (see also Chapter 10) developed a profound insight about mother-in-law triangles from her own mother, with whom she had an extremely difficult relationship for many years. Tan was the daughter of Chinese immigrant parents who themselves kept many family secrets from her and her siblings. When Amy met her husband, who was from a privileged white family, they strongly disapproved of her and she had a difficult time with them for years. She says that she remained angry at her husband's parents for their continued slights and at her husband for not standing up for her, but one day her own difficult mother told her she was being too sharp and fierce: "Be good to your mother-in-law, not for your mother-in-law, but for your husband. Don't make him choose. Don't make him one day regret what he did for you, when she is gone." Tan says she instantly knew her mother was right. She realized why her mother told her to let go. Her mother could not forget her own husband's pain and sorrow that she had forced him in the first years of their marriage to cut off his favorite sister, because she had felt insulted by her sister-in-law. Tan came to realize a deep truth about how in-law relationships had played out for two generations before. In time, Tan's mother-in-law did indeed come to love her and as exasperating as the mother-in-law was to her son, he remained devoted to his mother. Amy told him during his most trying moments how much she admired him for being not just a good son but a good person. When her mother-in-law died at 101, she says: "My husband had no regrets for how he had treated her. Nor did I."

She realized her mother had seen her own strong opinions and stubbornness and that of her own mother in Amy: "My mother saw her mother in me and no wonder. We are alike in so many ways. We have strong opinions. We can't tolerate insults. And look at what we did for love. We did not give up because of disapproval. We became more determined."

What Tan learned from her mother's message is something we all need to learn: to respect the complexity of our in-law relationships and be as supportive as possible of their connections rather than trying to resist them, because of their difficulty accepting us. This doesn't mean tolerating abuse, but it does mean taking the very broadest perspective on our spouse's (and our children's) commitment to their other family members.

Additionally, it is important to explore the triangles that so often develop in divorced and remarried families. It is extremely common for triangles to develop between children and their half-siblings or step-siblings and between the new spouse and the ex-spouse. Such patterns often continue on to the next generation, where the children on each side of the family continue the negativity without knowing anything about each other or having any idea of the reasons for the conflicts in the first place.

THE PROBLEM OF EITHER FUSION OR SEPARATION

Human beings need both connection and autonomy, and healthy relationships balance both needs. When relationships lean too heavily in one direction or the other, the result is either an over-connection, which is fusion, or an over-distancing, which is disconnection. Neither fusion nor separation are functional. As obvious as this may sound, modern Western culture romanticizes fusion by equating it with intimacy. From Hallmark to Hollywood we are bombarded with messages about how romantic it is for two people to merge together and "become one." Phrases of fusion such as "you are my world" and "I would be nothing without you" are extremely common. Yet we live in a culture where human interaction is increasingly controlled by technology and social media, which impair the kind of depth and vulnerability that lead to authentic relating. Hence, despite the illusion that we have a high degree of connection, in reality many people's lives are characterized by disconnection.

In healthy relationships, connection and autonomy are balanced by independent, differentiated thinking along with the ability to remain close. Each partner cares about how the other feels, but does need to control the other, nor to give up their own feelings to be connected.

In a balanced relationship. if one partner becomes depressed, the other partner has compassion for this, but does not assume she or he is the cause. Instead, the partner assumes, "There are many reasons to get depressed in life, this may have nothing to do with me." Such an assumption of not being responsible for the other's feelings permits a supportive response. Conversely, in a fused relationship there is a tendency to personalize the partner's problems, assuming, "I must be responsible for their depression." When partners start taking responsibility for each other's feelings, more and more areas of the relationship become tension-filled. The wife may feel inadequate, guilty, and resentful. She may decide to avoid dealing with her husband because she does not want to arouse his irritability or blame, or she may become protective of him and stay silent to keep from making him upset. He may avoid raising issues that create tension out of fear of her annoyance. In either case, the more the reactions of each are a response to the other, the more their communication will become constricted in emotionally charged areas and the less flexibility and freedom there will be in the relationship. On the other hand, in a relationship characterized by distance, partners tend to lack empathy or concern for how the other person feels. Hence, if one partner is depressed in a disconnected relationship, the other partner will likely not show empathy. In fact, there is likely to be minimal engagement overall and very little interest expressed in sharing or listening to each other.

GUSTAV AND ALMA MAHLER: A CASE OF INTENSE SEPARATION

Composer Gustav Mahler, one of the most gifted composers of the twentieth century, and Alma Schindler, also a great musical talent, are an example of a complex marriage that was fraught with too much distance on his part and too much giving up of self on hers. In 1902, Mahler, aged forty-two, married Schindler, aged twenty-three (**see Genogram 9.3: Mahler Marriage**).

For many years Mahler had avoided marriage, perhaps because his parents' marriage was extremely unhappy. His mother, Marie, had suffered from unrequited love for someone else, and married Gustav's father without loving him. She was a sweet, frail, quietly affectionate woman, who was born physically disabled. Gustav's irascible father brutalized her, beat his children, and ran after every servant. Mahler's love for his mother was as intense as his dislike for his father. Marie bore fourteen children in twenty-one years, losing eight sons in childhood. Gustav, the oldest surviving child, who had nursed his younger brother, Ernst, unceasingly until he died at fourteen, became the caretaker for the others. Until his marriage he lived with his sister Justine, who was his housekeeper, companion, and hostess for two decades. At age thirty-three Justine had begun to think she was doomed to the fate of tending to her brother and would never have a life of her own. She loved him but felt like his servant. She was in love with the first violinist at the Vienna Opera, which Gustav conducted. Not surprisingly, perhaps, she married the very day after her brother married Alma.

Gustav's attraction to Alma was immediate upon meeting her. She was beautiful, strong-minded, creative, and full of youth. The romance developed quickly, but trouble followed as soon as Alma let Gustav know her ambition was to continue being a musician and composer. His response was harsh, calling her arrogant and reminding her of his view of a wife: "You must become what I need if we are to be happy together. . . . The role of 'composer,' falls to me; yours is that of loving companion and understanding partner. . . . You must give yourself to me unconditionally, shape your future life in every detail entirely in accordance with my needs and desire nothing in return save my love" (Monson, 1983, pp. 42–44).

Alma was shocked. He was asking her to give up her work and herself, and requiring her instead to dedicate herself to him and his music, which she didn't even like. Alma had grown up devoted to her father, who had died when she

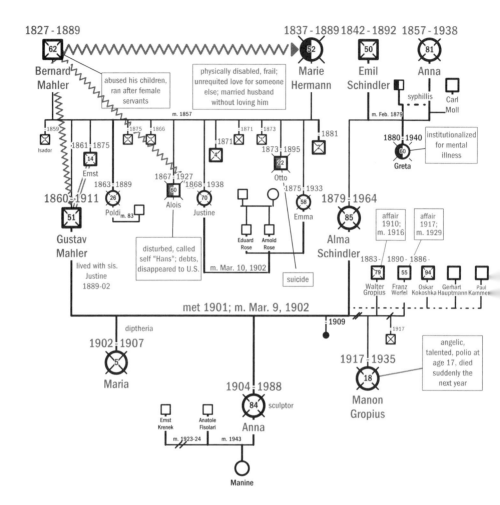

Genogram 9.2: Mahler Marriage

was thirteen. When she showed Gustav's letter to her mother, for whom she had always felt resentment, the mother urged her to end the relationship. But Alma, perhaps in defiance of her mother, chose to do the opposite. She soon paid heavily for her acquiescence!

As wedding plans proceeded, the tension between the couple continued. Gustav's friends found Alma rude and unappreciative of his work. His sister was jealous. In addition, as Alma soon realized, Gustav completely neglected his finances and was heavily in debt. It would take her five years to get him out of debt. And while he showed some flexibility during their brief courtship, as soon as they married he reverted to his rigid obsession with his work and acted more like her teacher than her partner.

In addition to copying his work for him, Alma's job was to keep everything running smoothly. She had become pregnant before they married and as the pregnancy developed, she felt her freedom disappearing. "Nothing has reached fruition for me, neither my beauty, nor my spirit, nor my talent. I am living what only appears to be a life. I hold so much inside of me. I am not free; I suffer, but I don't know why" (Monson, 1983, p. 65). Like so many women, she was mystified by her problem, which her husband invalidated. One day when Gustav found her crying, he accused her of being unhappy because she didn't love him enough. She wrote in her diary: "There is such a silent struggle going on inside me! And such a dreadful longing for someone who thinks about ME—that helps me find MYSELF! I am drowning beneath the altar of family life.... It came over me that I had crossed that bridge once and for all; someone had taken me roughly by the arm and led me far away from my own self" (Keegan, 1992, pp. 110–111).

Even when she did find words for her frustration, complaining to him the next year about his lack of acknowledgment of her or her work, his response was to blame her unhappiness on her: "Just because your budding dreams have not been fulfilled . . . that's entirely up to you" (Keegan, 1992, p. 115). Such a response, often referred to as "gaslighting" is typical in dys-

Gustav Mahler
Chronicle/Alamy Stock Photo

Alma Mahler
Lebrecht Music and Arts/Alamy Stock Photo

functional marriages, where the dominant partner conveys to the other that their response is their own fault and responsibility. The gaslighting partner takes no responsibility for their own behavior.

Over the next few years, the couple grew further and further apart. Gustav was preoccupied with his work. Alma was depressed and frustrated. Their first daughter, Maria, named for Gustav's beloved but frail mother, died in 1907, at the age of five. In his grief, Gustav withdrew further. The same year he was diagnosed with a life-threatening heart condition; Alma herself was often physically ill as well as depressed. Neither of them had much energy left over for their younger daughter, Anna, born in 1904, who, left to her own devices, blamed herself for years afterward for her sister's death, though it occurred when she was only three. Gustav became preoccupied with fear that he would die himself. He feared that, like Schubert, Beethoven, and Bruckner, having written eight symphonies he would not live past a ninth. He therefore chose to call his next work *The Song of The Earth*, convincing himself that he would thus not tempt fate. He did later complete a 9th Symphony, but he did not live to complete his tenth.

During this stormy period Alma became emotionally involved with one of Mahler's devotees, a common triangulating pattern in situations of couple conflict and loss or threatened loss.

Mahler was at the time preoccupied with his struggles with the Vienna Opera, and with the anti-Semitism in the socio–political atmosphere of the era in Austria, which was limiting his opportunities, contributing undoubtedly to his attempts to dominate in the marriage. For a time, they came to the United States, where he was much more appreciated, but where Alma was all the more isolated and cut off. In addition, in 1909, Alma had a miscarriage, which revived the pain of the loss of their first child.

In May 1910, Alma consulted a physician for what she called the "wear and tear of being driven on without respite by a spirit so intense as [Gustav's]." She feared she was on the brink of collapse. The doctor recommended a rest cure and she left for a spa. Not surprisingly, she became involved in a new romance, this time with Walter Gropius, a handsome, imaginative, talented German architect several years younger than she. Shortly afterward, Gropius wrote to Mahler, as if Mahler were Alma's father, asking permission to marry her.

Mahler went into a tailspin, obsessed with fear of losing his wife. He vowed to change, seeking consultation with Freud, whose intervention was interesting from a family systems perspective. Freud zeroed in on the unresolved issues the couple had with their own parents, which had drawn Gustav and Alma together in the first place. He posed the challenge: "How dared a man in your state ask a young woman to be tied to him? . . . I know your wife. She loved her father, and she can only choose and love a man of his sort.

Your age, of which you are so much afraid, is precisely what attracts her. You need not be anxious. You loved your mother and you looked for her in every woman. She was careworn and ailing, and unconsciously you wish your wife to be the same" (Monson, 1983, p. 111).

Gustav began writing love letters to Alma, saying he must sound like a "schoolboy in love," but no longer hiding his feelings. "Freud is quite right— you were always the light and the central point for me! That inner light, I mean, which rose over all" (Monson, 1983, p. 113). Here is the paradoxical aspect of so many marriages: though men may have controlled and inhibited their wives' personal development, their own unacknowledged and unarticulated dependence on their wives may be intense. This can leave the wife in a paradoxical situation: she is seen as vulnerable and emotionally dependent on her husband, yet paradoxically expected to survive with almost no emotional support, validation, or understanding from him.

The crisis led Gustav to begin playing the songs Alma had written years before, to convince her to return to composing, which he had forced her to give up years earlier. Far from feeling supported by this, Alma felt he was invading her privacy. She never gained the courage to return to composing, though gradually the marriage mellowed. Gustav became more supportive of her. He had long ignored her birthday and other holidays, but he now bought her a diamond ring and made elaborate preparations for a Christmas celebration. He also became more expressive to his daughter Anna. Then, shortly after Christmas in 1911, he contracted influenza and within a few months he died. Alma was 32.

Walter Gropius
Artokoloro/Alamy Stock Photo

Alma had relationships with several other men, including a dramatist Gerhardt Hauptman, a brilliant and controversial biologist, Paul Kammerer, and an artist, Oskar Kokoshka, whose demands were similar to Mahler's. Kokoshka wrote to her: "You must force yourself to give up every thought of every production from your past and of every advisor prior to me. . . . I want you very much when you find your own being, your peace, and your freedom in my existence. . . . I warn you to decide whether you want to be free from me or in me (Monson, 1983, pp. 145–146). He even took to signing his letters "Alma Oskar

Kokoshka," as if to fuse their two identities. Though deeply drawn to him, Alma had the wisdom, perhaps from hard experience, to resist his demands for fusion. She was deeply disturbed by the relationship, though she came to feel she could never be free of it: "I would like to break free from Oskar. . . . He makes me lose my momentum. . . . But now I know I will sing only in death. Then I'll be a slave to no man, because I will tend to my own well-being and to myself" (Monson, 1983, p. 164).

In an attempt to get away, she looked up Gropius again and convinced him within two weeks that they were in love with each other. It was not inconsequential to her that Gropius's birthday fell on May 18, Gustav's death day! She connected him with her loss in another way as well. Remembering her first meeting with him, she wrote: "I believed that I was old and hateful . . . and suddenly there came a man into my life who was new to me and immediately taken by me. When he first told me that he loved me, I was happy as I had not been in years. This happened right after I had lost my beautiful child. I was destroyed and suffering" (Monson, 1983, p. 175).

Since this relationship was built on her previous losses, it is perhaps not surprising that she wanted to end it soon after they married and had another daughter, Manon, in 1916. She tried to keep Gropius from getting close to their new daughter and turned her attention to a poet, Franz Werfel, eleven years her junior. Soon she became pregnant by him. Gropius was led to believe the child was his, but when he realized it was not, he graciously let Alma go without reproach. The baby, born premature, died after a few months.

Over the next few years, Alma struggled with herself about how to arrange her life. She could not marry Franz and she could not leave him. Several times a year the couple would part to do their own work and then they would reunite. Eventually, in 1929 they did marry, but their relationship was never really happy.

In Alma's last years, Oskar Kokoshka turned up in New York where she was living and asked to visit her. They had corresponded over the years in fits and starts, in letters full of dreams of reuniting and unfulfilled possibilities. In the end Alma refused to see him. Perhaps she preferred to hold on to her dream of their love than to confront once again it's complex reality.

COMPLEMENTARY RELATIONSHIPS

The old saying that "opposites attract" is not entirely true, since people generally choose partners who are similar to them in the most important ways.

Yet couples do often seem to choose each other to express hidden sides of themselves. Initially, differences may be quite alluring, novel, and exciting. But once the honeymoon phase of a relationship ends, the initial pleasure that differences generated may fade.

The issue is how a couple's similarities or differences organize their relational dynamics. Some couples are organized around their similarities, sharing work, values, and leisure activities. Others have more complementary relationships, their opposing characteristics creating the equilibrium. Whatever the patterns, you will want to explore their meaning to clarify what role you want to take in your relationships.

At age forty, George Bernard Shaw married Charlotte Payne-Townshend, who was one year younger. While the couple shared a number of things, their relationship dynamics were organized around their differences. As Shaw's wife wrote:

> The conflict of temperaments is nature's way of avenging the race. Nature thrusts men and women into the arms of their opposites . . . marriage causes untold unhappiness . . . brought about by the clash. . . . We constantly blame only one, and probably the wrong one. For the troubles of my youth my mother seemed entirely to blame, but on mature reflection I see that this is a wrong view. (Dunbar 1963, p. 252)

Like many oldests, Charlotte was responsible, accustomed to dominating and being the caretaker. Shaw, on the other hand, the younger brother of two sisters, was irreverent, creative, irresponsible, and used to having others take care of him. These complementary differences created a kind of balance that made them well-suited for each other, although ironically, one of the things they shared in common was a deep resistance to marriage.

Shaw had a long-tanding pattern of distancing from women who pursued him. One such admirer said of him: "The sight of a woman deeply in love with him annoyed him" (Holroyd, 1988, p. 428). His view of this woman was that "I give her nothing; and I do not even take . . . anything, which makes her most miserable. When I tell her so, it only mortifies and tantalizes and attracts her and makes her worse (p. 431).

This is the typical pattern of the pursuer/distancer relationship. The pursuer's pursuit distances the distancer, and his distancing attracts the pursuer more. What is most interesting about the pattern is that when either one changes role, the other seems to change as well. When Charlotte stopped pursuing, Shaw would begin to pursue her, and when he pursued her, she would tend to distance herself. Though Charlotte was in general the emotional pursuer, she also had money and liked to travel, which enabled her to distance physically from Shaw, and gave her a certain power over him.

George Bernard Shaw
Library of Congress, Prints and Photographs Division,
LC-USZ62-25210

Charlotte was the older of two sisters and had perceived her own parents' marriage as a disaster. Her mother, who was English, hated Ireland and everything Irish. Her father, who was Irish, adored Ireland and was like a fish out of water anywhere else. Charlotte adored her sweet Irish father, whose gentleness provoked her mother to rage. She longed for him to assert himself. Instead, he tried to deafen himself to his wife and make himself invisible (Holroyd, 1988, p. 433). He was a dreamer, who hummed mildly under his breath and drummed his fingers on the arms of chairs. As Charlotte saw it, her mother extinguished his dreams and finally squeezed all the life out of him. Later Charlotte wondered whether her hatred of her mother had killed her, as she thought her mother's hatred of her father had killed him.

Charlotte's mother pushed her relentlessly to marry and Charlotte just as vehemently resisted. It wasn't until her mother died that Charlotte let herself fall in love for the first time. When this love ended in rejection, she wandered about for several years, trying to establish a meaning for her life. A friend who soon introduced her to Shaw described her thus: "She found herself . . . alone in the world, without ties, without any definite creed, and with a large income. By temperament she is an anarchist, feeling any regulation or rule intolerable. . . . She is by nature a rebel. She has no snobbishness and no convention" (Dunbar, 1963, p. 98).

When she met Shaw, he was forty, she was thirty-nine. They had a remarkable amount in common, not least their loathing of marriage. Both were rebels, radicals, and nonconformists, who valued their independence. Shaw wrote of their early relationship:

She also being Irish does not succumb to my arts . . . but we get on together all the better, repairing bicycles, talking philosophy and religion . . . or, when we are in a mischievous or sentimental hour, philandering shamelessly and outrageously. . . . She knows the value of her unencumbered independence, having suffered a good deal from family bonds and conventionality. . . . The idea of tying herself up again by a marriage . . . seems to her intellect to be unbearably foolish. Her theory is that she won't do it. (Holroyd, 1988, p. 435)

This made their personalities sound ideally suited for each other. But, like most couples, they fell into complementary roles as their relationship evolved. Charlotte began seeking more connection and when she did, Shaw retreated, warning: "From the moment that you can't do without me, you're lost" (Holroyd, 1988, p. 438). When she took his advice and tried to resist him by suddenly leaving for Ireland, he was nonplussed and complained: "Why do you choose this time of all others to desert me, just now when you are most wanted." He tried to distance himself into other relationships, but the greater distance she kept, the more he found himself falling in love with her, though it petrified him. He wrote to her on the day before her return from Ireland: "I will contrive to see you somehow, at all hazards. I must, and that 'must' which 'rather alarms' you, terrifies me. . . . If it were possible to run away, if it would do any good, I'd do it; so mortally afraid am I that my trifling and lying and ingrained treachery and levity with women are going to make you miserable, when my whole sane desire is to make you hap—I mean strong and self-possessed and tranquil. . . . For there is something between us aside and apart from all my villainy" (p. 437).

He couldn't even admit that he cared enough to want to make her happy. That would imply too much dependence. Before seeing her, he instructed her on how she must keep her distance when they were alone together. But over the next few months their lives became more entwined. He ended his various relationships with other women, and she gradually made herself indispensable to him, becoming his secretary and caretaker, as well as his companion. Shaw believed the status of marriage was almost essential for a woman's greatest possible freedom—but, of course, he eschewed it for himself! When Charlotte finally tried to take his advice and proposed to him, he apparently responded "with shuddering horror and wildly asked the fare to Australia" (Holroyd, 1988, p. 442).

The couple were soon reconciled, but Charlotte was, as usual, in the position of emotional pursuer. When Shaw rebuffed her, she backed off again. In her absence, Shaw began to realize how much he missed her. He began having accidents and physical symptoms. First, he fell off his bicycle. Dramatist that he was, he played up his black eye and cut face to the hilt. But when Charlotte soon after invited him to go on a trip, he responded with sarcasm and avoidance: "No use in looking for human sympathy from me. I have turned the switch and am your very good friend, but as hard as nails" (p. 133). The longer Charlotte was away, the more unstable he grew. Finally, he wrote describing himself as "detestably deserted," and pleading, "Oh Charlotte, Charlotte: is this a time to be gadding about in Rome?" (Holroyd, 1988, p. 455). Soon both of them were becoming symptomatic; he with headaches, toothaches, accidents, and finally gout, she with neuralgia, restlessness, and depression. As much as he missed her, he also feared her: "But then I think of the other Charlotte, the terrible Charlotte, the lier-in-wait, the soul hypochondriac, always watching and dragging me into bondage, always planning nice, sensible, comfortable, selfish destruction for me, wincing at every accent of freedom in my voice, so that at last I get the trick of hiding myself from her, hating me and longing for me with the absorbing passion of the spider for the fly" (p. 455).

By the time she returned from Rome, he was desperate for her and almost an invalid by virtue of an infected foot. Charlotte was appalled when she saw the circumstances in which he was living—filthy, wretched, malnourished, uncared for. His mother, with whom he lived, did nothing for him, if she even noticed his condition at all. Charlotte could never forgive her for her neglect of her son, though from the time of their marriage she provided her mother-in-law an annuity. In fact, both families of origin had a lasting antagonism for the couple. Charlotte's sister never even wanted to meet Shaw, and his sister, who resented him in the first place, resented Charlotte even more.

Exactly how the couple came to their final decision to marry we will never know. Charlotte never spoke of private things and Shaw always hid the deeply emotional events of his life in clownish descriptions. At the time he was also in constant pain and needed a serious operation, which Charlotte finally arranged. Shaw said his situation was somehow changed: "I found that my own objection to my own marriage had ceased with my objection to my own death" (Dunbar, 1963, p. 148). "Death did not come; but something which I had always objected to far worse: to wit, Marriage did" (Holroyd, 1988, p. 461).

Shaw later told the story that he married because, being a wretch on crutches, stifled by chloroform and determined to die: "I proposed to make her my widow" (Holroyd, 1988, p. 461). This is remarkably reminiscent of the Irish joke of asking a woman to marry by saying, "How'd you like to be buried with my folks?" (For details see McGoldrick, 2004.) Even years later Shaw insisted that he had made the decision to marry as a dying man. Charlotte had predicted he would otherwise become a permanent invalid. He wrote his own humorous announcement describing his wedding as a totally chance event:

> As a lady and gentleman were out driving in . . . Covent Garden yesterday, a heavy shower drove them to take shelter in the office of the . . . Registrar there, and in the confusion of the moment married them. The lady was . . . Miss Payne Townshend and the gentleman was George Bernard Shaw. . . . Miss Payne Townshend is an Irish lady with an income many times the volume of that which "Corno di Bassetto" used to earn, but to that happy man, being a vegetarian, the circumstance is of no moment. (Dunbar, 1963, p. 151)

Despite the things they shared in common, it was their differences that defined the dynamics in their marriage. Perhaps Charlotte married Shaw for his unpredictability and creative genius and his seeming need for a caretaker. Though Shaw had finally achieved economic stability through the success of one of his plays a few months before the marriage, his decision may have been facilitated by Charlotte's wealth, which enabled him to provide for his mother with whom he had always lived.

However, the complementary differences that brought the couple together were not enough to make for a successful marriage. Although the marriage lasted for forty-five years, and Shaw insisted to the end of his life that he could not have married anyone else, the couple grew less intimate as the years went by. Charlotte loved to travel; he hated it. She, like her father, loved to be in Ireland; Shaw was ambivalent about ever returning to his homeland. Most important, Shaw came to believe that his wife was not a worthy discussant on one topic after another: religion, politics, and so forth; he closed her out. Charlotte did handle Shaw's one major affair, with Mrs. Patrick Campbell, with great skill, continuing to socialize with him and refusing to be put off by the rumors of the affair. She was meanwhile preoccupied with her own spiritual search, which she did not share with her husband. From about 1922 she developed an intimate friendship with T. E. Lawrence (Lawrence of Arabia), twenty years her junior, certainly one of the geniuses of the era, sharing with him the personal thoughts she could not share with her husband. This relationship lasted until Lawrence's death in 1935.

It was not until Charlotte's death in 1943, that Shaw, then in his eighties, read her correspondence with Lawrence and realized he had misjudged her. He saw that he had missed out on the intellectual and emotional richness that she obviously had to share. He wrote:

> From a diary I discovered lately and some letters which she wrote to T. E. Lawrence, I realize that there were many parts of her character that even I did not know, for she poured out her soul to Lawrence. . . . I lived with Charlotte for forty years and I see now that there was a great deal about her that I didn't know. It has been a shock. (Dunbar, 1963, p. xi)

Shaw had expected someone to take care of him, not someone to be his intellectual companion. Unable to move beyond the expectations of his own unhappy family, he had not seen his wife for who she was. One might hypothesize that sibling complementarity (he a youngest, she an oldest), enabled them to remain married for forty-five years, but the family legacy of marital unhappiness seems to have influenced their low expectations of marriage, and they were unable to be really intimate with each other.

Mrs. Patrick Campbell
Lebrecht Music and Arts/Alamy Stock Photo

SUCCESSFUL COUPLES: BALANCING CONNECTION AND AUTONOMY

Some people continue to remake the same mistakes as they go through life. Others seem able to improve their circumstances, though the path is not necessarily straight. One of the keys to success for couples in achieving and sustaining a satisfying relationship over time and circumstance is being able to balance connection and autonomy. Sometimes, like Agatha Christie, they have to cycle through one or more relationships to achieve this state of balance. Christie was the youngest of three, with two much older siblings. She described her childhood as very happy, and her parents as having loved each other

dearly **(see Genogram 9.3: Agatha Christie Family)**. She especially loved her father
who had, she thought, a wonderful sense of
humor and a natural happiness and serenity. But he died when Agatha was eleven.
He had come from an American family and
lived on income from the family's business,
but his income had dwindled and when he
died, Agatha and her mother were left in
very strained circumstances.

Agatha saw her mother Clara as "an enig-
matic and arresting personality, more forceful than my father, startlingly original in
her ideas, shy and miserably diffident about
herself, and at bottom . . . with a natural
melancholy . . . and as my father used to tell
her, absolutely no sense of humor" (Christie,
1977, p. 3).

T. E. Lawrence (Lawrence of
Arabia)
*The History Collection/Alamy
Stock Photo*

As it happened, Agatha's parents had
grown up as step-siblings. Agatha's mother was one of five children and the
only girl. Her father died suddenly when she was still young. At that time,
her mother's older sister (Mary Ann, known as Polly), had just married a
wealthy American and because she could not have children, she offered to
adopt one of Polly's children. Polly chose Clara, and Margaret agreed. Hence,
for the rest of her life, Clara had an ongoing sense of having been rejected by
her mother.

She did, however, become enamored early on with her much older adoptive stepbrother Fred, son of her father's first wife, who had died. Clara eventually married this stepbrother, who became Agatha's beloved father. Agatha
wrote in her autobiography that her parents' marriage was one of only four
completely happy marriages she had ever known, an assessment her mother
might not have agreed with (Christie, 1977, p. 4).

Agatha, ten years younger than her next sibling, grew up basically as an
only child. She was educated primarily at home and without anyone paying
much attention to her. As a young woman she became engaged to four different men, one after the other, finding a man being the primary role for a
woman in her situation. During World War I she married the last of these
fiancés, Archie Christie, with whom she seems to have had little in common,
and who could not stand, as he said, to be unhappy (Christie, 1977, p. 423).

He also had no ability to support a wife, being at a low level in the military. This was similar to the situation of Agatha's own father, who had basically never worked much. Christie's lack of promise as a husband was a serious issue as Agatha's mother's health was failing. The couple married in what seemed like an impulsive decision over a Christmas holiday. In 1919 when the war ended and Archie returned, the couple had a daughter, but they do not seem to have had much connection with each other and he opposed her having a second child.

Agatha Christie
Photo 12/Alamy Stock Photo

Meanwhile, Agatha described in her autobiography that she began writing one day on a dare from her mother, because she had nothing to do. Before long, and much to everyone's surprise, she became a successful mystery writer and over her lifetime wrote almost 100 books. Her first big success, *The Mysterious Affair at Styles*, published in 1920, introduced her famous detective Hercule Poirot. Christie kept writing, but her marriage did not seem to improve. In early 1926, her book *The Murder of Roger Ackroyd*, another Poirot mystery, became very successful, and she wanted to take a vacation, but her husband did not want to go. So she took her older sister who had begun writing as well. By the time they returned, her mother's health was failing badly and in April she died. Archie took this opportunity to go traveling, since he did not like unhappiness. He did not even attend her mother's funeral. Agatha's longtime secretary and caretaker for her daughter (and by now close friend), Carlo, also had to leave at this time because of family illness. Agatha was beside herself with her losses, as well as dealing with disposal of her mother's things and managing her daughter.

That August, while she was still struggling with her grief and trying to go through her mother's belongings, her husband returned for the weekend of their daughter's seventh birthday, to tell her he wanted a divorce. He said he had fallen in love with one of their friends and had to be with her. Agatha seems to have gone from depression into a kind of nervous collapse, trying desperately to convince Archie not to divorce her, but by early December he came to the house to say he was now leaving for good.

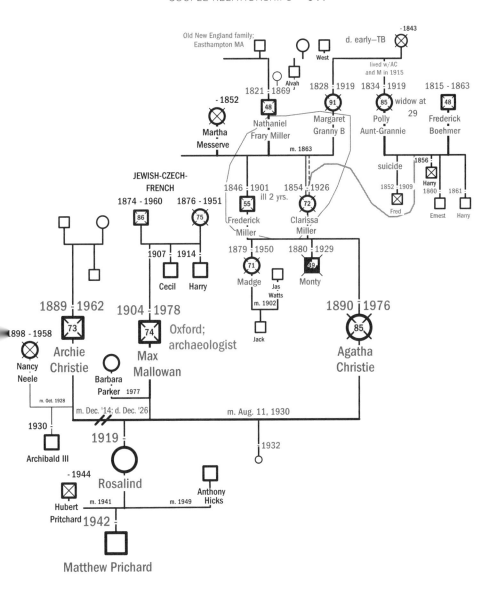

Genogram 9.3: Agatha Christie Family

Agatha came up with a plan she seems to have thought would help Archie change his mind. She took off, first with her car and then by train, for a Yorkshire spa where she signed in using the last name of her husband's lover, Neale, perhaps knowing that the name, which he was trying to keep secret would now become known. She sent a letter to her husband's brother, Clarence, the only one to whom she explained her plan, telling him that she was okay but not to look for her till after the weekend, giving her husband time to hopefully regret his decision to leave her and their daughter. She then bought what she needed for the trip and took a train to the spa. She remained there while all of Britain became involved in the search for the famous mystery writer who had disappeared. Her brother-in-law did not contact Archie, but eventually her whereabouts were discovered, and she returned home, giving in finally to the divorce. The whole story could have been right out of one of her mystery novels. (In fact, she did tell parts of the story in her book *Giant's Bread*, under her pseudonym Mary Westmacott a few years later.)

In her autobiography, written toward the end of her life, she describes her response to the trauma of Archie's insistence on ending the marriage in the way he did: "After illness came sorrow, despair, and heartbreak. There was no need to dwell on it. I stood out for a year, hoping he would change, but he did not. So ended my first married life" (Christie, 1977, p. 423). Archie remarried two weeks after the divorce came through and moved on.

That fall Agatha's daughter began boarding school, as had been planned, and Agatha thought to go to the West Indies where she had gone many times before, but two days before leaving she had by chance had dinner with a couple, just back from Baghdad, where she had never been. On the spot she decided to change her plans and take the Orient Express train to Istanbul, Damascus, and Baghdad. Agatha's family and friends thought this was an absurd idea, but after the stress of her divorce, she felt a real need to expand:

> One must do things by oneself sometimes, mustn't one? I never had before—I didn't much want to now—but I thought: It's now or never. Either I cling to everything that's safe and that I know, or else I develop more initiative, do things on my own . . . I should find out now what kind of person I was. Whether I had become entirely dependent on other people, as I feared. I could indulge my passion for seeing places—any place I wanted to see. I could change my mind at a moment's notice, just as I had done when I chose Baghdad instead of the West Indies. I would have no one to consider but myself. I would see how I liked that. I knew well enough that I was a dog character. Dogs will not go for a walk unless someone takes them. Perhaps I was going to be like that. I hoped not. (Christie, 1977, pp. 433–434)

Agatha did indeed travel around Baghdad, befriending a well-known archae-ologist, Leonard Woolley, who was working there, and his wife. Agatha loved the region, and the next year the Woolleys invited her back, the second trip including Woolley's young protegee, Max Mallowan, who was working with Woolley and with whom to her great surprise she was very compatible. Mal-lowan reconnected with her back in London and on his first visit stunned her by asking to marry her. She said his idea was nonsense, as he was four-teen years younger than she and had gone to Oxford with her nephew! She thought Mallowan's suggestion that they marry ridiculous and hesitated for months, but he did not waver. Within a few months Agatha agreed, resisting even her family's resistance to the marriage. She was a world-famous writer with almost no formal education, and he was a highly educated aspiring aca-demic and researcher in the Middle East.

They married quietly in Scotland in September 1929, with only her daughter Rosalind present. For the next forty-seven years they shared a deep compatibility, both physically and intellectually. One of the interesting aspects of their relationship seems to have been their ability to go off on their separate tracks and then come back together. We think of differentiation increasing our ability for good connection. It was perhaps a major factor in the success of their relationship that by the time they met they both had well-developed and independent personalities, interests, projects, and a sense of professional and cultural identity (Gill, 1990). Agatha continued to publish about a book a year, and Mallowan became a distinguished archaeologist, the two of them spending a great deal of time on digs in the Middle East, which Agatha came to love.

Mallowan was not threatened by his wife's international fame as a mys-tery writer and was comfortable in her world of writers. For her part, she shared his passion for ancient cultures. Both were humorful, energetic, independent people and their compatibility lasted the rest of their lives. It is interesting that Christie's daughter, Rosalind, seems to have been positive about Mallowan becoming her father from the beginning. Though Rosa-lind's first husband unfortunately died in World War II, she remarried a man apparently very like her stepfather, and with whom she had a similar compatibility. The four of them shared close connections.

DIVORCE AND REMARRIAGE

It has been said that the twenty-first century will be about the invention of the marriage–divorce cycle as the normal pattern of life for families in the U.S., since this has become such a common process in family life. Families do not generally handle the breakdown of a marriage very well, and unresolved relationships often come back to haunt them later. Divorce most often leaves a legacy of dangling ends—the bric-a brac of a lifetime, along with bitterness, pain, and cutoff that have to be gotten past. As one young man summed up his father's second wife: "There she was, redecorating my past with all her fake antiques."

When there are new or missing marital partners in a family brought on by separation, divorce, or early death, bridging the cutoffs in the family will open up another set of connections to people who belong, people with an investment in the members' past as well as their future. Getting to know about every branch of your family may involve getting past some intense reactions of other family members and holding yourself steady in pursuit of the missing information on your family tree. Others may resent your reconnecting with your divorced and remarried father or with your grandmother's step-grandchildren, but they may be relevant to your going home again.

QUESTIONS TO ASK ABOUT COUPLE RELATIONSHIPS IN YOUR FAMILY

- What unresolved issues from their families of origin did members of the family bring into their couple relationships?
- Are there coincidences in timing between marriage decisions (when partners met, fell in love, decided to marry, or began to have marital problems) and other family events, particularly loss (deaths, moves, family traumas, or other life cycle transitions)?
- What unresolved issues from their families of origin did members of the family bring into their couple relationships/marriages?
- Have family weddings typically been traumatic affairs or happy gatherings? Large and lavish? Elopements? Plain-clothes affairs with a justice of the peace? Did anyone not go to a wedding who should have been there? Have any cutoffs occurred around a wedding?
- What are the typical patterns of marriage in the family? Are there certain typical patterns of symmetry or complementarity: the tyrant/battle-ax and the doormat/mouse? The silent clam and the babbler?
- Are there patterns of divorce? Remarriage? Late marriage? Non-marriage? Long marriage? Happy marriage?

- How did couples handle differences? How did they handle conflict (e.g., avoiding it, duking it out, negotiating it)? What are the sources of conflict (e.g., money, sex, child-rearing practices, food, religion, politics, work/leisure time, in-laws)? Are parts of the family tree missing or blurry because of divorce, dysfunction, or in-law triangles? Can you see ways to gain access to the missing information? Who would be most upset if you connected with these sources? Can you deal with the loyalty conflicts, jealousy, or sense of betrayal others may feel in order to reclaim the missing parts of your family?
- Are there typical gender patterns in your family's marriages? Are men impulsive, frightening, invisible? Do they leave? Are the women long-suffering, frustrated impresarios? How did couples manage childcare, housework, and chores?

Chapter 10
Reconnecting with Your Family

If you have a family gathering and a distant cousin comes who has been kept out of the family for a long time, it's a little uncomfortable. Let's bear the discomfort. It's worth it.

—PAUL ROBESON JR.

What if they'd stayed? Who would I be if I grew up in Vega Alta, Puerto Rico? The nuance that we always fought for is to say, "I can accept the sacrifice of my ancestors. I can accept the responsibility that bestows upon me and still find my own way in the world." It's not an either-or, it's not about, "Forget your dreams. It's my dreams." It's thinking, "I accept the incredible journey you had to take for me to even be standing here and still my job is to make my own way in the world and define home for what it is for me."

—LIN-MANUEL MIRANDA
cited in Aguilar (2021)

Composing a life involves a continual reimagining of the future and reinterpretation of the past to give meaning to the present.... Storytelling is fundamental to the human search for meaning. Each [of us] is involved in inventing a new kind of story.

—MARY CATHERINE BATESON
Composing a Life

We would all like to be able to be ourselves with our families, to have them accept us for who we really are. But we may lose sight of the prerequisite—that we accept them for who they really are, getting past the anger, resentment, and regret of their not being the family we wish they were. Visiting home, even for those who are highly successful in careers and other relationships, may mean reverting to childish responses. A daughter tenses up within a few minutes in reaction to her mother's implied criticism of her clothes, her haircut, or her partner. A son returns for Thanksgiving with the image of other families who always seem happy, while he experiences the subtle bitterness of his parents' ongoing war and his sister's disgruntlement with her life.

A part of us always longs to go back to the family, but to have it be different. This time, you tell yourself, you'll hold on to your adult perspective and not become defensive. You won't get caught up in your parents' battles or in competing with your siblings for attention. Maturity, objectivity, humor, and serenity will carry the day, if only you can keep your distance.

Sometimes you can even manage to hold on to your sense of self for a while. But then something seemingly trivial happens. Perhaps your father makes a sarcastic joke at your mother's expense, and she goes silent. This little scene may have occurred a hundred times in the past. In a second you fall into the role you played growing up, moving in to protect your mother. In your frustration you gossip with your siblings about how impossible your parents are and you wonder how you managed to survive all the underlying hostility in your family for so long.

If you want to reconnect with your family, you will need to develop a kind of empathy, which recognizes that you and your family belong to each other. This requires an acceptance of our fundamental human connectedness as people that is almost mystical. It means accepting that whatever terrible things another person may do, we could be in their shoes. It means accepting our parents *with* all their imperfections, which is not the same thing as accepting specific qualities or behaviors that are hurtful or harmful. It means, for example, accepting your father as a whole, without needing to even the score for his emotional neglect or physical abuse or for his irrational demands and attempts at intimidation. This is not the same thing as accepting the abuse or not holding him accountable for what he did. It is a matter of acknowledging that the relationship is about more than just the abuse. The grown-up child who truly has an individual identity can be generous to a critical, distant father without becoming defensive, even when that father continues to be critical.

This requires an approach that allows you to see the world from the perspective of each person in your family, accepting that others did not always meet your needs or understand your feelings or those of others in the family. Too often, people try to change their family as a way of changing themselves, rather than changing themselves as a way of changing family patterns. There is a story of an old Hasidic rabbi who said that when he was young, he set out to change the world, but as he got older he realized that was too ambitious and set out to change his state. Older yet, he realized this was still grandiose and decided to limit himself to his family. As a very old man, he realized he should have started with himself, and maybe he could have succeeded in changing his family, his state, or even the whole world.

Change requires letting go of our wishes that family members had been different and had met our needs, understood our feelings, and always made us proud. It requires arriving at a new perspective from which it is possible to evaluate your personal worth for yourself. It also means risking family disapproval, rejection, or inattention, without becoming disapproving, rejecting, or inattentive in return.

The fundamental guideline for going home again, as we have repeated through this book is: Don't attack, don't defend, don't placate, and don't shut down. Going home again means finding a way to be yourself and still stay connected to your family without defending yourself or attacking others. We develop dysfunctional roles because we have not evolved sufficient sense of self to function for ourselves, playing the wounded daughter to the arrogant and uncaring father, or the dutiful brother to a prodigal sibling.

Defining your actual responsibility toward your family is a very personal matter. Only you can decide what obligation you have to be generous, loving, or thoughtful toward others, no matter what hurt they have caused you. If your father is a depressed and withdrawn alcoholic, you may decide to treat him with compassion, and to do whatever is possible to discourage his self-destructive behavior, realizing also that his destiny is beyond your control. At the same time, you must appreciate your limitations. The Alcoholics Anonymous serenity prayer is a great basic rule for anyone facing difficult family circumstances: "May I have the serenity to accept the things I cannot change, courage to change the things I can, and wisdom to know the difference."

An important place to reconnect with family is at the celebrations that mark family holidays and transitions: weddings, funerals, and reunions. Family rituals are important, often incorporating familiar as well as symbolic meanings. Such occasions tend to involve intentional repetition of words, music, food, drink, ceremony, and behavior that suggests continuity. While this can be stifling if the rituals are hollow, it can also be healing and enriching if you make the rituals personally meaningful. Family gatherings also offer a good opportunity to hear family stories, observe your family in action and work on your part in family relationships.

Consider what family stories might be like from the angle of a different participant, the so-called villains, for example. Imagine what Cinderella's stepmother's perspective might be on her "spoiled stepdaughter" to whom everything came so easily and whom everyone adored for her "sweetness," her beauty, her and her goody-two-shoes behavior (Friedman, 1990). Consider also the dilemma her stepsisters were in, because they didn't conform to the culture's requirements of a woman—to be small, beautiful, gentle, long suffering, and unassertive!

You can also think about what would happen if you changed your part in family relationships. If you always lock horns with your father, you could say: "You've got a point, Dad." If you have had a poor relationship with a family member for a long time, you will need to proceed slowly and with patience. Do not expect too much too soon. No relationship can be forced and if the other person expects you to be negative, they are likely to be suspicious if you suddenly become gracious.

Letters can sometimes be useful in reconnection efforts. They can be a way to repair a rift with an estranged or difficult parent, for example. They enable you to express exactly what you want, without accusation or defense. Most important, they allow you to convey the whole message before you have to deal with the other's reactions. With luck, the letter will be a first step, leading to further, more personal communications.

Pictures are also wonderful triggers for memories and may help family members feel they are being given to, even as they share difficult memories. By enlarging old family photographs and distributing them to the family, new messages can be conveyed about continuity.

In most families there are few pure saints or sinners. While we all need to protect ourselves from a relative who might actually hurt us, an active alcoholic or drug addict, for example, it is important not to write these people off as family members. You never know when they might change their ways, even after a lifetime of destructive behavior. Various events, especially aging and loss, can trigger a transformation. And you want to be ready to receive someone who makes a turn in life toward relating.

OBAMA'S COMING HOME TO HIS FAMILY

In his book, *Dreams from My Father* (1995), Obama discusses his trip to Africa to understand himself, his family, and his African father, whom he had never known and who had by then died. He wondered to himself,

> What is a family? Is it just a genetic chain, parents and offspring, people like me? Or is it a social construct, an economic unit, optimal for child-rearing and divisions of labor? Or is it something else entirely: a store of shared memories, say? An ambit of love? A reach across the void? (p. 327)

In Africa, Obama encountered a definition of family much broader than anything he had experienced in the U.S., underscoring the point that while family may or may not always have a genetic component, it most certainly has a cultural component. How we understand what family is, who is included in it, and the role it plays in our lives is shaped by our cultural context. In making a journey home again, we must therefore consider our families within their cultural contexts. This means working to reconnect to our families in ways that are both detailed and broad, literal and symbolic, personal and cultural. It is both unique and simultaneously connected to the broader story of our relations with each other. The more fully we can relate to our families' lives, the more we will understand— and perhaps empathize with their struggles.

Barack Obama
Library Congress, Prints and Photographs Division,
LC-DIG-ppbd-00603

Without that empathy we are left with a sense of mystification. Yet parents always matter.

Obama's father had left Hawaii by the time his son was two and visited him only once more in his life. Though he had his mother, stepfather, and grandparents, Obama was haunted throughout his childhood by his absent father. As Obama saw it, the problem was that his father was missing, and nothing his mother and grandparents told him could obviate what had happened: his father had left him. They couldn't explain why his father left or why he had become a "prop" in someone else's story—an attractive person, a figure with a "heart of gold," and a "mysterious stranger" (Obama, 1995, p. 26). Obama is very clear that when someone is absent in a family, you are left with myths and fantasies, unless you make real effort to fill in the blanks. He didn't blame his mother or grandparents for the mythology and imagined his father as complicit in its creation. In fact, he thought he might have preferred the image they created for him, or even participated in the myth they created.

He first began to learn about his father when, as a young adult, he met his half-sister, Auma, who had grown up with the father in Africa. What she told him about his father shocked him. All his life he had carried a single image of his father as a brilliant scholar, a generous friend, and an upstanding leader. He had at times rebelled against the image, but never really questioned it. Except for one brief visit from his father when he was eight, his father had never been present in his life to challenge the image (Obama, 1995).

He had seen weakness in other men, his grandfather's disappointments and drinking, his stepfather's compromise. But he saw those men as object lessons for him. Those were men he might love but would never emulate; white and brown men whose lives did not speak to his own life. Obama spoke of how he took admirable qualities from such legendary figures as Martin, Malcolm, Mandela, and Du Bois, and that he projected these qualities onto his image of his father. And then, the image of a man who was beyond rebuke evaporated and was replaced by a tarnished image of a fallen hero: a drunk, an abuser; an embittered and lonely man. At that point Obama realized: "All my life I had been wrestling with nothing more than a ghost" (Obama, 1995, p. 105).

Barack Obama's father, Barack Obama Sr.
Polaris Images

In 1987, Obama went to Kenya in a search to understand himself. It had taken him until he was in his late twenties, and some years after his father's death, to be ready to learn about him. He realized only when he was en route how strong his avoidance of this journey had been, to delay his coming to terms with his father: "The incompleteness of my own history stood between me and the sites I saw like a hard pane of glass" (Obama, 1995, p. 301).

Even though his trip came too late for him to see his father, he was able to meet a great many family members. **Genogram 10.1: Obama Family** shows with the connection lines all the family members Obama connected with during his visit.

He was immediately drawn into triangles set up by the conflicts among several different parts of his father's multiply divorced family. His father's sister complained that he should have visited her first, instead of connecting to his father's first wife, Kezia, and her family. But that family included Obama's half-sister, Auma, the only one he had met before and the one with whom he had the most connection.

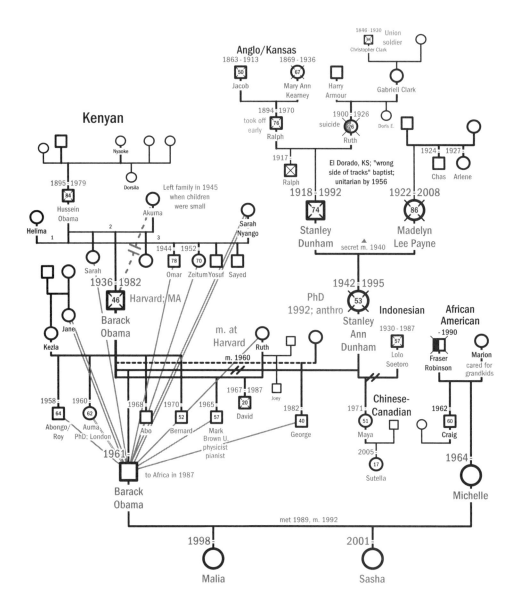

Genogram 10.1: Obama Family

All sorts of conflicts developed about who he would spend more time with
and to whom he would be more generous. There was also conflict during his
father's relationship with his third wife, Ruth, who was white, Obama Sr. had
continued his relationship with his first wife, Kezia, with whom he had two

younger sons, Abo and Bernard. There was a question about whether Bernard was really his son or not. Obama struggled with the question, wondering whether the truth should impact his relationship with Bernard, whom he was just getting to know. The family reassured him that his father had been very accepting of Bernard and did not let it become an issue to him: accepting all the children as his own, though he had earlier taken Kezia's two oldest children Roy and Auma away from their family home to live with him and his third wife Ruth in Nairobi, so the two oldest had been separated from their mother and had not known their other brothers.

During Obama's visit word came that Ruth resented that he was in Africa, but not coming to visit her. She was a white woman the father had met at Harvard, married, and brought to Africa, but later divorced, when their two sons were still children. Obama had been told that his father's divorce from her was very bitter. Ruth had become involved with another man and tried to get her two sons, Mark and David, to change their name to that of her new husband. Mark did so, but David refused, actually moving back to live with his half-brother Roy (Auma's brother), where he tragically died at age eighteen in 1983, just a year after Obama Sr. died.

So Obama went to visit Ruth, who took out an album of family pictures from her years with his father. He was spooked by the pictures. They were all of happy times, and strangely, they were familiar, as if he was glimpsing into some alternative universe that had been playing out behind his back. He was seeing the fantasies that he had been clinging to of his father taking him and his mother back to Kenya and he realized his underlying yearning for a reunification of his family.

It was a rude awakening: "The recognition of how wrong it had all turned out, the harsh evidence of life as it had really been lived, made me so sad that after only a few minutes I had to look away" (Obama, 1995, p. 343). What is sad, touching, and very common about this is that parents so often live large in the hearts and fantasies of their children, even if they have physically disappeared.

In fact, Obama spent much of his childhood living away from his mother as well as his father, raised by his maternal grandparents in Hawaii. So his search for his mother was also a part of his journey. He writes of a visit she made to him while he was in college when it became clear to him that she had never stopped loving his father. "She saw my father as everyone hopes at least one other person might see him; she had tried to help the child who never knew him see him the same way" (Obama, 1995, p. 137).

He was struggling to understand his mother as well. Obama could see in her face what he thought all children must come to see in their parents as they

grow up: that their parents' lives are separate from theirs, and they go way
beyond their birth as children to their parents, to an infinite legacy of grandparents and great-grandparents with a long history of projected hopes, hap-
penstance, and limitations. He saw his mother as a young woman who was
flattered by his father's attention and struggling with confusion as she tried to
break away from her parents and the grip of their lives on hers.

Obama learned a great deal about himself as he sought to learn who his
parents were and about his multicultural family and the cultures they came
from in Kenya and Kansas.

Obama Sr.'s death had left all the triangles and conflicts of the divorced
and multiply remarried family in a very unresolved place. Luckily, through
Obama's efforts to make connections with each part of the family and his
willingness to visit each side and listen to them without choosing sides
(though he was told all the stories about who did what to whom!), he was able
to learn a great deal about his family and thus about himself. He even took
the opportunity to question his half-brother Mark about his lack of interest in
their father. Mark, like Obama, had hardly known their father, since his parents divorced when he was still young, and he hardly saw his father after the

Barack Obama as a boy, with his sister Maya, his mother Stanley Ann Dunham,
and her second husband, Lolo
UPI/Alamy Stock Photo

divorce. Mark explained that he had made a decision at a certain point to not think about his father, because in reality, his father was more dead than alive to him. He said: "I knew he was a drunk and showed no concern for his wife or children. That was enough. . . . I don't ask myself a lot of questions about what it all means. About who I really am" (Obama, 1995, p. 344).

Such responses are very common and understandable in the painful aftermath of losing a parent in a divorce. Obama felt the same pain, but the effort to reconnect, even when the parent is gone, can make a tremendous difference, as Obama's efforts in his memoir reveal.

After learning a lot about the family history of painful parental cutoffs from "granny" and visiting his father's grave, Obama wrote to his dead father about what he now understood. In the letter he told his father of the damage that silence among the generations of men in his family had caused, how silence had robbed fathers from teaching their sons important lessons. There was too much clinging to the past with all its limitations and not enough embracing of the goodness around them emanating from their families and connections with their community: "For all your gifts—the quick mind, the powers of concentration, the charm—you could never forge yourself into a whole man by leaving those things behind" (Obama, 1995, p. 429).

In Obama's narrative we see his reflections on the complexities of identity. We see family ties, binds and triangles, conflicts, cutoffs, divorce, death and other losses, family stories, myths, secrets, silence and the intersection of race, social class, ethnicity, gender, religion, migration, and geographic locations are all woven together across generations, forming the complexity of identity.

His story also highlights how a person can become exiled, both in familial and cultural terms, and how painful and dispiriting that can be. Most importantly however, Obama's story provides a powerful example of how we can take the journey home, by probing to learn our history, and embracing the parts that reflect both pride and shame, joy and pain. His story illustrates how we can take similar journeys of courage, by risking to wonder about things we perhaps never dared to let ourselves consider, and reaching out to those we may never really have talked to before, to ask long withheld questions and daring to hear the answers. His is a powerful example of how we can work to find our way back home, not in the sense of returning to the fantasy that never was, but in facing the truth of what was and building something meaningful from it. Our sense of self needs to be inclusive of what came before and what may lie ahead, allowing us to transform our relationships with our past familial and cultural legacies.

GOING HOME AGAIN TO FIND A TRANSGENDER, BICULTURAL, AND ABUSIVE PARENT AND FAMILY HISTORY

Pulitzer Prize winning journalist and author Susan Faludi had a twenty-five-year cutoff from her abusive and volatile father. Then, in 2004, when he was seventy-six, he sent her an email entitled "Changes," which began: "Dear Susan, I've got some interesting news for you. I have decided that I have had enough of impersonating a macho aggressive man that I have never been inside."

In the course of a lifetime, her father had, she said, "pulled off many reinventions, and laid claim to many identities" (Faludi, 2016. p. 2). He proceeded to tell her he had had gender-reassignment surgery in Thailand and from now on would be Stefanie. He enclosed various snapshots of himself in hyper-feminine outfits. He said he wanted her to visit him in Budapest, the city where he had grown up during the Nazi era, before emigrating in his twenties to New York. He said he had returned to Hungary in 1990 as the Soviet era ended. He added that he wanted her to write his story!

Susan Faludi
Courtesy Russ Rymer

His email raised a question many have in considering whether to try to go home again: Which part of what the family tells is true? Which part is myth? Which part to expose and tell and which part to keep hidden, even when you can find it out?

Twelve years later, Susan published her memoir about her father, called *In the Darkroom* (2016). She had gone to Hungary to confront her father, only to find that Steven, the man who had been her father, was "gone," having been replaced by Stefanie. Faludi's father had been a photographer, or rather a man who was the master of modifying photographs, or "trick photography," as he called it, and at age of seventy-six, it seemed he had mastered his most compelling modification yet via his gender transformation.

Istvan Friedman had changed his name in the U.S. to Steven Faludi and met his wife, who had grown up in New Jersey, the daughter of a Jewish father and a mother descended from German ancestors. Because her father had cut off from his Jewish roots, changing his name from Levi to Lanning, he had refused to attend his daughter's wedding when she married a Jew.

Steven had a successful career as a photographic developer and fixer, with many outside interests in electronics, rock climbing, cycling and other sports, but not much interest in his family. He had refused even to let his wife work and was self-centered, distant, and finally violent, before disappearing from Susan's life altogether when she was still in her teens.

Steven Faludi as a young photographer
Courtesy Russ Rymer

The year after the parents' divorce, when Susan was sixteen, he violated a restraining order, breaking into the family's home, and trying to kill the mother's new partner with a baseball bat and knife. Remarkably, he got away with no punishment and never fully paid even the minimal court-mandated child support.

Susan managed to put herself through Harvard and became a prize-winning writer. Now after all these years of no contact, she made the audacious choice to visit her father in Budapest. She found the attempt at reconnection even harder than she could have imagined, but she did not give up in her efforts to get to know and understand her father and his history.

He, now she, was still completely self-preoccupied, refusing to make even small efforts to respond to Susan's questions or requests to go out and see the city where the father had grown up. She even tried to get Susan to leave the door open so there could be a "womanly open connection," while paying no attention to Susan's feelings or questions about the father's history or life.

As Susan attempted to reconnect with her father, she thought about how her own writing had always been to expose, rather than conceal societal flaws, while her father's creativity as a photograph editor had always been in hiding and concealing blemishes and imperfections to make a good picture. Susan began to ask herself questions about her own identity as well as her father's. She thought, for example, that her own two primary identities were as a woman and as a Jew. But then, she thought that by Jewish standards she would not even be considered a Jew, since her mother was not Jewish, and Jewish heritage officially continues only through the maternal line.

As for being a woman, though she had always been a strong feminist, she had not done the things women are supposed to do, such as marry and have children. Even when she eventually married her boyfriend after twenty years, she did not do it according to our society's rules for womanly behavior. And she did not have children, which is generally considered another "basic" role of womanhood.

In fact, Stefanie Faludi saw her daughter as going against the requirements for women, even taking her to her own Hungarian gynecologist under the ruse that the visit was for the father, while trying to pressure her to have a baby, although she was already forty-nine by that time.

In spite of Susan's great difficulty connecting with her father or getting her to answer even her most basic questions, she committed herself to trying to understand her father better. When she returned to the U.S., she interviewed other transgender people her father had known, and contacted classmates, going back to her father's school days in Budapest. Through them she learned that Steven had not been a particularly popular student in his school days. He had, in fact, been sent to live away from his family as a child for his violent behavior toward one of the family servants. Her father misremembered this experience, telling Susan he had been sent away because his parents were separating and that he was the one who had managed to get them back together.

Exploring her family's cultural history, Susan learned that after the ancestors of the Hungarians, the Magyars, settled in the area, their country was ravaged by invasions, defeats, and occupations for the next 1,000 years. The last half of the nineteenth century marked the "Golden Age" of Hungarian Jewry, when, in exchange for embracing the Magyar language and promoting Magyar culture, assimilated Jews were welcomed, temporarily, into Hungarian society. Jews were 20 percent of the population, but 40 percent of the voters. Seventy-five percent of Jews declared Hungarian their language, taking the Magyars over the 50 percent mark. During this period, Hungary was the most hospitable of all European countries to Jews, and Hungarian Jews did much to bring the country into the industrial age. They were doctors, lawyers, engineers, industrialists, and artists. Steven Faludi's grandparents and parents were all part of this evolution. But in the buildup to World War II, Hungarian Jews went from being the most assimilated in Europe to being among the most reviled, subject to the earliest anti-Semitic legislation, deprived by the late 1930s of their property, professions, and freedoms. This was the context in which Istvan (Steven) Friedman Faludi grew up, coming of age just as his family's property was being stolen and his parents forced into ghettoized "yellow star houses" and hid in "safe houses" until they were no longer safe.

Faludi's memoir traces the decimation of her father's prosperous, assimilated Jewish clan during World War II, his improbable survival, and then his reinvention first in Denmark, next in Brazil, and finally in the U.S. We might think of her efforts to understand her father's gender metamorphosis at seventy-six and gradually learning parts of his history as a complex act of forgiveness, as Michelle Goldberg (2016) put it.

At some point in Faludi's journey, her father told her the story of dressing up as a Hungarian Nazi to rescue his parents from the fascist Arrow Cross. She could not believe it, but, as she explored her father's history, she came to realize that he had understated his valor in saving his parents. As a young teenager, Istvan had dared to impersonate an Arrow Cross officer to save his parents and succeeded. Young as he was, he had taken the bold step of dressing up as a Hungarian Nazi with a swastika armband and fake ID papers, daring to come to where the parents were being held and steal them away, pretending to be a Nazi soldier, who had been ordered to take them off to prison. Susan had heard this amazing story before but hadn't known it was true.

Over the course of her efforts, Susan deepened her understanding of herself as well as of her father. She had thought it impossible to tease apart the different threads that make up our "identity." Do we choose it, or is it something we cannot escape? She wondered how much of who we are is what we are born with, how much is imposed on us, and how much is determined by our own actions. "My father like that other Hungarian, Houdini, was a master of the breakout. For my part I kept up the chase. I had cast myself as a posse of one, tracking my father's many selves to their secret recesses" (Faludi, 2016, p. x).

Stefanie Faludi
Courtesy Russ Rymer

When she completed a draft ten years later, Susan warned her father that there were things in what she had written that would be hard for the father to take. Stefanie had as a photographer devoted a lifetime to altering images—moving between masculine and feminine, Jewish and Christian, Hungarian and American, family savior and family outsider, survivor and abuser. Through Susan's journey to get to know her father's past history, she tried to disentangle her own experience of the violent father she remembered from her youth, from the person her father had been growing up in his family and culture of origin during Nazi-era Hungary and engaging with an emerging older woman she had never known.

Faludi's journey home in the end helped her realize that we do not create ourselves, but always evolve through our cultural heritage and family history. Her efforts did not end in closure. But what was powerful was her willingness to stay present to try to understand her complicated father from multiple perspectives. However frustrated she was with her father's way of presenting herself, Susan never stopped her efforts to get to know and understand her and to learn more about herself from her history. While her reconnection with her father did not offer the kind of relational healing and closeness she would have hoped for, her persistent effort to understand and contextualize her father's life is a powerful example of resilience and of what you can gain through such an effort to understand and connect with your family.

Susan Faludi and Stefanie Faludi
Courtesy Russ Rymer

WHERE THE PAST AND FUTURE BEGIN AND END: THE JOURNEY OF AMY TAN

The writer Amy Tan, whose insights about her mother-in-law we discussed in the last chapter, has spent much of her life trying to contend with the traumas, mysteries, and secrets of her family. She has written a memoir, *Where the Past Begins: A Writer's Memoir* (2017), from which she has made an extraordinary video, *An Unintended Memoir* (2021), about her family and her life experiences.

During the writing of her memoir, Tan went through all sorts of memorabilia, letters, and photos, and says that what she found "had the force of glaciers caving." Many readers think of her as writing about Chinese culture or about mother–daughter issues. But she sees herself as a writer "compelled by a subconscious neediness to know."

Lou DeMattei and Amy Tan
WENN Rights Ltd/Alamy Stock Photo

She always tries to understand how things come together to bring you to where you are.

Amy's mother had had a whole previous life in China with a brutal husband. She had had six children with him, but only three survived. She then met Amy's father and left her husband and three daughters for him, for which she was jailed, but managed to escape and leave China for the U.S. with her second husband. The couple together had three children, of whom Amy was the middle child and only girl. Amy's mother never told her or her brothers about her other children or her life in China.

The family struggled as immigrants to raise their three children in California. The mother was at times seriously depressed and even suicidal, once attempting to jump out of the moving car while her children were sitting in the back. What Amy found most mystifying about that traumatic experience was that afterward her father focused on reassuring his wife, rather than on his children's trauma.

Amy's father was an engineer who had passed up the opportunity to go to MIT in order to become a minister but struggled to support his family. When many years later Amy read her father's papers, she concluded that a key motivation for his decision to change professions and become a minister was his spiritual struggle with having broken one of the ten commandments in his relationship with his wife, who was already married to someone else.

Then, within a six-month period, Peter, the star oldest son, developed a brain tumor at age fifteen and died very quickly. While Peter was dying, their father developed a similar brain tumor and died two months after Peter, leaving Amy's already traumatized and dysfunctional mother alone with two children. Multiple traumas and disruptions followed in the family and Amy struggled, especially with her mother, for many years. As she later described it, they had an emotional seesaw relationship that continued until long after Amy married her husband Lou, whom she had met in college, and developed her career as a writer.

Then one day Amy's younger brother called to say their mother had had a heart attack, which sounded life threatening. As Amy waited to hear news about her mother, she "made a vow to God and whoever was listening: If my mother lives, I will get to know her. I'll ask her about her past, and this time I'll actually listen to what she has to say. Why, I'll even take her to China and, yes, I'll even write stories about her."

A transformation began for Amy. "I started asking her about her life, and I really listened, instead of saying: 'I'm really busy now, I can't listen to you,' and that profoundly changed everything. I wasn't fighting it anymore, and

I learned a lot by simply being quiet and listening." And she went to China with her mother, learning her mother's story and meeting the relatives.

Amy's strained relationship with her mother had been a barrier to her being able to "go home again"—but things started to change after she began applying the rules of healthy relating. She did this by reaching out and really listening to her mother, and not judging as she focused on trying to hear and understand her mother's perspective. Through that she was able finally gain information and insight, to develop a deeper connection with her mother and with herself. The "neediness to know" and make sense of things had always been Tan's driving force. Her efforts to go home again and to learn about her mother's very traumatic history are profoundly inspiring.

A LIFE JOURNEY TO GO HOME AGAIN

Mary Catherine Bateson (**see Genogram 10.2: Bateson Family**), the only daughter of two world-renowned anthropologists, Margaret Mead and Gregory Bateson, did not have an easy childhood. The relationship between her parents was not harmonious. Her father left her mother when she was seven and they divorced when she was eleven. Her mother often left her with other caretakers for long periods. Catherine's parents were preoccupied with their own concerns and attended to her needs only intermittently. As an infant, she was mostly cared for by a nurse. After her parents separated, she would periodically visit her father, who soon remarried and fathered another child, a son. On at least two occasions her father made inappropriate sexualized suggestions to her. However, she was able to maintain emotionally important, if sometimes physically distant, relationships with both her parents. She is a striking example of a person who as an adult worked hard to go home again.

Catherine was surprised when she read in her mother's autobiographical writings that she described herself and Gregory Bateson as nurturing personalities. Mead and Bateson felt that Catherine was a perfectly contented child, and she admits she never complained. She felt she had to be the non-whining "good girl" to encourage her parents to want to be with her as much as possible. If she was unpleasant to be with, she would lose them to

Mary Catherine Bateson
Steve Liss/Getty Images

other activities. Throughout her own memoir, Catherine Bateson shows an astute perception of the need to remain her own self—and not be a replica of her parents.

Bateson's story is one of acceptance of her parents as they were, with their faults and limitations, and of looking for the value in her relationship with each of them: "The voices of my parents are still very much with me, for I hear their echo in so much that I see and encounter"... (Bateson, 1984, p. 220).

In the end, Bateson remembered more about what she got than what she did not get from her parents. She felt that she got a sense of basic trust, self-confidence, faith, strength, and resiliency from her mother. As a professional anthropologist and mother herself, she came to appreciate how well-organized and masterful Mead had been, to have kept her always well cared

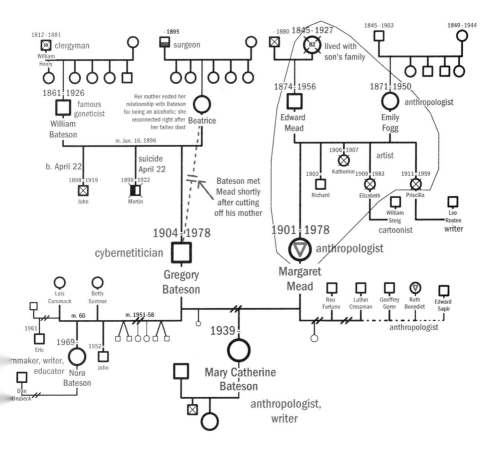

Genogram 10.2: Bateson Family

Gregory Bateson and Margaret Mead, with her previous husband, Reo Fortune
(right)
Library of Congress

for in the "extended family" of professional colleagues she had created. Catherine made her own synthesis from the models offered by her parents and
others around her. Like her mother, she had to combine multiple commit-
ments and to adapt and improvise in a culture in which she could be only
partly at home.

As for her father, although she spent less time with him, she was grateful for their long walks and talks, where he taught her about nature and science and answered her difficult questions about the way the world works.

Having struggled greatly with her parents' separation and divorce, Catherine came to fear she would follow in their footsteps with numerous failed marriages. She spent a lot of time trying to understand their marriages and their differences. Bateson's memoir demonstrates in a most touching way her effort to see her parents from many perspectives: as children in their own families, as lovers and marital partners, as siblings, and as professionals.

In many ways Mead and Bateson were opposites. She was American, practical, effusive, poetic. He was British, impractical, detached, scientific. Margaret thought that problems usually have a solution, whereas Gregory thought that people's efforts to improve things usually made them worse. Margaret appreciated the various conventions and rules of different societies, while Gregory lived his life as unconventionally as possible. Margaret loved religious ritual; Gregory was an atheist. Margaret loved people; Gregory preferred animals. Margaret's moral concerns focused on the development of societies; Gregory focused on ecology or the world as a whole. Margaret loved to be an organizer. Gregory came to see her organizing abilities as controlling. He was more abstract, more interested in finding the patterns of life than in controlling the particulars.

Margaret Mead with her young daughter, Mary Catherine Bateson
National Anthropological Archives, Smithsonian Institution

Catherine was forced to wonder how two such different people ever married. She speculated that her mother was most attracted to Bateson's cultural difference and noted that she too had also married a man from a different culture (Iran).

In her attempt to understand her parents' differences, Catherine noted their different sibling positions and roles in their families, Margaret was the oldest of five, all but one female. Gregory was the youngest of three, all boys. She said of her parents differing approaches to solving problems: "Margaret's approach must have been based on early success in dealing with problems, perhaps related to the experience of being an older child and amplified by years of successfully organizing the younger ones. Gregory's experience was that of a youngest child with relatively little capacity to change what went on around him. Instead, he would seek understanding" (Bateson, 1984, p. 176).

Catherine speculated further on the influence of early family events on her father's approach to life, including the suicide of his brother Martin in 1922 and intrusive parental attempts at guidance. Gregory Bateson was the youngest and considered the least promising of three sons of a famous British geneticist. He was sickly in childhood and not an outstanding student. The highest expectations were for the oldest son, John, who seemed to excel in every way. He and the middle brother, Martin, just two years apart in age, were extremely close. Gregory was four years younger and grew up somewhat separately. At age twenty John was killed in World War I. A few days later his mother wrote to Martin: "You and Gregory are left to me still and you must help me back to some of the braveness that John has taken away" (Lipset, 1980, p. 71).

Following John's death, a rift developed between Martin and his father, whose mother had coincidentally died just two months before. The father, now doubly bereft, began to pressure Martin, who was a poet, to take over his brother's role and become a zoologist. Relations between father and son deteriorated. When, in addition, Martin felt rebuffed by a young woman he admired, he took a gun and shot himself in Trafalgar Square on his brother John's birthday, April 22, 1922, in what was described as "probably the most dramatic and deliberate suicide ever witnessed in London" (Lipset, 1980, p. 93). This was the legacy for Gregory, "the runt," as he called himself. All the family's expectations that their oldest son would become a great scientist and follow in the father's footsteps now came down upon Gregory. His solution was to study anthropology, a science different from his father's field, biology, which also allowed him to escape from the family pressure into field work. All his life, Gregory would resist the expectations of others. The shift in his sibling position in early adult life may indeed have contributed to the incompatibility between him and Margaret, even though their birth positions were initially complementary, until his two older brothers' early and tragic deaths. There is also some similarity between Gregory, whose role in his family as the only surviving child intensified his relationship with his mother to the point of toxicity, and he ended up cutting her off.

Margaret Mead's father, an only child, was doted on by his mother after his father's early death when the boy was only six. While Bateson cut off his mother to avoid the pressure of the legacy, his future father-in-law,

Edward Mead, was so connected to his widowed mother that he brought her with him into his marriage. She lived in the Mead household for the rest of her life.

If we trace marital relationships in the Bateson family back, we observe problematic issues also in the previous generation. Gregory's parents had a prolonged courtship, which would lead one to suspect potential difficulties in the family relationships. His maternal grandmother had married an alcoholic, and when her daughter Beatrice got engaged to William Bateson, the mother called off the engagement, because he got drunk. She was trying to protect her daughter from her own fate of marrying an alcoholic. However, Beatrice recontacted William shortly after her father died, and married him soon afterward.

In the next generation, Gregory met and fell in love with Margaret just after becoming estranged from his mother, Beatrice. Margaret and her second husband were doing anthropological work in a remote area of the world at that time.

Catherine made an enormous effort to understand her parents through an exploration of their lives. She worked to see them as individuals, each with their own set of problems. Most important, she tried to see them in the multigenerational context of their families, struggling to come to terms with their parents, in much the same way that she struggled to come to terms with hers. She was able to accept their differences without blaming either of them. Although it was her father who left her mother, she tried not to judge, but only to understand him. Throughout their lives, she maintained connections with both parents. Gregory always sought to interest his daughter in what *he* considered "important matters," but never paid attention to her interests. She did not reject her father for not validating her interests. Nor did she try to change him. When, toward the end of his life, he became interested in ecology, he elicited and got her help in organizing his project.

Catherine maintained both personal and professional contact with her mother as well. They did presentations together. They planned a conference on rituals together. Particularly important, Catherine was able to appreciate her mother's efforts not to dominate her life. She says of her:

> In any quarrel between us, the thing that would have hurt her most, because it had been said to her so many times, would have been to accuse her of dominating me or interfering with my life. (Bateson, 1984, pp. 110–111)

We see here that Margaret herself was concerned about differentiation in the sense of not intruding on her daughter's personhood, which probably was important modeling for Catherine. It may also reflect an Anglo sensibility to privacy and not intruding on anyone else's space, which might be viewed very differently in other cultures. Mother and daughter both worked at their separateness. Through these efforts not to have a parent–child relationship of control, they were able to avoid the power struggle that had so plagued the parents' marriage.

One of the most touching issues Bateson explores is her mother's secrecy and what it cost both of them. Margaret's sexual liaisons and particularly her bisexuality were discovered by her daughter only after her mother's death in 1978, when a close family friend gave Catherine a letter that Margaret had written many years earlier, intended for those she loved in the event of her death. The letter seemed to Catherine to be an expression of her mother's concern that details of her life might be revealed under circumstances of scandal, without her being able to provide explanation or reassurance. Margaret apparently became increasingly grieved that many aspects of her life could not be shared. She was troubled about the pain the revelation of her secret might cause to others.

> It has not been my choice of concealment that any one of you have been left in ignorance of some part of my life which would seem, I know, of great importance. Nor has it been from lack of trust, in any person, on my part, but only from the exigencies of the mid-twentieth century when each one of us, at least those of us who are my age, seems fated for a life, which is no longer sharable. (Bateson, 1984, p. 115)

Catherine, who was only fifteen when her mother wrote this letter, was one of the ones to whom it would have been given. She wrote in her memoir: "I knew little until after her death of the pattern of relationships to male and female lovers that she had developed, so that trying to look back on who she was as a person and as my mother has been complicated by the need to revise my picture of her in important ways and by the need to deal with the fact of concealment. I have been at times angered at the sense of being deliberately deceived and at having been without doubt a collaborator in my own deception, limiting my perceptions to the images she was willing to have me see" (Bateson, 1984, p. 119). Margaret's concern about the possible negative impact of the secrets in her life is impressive as is her effort to counteract their negative potential by her letter.

Margaret Mead and Gregory Bateson
Courtesy of Carrie Humphrey

But what is most impressive about Catherine's commentary is her recognition of the part she played in her mother's secrecy and her willingness to explore her own complicity: "I have sometimes felt myself doubly bereaved as well, having radically to reconsider my convictions about who she was and therefore, in relationship to her, about who I was and am, surprised at last by the sense of continuing recognition" (Bateson, 1984, p. 119).

In the end, Catherine Bateson was able to accept both her mother and her father for who they were. They were far from perfect as parents, but their daughter's ability to take what they had to offer her and transform it into a significant part of her own self is most impressive. She used this acceptance to deal with their deaths:

> The contained world of early childhood no longer exists, but my concerns remain similar to theirs and the analogies that bridge from the microcosm to the wider world continue. (Bateson, 1984, p. 227)

We and our families are always struggling to reinvent ourselves and transform our difficult and painful experiences into something creative and positive. As Bateson says: "Part of the task of composing a life is the artist's need to find a way to take what is simply ugly and instead of trying to deny it, to use it in the broader design" (Bateson, 1984, p. 211).

Bateson's words and efforts hopefully suggest the value of taking a journey home and engaging with all of what we find, the good and the bad, the hopeful and the disappointing, the hurtful and the healing, and to make peace with all of it.

CONCLUDING REMARKS

The idea of reconnecting with our families is so that "hope and history will rhyme," that is, so that connections to our history will open up the future. This requires creating a sense of family and "home" in which no one's experience is outside history, whether because of race, class, gender, shame, or secrecy, a place where the complex and ambiguous connections that entwine your family can be validated.

The work of understanding and reconnecting is a lifetime project. To create something new you will have to struggle against the definitions you are given, so that you can define connectedness in ways that *you* find meaningful.

Home: it is that place we never really left because it is always within us, but hopefully by taking the journey we have laid out in this book, you will find a way to go home again in the sense of finding yourself as you find your family in new, deeper, fuller, and more accepting ways.

REFERENCES

General

Aguilar, C. (2021, June 11). They fought to make "In the Heights" both dream-like and authentic. *New York Times,* C6.

Anderson, R. (1968). *I never sang for my father.* New York: Random House.

Arons, R. (2016). *The Jews of Sing Sing.* Barricade Books.

Bernikow, L. (1980). *Among women.* New York: Harper & Row.

Bowen, M. (1978). *Family therapy in clinical practice.* New York: Jason Aronson.

Brooks, D. (2021). What's ripping American families apart? *New York Times.* Retrieved 12/20/21. https://www.nytimes.com/2021/07/29/opinion/estranged-american-families.html

Burton, L., Winn, D. M., Stevenson, H., & Clark, S. L. (2004). Working with African American clients: Considering the "homeplace" in marriage and family therapy practices. *Journal of Marital and Family Therapy, 30*(4), 113–129.

Carter, B., & McGoldrick, M. (2001). Family therapy with one person and the family therapist's own family. *Journal of Marital and Family Therapy, 27*(3), 281–300.

Carter, B., & Peters, J. K. (1996). *Love honor and negotiate: Making your marriage work.* New York: Pocket Books.

Carter, E. A., & McGoldrick Orfanidis, M. (1976). Family therapy with one person and the family therapist's own family. In: P. J. Guerin (Ed.), *Family therapy* (pp. 193–219). New York: Gardner.

Conroy, P. (1988). *The prince of tides.* New York: Houghton Mifflin.

Dahl, G. B., & Moretti, E. (2008). The demand for sons. *Review of Economic Studies, 75,* 1085–1120.

De Bernicres, L. (2005). *Birds without wings.* New York: Vintage.

Denborough, D. (2020). *Unsettling Australian histories: Letters to ancestry from a great great grandson.* Adelaide, Australia: Dulwich Center Publications.

Duckworth, T. (2021). *Every day is a gift: A memoir.* Twelve Press.

Eagan, T. (2021, May 28). Scenes from a mogul's marriage or: The troubling fourth act of Bill Gates. *The New York Times.* Retrieved from: https://www.nytimes.com/2021/05/28/opinion/bill-melinda-gates-divorce.html

Fishel, E. (1979). *Sisters: Love and rivalry inside the family and beyond.* New York: William Morrow.

Flanagan, T. (1979). *The year of the French.* New York: Holt, Rinehart & Winston.

Friedman, E. (1990). *Friedman's fables.* New York: Guilford.

Garrett, R. E., Klinkman, M., & Post, L. (1987). If you meet Buddha on the road, take a genogram: Zen and the art of family medicine. *Family Medicine, May-Jun, 19*(3), 225–226.

Gates, H. L. (Director). (2019, February 26). Michael Moore: Hard times (Season 5, Episode 8). [TV Series Episode] *Finding your roots with Henry Louis Gates, Jr.* McGee Media, Inkwell Media, Kunhardt Films.

Gates, H. L. (Director). (2021, February 16). Pharrell Williams: Write my name in the book of life (Season 7, Episode 5). [TV Series Episode] *Finding Your Roots with Henry Louis Gates, Jr.* McGee Media, Inkwell Media, Kunhardt Films.

Gates, H. L. (Director). (2021, February 23). Roseanne Cash: Country roots (Season 7, Episode 6). [TV Series Episode] *Finding Your Roots with Henry Louis Gates, Jr.* McGee Media, Inkwell Media, Kunhardt Films.

Gates, H. L. (2021). *The black church. This is our story, this is our song.* New York: Penguin Press.

Giamatti, A. B. (1989). *Take time for paradise: Americans and their games.* New York: Summit.

Gilles-Donovan, J. (1991, Summer). Common misunderstandings. *American Family Therapy Academy Newsletter, 7–14.*

Gold, D. T. (1989). Sibling relationships in old age: A typology. *International Journal of Aging and Human Development, 28*(37), 37–51.

Golden, M. (2003). *Don't play in the sun: One woman's journey through the color complex.* Garden City, NY: Anchor Press.

Goleman, D. (2006). *Social intelligence.* New York: NY: Random House.

Gottman, J. (2007). *Why marriages succeed or fail, and how to make them last.* London: Bloomsbury.

Griffin, S. (1992). *A chorus of stones.* New York: Doubleday.

Haley, A. (1976). *Roots: The saga of an American family.* New York: Doubleday.

Haskell, M. (1990). *Love and other infectious diseases.* New York: William Morrow.

Heilbrun, C. G. (1988). *Writing a woman's life.* New York: Norton.

Kleiner, P. *Good mother, good daughter.* Unpublished manuscript.

Kolker, R. (2020). *Hidden valley road: Inside the mind of an American family.* Vintage Canada.

Kotre, J., & Hall, E. (1990). *Seasons of life.* Boston: Little, Brown.

Liem Borshay, D. (Director). (2000). *First person plural.* Retrieved from: https://www.mufilms.org/films/firstpersonplural/

Liem Borshay, D. (Director). (2010). *In the Matter of Cha Jung Hee*. Retrieved from: https://www.amdoc.org/watch/chajunghee/

Lott, T. (2012, August 18). Get over it: Brotherhood is the greatest relationship you can share. *The Guardian*. Retrieved from: https://www.theguardian.com/commentisfree/2012/aug/18/brotherhood-rivalry-love-hate

Mancini. J. (2021). *Immigrant secrets: The search for my grandparents*. Self-published.

McHale, S. M., Updegraff, K., & Whiteman, S. D. (2012). Sibling relationships and influences in childhood and adolescence. *Journal of Marriage and Family, 74*(5), 913–930.

McGoldrick, M., Carter, B., & Garcia Preto, N. (Eds.). (2016). *The changing family life cycle* (5th ed.). Boston: Allyn & Bacon.

McGoldrick, M., Gerson, R., & Petry, S. (2021). *Genograms: Assessment and intervention*. New York: Norton.

McGoldrick, M., Giordano, J., & Garcia Preto, N. (2005). *Ethnicity and family therapy* (3rd ed.). New York: Guilford.

Nabokov. V. (1992). *The real life of Sebastian Knight*. New York: Vintage.

Osterweis, M., Solomon, F., & Green, M. (Eds.). (1984). *Bereavement: Reactions, consequences, and care*. Washington, DC: National Academy Press/Solomon & Green.

Rawat, S., Yadav, A., Parve, S., & Bhate, K. (2021). Epidemiological factors influencing gender preference among mothers attending under-five immunization clinic: A cross-sectional comparative study. *Journal of Education and Health Promotions, 10*(190).

Rose, P. (1984). *Parallel lives: Five Victorian marriages*. New York: Vintage.

Russell, K., Wilson, M., & Hall, R. (1993). *The color complex: The politics of skin color among African Americans*. Garden City, NY: Anchor Press.

Schapiro, D. (2019). *Inheritance: A Memoir of Genealogy, Paternity and Love*. New York: Knopf.

Siegel, D. J. (2017). *Mind: A journey to the heart of being human*. New York: Norton.

Siegel, D. J. (2018). *Aware: The science and practice of presence—the groundbreaking meditation practice*. New York: Tarcher-Perigree.

Sulloway, F. (1997). *Born to rebel: Birth order, family dynamics, and creative lives*. Vintage Books: New York, NY.

Teege, J. & Sellmair, N. (2015). *My grandfather would have shot me: A black woman discovers her family's Nazi past*. New York: The Experiment Publishing.

Tucker, A. (Director). (2013). *Closure*. Retrieved from: https://www.angelatucker.com/films

Valliant, G. E. (1977). *Adaption to life*. Boston: Little, Brown.

Walmsley, J. (2003). *Brit-think, Ameri-think.* New York: Penguin.

Walsh, F. (2023). *Complex and traumatic loss.* New York: Guilford.

Walsh, F., & McGoldrick, M. (Eds.). (2004). *Living beyond loss: Death and the family* (2nd ed.). New York: Norton.

Washington, E. L (2007). Female socialization: How daughters affect their legislator fathers' voting on women's issues. *American Economic Review, 86*(3), 425–441.

Witchel, A. (1989, November 12). Laughter, tears and the perfect martini. *New York Times Magazine,* 102–105.

Younger, S. (2016). Six inspiring quotes by J. K. Rowling. Retrieved 12/19/21 from: https://www.chicagonow.com/between-us-parents/2016/01/inspiring-quotes-from-j-k-rowling/)

Adams Family Sources

Adams, J. T. (1976). *The Adams family.* New York: Signet.

Butterfield, L. H., Friedlaender, M., & Kline, M. (Eds.). (1975). *The book of Abigail and John: Selected letters of the Adams family: 1762–1784.* Cambridge: Harvard University Press.

Conroy, S. B. (1993). *Refinements of love: A novel about Clover and Henry Adams.* New York: Pantheon.

Homans, A. A. (1966). *Education by uncles.* Boston: Houghton Mifflin.

Levin, P. L. (1987). *Abigail Adams.* New York: St. Martin's.

McCullough, D. (2001). *John Adams.* New York: Simon & Schuster.

Musto, D. (1981). The Adams family. *Proceedings of Massachusetts Historical Society, 93,* 40–58.

Nagel, P. C. (1983). *Descent from glory: Four generations of the John Adams family.* New York: Oxford University Press.

Nagel, P. C. (1987). *The Adams women.* New York: Oxford University Press.

Nagel, P. C. (1997). *John Quincy Adams: A public life.* New York: Knopf.

O'Faolain, N. (1996). *Are you somebody: The accidental memoir of a Dublin woman.* New York: Henry Holt & Company.

O'Faolain, N. (2001). *My dream of you.* New York: Penguin Putnam.

O'Toole, P. (1990). *The five of hearts: An intimate portrait of Henry Adams and his friends 1880–1918.* New York: Ballantine.

Richards, L. L. (1986). *The life and times of congressman John Quincy Adams.* New York: Oxford University Press.

Shaw, P. (1976). *The character of John Adams.* New York: Norton.

Shepherd, J. (1975). *The Adams chronicles: Four generations of greatness.* Boston: Little, Brown.

Withey, L. (1981). *Dearest friend: A life of Abigail Adams.* New York: Free Press.

Angelou Sources

Angelou, M. (1970). *I know why the caged bird sings*. New York: Random House.

Angelou, M. (1974). *Gather together in my name*. New York: Bantam.

Angelou, M. (1981). *The heart of a woman*. New York: Bantam.

Angelou, M. (1986a). *All God's children need traveling shoes*. New York: Vintage.

Angelou, M. (1986b). *Poems: Maya Angelou*. New York: Bantam.

Angelou, M. (1993). *Wouldn't take nothing for my journey now*. New York: Random House.

Angelou, M. (2007). *Letter to my daughter*. New York: Random House.

Elliott, J. M. (1989). *Conversations with Maya Angelou*. Jackson, MI: University of Mississippi Press.

Kite, L. P. (1999). *Maya Angelou*. Minneapolis, MN: Lerner.

McPherson, D. A. (1999). *Order out of chaos: The autobiographical works of Maya Angelou*. New York: Peter Lang.

Oliver, S. S. (1989). Heart of a woman. In: J. M. Elliott (Ed), *Conversations with Maya Angelou* (135–39). Jackson, MI: University of Mississippi Press.

Shuker, N. (1990). *Maya Angelou*. Englewood Cliffs, NJ: Silver Burdett Press.

Baldwin Sources

Baldwin, J. (1962). *The fire next time*. New York: Vintage Books.

Baldwin, J. (1991). Sonny's blues. In: Minnesota Humanities Commission (Ed.), *Braided lives: An anthology of multicultural American writing*. St. Paul, Minnesota: Minnesota Humanities Commission.

Baldwin, J. (1998a). *Collected essays*. New York: The Library of America.

Baldwin, J. (1998b). *Collected essays: Notes of a native son, Nobody knows my name, The fire next time, No name in the street, The devil finds work, Other essays*. New York: Library Classics of the United States.

Baldwin, J. (2017). *I am not your negro*. New York: Vintage Books.

Glaude, E. S. (2020). *Begin again: James Baldwin's America and its urgent lessons for our own*. New York: Crown.

Leeming, D. (1994). *James Baldwin, a biography*. New York: Arcade.

Barrett and Browning Sources

Browning, R., & Barrett Browning, E. (1902). *The letters of Robert Browning and Elizabeth Barrett Browning, 1845–1846*. New York: Harper and Brothers.

Browning, V. (1979). *My Browning family album*. London: Springwood.

Buchanan, A., & Buchanan-Weiss, E. (2011). Elizabeth Barrett Browning's illness deciphered after 150 years. Penn State University. Retrieved: https://www.eurekalert.org/pub_releases/2011-12/ps-ebb121911.php

Forster, M. (1988). *Elizabeth Barrett Browning: A biography.* New York: Doubleday.

Hewlett, D. (1953). *Elizabeth Barrett Browning.* New York: Cassell.

Honan, P., & Irvine, W. (1974). *The book, the ring and the poet: A biography of Robert Browning.* New York: Bodley Head.

Karlin, D. (1987). *The courtship of Robert Browning and Elizabeth Barrett.* New York: Oxford University Press.

Leighton, A. (1986). *Elizabeth Barrett Browning.* New York: Harvester Press.

Mander, R. (1980). *Mrs. Browning: The story of Elizabeth Barrett.* London: Weidenfeld & Nicolson.

Marks, J. (1938). *The family of the Barrett.* New York: Macmillan.

Markus, J. (1995). *Dared and done: The marriage of Elizabeth Barrett and Robert Browning.* New York: Knopf.

Maynard, J. (1977). *Browning's youth.* Cambridge, MA: Harvard University Press.

Miller, B. (1973). *Robert Browning: A portrait.* New York: Scribner.

O'Faolain, N. (1998). *Are you somebody? The accidental memoir of a Dublin woman.* New York: Henry Holt.

Orr, S. (1908). *Life and letters of Robert Browning* (Rev. ed.). New York: John Murray.

Robinson, J. (1894, August 18). Mrs. Barrett Browning's parentage. *Athenaeum, 3486,* 223–224.

Ryals, C. de L. (1993). *The life of Robert Browning.* Cambridge, MA: Blackwell.

Taplin, G. B. (1957). *The life of Elizabeth Barrett Browning.* New York: John Murray.

Teege, J. (2015). *My grandfather would have shot me: A black woman discovers her family's Nazi past.* The Experiment Press.

Thomas, D. (1982). *Robert Browning: A life within a life.* London: Weidenfeld & Nicolson.

Turner, W. C. (Ed.). (1983). *The poet Robert Browning and his kinsfolk by his cousin Cyrus Mason.* Waco, TX: Baylor University Press.

Ward, M. (1955). *Robert Browning and his world: The private face (1812–61).* New York: Holt, Rinehart & Winston.

Ward, M. (1972). *The tragi-comedy of pen Browning.* New York: Sheed & Ward Browning Institute.

Bateson and Mead Sources

Bateson, M. C. (1984). *With a daughter's eye.* New York: William Morrow.

Bateson, M. C. (1990). *Composing a life.* New York: Atlantic Monthly Press.

Bateson, M. C. (1994). *Peripheral visions.* New York: William Morrow.

Cassidy, R. (1982). *Margaret Mead: A voice for the century.* New York: Universe Books.

Grosskurth, P. (1988). *Margaret Mead: A life of controversy.* London: Penguin.

Howard, J. (1984). *Margaret Mead: A life.* New York: Ballantine.

Lipset, D. (1980). *Gregory Bateson: The legacy of a scientist.* Englewood Cliffs, NJ: Prentice.

Mead, M. (1972). *Blackberry winter, my earlier years.* New York: Simon & Schuster.

Rice, E. (1979). *Margaret Mead: A portrait.* New York: Harper & Row.

Beethoven Sources

Caeyers, J. (2009). *Beethoven: A life.* University of California Press.

Ciardello, J. A. (1985). Beethoven: Modern analytic view of the man and his music. *Psychoanalytic Review, 72*(1), 129–147.

Cooper, M. (1985). *Beethoven: The last decade: 1817–1827.* New York: Oxford University Press.

Editore, A. M. (1967). *Beethoven: Portraits of greatness.* New York: Curtis.

Forbes, E. (Ed.). (1969). *Thayer's life of Beethoven.* Princeton: Princeton University Press.

Hamburger, M. (Ed.). (1951). *Beethoven: Letters, journals and conversations.* New York: Thames & Hudson.

James, R. M. (1983). *Beethoven.* New York: St. Martin's Press.

Kerst, F., & Krehbiel, H. E. (Eds.). (1964). *Beethoven: The man and artist as revealed in his own words.* New York: Dover.

MacArdle, D. W. (1949). The family van Beethoven. *Musical Quarterly, xxxv* (4), 528–550.

Marek, G. R. (1969). *Beethoven: Biography of a genius.* New York: Thomas Y. Crowell.

Matthews, D. (1988). *Beethoven.* New York: Vintage.

Rodman, S., & Kearns, J. (1962). *The heart of Beethoven.* New York: Shorewood.

Solomon, M. (1977). *Beethoven.* New York: Schirmer.

Solomon, M. (1988). *Beethoven essays.* Cambridge: Harvard University Press.

Sterbe, E., & Sterbe, R. (1954). *Beethoven and his nephew.* New York: Pantheon.

Sullivan, J. W. N. (1960). *Beethoven: His spiritual development.* New York: Vintage.

Swafford, J. (2014). *Beethoven: Anguish and triumph.* New York: Houghton Mifflin Harcourt.

Blackwell, Stone, and Brown Sources

Binns, T. B. (2005). *Elizabeth Blackwell.* New York: Franklin Watts.

Cazden, E. (1983). *Antoinette Brown Blackwell: A biography.* Old Westbury, NY: Feminist Press.

Hays, E. R. (1967). *Those extraordinary Blackwells.* New York: Harcourt Brace.

Horn, M. (1980). *Family ties: The Blackwells, a study of the dynamics of family life in nineteenth century America.* Unpublished doctoral dissertation, Tufts University.

Horn, M. (1983). Sisters worthy of respect: Family dynamics and women's roles in the Blackwell family. *Journal of Family History, 8*(4), 367–382.

Kerr, A. M. (1992). *Lucy Stone: Speaking out.* New Brunswick, NJ: Rutgers University Press.

Lasser, C., & Merrill, M. D. (1987). *Friends & sisters: Letters between Lucy Stone and Antoinette Brown Blackwell 1846–93.* Chicago: University of Illinois.

Nimura, J. P. (2021). *The doctors Blackwell: How two pioneering sisters brought medicine to women and women to medicine.* New York: Norton.

Wheeler, L. (1981). *Loving worriers: Selected letters of Lucy Stone and Henry B. Blackwell, 1853 to 1893.* New York: Dial.

Brontë Sources

Bentley, P. (1969). *The Brontës and their world.* New York: Viking.

Brontë, C. (1922). *Villette.* New York: E. P. Dutton.

Cannon, J. (1980). *The road to Haworth: The story of the Brontës' Irish ancestry.* London: Weidenfeld and Nicolson.

Chadwick, E. H. (1914). *In the footsteps of the Brontës.* London: Sir Isaac Pitman & Sons.

Chitham, E. (1986). *The Brontës' Irish background.* New York: St. Martin's Press.

Chitham, E. (1988). *A life of Emily Brontë.* New York: Basil Blackwell.

Chitham, E., & Winnifrith, T. (1983). *Brontë facts and Brontë problems.* London: Macmillan.

du Maurier, D. (1961). *The infernal world of Branwell Brontë.* Garden City, NY: Doubleday.

Frazer, R. (1988). *The Brontës: Charlotte Brontë and her family.* New York: Crown.

Gaskell, E. (1975). *The life of Charlotte Brontë.* London: Penguin.

Gerin, W. (1961). *Branwell Brontë.* London: Thomas Nelson & Sons.

Gerin, W. (1971). *Emily Brontë: A biography.* London: Oxford University Press.

Hannah, B. (1988). *Striving toward wholeness.* Boston: Signpress.

Hanson, L., & Hanson, E. (1967). *The four Brontës.* New York: Archon Press.

Hinkley, L. L. (1945). *The Brontës: Charlotte and Emily.* New York: Hastings House.

Hopkins, A. B. (1958). *The father of the Brontës.* Baltimore: Johns Hopkins Press.

Lane, M. (1969). *The Brontë story*. London: Fontana.

Lock, J., & Dixon, W. T. (1965). *A man of sorrow: The life, letters, and times of Reverend Patrick Brontë*. Westport, CT: Meckler Books.

Mackay, A. M. (1897). *The Brontës: Fact and fiction*. New York: Dodd, Mead.

Maurat, C. (1970). *The Brontës' secret* (M. Meldrum, Trans.). New York: Barnes & Noble.

Moglen, H. (1984). *Charlotte Brontë: The self conceived*. Madison, WI: University of Wisconsin Press.

Morrison, N. B. (1969). *Haworth harvest: The story of the Brontës*. New York: Vanguard.

Peters, M. (1974). *An enigma of Brontës*. New York: St. Martin's Press.

Peters, M. (1975). *Unquiet soul: A biography of Charlotte Brontë*. New York: Atheneum.

Ratchford, F. W. (1964). *The Brontës' web of childhood*. New York: Russell & Russell.

Raymond, E. (1948). *In the steps of the Brontës*. London: Rich & Cowan.

Spark, M., & Derek, S. (1960). *Emily Brontë: Her life and work*. London: Arrow Books.

White, W. B. (1939). *The miracle of Haworth: A Brontë story*. New York: E. P. Dutton.

Wilks, B. (1986a). *The Brontës: An illustrated biography*. New York: Peter Bedrick Books.

Wilks, B. (1986b). *The illustrated Brontës of Haworth*. New York: Facts on File Publications.

Winnifrith, T. Z. (1977). *The Brontës and their background: Romance and reality*. New York: Collier.

Wright, W. (1893). *The Brontës in Ireland*. New York: D. Appleton & Company.

Broyard Sources

Broyard, A. (1979, April 19). The advantage of growing up irrational. *The New York Times, Section C*, p. 1.

Broyard, A. (1992). *Intoxicated by my illness and other writings on life and death*. New York: Fawcett Columbine.

Broyard, B. (2007). *One drop: My father's hidden life—A story of race and family secrets*. New York: Little Brown.

Broyard, B. (1999). *My father dancing*. New York: Alfred A. Knopf.

Gates, H. L. (1996, June, 17). White like me. *The New Yorker*.

Maslin, S. (2007, September 27). A daughter on her father's bloodlines and color lines. *The New York Times,* Best of the Times.

Chaplin Sources

Bessy, M. (1983). *Charlie Chaplin*. New York: Harper & Row.

Chaplin, C. (1964). *My autobiography*. New York: Simon & Schuster.

Chaplin, C., Jr., Rau, N., & Rau, M. (1960). *My father, Charlie Chaplin*. New York: Random House.

Chaplin, L. G., & Cooper, M. (1966). *My life with Chaplin: An intimate memoir*. Brattleboro, VT: Book Press.

Epstein, J. (1989). *Remembering Charlie*. New York: Doubleday.

Haining, P. (Ed.). (1982). *The legend of Charlie Chaplin*. London: W. H. Allen.

Karney, R., & Cross, R. (1992). *The life and times of Charlie Chaplin*. London: Green Wood Publishing.

Maland, C. (1989). *Chaplin and American culture: The evolution of a star image*. Princeton, NJ: Princeton University Press.

McCabe, J. (1978). *Charlie Chaplin*. New York: Doubleday.

Robinson, D. (1983). *Chaplin: The mirror of opinion*. Bloomington, IN: Indiana University Press.

Robinson, D. (1985). *Chaplin: His life and art*. New York: McGraw-Hill.

Smith, J. (1984). *Chaplin*. Boston: Twayne Publishers.

Christie Sources

Cade, J. (1998). *Agatha Christie and the eleven missing days*. London: Peter Owen Publishers.

Christie, A. (1974). *Come tell me how you live*. New York: Bantam Books.

Christie, A. (1977). *An autobiography*. New York: Dodd, Mead & Co.

Curran, J. (2009). *Agatha Christie's secret notebooks*. New York: Harper.

Gill, G. (1990). *Agatha Christie: The woman and her mysteries*. New York: The Free Press.

Hack, R. (2009). *Duchess of death: The unauthorized biography of Agatha Christie*. Beverly Hills, CA: Phoenix Books.

Macaskill, H. (2009). *Agatha Christie at home*. London: Frances Lincoln Limited.

Mallowan, M. (2012). *Mallowan's memoirs*. New York: Harper Collins.

Morgan, J. (1984). *Agatha Christie: A biography*. New York: Knopf.

Osborne, C. (1999). *The life and crimes of Agatha Christie: A biographical companion to the works of Agatha Christie*. New York: St. Martin's Press.

Robyns, G. (1978). *The mystery of Agatha Christie: An intimate biography of the duchess of death*. New York: Penguin.

Sova, D. B. (1996). *Agatha Christie A to Z: The essential reference to her life and writings.* New York: Checkmark Books.

Thompson, L. (2007). *Agatha Christie: A mysterious life.* London: Headline Publishing Group.

Curie Sources

Curie, E. (1939). *Marie Curie: A biography.* New York: Doubleday.

Giroud, F. (1986). *Marie Curie: A life.* New York: Holmes & Meier.

Pflaum, R. (1989). *Grand obsession: Madame Curie and her world.* New York: Doubleday.

Reid, R. (1974). *Marie Curie.* New York: E. P. Dutton.

Steinke, A. E. (1987). *Marie Curie.* New York: Barrons.

De Beauvoir Sources

Appignanesi, L. (1988). *Simone de Beauvoir.* New York: Viking Penguin.

Ascher, C. (1981). *Simone de Beauvoir: A life of freedom.* Boston: Beacon.

Bair, D. (1990). *Simone de Beauvoir: A biography.* New York: Summit.

de Beauvoir, S. (1959). *Memoirs of a dutiful daughter.* New York: Harper & Row.

de Beauvoir, S. (1973). *A very easy death.* New York: Warner Paperback Library.

de Beauvoir, S. (1974). *The second sex.* New York: Vintage.

Francis, C., & Gontier, F. (1987). *Simone de Beauvoir: A life, a love story.* New York: St. Martin's Press.

Dickens Sources

Johnson, E. (1980). *Charles Dickens: His tragedy and triumph.* New York: Penguin.

Hawksley, L. (2016a). *Charles Dickens and his circle.* London: National Portrait Gallery.

Hawksley, L. (2016b). *The forgotten Catherine Dickens.* Retrieved 7/31/21 from: https://www.bbc.com/culture/article/20160519-the-forgotten-wife-of-charles-dickens

Kaplan, F. (1988). *Dickens: A biography.* New York: William Morrow.

Mackenzie, N., & Mackenzie, J. (1979). *Dickens: A life.* New York: Oxford.

Storey, G. (1939). *Dickens and daughter.* London: Frederick Muller Ltd.

Tomalin, C. (1991). *The invisible woman: The story of Nelly Ternan and Charles Dickens.* New York: Knopf.

Edison Sources

Conot, R. (1979). *Thomas A. Edison: A streak of luck.* New York: Plenum.

Frost, L. A. (1984). *The Edison album: A pictorial biography of Thomas Alva Edison*. Mattituck, NY: Amereon House.

Josephson, M. (1959). *Edison: A biography*. New York: McGraw-Hill.

Venable, J. D. (1961). *Mina Miller Edison: Daughter, wife and mother of inventors*. East Orange, NJ: Charles Edison Fund.

Wachhorst, W. (1984). *Thomas Alva Edison: An American myth*. Cambridge, MA: MIT Press.

Faludi Sources

Clark, W. (2017). Navigating identities past and present in Susan Faludi's "In the Darkroom." *Los Angeles Review of Books*, May 20, 2017.

Corrigan, M. (2016, June 15). "In the darkroom" explores the concept of identity—both fixed and fluid. *NPR*.

Faludi, S. (2016). *In the darkroom*. New York: Metropolitan Books, Henry Holt & Co.

Goldberg, M. (2016, June 19). In the darkroom: A father's legacy. *New York Times*. Retrieved from: https://www.nytimes.com/2016/06/19/books/review/susan-faludis-in-the-darkroom.html

Haldeman, P. (2016, December 31). My father, the shapeshifter. *New York Times*.

Harman, C. (2016). In the darkroom by Susan Faludi review—my father, the woman. *The Guardian*, U.S. Edition.

Senior, J. (2016, June 12). Review: Father was a vicious bully. Then he became a woman. *New York Times: Books of the Times*.

Sluhovsky, M. (2017, June 28). The fascinating tale of Steve, a shul-going Holocaust survivor, who became Stefanie, a Jew-hating lady. *HAARETZ*.

Fonda Sources

Collier, P. (1992). *The Fondas*. New York: Putnam.

Fonda, A. (1986). *Never before dawn: An autobiography*. New York: Weindenfeld & Nicolson.

Fonda, J. (2006). *My life so far*. New York: Random House.

Fonda, P. (1998). *Don't tell dad*. New York: Hyperion.

Guiles, F. L. (1981). *Jane Fonda: The actress in her time*. New York: Pinnacle.

Hayward, B. (1977). *Haywire*. New York: Knopf.

Kiernan, T. (1973). *Jane: An intimate biography of Jane Fonda*. New York: Putnam.

Sheed, W. (1982). *Clare Booth Luce*. New York: E. P. Dutton.

Springer, J. (1970). *The Fondas*. Secaucus, NJ: Citadel.

Teichman, H. (1981). *Fonda: My life*. New York: New American Library.

Franklin Sources

Bowen, C. D. (1974). *The most dangerous man in America: Scenes from the life of Benjamin Franklin.* Boston: Little, Brown.

Clark, R. W. (1983). *Benjamin Franklin: A biography.* New York: Random House.

Fay, B. (1969). *The two Franklins: Fathers of American democracy.* New York: AMS Press.

Franklin, B. (1964). *The autobiography of Benjamin Franklin.* New Haven, CT: Yale University Press.

Hall, M. (1960). *Benjamin Franklin and Polly Baker.* Chapel Hill, NC: University of North Carolina Press.

Labaree, L. W., Ketcham, R. L., Boarfield, H. C., & Fineman, H. H. (Eds.). (1964). *The autobiography of Benjamin Franklin.* New Haven, CT: Yale University Press.

Lopez, C. A., & Herbert, E. W. (1975). *The private Franklin: The man and his family.* New York: Norton.

Middlekauf, R. (1996). *Benjamin Franklin and his enemies.* Berkeley, CA: University of California Press.

Osborne, M. P. (1990). *The many lives of Benjamin Franklin.* New York: Dial.

Randall, W. (1984). *A little revenge: Benjamin Franklin and his son.* Boston: Little, Brown.

Seavey, O. (1988). *Becoming Benjamin Franklin: The autobiography and the life.* University Park, PA: Pennsylvania State University Press.

Skemp, S. L. (1990). *William Franklin, son of a patriot, servant of a king.* New York: Oxford University Press.

Stevenson, A. (1987). *The real Benjamin Franklin: The true story of America's greatest diplomat.* Washington, DC: National Center for Constitutional Studies.

Van Doren, C. (1938). *Benjamin Franklin.* New York: Viking.

Wright, E. (1986). *Franklin of Philadelphia.* Cambridge, MA: Harvard University Press.

Wright, E. (1990). *Benjamin Franklin: His life as he wrote it.* Cambridge, MA: Harvard University Press.

Freud Sources

Anzieu, D. (1986). *Freud's self analysis.* Madison, CT: International Universities Press.

Appignanesi, L., & Forrester, J. (1992). *Freud's women.* New York: Basic.

Bernays, A. F. (1940, November). My brother Sigmund Freud. *The American Mercury, 51,* 335–342.

Bernays, Edward. Personal interview.

Bernays, Hella. Personal interview.

Burlingham, M. J. (2002). *Behind glass: A biography of Dorothy Tiffany Burlingham.* New York: Other Press.

Carotenuto, A. (1982). *A secret symmetry: Sabina Spielrein between Jung and Freud.* New York: Pantheon.

Clark, R. W. (1980). *Freud: The man and the cause.* New York: Random House.

Eissler, K. R. (1978). *Sigmund Freud: His life in pictures and words.* New York: Helen & Kurt Wolff Books, Harcourt Brace, Jovanovich.

Freeman, L., & Strean, H. S. (1981). *Freud and women.* New York: Frederick Ungar Publishing.

Freud, E. L. (1960). *The letters of Sigmund Freud.* New York: Basic.

Freud, M. (1982). *Sigmund Freud: Man and father.* New York: Jason Aronson.

Freud, S. (1988). *My three mothers and other passions.* New York: New York University Press.

Gay, P. (1988). *Freud: A life for our time.* New York: Norton.

Gay, P. (1990). *Reading Freud.* New Haven, CT: Yale University Press.

Gicklhorn, R. (1979) The Freiberg period of the Freud family. *Journal of the History of Medicine, 24,* 37–43.

Jones, E. (1953, 1954, 1955). *The life and work of Sigmund Freud.* (Vols. 1–3). New York: Basic.

Jones, E. (Ed.). (1975). *Letters of Sigmund Freud.* London: Cambridge University Press.

Krüll, M. (1986). *Freud and his father.* New York: Norton.

Mannoni, O. (1974). *Freud.* New York: Vintage.

Margolis, D. P. (1996). *Freud and his mother.* Northvale, NJ: Jason Aronson.

Masson, J. (Ed.). (1985). *The complete letters of Sigmund Freud to Wilhelm Fleiss: 1887–1904.* Cambridge, MA: Belnap Press.

Masson, J. (1992). *The assault on truth.* New York: Harper Collins

Peters, U. H. (1985). *Anna Freud: A life dedicated to children.* New York: Shocken.

Roazen, P. (1993). *Meeting Freud's family.* Amherst, MA: University of Massachusetts Press.

Ruitenbeek, H. M. (1973). *Freud as we knew him.* Detroit: Wayne State University.

Schur, M. (1972). *Freud: Living and dying.* New York: International Universities Press.

Swales, P. (1982). Freud, Minna Bernays, and the conquest of Rome: New light on the origins of psychoanalysis. *The New American Review, 1*(2/3), 1–23.

Swales, P. (1986, November 15). *Freud, his origins and family history.* Presentation at UMDNJ Robert Wood Johnson Medical School, Piscataway, NJ.

Swales, P. (1987, May 15). *What Freud didn't say*. Presentation at UMDNJ Robert Wood Johnson Medical School, Piscataway, NJ.

Young-Bruel, E. (1988). *Anna Freud: A biography*. New York: Summit.

Gandhi Sources

Chadha, Y. (1997). *Gandhi: A life*. New York: John Wiley.

Easwaran, E. (1972). *Gandhi the man* (2nd ed.). New York: Nilgiri/Random House.

Erikson, E. H. (1969). *Gandhi's truth: On the origins of militant nonviolence*. New York: Norton.

Gandhi, M. K. (2008). *An autobiography: On my experiments with truth*. Ahmedabad, India: Navajivan.

Gold, G., & Attenborough, R. (1983). *Gandhi: A pictorial biography*. New York: Newmarket.

Kripalani, K. (1999). *Gandhi*. New Delhi, India: Interprint.

Woodcock, G. (1971). *Mohandas Gandhi*. New York: Viking.

Guevara Sources

Anderson, J. L. (1997). *Che Guevara: A revolutionary life*. New York: Grove.

Deutschmann, D. (Ed.). (2006). *Che: A memoir by Fidel Castro*. Melbourne, Australia: Ocean Press.

James, D. (2001). *Che Guevara: A biography*. New York: Cooper Square Press.

Ortiz, V. (1968). *Che Guevara: Reminiscences of a Cuban revolutionary war*. New York: Monthly Review Press.

Sinclair, A. (1970). *Che Guevara*. New York: Viking.

Hawthorne Sources

Bassan, M. (1970). *Hawthorne's son: The life and literary career of Julian Hawthorne*. Columbus, OH: Ohio State University Press.

Cowley, M. (Ed.). (1983). *The Hawthorne reader*. New York: Viking.

Erlich, G. (1986). *Family themes and Hawthorne's fiction: The tenacious web*. New Brunswick, NJ: Rutgers University Press.

Hawthorne, J. (1888) *Nathaniel Hawthorne and his wife: A biography* (Vols. 1–2). Grosse Pointe, MI: Scholarly Press.

Hawthorne, N. (1969). *The portable Hawthorne*. New York: Viking.

Maynard, T. (1948). *A fire was lighted: The life of Rose Hawthorne Lathrop*. Milwaukee, WI: Bruce.

McFarland, P. (2004). *Hawthorne in Concord*. New York: Grove.

Mellow, J. R. (1980). *Nathaniel Hawthorne in his times*. Boston: Houghton Mifflin.

Wagenknecht, E. (1961). *Nathaniel Hawthorne: Man and writer.* New York: Oxford University Press.

Wineapple, B. (2004). *Hawthorne: A life.* New York: Random House.

Young, P. (1984). *Hawthorne's secret: An untold tale.* Boston: David R. Godine.

Hepburn and Tracy Sources

Anderson, C. (1988). *Young Kate.* New York: Henry Holt.

Anderson, C. (1997). *An affair to remember.* New York: Morrow.

Carey, G. (1983). *Katharine Hepburn: A Hollywood Yankee.* New York: Dell.

Davidson, B. (1987). *Spencer Tracy: Tragic idol.* New York: E. P. Dutton.

Edwards, A. (1985). *A remarkable woman: A biography of Katharine Hepburn.* New York: Simon & Schuster.

Hepburn, K. (1991). *Me.* New York: Knopf.

Higham, C. (1981). *Kate: The life of Katharine Hepburn.* New York: Signet.

Kanin, G. (1988). *Tracy and Hepburn: An intimate memoir.* New York: Donald I. Fine.

Leaming, B. (1995). *Katharine Hepburn.* New York: Crown.

Mann, W. J. (2006). *Kate: The woman who was Hepburn.* New York: Henry Holt.

Morley, S. (1984). *Katharine Hepburn.* London: Pavilion Books.

Parish, J. R. (2005). *Katharine Hepburn: The untold story.* New York: Advocate Books.

Porter, D. (2004). *Katharine the great.* New York: Blood Moon Productions.

hooks Sources

hooks, b. (1990). *Yearning: Race, gender and cultural politics.* Boston: South End Press.

hooks, b. (1996). *Bone black: Memories of girlhood,* New York: Henry Holt.

hooks, b. (1997). *Wounds of passion: A writing life.* New York: Henry Holt.

hooks, b. (1999). *Remembered rapture: The writer at work.* New York: Henry Holt.

hooks, b. (2009). *Belonging: A culture of place.* New York: Taylor & Francis.

Hughes Sources

Hughes, L. (1945). *The big sea: An autobiography.* New York: Knopf.

McClatchy, J. D. (2002). *Langston Hughes: Voice of the poet.* New York: Random House.

Rampesad, A., & Roessel, D. (2002). *The collected poems of Langston Hughes.*

Jefferson Sources

Brodie, F. M. (1974). *Thomas Jefferson: An intimate history.* New York: Norton.

Fleming, T. J. (1969). *The man from Monticello.* New York: Morrow.

Gordon-Reed, A. (1997). *Thomas Jefferson and Sally Hemings*. Charlottesville, VA: University of Virginia Press.

Gordon-Reed, A. (2008). *The Hemingses of Monticello*. New York: Norton.

Halliday, E. M. (2001). *Understanding Thomas Jefferson*. New York: Harper Collins.

Lanier, S., & Feldman, J. (2000). *Jefferson's children*. New York: Random House.

Lanning Binger, C. A. (1970). *Thomas Jefferson: A Well-Tempered mind*. New York: Norton.

Lemon, T. (Producer). (2013). *Jefferson's blood* [Film]. https://www.pbs.org/wgbh/pages/frontline/shows/jefferson/etc/synopsis.html

Meacham, J. (2013). Thomas Jefferson: The Art of Power: New York: Random House.

Smith, D. (1998, November 7). The enigma of Jefferson: Mind and body in conflict. *New York Times*, B7–8.

Wills, G. (2003). *Negro president*. Boston: Houghton Mifflin.

Woodson, B. W. (2001) *A president in the family: Thomas Jefferson, Sally Hemings and Thomas Woodson*. Westport, CT: Praeger.

Joplin Sources

Berlin, E. A. (1994). *King of ragtime: Scott Joplin and his era*. New York: Oxford University Press.

Curtis, S. (2004). *Dancing to a black man's tune: The life of Scott Joplin*. Columbia, MO: University of Missouri Press.

Gammond, P. (1975). *Scott Joplin and the ragtime era*. New York: St. Martin's Press.

Haskins, J. (1978). *Scott Joplin: The man who made ragtime*. Briarcliff Manor, NY: Scarborough.

Preston, K. (1988). *Scott Joplin: Composer*. New York: Chelsea House.

Websites:

www.personal.psu.edu/users/j/n/jnm144/scott%20joplin.htm

www.scottjoplin.org/biography.htm

Kafka Sources

Citati, P. (1989). *Kafka*. New York: Knopf.

Glazer, N. N. (1986). *The loves of Franz Kafka*. New York: Schocken Books.

Gray, R. (Ed.). (1962). *Kafka: A collection of critical essays*. Englewood Cliffs, NJ: Prentice Hall.

Heller, E. (1974). *Franz Kafka*. Princeton, NJ: Princeton University Press.

Kafka, F. (1953). *Letter to his father.* New York: Schocken Books.

Kafka, F. (1982). *Letters to Ottla and the family* (R. Winston & C. Winston, Trans.). New York: Schocken Books.

Pawel, E. (1984). *The nightmare of reason: A life of Franz Kafka.* New York: Vintage.

Robert, M. (1986). *As lonely as Franz Kafka: A psychological biography.* New York: Schocken Books.

Wagenbach, K. (1984). *Franz Kafka: Pictures of a life.* New York: Random House.

Kahlo and Rivera Sources

Alcantara, I., & Egnolff, S. (1999). *Frida Kahlo and Diego Rivera.* New York: Prestel Verlag.

Drucker, M. (1991). *Frida Kahlo.* Albuquerque, NM: University of New Mexico Press.

Fris, R. (2004). The fury and the mire of human veins: Frida Kahlo and Rosario Castellanos (PDF). *Hispania, 87*(1): 53-61. Doi:10.2307/20062973. JSTOR Archived from the original PDF on July 6, 2019.

Grimberg, S. (2002). *Frida Kahlo.* North Digton, MA: World Publications Group.

Helland, J. *(1990–1991).* Aztec imagery in Frida Kahlo's paintings: Indigenity and political commitment" (PDF). *Woman's Art Journal, 11*(5), 8–13. JSTOR 3690692. Archived from the original PDF on July 6, 2019.

Herrera, H. (1983). *Frida: A biography of Frida Kahlo.* New York: Harper & Row.

Herrera, H. (1984). *Frida.* New York: Harper Collins.

Herrera, H. (1991). *Frida Kahlo: The paintings.* New York: Harper Collins.

Johnson, J. (1996). The diary of Frida Kahlo: An intimate self-portrait [Review of *The diary of Frida Kahlo: An intimate self-portrait*]. *Art in America.* Retrieved from: http://findarticles.com/p/articles/mi_m1248/is_n3_v84/ai_18119049/

Kahlo, F. (1995). *The letters of Frida Kahlo: Cartas apasionadas.* San Francisco: Chronicle Books.

Kahlo, F. (2001). *The diary of Frida Kahlo: An intimate self-portrait.* Toledo, Spain: Abradale Press.

Kettenmann, A. (2002). *Frida Kahlo, 1907–1954: Pain and passion.* New York: Barnes & Noble Books. (Original publication 1992, Cologne, Germany: Benedikt Taschen Verlag GmbH.)

Marnham, P. (1998). *Dreaming with his eyes open: A life of Diego Rivera.* New York: Knopf.

Rivera, D. (1991). *My art, my life: An autobiography.* New York: Dover.

Tibol, R. (1983). *Frida Kahlo: An open life.* Albuquerque, NM: University of New Mexico Press.

Kennedy Family Sources

Andrews, J. D. (1998). *Young Kennedys: The new generation*. New York: Avon.

Collier, P., & Horowitz, D. (1984). *The Kennedys*. New York: Summit Books.

Davis, J. (1969). *The Bouviers: Portrait of an American family*. New York: Farrar, Straus, Giroux.

Davis, J. (1984). *The Kennedys: Dynasty & disaster*. New York: McGraw-Hill.

Davis, J. (1993). *The Bouviers: From Waterloo to the Kennedys and beyond*. Washington, DC: National Press Books.

DuBois, D. (1995). *In her sister's shadow: The bitter legacy of Lee Radziwell*. New York: St. Martin's Press.

Gibson, B., & Schwarz, T. (1993). *The Kennedys: The third generation*. New York: Thunder Mouth's Press.

Gibson, B., & Schwarz, T. (1995). *Rose Kennedy and her family*. New York: Birch Lane Press.

Hamilton, N. (1992). *JFK: Reckless youth*. New York: Random House.

Heymann, C. D. (1989). *A woman named Jackie*. New York: New American Library.

James, A. (1991). *The Kennedy scandals and tragedies*. Lincolnwood, IL: Chicago Publications International.

Kearns Goodwin, D. (1987). *The Fitzgeralds and the Kennedys*. New York: Simon & Schuster.

Kelley, K. (1978). *Jackie Oh!* Secaucus, NJ: Lyle Stuart.

Kennedy, R. (1974). *Times to remember*. New York: Bantam.

Klein, E. (1998). *Just Jackie: Her private years*. New York: Ballantine.

Klein, E. (2003). *The Kennedy curse*. New York: St. Martin's Press.

Latham, C., & Sakol, J. (1989). *Kennedy encyclopedia*. New York: New American Library.

Leamer, L. (2001). *The Kennedy men: 1901–1963*. New York: Harper Collins.

Maier, T. (2003). *The Kennedys: America's emerald kings*. New York: Basic Books.

McTaggart, L. (1983) *Kathleen Kennedy: Her life and times*. New York: Dial.

Moutsatos, K. F. (1998). *The Onassis women*. New York: Putnam.

Rachlin, H. (1986). *The Kennedys: A chronological history 1823–present*. New York: World Almanac.

Rainie, H., & Quinn, J. (1983) *Growing up Kennedy: The third wave comes of age*. New York: G.P. Putnam's Sons.

Saunders, F. (1982). *Torn lace curtain: Life with the Kennedys*. New York: Henry Holt.

Wills, G. (1981). *The Kennedy imprisonment: A meditation on power*. New York: Little, Brown.

King Family Sources

Carson, C. (Ed.). (2001). *The autobiography of Martin Luther King.* New York: Warner Books.

Franklin, V. P. (1998). *Martin Luther King, Jr. biography.* New York: Park Lane Press.

King, M. L., Sr., & Riely, C. (1980). *Daddy King, an autobiography.* New York: Morrow.

Lewis, D. L. (1978). *King: A biography* (2nd ed). Chicago: University of Illinois Press.

Oates, S. B. (1982). *Let the trumpet sound: The life of Martin Luther King, Jr.* New York: New American Library.

Ann Landers and Dear Abby Sources

Howard, M. (2003). *Ann Landers in her own words.* New York: Warner.

Kogan, R. (2003). *America's mom.* New York: HarperCollins.

Pottker, J., & Speziale, B. (1987). *Dear Ann, Dear Abby: The unauthorized biography of Ann Landers and Abigail Van Buren.* New York: Dodd, Mead & Company.

Lincoln and Todd Sources

Baker, J. (1987). *Mary Todd Lincoln: A biography.* New York: Norton.

Eliot, A. (1985). *Abraham Lincoln: An illustrated biography.* New York: W. H. Smith.

Neely, M. E., & McMurtry, R. G. (1986). *The insanity file: The case of Mary Todd Lincoln.* Carbondale, IL: Southern Illinois University Press.

Oates, S. B. (1977). *With malice toward none: The life of Abraham Lincoln.* New York: New American Library.

Oates, S. B. (1984). *Abraham Lincoln: The man behind the myths.* New York: Harper & Row.

Sandburg, C. (1926). *Abraham Lincoln: The prairie years* (Vols. I–II). New York: Harcourt, Brace & Company.

Schreiner, S. A. (1987). *The trials of Mrs. Lincoln.* New York: Donald I. Fine.

Lindbergh Sources

Lindbergh, R. (1998). *Under a wing: A memoir.* New York: Dell/Random House.

Lindbergh, R. (2003). *Forward from here.* New York: Simon & Schuster.

Mahler Sources

Blaukopf, K. (1985). *Gustav Mahler.* New York: Limelight Editions.

De La Grange, H. (1976). *Mahler.* London: Victor Gollancz Ltd.

De La Grange, H. (1995). *Gustav Mahler: Letters to his wife.* Ithaca, NY: Cornell University Press.

Keegan, S. (1992). *The bride of the wind: The life of Alma Mahler.* New York: Viking.

Mahler, A. (1971). *Gustav Mahler: Memories and letters.* Seattle, WA: University of Washington Press.

Martner, K. (Ed.). (1979). *Selected letters of Gustav Mahler.* New York: Farrar, Straus, Giroux.

Monson, K. (1983). *Alma Mahler: Muse to genius.* Boston: Houghton Mifflin.

Secherson, E. (1982). *Mahler.* New York: Omnibus Press.

Mead Sources: see Bateson and Mead

Monroe Sources

Barris, G. (1995). *Marilyn: Her life in her own words: Marilyn Monroe's revealing last words and photograph.* New York: Citadel Press.

Leaming, B. (1998). *Marilyn Monroe.* New York: Three Rivers Press.

McDonough, Y. Z. (Ed.). (2005). *All the available light: A Marilyn Monroe reader.* New York: Simon & Schuster.

Monroe, M. (1976). *My story.* Briarcliff Manor, NY: Stein & Day.

Monroe, M. (2001). *My story: Marilyn Monroe.* New York: Cooper Square Press.

Spoto, D. (1993). *Marilyn Monroe.* New York: Harper.

Spoto, D. (2001). *Marilyn Monroe: The biography.* New York: Cooper Square Press.

Summers, A. (2000). *Goddess: The secret lives of Marilyn Monroe.* London: Phoenix Press.

Zimroth, E. (2005). Marilyn at the Mikvah. In Y. Z. McDonough. (Ed.), *All the available light: A Marilyn Monroe reader.* New York: Simon & Schuster.

Nehru-Gandhi Family Sources

Ali, T. (1985). *An Indian dynasty.* New York: Putnam.

Frank, K. (2002). *Indira: The life of Indira Nehru Gandhi.* New York: Houghton-Mifflin.

Gopal, S., & Iyengar, U. (Eds.). (2003). *The essential writings of Jawaharlal Nehru.* Oxford, UK: Oxford University Press.

Nehru, J. (1958). *Autobiography: Toward freedom.* Boston: Beacon.

Nehru, J. (2004). *Letters from a father to his daughter.* Viking Press.

Wolpert, S. (1996). *Nehru.* New York: Oxford University Press.

Obama Sources

Grimes, N., & Collier, B. (2008). *Barack Obama: Son of promise, child of hope.* New York: Simon & Schuster.

Obama, B. (1995). *Dreams from my father: A story of race and inheritance.* New York: Three Rivers Press.

Obama, B. (2008). *The audacity of hope: Thoughts on reclaiming the American dream* (Reprinted ed.). New York: Vintage.

Wolfe, R. (2009). *Renegade: The making of a president.* New York: Crown.

O'Neill Family Sources

Black, S. (1999). *Eugene O'Neill: Beyond mourning and tragedy.* New Haven, CT: Yale University Press.

Bowen, C. (1959). *The curse of the misbegotten.* New York: McGraw-Hill.

Gelb, A., & Gelb, B. (1987). *O'Neill.* New York: Harper & Row.

Scovell, J. (1999) *Oona: Living in the shadows: A biography of Oona O'Neill Chaplin.* New York: Grand Central Publishing.

Sheaffer, L. (1968). *O'Neill: Son and playwright.* Boston: Little, Brown.

Sheaffer, L. (1973). *O'Neill: Son and artist: Volume II.* Boston: Little, Brown.

Rivera Sources: see Kahlo and Rivera

Robeson Sources

Dean, P. H. (1989). Paul Robeson. In: E. Hill (Ed.), *Black heroes: Seven plays* (pp. 27–353). New York: Applause Theatre.

Duberman, M. B. (1988). *Paul Robeson.* New York: Knopf.

Ehrlich, S. (1988). *Paul Robeson: Singer and actor.* New York: Chelsea House Publishers.

Larsen, R. (1989). *Paul Robeson: Hero before his time.* New York: Franklin Watts.

Ramdin, R. (1987). *Paul Robeson: The man and his mission.* London: Peter Owen.

Robeson, P. (1988). *Here I stand.* Boston: Beacon.

Robinson Sources

Falkner, D. (1995). *Great time coming: The life of Jackie Robinson from baseball to Birmingham.* New York: Simon & Schuster.

Rampersad, A. (1997). *Jackie Robinson: A biography.* New York: Knopf.

Robinson, J. (1972). *I never had it made: An autobiography of Jackie Robinson.* New York: Putnam.

Robinson, R. (1996). *Jackie Robinson: An intimate portrait.* New York: Abrams.

Robinson, S. (1996). *Stealing home.* New York: HarperCollins.

Tygiel, J. (1997). *Baseball's great experiment: Jackie Robinson and his legacy.* New York: Oxford University Press.

Roosevelt Family Sources

Asbell, B. (Ed.). (1982). *Mother and daughter: The letters of Eleanor and Anna Roosevelt.* New York: Coward McCann & Geoghegan.

Bishop, J. B. (Ed.). (1919). *Theodore Roosevelt's letters to his children.* New York: Charles Scribner's Sons.

Brough, J. (1975). *Princess Alice: A biography of Alice Roosevelt Longworth.* Boston: Little, Brown.

Collier, P., & Horowitz, D. (1994). *The Roosevelts.* New York: Simon & Schuster.

Cook, B. W. (1992). *Eleanor Roosevelt 1884–1933: A life: Mysteries of the heart, Vol. 1.* New York: Viking Penguin.

Cordery, S. A. (2007). *Alice.* New York: Viking.

Donn, L. (2001). *The Roosevelt cousins.* New York: Knopf.

Feldman, E. (2003). FDR and his women. *American Heritage, 54*(1). Retrieved from: https://www.americanheritage.com/content/march-2003

Felsenthal, C. (1988). *Alice Roosevelt Longworth.* New York: G. P. Putnam's Sons.

Fleming, C. (2005). *Our Eleanor.* New York: Simon & Schuster.

Fritz, J. (1991). *Bully for you, Teddy Roosevelt.* New York: G.P. Putnam's Sons.

Hagedorn, H. (1954). *The Roosevelt family of Sagamore Hill.* New York: Macmillan.

Kearns Goodwin, D. (1994). *No ordinary time. Franklin and Eleanor Roosevelt: The home front in World War II.* New York: Simon & Schuster.

Lash, J. P. (1971). *Eleanor and Franklin.* New York: Norton.

McCullough, D. (1981). *Mornings on horseback.* New York: Simon & Schuster.

Michaelis, D. (2020). *Eleanor.* New York: Simon & Schuster.

Miller, N. (1979). *The Roosevelt chronicles.* Garden City, NY: Doubleday.

Miller, N. (1983). *FDR: An intimate biography.* Garden City, NY: Doubleday.

Miller, N. (1994). *Theodore Roosevelt: A life.* New York: Morrow.

Morgan, T. (1985). *FDR: A biography.* New York: Simon & Schuster.

Morris, E. (1979). *The rise of Theodore Roosevelt.* New York: Ballantine.

Pringle, H. F. (1931). *Theodore Roosevelt.* New York: Harcourt, Brace, Jovanovich.

Roosevelt, E. (1984). *The autobiography of Eleanor Roosevelt.* Boston: G. K. Hall.

Roosevelt, E., & Brough, J. (1973). *The Roosevelts of Hyde Park: An untold story.* New York: Putnam.

Roosevelt, E., & Brough, J. (1975). *A rendezvous with destiny: The Roosevelts of the White House.* New York: Dell.

Roosevelt, J. (1976). *My parents: A differing view.* Chicago: The Playboy Press.

Roosevelt, T. (1925). *An autobiography.* New York: Charles Scribner's Sons.

Streitmatter, R. (Ed.). (1998). *Empty without you: The intimate letters of Eleanor Roosevelt and Lorena Hickok.* New York: Da Capo Press.

Teichman, H. (1979). *Alice: The life and times of Alice Roosevelt.* Englewood Cliffs, NJ: Prentice-Hall.

Youngs, W. T. (1985). *Eleanor Roosevelt: A personal and public life.* Boston: Little, Brown.

Sartre Sources

Cohen-Solal, A. (1987). *Sartre, a life.* New York: Pantheon.

Sartre, J. P. (1964). *The words.* Greenwich, CN: Fawcett.

Shaw and Payne-Townshend Sources

Brown, M. (2005). *Lawrence of Arabia: The life, the legend.* London: Thames & Hudson.

Colbourne, M. (1949). *The real Bernard Shaw.* New York: Philosophical Library.

Dervin, D. (1975). *Bernard Shaw: A psychological study.* Lewisburg, PA: Bucknell University Press.

Dunbar, J. (1963). *Mrs. G.B.S.: A portrait.* New York: Harper & Row.

Holroyd, M. (1988). *Bernard Shaw, Vol. I: The search for love, 1856–1898.* New York: Random House.

Holroyd, M. (1989). *Bernard Shaw, Vol. II: The pursuit of power, 1989–1918.* New York: Random House.

Holroyd, M. (1991). *Bernard Shaw, Vol. III: The lure of fantasy, 1918–1951.* New York: Random House.

Shaw, G. B. (1968). *Complete plays, Vol. 3.* New York: Dodd, Mead.

Shaw, G. B. (2007). *John Bull's other island.* Charleston, SC: Bibliobazaar.

Smith, J. P. (1965). *The unrepentant pilgrim: A study of the development of Bernard Shaw.* Boston: Houghton-Mifflin.

Tan Sources

Redford, J. (2017, May 3). Amy Tan: An unintended memoir (Season 35, Episode 7) [TV Series Episode]. In: Kantor, M. (Executive Producer), *American Masters.* Thirteen Productions LLC.

Tan, A., (2017). *Where the past begins: Memory and imagination.* Ecco Press.

Tolstoy Sources

Citati, P. (1986). *Tolstoy*. New York: Schocken Books.

de Courcel, M. (1980). *Tolstoy: The ultimate reconciliation*. New York: Charles Scribner's Sons.

Edwards, A. (1981). *Sonya: The life of countess Tolstoy*. New York: Simon & Schuster.

Maude, A. (1987). *The life of Tolstoy* (Vols. I and II). New York: Oxford University Press.

Simmons, E. J. (1960). *Leo Tolstoy* (Vols. I and II). New York: Vintage.

Smoluchowski, L. (1987). *Lev & Sonya: The story of the Tolstoy marriage*. New York: G. P. Putnam's Sons.

Stilman, L. (Ed.). (1960). *Leo Tolstoy: Last diaries*. New York: G. P. Putnam's Sons.

Tolstoy, L. (1964). *Childhood, boyhood, youth*. Baltimore: Penguin.

Tolstoy, N. (1983). *The Tolstoys: Twenty-four generations of Russian history*. New York: William Morrow.

Troyat, H. (1967). *Tolstoy*. New York: Dell.

Wilson, A. N. (1988). *Tolstoy*. New York: Norton.

Queen Victoria Sources

Auchincloss, L. (1979). *Persons of consequence: Queen Victoria and her circle*. New York: Random House.

Benson, E. F. (1987). *Queen Victoria*. London: Chatto & Windus.

Ferguson, S., & Stoney, B. (1991). *Victoria and Albert: Family life at Osborne House*. New York: Prentice-Hall.

Hibbert, C. (1984). *Queen Victoria in her letters and journals*. London: Penguin.

James, R. R. (1983). *Prince Albert*. New York: Knopf.

Strachey, L. (1921). *Queen Victoria*. New York: Harcourt, Brace, Jovanovich.

Weintraub, S. (1987). *Victoria*. New York: E. P. Dutton.

Wilson, E. (1990). *Eminent Victorians*. New York: Norton.

Woodham-Smith, C. (1972). *Queen Victoria*. New York: Donald Fine.

Washington Sources

Bourne, M. A. (1982). *First family: George Washington and his intimate relations*. New York: Norton.

Ellis, J. J. (2004). *His excellency: George Washington*. New York: Knopf.

Furstenberg, F. (2006). *In the name of the father: Washington's legacy, slavery and the making of a nation*. New York: Penguin.

Johnson, P. (2005). *George Washington: The founding father*. New York: Harper Collins.

McCullough, D. (2005). *1776*. New York: Simon & Schuster.

Mitchell, S. W. (1904). *The youth of Washington*. New York: The Century Company.

Moore, C. (1926). *The family life of George Washington*. Boston: Houghton-Mifflin.

Randall, W. S. (1997). *George Washington: A life*. New York: Henry Holt.

Wiencek, H. (2003). *An imperfect god: George Washington, his slaves and the creation of America*. New York: Farrar, Strauss & Giroux.

Wright Sources

Crouch, T. D. (1989). *The Bishop's boys: A life of Wilbur and Orville Wright*. New York: Norton.

Freedman, R. (1991). *The Wright brothers: How they invented the airplane*. New York: Holiday House.

Goulder, G. (1964). *Ohio scenes and citizens*. Cleveland, OH: World.

Howard, F. (1987). *Wilbur and Orville: A biography of the Wright brothers*. New York: Knopf.

Kelly, F. C. (1989). *The Wright brothers: A biography*. New York: Dover.

Kinnane, A. (1982). *The crucible of flight*. Unpublished manuscript.

Kinnane, A. (1988). A house united: Morality and invention in the Wright brothers' home. *Psychohistory Review (Spring)*, 367–397.

Mackersey, I. (2003). *The Wright brothers: The remarkable story of the aviation pioneers who changed the world*. New York: Time/Warner.

Maurer, R. (2003). *The Wright sister*. Brookfield, CT: Millbrook Press.

McMahon, J. R. (1930). *The Wright brothers: Fathers of flight*. Boston: Little, Brown.

Miller, I. W. (1978). *Wright reminiscences*. Dayton, OH: Privately printed.

Renstrom, A. G. (1975). *Wilbur and Orville Wright: A chronology commemorating the one hundredth anniversary of the birth of Orville Wright*. Washington, DC: Library of Congress.

Reynolds, Q. (1950). *The Wright brothers*. New York: Random House.

Walsh, J. E. (1975). *One day at Kitty Hawk: The untold story of the Wright brothers and the airplane*. New York: Crowell.

Wilson, A. N. (1988). *Tolstoy*. New York: Norton.

Wright, M. (1999). *Diaries: 1857–1917*. Dayton, OH: Wright State University.

INDEX

gender fluidity, 205
genogram, 199
and Spencer Tracy, 40–41, 62,
122, 205–206
historical context of family, 43–47,
53
Holocaust, 46, 166, 238
homosexuality
of Langston Hughes, 62–63
of Katherine Hepburn, 205–206
of Eleanor Roosevelt, 62, 122,
278
of Margaret Mead, 62, 122
hooks, bell, 35–38
Belonging: The Culture of Place, 35
Hughes, Langston, 62–63
Hungarian culture, 327–329

"Identified Patient", 170
illegitimacy, in family of Benjamin
Franklin, 81–83
immigrants, homeplace, 37, 40, 62,
68, 331
incest
in Hawthorne manuscripts, 140
multigenerational, 138–141
Indigenous Americans, 46
Irish Americans
migration, 46
overprotection of sons, 254

Jefferson, Thomas, 112
and John Adams, death of, 195
and Sally Hemings, 128–129
Jefferson's Blood (Shelby Steele),
128–129
Jewish families, 38, 44
of Faludi, Susan, 327–329
migration of, 46

speeches by Charles Lindbergh, 63
Joplin, Scott, 45–46
genogram, 45

Kafka, Franz, 235–239
parents, 235–238
Kahlo, Frida
and Diego Rivera, 47–52
genogram, 48
mixed culture, 49–50
resilience to loss, 223–225
Kennedy, Eunice, 214
Kennedy, Honey Fitz, 210–211
Kennedy, John, 195, 207, 218
Kennedy, Joseph, 209
Kennedy, Kathleen, 163, 207,
216–217
Kennedy, Patrick Joseph, 208–210
Kennedy, Robert, 196, 218
Kennedy, Rose Fitzgerald, 210–
213, 217
Kennedy, Rosemary, 212–213
Kennedy, Ted, 196, 207, 219
Kennedy family, 206–219
genogram, 207
multiple deaths, 196, 206–219
religion of, 57
King, Martin Luther, 271
King Charles III, 26
Krasner, Barbara, 144

Lawrence, T. E., 307–309 308
lesbian relationships, 37, 122, 286,
288
Lester, Jane, Aboriginal Australian, 66–67
Lincoln, Abraham
cutoff of father, 22–23
genogram, 273

informal family and, 3, 76, 145

triangle between Eleanor Roosevelt and, 230–235

identification with children and sibling position of, 87–88, 280

oldest sons and daughters identifying with, 256–262

problematic, readiness for engaging with, 249, 287, 330, 337

questions about, 246, 327, 335

reconciling with, before deaths of, 244

reconnections after conflictual relationships with, 75, 319, 327, 330

religious and spiritual orientations and, 57–62, 68–69, 89, 287

seeing in context of their own lives, 68

sibling patterns perpetuated by, 283

siblings, birth order and expectations of, 88–89, 121, 113, 210, 254–256, 269, 308, 336

Payne-Townshend, Charlotte, and George Bernard Shaw, 303–308

pregnancy, Alma Mahler, 299

prodigal son, 251

Queen Victoria

dysfunctional mourning, 198

family cutoff, 24–26

race

denial of, 129–133

family messages conveyed about, 43, 102

secrets involving, 128–133

skin color and, 41–43, 68

religion

family culture and, 33, 43, 44, 57–60, 69, 75, 286, 307

of Marilyn Monroe, 60–62

in Gandhi family, 58–60

in Kennedy family, 163, 212, 215

remarriage

divorce and, 50, 52, 135, 196, 295, 312, 313–314, 324, 332

sibling relationships and, 249

of Theodore Roosevelt, 159–160

reversal of family roles, 94

rituals of family, 318

Rivera, Diego, and Frida Kahlo, 47–52

genogram, 48

Robeson, Paul, 267–270, 316

genogram, 269

Robinson, Jackie, 252–255

genogram, 253

roles in family, 250–251

twins, 255

youngest children, 262–265

See also sisters and brothers

Romeo and Juliet, families of, 285–286

Roosevelt, Eleanor, 122, 230–235

autobiography, 230

bisexuality, 62, 122

daughter Anna, 234–235

death of mother, 233

dysfunctional parents, 233–234

father, 230–233

and Franklin, 276–280

genogram, 231, 277

uncle with second family, 233

Roosevelt, Franklin, 276–280

genogram, 277

ABOUT THE AUTHORS

Monica McGoldrick, MA, MSW, PhD, (hc), is cofounder and director of the Multicultural Family Institute in Highland Park, New Jersey, and adjunct faculty of the Robert Wood Johnson Medical School. Her books include *Ethnicity and Family Therapy, Genograms: Assessment and Intervention, The Expanded Family Life Cycle,* and *Revisioning Family Therapy,* all of which have appeared in multiple editions. She received her BA from Brown, and MA from Yale in Russian Studies, as well as her MSW and honorary PhD from Smith. McGoldrick is known internationally for her writings and videos on topics including culture, gender, the family life cycle, loss, and remarried families.

Tracey A. Laszloffy, PhD, maintains a private practice in individual and relationship therapy in Norwich, Connecticut where she directs the Center for Healing Connections. Dr. Laszloffy received her master's and doctoral degrees in Marriage and Family Therapy from Syracuse University. She has been a professor of family therapy at various universities; has presented workshops and seminars nationally and internationally on issues of diversity, oppression, and trauma; and she has published extensively in academic journals. Dr. Laszloffy has also coauthored four books including *Teens Who Hurt: Breaking the Cycle of Adolescent Violence* and *Eco-Informed Practice: Family Therapy in an Age of Ecological Peril.*